D1271406

How to Sell
to the Government

HOW TO SELL
TO THE GOVERNMENT
A Step-by-Step Guide
to Success

William A. Cohen

Foreword by

Paul L. Smith
Vice-President, Program Development and Marketing
McDonnell-Douglas Astronautics Company

A Ronald Press Publication

JOHN WILEY & SONS

New York • Chichester • Brisbane • Toronto

Library of Congress Cataloging in Publication Data:

Cohen, William A   1937–
  You can do millions of dollars in business with
  the U.S. Government.

  "A Ronald Press publication."
  Includes index.
  1. Government purchasing—United States.

I. Title.
JK1671.C63   353.0071'2   80-22997
ISBN 0-471-08103-5

Printed in the United States of America

10 9 8 7 6 5 4 3 2 1

FOREWORD

The federal government has been, and continues to be, the largest buyer of goods and services in our economy. Although it is an attractive marketplace, its size and the complexity of its needs have led to the creation of a multitude of rules and constraints, making it seem overwhelmingly complicated and difficult to penetrate. Nonetheless, for the businessman who has mastered its requirements, the government market can be very profitable.

The entrepreneur, hopeful of winning government business, usually starts with an idea, a product, a process, or a service that he believes the government may need. But his problem is, who should he see, and how should he get started?

A small business, already selling a product to the government, may decide to expand its activities and sell a major component or subsystem that requires the preparation of a proposal. How does it prepare a winning proposal?

A larger company, regularly turning out quality proposals, may find it is not winning enough competitions. Does it understand how to do preproposal marketing effectively? Does it have the right marketing strategy? Is the strategy being properly implemented by means of workable market-action plans?

When a competition is won, what type of contract best matches the needs and requirements of the winner as well as the needs and requirements of the government? What options does the contractor have in this regard and how does he negotiate to secure the most favorable options?

There is a law, a regulation, a rule, a practice, a procedure, or a tradition that governs every phase of the government's acquisition process. Successful marketing requires not only a thorough understanding of the rules, but the ability to create winning strategies and implement them profitably.

Many books have been written to describe the various activities that must be mastered to succeed in marketing to the government—how to make presentations, where to look for requirements, how to write proposals, and how to negotiate effectively. But *How to Sell to the Government* puts all of these activities, and more, together, gives them relevance, and provides comprehensive guidance.

This is a book on the ABCs of government marketing that truly goes from A to Z. Its breadth and its depth ensure value for the professional as well as the novice, and its instructions should dependably lead to success, for they have been derived from on-the-firing-line experience.

PAUL L. SMITH, Vice President Program Development and Marketing
McDonnell Douglas Astronautics Company

PREFACE

As a young man, I would never have imagined that I would ever have anything to do with marketing or sales to the U.S. Government. Yet while starting as neither buyer nor seller, I can trace my own involvement with government-purchased goods back to the fifth of July, 1955, when I entered the United States Military Academy at West Point as a cadet. That very first day, we were issued woolen uniforms. The mismatch of the woolen material with the weather was so great that I still remember the physical discomfort. But the quality of this government-issue uniform was such that despite four years of hard use, it was not once in need of repair. Though I hardly had occasion to think of it at the time, the manufacturer of these goods was not the Government but an industrial firm that marketed, sold to, and, at least in this instance, made its living from doing business with the Federal Government.

Six years later, another aspect of Government business came to my attention. A significant portion of the nation's defense was vested in the B-52 strategic bomber, an Air Force plane that is still flying. One of the B-52 weapons systems was the air-to-ground missile system known as the "Hound Dog." Assigned to B-52s, I was packed off to learn the operation of the Hound Dog missile system in a special course taught by the contractor. The navigator of the aircraft programed and launched these missiles, but the copilot controlled the missile engines until launch. At the navigation console there were two green lights, each containing the inscription "Missile Ready For Launch." These lights went on when the copilot manually flipped a switch exactly like the ones found in any American home. We were amazed to learn that such of these "house switches" cost the Government $10,000! To outfit all the B-52s carrying Hound Dogs with this single switch probably cost the Air Force no less than $6 million—a small fortune in 1961. Clearly there was more to Government contracting than at first met the eye.

It took another seven years before I became directly involved in that process in the Government that was then called "procurement" and is now known as "acquisition." Returning from a combat tour in Southeast Asia, the Air Force decided to recoup part of the investment it had made in my getting an M.B.A. several years earlier. I was assigned to duty as a program manager in the Aerospace Systems Division at Wright-Patterson Air Force Base, Ohio; this division was, and is, the center for systems development within the research and development command of the Air Force. It is responsible for billions of dollars in the acquisition and performance of research and development services. My share of the total expenditure was several million dollars a year for my own "small" programs and management of part of the design and acquisition of such major weapon systems as the F-15, the B-1, and AWACS aircraft. During my time at Wright-Patterson, I participated in every phase of the procurement process. I helped prepare and directed the preparation of "data packages" and statements of work upon which invitation for bids (IFBs) and requests for proposals (RFPs) are based. I fought with my superiors and higher headquarters for money for my programs. I successfully defended the 18 different programs for which I was personally responsible. I had hundreds of meetings with contractors and potential contractors from companies of all sizes and description. I evaluated competitive proposals and was either impressed or unimpressed with various contractors' solicited and unsolicited solutions to our problems. I helped negotiate contracts and helped kill potential contracts. I sat as a member of source selection evaluation boards for major multibillion dollar weapons systems, and for programs costing the Government no more than $20,000. In short, I was involved in all aspects of marketing to the Government from the Government side of the table.

The following years were spent on the other side—in industry—in a succession of senior marketing and engineering management positions, all dealing with Government contracting. At first, I headed up research and development with a small company. Our first year, we bid for three important R&D contracts with the Air Force totaling about a quarter of a million dollars. We won all three. Two years later, we bid for what was then the largest single R&D contract in the history of that 40-year-old Government contractor that held it. We won that contract with the U.S. Army for $1.8 million. As marketing manager of Advanced Technology at the McDonnell Douglas Astronautics Company, I was involved with 123 small contracts with 26 different Government agencies, totaling about $16 million. The major agencies included not only the Department of Defense but also units of NASA; the Department of Energy; Department of Transportation; Health, Education, and Welfare; National Science Foundation; and others. As a result, my education on the industrial side has been no less thorough than the education in Government marketing I acquired while working for the Government.

Most recently, in addition to teaching marketing full time as an associate professor of marketing and conducting a course on Government marketing nationwide, I am still personally involved in Government contracting as the director of the Bureau of Business and Economic Research at California State University, Los Angeles.

I have outlined my background in Government marketing to emphasize the purpose of the book. Exactly as stated, it is to show you how you can do millions of dollars in business with the U.S. Government. I believe absolutely that if you follow the techniques and procedures outlined in this book and apply them to your business, you will succeed in doing exactly what the title of the book states.

In showing you how to market successfully to Uncle Sam, I believe that the benefit will accrue not only to you in increased business but also to the Federal Government in increased and more efficient satisfaction of the needs for goods and services that the Government must have in order to fulfill its function.

Specifically, here is what you will learn from this book:

- How to apply marketing theory in the Government marketplace.
- Where and how to get help from the Government itself.
- Where the Government customers are and how to approach them.
- The most effective process for locating new Government customers.
- How to perform initial customer screening.
- How to conduct briefings and presentations for potential customers.
- Government forms and how to use them.
- How to do a situation analysis.
- How to develop a marketing strategy.
- How to make consumer acceptance theory work for you.
- How to use merchandising theory.
- What research says about the value of customer contacts.
- When, how, and who should make what kinds of contacts with the customer.
- The intelligence operation and how to perform it properly.
- Uses and processes of market research in Government contracting.
- Different types of requests for proposals from the Government and how to respond to each type.
- Unsolicited proposals and when to make them.
- How to organize your proposal team.
- The functions of each member of the proposal team.
- The critical function of the Gold Team in your proposal.
- How to write a proposal.
- How to price your proposal or bid.
- How the Government evaluates your proposal and the criteria it uses.
- How a source selection evaluation board scores your proposal.
- Bid strategies for winning contracts.
- How to negotiate a winning contract.
- How to handle "orals" and post-bid questions.
- What to do about "best and finals."
- The pre-award survey, what it is, how to prepare, and how to score well on it.
- Negotiation principles and techniques.
- What to do after your first win with a new customer to encourage subsequent wins and follow-up business.
- How to manage and administer the contract.
- Basics of contract law.
- How to win follow-up contracts . . . and much, much more.

Now, let's not lose any more time. Please begin reading the introduction. This is your first step toward doing millions of dollars in additional business with the U.S. Government.

WILLIAM A. COHEN

Pasadena, California
November 1980

CONTENTS

How to Sell
to the Government

INTRODUCTION

The U.S. Government is the largest buyer of goods and services in the world. As I am writing this, yearly procurement of goods and services by the General Services Administration (GSA) alone approaches $80 billion. This incredible level of buying is possible through a GSA catalogue of four million different items that can be ordered by federal agencies. Over 20,000 of the common-use items stocked at GSA supply depots are described and priced in the GSA stock catalogue, which can be purchased by anyone from the Superintendent of Documents at the Government Printing Office. The Defense Supply Agency, which has the responsibility for providing effective and economical support for common supplies and services to the military departments and other Department of Defense components, manages approximately 800,000 separate procurement items. Government research and development activity, much of which is procured from industry is expected to be more than $30 billion next year, while federal grants of all types will be in excess of $70 billion. In 1977 the total U.S. Government procurement of goods and services for that year was published in the official *Statistical Abstract of the United States*, prepared by the Bureau of Census of the Department of Commerce. The total was a staggering $365.5 billion! What a market! Enough to keep both the small businessman and the large industrial firm busy with millions of dollars left over.

Does the U.S. Government buy what you want to sell? Without even knowing your product or service, I can state with some confidence that the answer is probably yes. Almost everything that anyone could possibly make or provide as a service is wanted by someone in the Government marketplace. For example, the Small Business Administration publishes a purchasing and sales directory as an aid to small businesses that want to sell to the Federal Government, or buy property being sold by the Government. One section lists only products and services wanted by the military. The list of approximately 1500 products and services currently bought by major military purchasing offices begins with "abrasive materials" and ends with "yarn." A similar listing of about 4000 products and services bought by major federal civilian purchasing offices begins with "ablative heat shields" and ends with "zinc ribbon." A separate section in their directory lists research and development opportunities with the Department of Defense and

1

federal civilian agencies. These listings run the gamut from a medical research program that deals in clinical medicine and human factors for the Air Surgeon General's office of the FAA to applied research and development and engineering for the development of an advanced tank for the Army, a submarine for the Navy, and a missile and aircraft for the Air Force.

What if you have something unique and so different that it's not one of the millions of items listed in any of the Government procurement catalogues? The Government may still be interested. Joe Cossman, the mail-order millionaire who sold over 40 million toy soldiers by mail and to key stores around the country, sold even more than 40 million toy soldiers to the Military Exchange Services.

The *Commerce Business Daily* is a Government publication that lists current Government business opportunities and awards of all types. Here is a sampling for one single issue of what the U.S. Government buys, as advertised in that publication.

Under "Experimental, Developmental, Test and Research Work," the following opportunities were listed:

Site participation in an experimental one-megawatt solar thermal electric power plant; alkaline battery separator development; quick response policy economic and technical analyzer support; mission application of limited energy vehicles; support for the Phalanx close-in-weapon system (CIWS) program; support services to ASW: support of the AEGIS shipbuilding project related to AN/SPY–1A radar; support to the NAVSEA surface effect ship program office by evaluating the latest design requirements and ship design configurations; systems engineering and technical services for the submarine ASW standoff weapon development program; investigation and analysis of radiation effects; preparation of a handbook of methods for private population surveys; contract definition study for an active electronic decoy (AED) full-scale engineering development; technical studies on HF system architecture; testing modifications to VLF/LF transmitter; design, development, fabrication, and testing of an automatic message switching set; engineering and technical support of the cincusnaveur intelligency support system; automotive gas turbine programs; and 39 other research and development activities.

Under the heading "Expert and Consultant Services," the Government was looking for contractors to do the following:

Take four soil borings, make soil analysis and recommend construction methods and procedures for two proposed buildings; serve as an information clearinghouse for existing patient educational materials; develop an outreach program to attract women into male-intensive vocational educational programs; provide the Fish and Wildlife Service with information on the types and degree of impacts of peat mining on fish and other aquatic organisms and the mitigation of these impacts; investigate U.S. Air Force living and family patterns; present an engineering design for a 45,000 SHP controller pitch propeller; inquire into commercial television network practices; prepare a DOE advisory committee manual; make concept definition studies for standoff jammer suppression; initiate selective vegetation control in Oregon; select, perfect, replicate, and evaluate five smoking and youth demonstration projects; provide responses to routine phone and written inquiries received under the seven federal Student Financial Assistance Programs; develop a plan for the independent certification and validation of the ALQ-131 electronic warfare system; inventory and analyze rock art in three locations in Wyoming; provide EDP support services; and respond to any of the 27 other opportunities that were also listed under this classification.

One hundred and eighty-seven other potential business opportunities were listed under other headings such as "Maintenance and Repair of Equipment"; "Modification, Alteration, and Rebuilding of Equipment"; "Technical Representative Services"; "Operation and Maintenance of Government Owned Facility"; "Installation of Equipment"; "Medical Services"; "Architect-Engineering Service"; "House keeping Services"; "Photographic, Mapping, Printing, and Publications Services"; "Training Services"; "Transportation Services"; "Lease or Rental Equipment"; "Miscellaneous Not Included in Other Categories"; "Construction"; and "Maintenance, Repair and Alteration of Real Property."

Finally we come to a heading called "Supplies, Equipment, and Material." Here, under various subheadings such as "Weapons," "Fire Control Equipment," "Guided Missiles," "Tires and Tubes," "Metalworking Machinery," and many others, there were no fewer than 722 different opportunities to sell hardware in various quantities to Uncle Sam.

Remember, all this was in one typical daily issue of the *Commerce Business Daily.* Each and every issue of that daily publication has a similar number of activities.

Are these opportunities just "pie in the sky," or can small businesses and larger firms really make a bundle selling to the huge federal market? Well, we know about the larger firms. Those big corporations that sell major systems are publicly owned, and their annual stockholder reports show that they are doing at least $2-3 billion each in business with Uncle Sam every year. But what about the smaller firms?

Here again are some documented facts from one issue of the *Commerce Business Daily.* Only a few of the more than 900 awards listed are reproduced here. (I should also mention that the *Commerce Business Daily* doesn't even bother to list civilian awards under $10,000 or military products and services under $15,000.)

- Camouflage development awarded to the Brunswick Corporation of Deland, Florida, for $51,018 by the U.S. Army Mobility Command.
- A study on training applications for automated speech technology awarded to Toquon, Inc. of San Diego for $195,162 by NASA.
- Evaluation of the feasibility of increasing the permeability of coal awarded to Physics, International for $99,521 by the Department of Energy.
- Fabrication of an artificial left-ventricular assist device awarded to Thorater Laboratories Corporation for $209,951 by the National Institutes of Health.
- Prepare and/or revise technical publications awarded to Two D Engineering Company of Oxnard, California, for $150,000 by Naval Regional Contracting.

- Control Related Computer Technology awarded to Bold, Beranek and Newman, Inc. of Cambridge, Massachusetts, by the Defense Supply Agency.
- Provide training and technical assistance pertaining to a national brokerage system awarded to Capla Associates, Inc. of Pochell Park, New Jersey, for $1.2 million by the Department of Health, Education, and Welfare.
- Radiation monitoring services awarded to Radiation Management Corporation of Philadelphia, Pennsylvania, for $50,000 by Nuclear Regulatory Commission.
- Maintenance, repair, and rebuilding of aircraft equipment awarded to Bridges Enterprises, Inc. of Midwest City, Oklahoma, for $759,240 by the Air Force Logistics Command.
- Tree thinning awarded to Marmot Construction Works, Ltd., of Puerto Rico for $72,799 by a U.S. Army procurement division.
- Purchase of 20,000 binder jackets from DVC Industries Inc., of Bay Shore, New York, for $36,000 by the General Services Administration.
- Preparation of a propagation handbook for satellite engineers for $74,998 awarded to ORI, Inc., of Silver Spring, Maryland by NASA.
- Rental of one airplane without pilot from Alaska Air Service, Inc., for $27,336 by the Department of the Interior.
- Purchase of 5333 shotguns from O. F. Mossberg and Sons, Inc., for $475,383 by the U.S. Army.
- Purchase of 35 hydraulic swivel joints from Akwin Industries, Inc., of Westbury, New York, for $54,907 by the Naval Aviation Supply Office.
- Purchase of a crane barge from Fred Selton, Inc., of Piene Port, Louisiana for $401,341 by the U.S Army Engineer District.
- Purchase of 21,600 weighted canvas bags used for submarine garbage and trash disposal from the U.S. Lock and Hardware Company of Columbia, Pennsylvania, for $384,480, by the Naval Ships Parts Control Center.
- Purchase of 520 washcan units from Global Housing, Ltd., of The Dalles, Oregon, for $38,870 by the Bureau of Land Management.
- Purchase of 50 trailer-inserted pumps from the Gorman-Rupp Company of Mansfield, Ohio, for $824,773 by the Marine Corps.
- Purchase of animal bedding from the Shurfire Products Corporation of Beltsville, Maryland, for $288,660 by the National Institutes of Health.
- Purchase of 3344 storage batteries from Eagle-Picher Industries, Inc., of Joplin, Missouri, for $77,046 by the Defense General Supply Center.
- Purchase of 442,400 pounds of insecticide bait from A. E. Staley Manufacturing Company of Decatur, Illinois, for $96,000 by the Animal and Plant Health Inspection Service.
- Purchase of 553,800 boxes of rubber bands from the Plymouth Rubber Company, Inc., of Canton, Massachusetts, for $749,780 by the General Services Administration.

- Purchase of 2350 bundles of polyethylene bags from Park Poly Bag Corporation of Duneller, New Jersey, for $94,986 by the National Institutes of Health.
- Purchase of 729,000 yards of cotton tape from the Elizabeth Wabbeing Mills Company of Central Falls, Rhode Island for $66,992 by the Defense Personnel Support Center.
- Purchase of 4264 women's overcoats from VI-MIL, Inc., of Cambridge, Massachusetts, for $359,199 by the Defense Personnel Support Center.

In addition to thousands of business opportunities involving billions of dollars, there are other advantages to doing business with the Government:

- If you are already selling something, you can reduce the cost of your product and service by adding this new market without appreciably increasing your overhead.
- You don't have to worry about your customer's ability to pay. In fact, under some conditions the Government will fund start-up costs, pay in advance, or make payments during the period of performance.
- Your sale is guaranteed before you start producing anything.
- Under some types of Government contracts, you have no risk of loss.
- The customer spends a goodly amount in various types of advertising in order to try to locate you rather than the reverse.

With these proven opportunities and the advantages of Government business, one would think that just about every firm would be fighting to get its share of the Government market. Yet this just isn't so. One year the GSA identified $73 million worth of contracts, each worth $50,000 or more, for which there had been fewer than four bidders. As a program manager in the Government in the late 1960s, I can even say there were times that ten or more bidders were solicited and only one or two—and sometimes not a *single* bidder—responded. Many Government agencies today claim that the number of bidders for Government business, which has never been great, is declining.

Why should this be so? If there is so much money in Government business and so many additional advantages, why aren't businesses going after it? There are two main reasons why companies have failed to take advantage of dealing with Uncle Sam:

1. The Government marketing process is complicated, and relatively few firms understand the process. When doing business with the Government, the seller must contend with a library of procurement regulations, a significant amount of forms and paper work, and an established ritual of bidding and submission of proposals that must conform to policies and directives.
2. There are important methods and techniques for successful marketing and selling to the Government, just as in selling to any other market. Even if the

procedures are known, you can still fail if you do not employ successful marketing and selling methods. In conducting interviews for a study on defense contracting, J. Ronald Fox, a former Associate Professor of Business Administration at the Harvard Business School, found that only 25% or fewer proposals submitted to the Department of Defense were successful. In fact, representatives from several firms indicated their success rate was 15% or less. Yet my own research showed some firms with success at winning Government bids in excess of 70%, and Hyman Silver, a Government contracting proposal consultant, claims a success rate for his clients of over 90%.

This book was written to solve both of these problems. It will not only take you step by step through the process of doing business with the Federal Government, it will also show you the methods and techniques that will make your efforts pay off.

Here's how you should use this book. If you are considering doing Government business, then read the book straight through. You needn't read every word when it comes to specifics. You can always go back and deal with the specifics later when you need them. In this way, in a relatively short period of time, you'll get a general overview of the entire Government market, how to get into it, and what steps you must take in your specific case to do so.

If you are already on the front line in dealing with the Government, it's entirely possible that you have immediate need for some of the information presented. In that case, you should turn to the appropriate chapter dealing with your current needs and make use of the information immediately. You can go back later and read other areas in which the book can help you.

Whether you are a small businessman or a member of a giant corporation, someone who has been contracting with the Government for years or someone who has not yet won a first contract, this book can be worth millions of dollars to you. But only you can put the procedures, techniques, and methods of Government marketing that are presented here into practice. The book can show you how, but reading alone is insufficient. You must actually take action in order to accomplish anything. With full confidence that you *will* take action, let's begin now to find out how you can do millions of dollars in business with the U.S. Government.

Chapter 1

HOW TO GET STARTED

FIRST STEPS

If you have read the introduction to this book, then I assume you are serious, or are at least willing to stay with me a while longer to see if what I say will make it possible for you to make the money I say you will by doing business with the Government. The steps you will follow to get started in Government contracting are simple!

1. Read Chapter 1 of this book and get an overview of what the Government market is like and how the process works.
2. Find Government customers for your product or service.
3. Develop a market plan and initiate your marketing campaign.
4. Bid and register your Government contract.
5. Complete the requirements of the contract and collect your money.
6. Go after new customers, while continuing to do business with the Government customers you already have.

MAJOR FEATURES OF THE GOVERNMENT MARKET
AND GOVERNMENT CONTRACTING

If doing business with the Government were identical with doing business in the consumer or industrial market, you might not need this book. But the fact is that while there are certain fundamental similarities between Government and nongovernment marketing and contracting, there are some significant and very important differences. Similarities include:

- Contractual elements. The essential elements of a contract are identical in both Government and nongovernment contracting. This means that there must be an agreement between both parties for something of value to be exchanged, and that the terms and conditions of the contract must be clearly defined.

7

Also, what is agreed to must be lawful and it must be carried out in the form required by law.

- Rules of contract interpretation. The same rules of interpretation applicable to contracts in the private sector are applicable to Government contracts. This means that doubtful or ambiguous terms of the contract are generally interpreted (under the law) against the drafter, and if the drafter is the Government, the Government is liable.
- Performance obligations. Both you and the Government are obligated to perform according to the terms of the contract. If either you or the Government fails to do this, you both have the same legal options that are available under private contract.
- Price may not be the dominant factor. Government contracts may be negotiated, and as provided for under various Government regulations, price may not be the factor that governs selection of the winning contractor. If you have done business in other markets, you know that price is not always the whole story in those markets either.
- Basic marketing functions and theory. Basic marketing functions, as developed in the nongovernmental area, are the same. Only the applications of these functions and theories have changed.

Important differences in the Government marketplace include:

- Nonliability due to sovereign immunity. This may tend to discourage you, but when Uncle Sam in his sovereign capacity causes damages to you as a contractor, he is not liable for that damage. This concept is derived from an ancient rule of law that states that the Government is not liable for general acts pertaining to the public good. Now don't worry too much about this. For one thing, the Government act must indeed be a general one—it must affect everyone in a given class. You, as an individual contractor, cannot be singled out. Also, the act must be specifically intended for the public good. This isn't a general catchall to allow your customer to run rampant over you. Finally, any nonperformance on your part growing out of Uncle Sam's act of sovereign immunity will be forgiven, and you will not be liable either for delivery or for any resulting delay. Practically speaking, the type of sovereign immunity that is likely to affect you will be the sort that will have a detrimental effect on your business whether you are engaged in Government business or not. For example, if the Government limits your hours of operation because of an energy shortage, you're going to be hurt whether your customer is Uncle Sam or someone else. The difference is that if you *are* dealing with Uncle Sam, late deliveries resulting from governmental curtailment of your hours of operation may be forgiven.
- Governing law. When dealing with the Government, federal law governs the obligations and rights of both you and the Government rather than state law. As you may have guessed, this was determined by no less an authority than the United States Supreme Court.

- The authority of agents. The authority of agents is an area in which there is a significant distinction between Government and commercial contracts, and this distinction can get you into a lot of trouble if you aren't careful. In the world of commerce, an agent has the authority that is derived from the principal whom he represents. He can represent the principal in all matters within the scope of his authority, or by his conduct be given apparent authority under the law, which his poor old principal is liable for. In a nutshell, the principal's agent can perform all acts except those that are specifically denied him. Not so in dealing with the Government. The Government agent is permitted to do only certain things. All else is denied him. Most important of all is that where acts of Government agents are required by law, regulation, or the contract itself to be approved by higher authority, the Government is not bound until that approval is obtained. Frequently a company will get in trouble as a result of this difference in dealing with such Government agents as project engineers, who by their position and conduct apparently have certain authority, but in fact do not.

  For example, a small company modifying commercial vehciles by the addition of armor had a contract with the Government to furnish an armored vehicle conforming to Government specifications. The contract stated that all changes or additions had to have approval of the Government headquarters that had let the contract. A Government engineer was assigned full time to the company during the period of contract performance. He flatly stated that unless certain changes were made to the vehicle, he would not approve acceptance of the product. By his position and conduct, the engineer apparently had the authority to order these changes. The company complied with his directions, assuming that they constituted approval for the changes by the contracting agency of the Government. When the company billed the agency for approximately $5000 in additional charges, the agency refused, citing the terms of the contract requiring approval, and that the Government engineer did not have the authority to order changes or additions to the contract without the approval of the Government contracting officer.

  I'll discuss how to handle this type of problem in a later chapter. For the moment, you should understand that this is a crucial difference between commercial and governmental contracting, and that this difference can lead to problems and cost you money unless you stick to the exact terms of your contract regarding the authority of the Government contracting officer.

- Direct customer control of the market and the contracting process. In the Government marketplace, the Government totally controls the market, the process of bidding and submittal of a proposal, and to the extent that it can, even regulates how the process of marketing will be accomplished. This means that certain strategic variables that you can manipulate and control in the private sector must be viewed as environmental variables that, while you do not control them, you must allow for them and make them a part of your overall marketing campaign.

- Long procurement cycles. Some Government procurements now in the planning stages are years in the future. Yet to win big production contracts then, you must start your planning, marketing campaign, and expenditure of resources now, if you hope to have any chance of winning them in the future.

- Production is accomplished after the sale. This is clearly an advantage that, among other advantages, lowers your risk and means that you need not have large amounts of financial resources tied up in inventory.
- Customer sophistication. In most instances your customer will have a very good understanding of your product or service and what you are offering him. Often you will find that your potential customer know as much about a particular class of products as you do. In a few instances he will know more. This is, in part, because as a customer, the Government sees not only what you are offering, but also exactly what your competition is doing. Your customer, therefore, has a good idea of alternative approaches and solutions and their costs. Also, because the customer is involved in theuse of the product operationally (and frequently you and I are not), he may have firsthand knowledge of employment, tactical use of the product, and so on, which we, as Government contractors, can only obtain secondhand. Examples of these kinds of products would be airplanes, missiles, and space vehicles. Even the Government's knowledge of business and management procedures may also surprise you. Paul R. McDonald in his publication, *Government Marketing Service*, states that this customer sophistication is increasing, as evidenced by ". . . detailed source selection procedures and by sophisticated techniques such as program management, systems engineering, configuration management, cost measurement, schedule performance control, and technical performance systems."
- Ease of entry into the marketplace. Although many firms that have the potential for doing big business avoid Government contracting, it is relatively easy to enter the market. The Government, having established the market, will sometimes finance your entry, provide detailed manufacturing specifications, help you find specific Government customers for your product or service, maintain the marketing distribution system for you, and help you in many other ways that will make it easier to enter the Government market than many other markets in the private sector. More about the various methods that the Government will help you with and how to obtain this help will be found in Chapter 3.
- Customer financed product development, equipment and facilities. The governmental customer will frequently fund your new-product ideas that he is interested in and will lend you or give you the equipment and facilities to do the job. Although Government funding of the development of a new product will generally mean that you must compete with other Government contractors for a production contract later, allowing the Government to participate in funding a new product puts you in a very competitive position for winning these later production contracts—and may also give you a new product that you can sell in the consumer market. Borrowing or receiving free Government

equipment or the free use of facilities for performance of your contract means that you have no investment at the front end for items that might otherwise be a major portion of your cost.

- A market composed of a few big customers operating under similar regulations and procedures. This is both an advantage and a disadvantage. It means that once you master the procedures of doing business with the Government this whole giant market, with relatively minor differences between segments, is open to you. On the other hand, because of the limited number of customers, loss of a single customer can have a significant negative impact on your business.

- The potential for rapid changes and fluctuation in demand for product or services. International tension or conflict resolution can cause requirements to rise or fall with great rapidity. A change in the Government administration, in policy, doctrine, tactics, or political factors, can cause dramatic and immediate changes in the fortunes of any planned or active procurement. The advancement of technology, especially in the defense area, may cause product obsolescence long before a product would enter the final stages of its life cycle in other markets. In fact, the product may even be obsolete when the prototype is produced. If a redirection is made at this late stage, you could end up completing a research and development contract without the possibility of future production. The risk of any program not proceeding all the way from basic research to production must always be considered in dealing with the Government if in your particular program you do not make your money at the front end.

WHAT YOU MUST KNOW IN ORDER TO DO BUSINESS

In order to do business with the Government, you must know where to market your products or services within the federal structure, how to make these products or services known, which forms and papers to use and where to get them, and how to bid on procurements. Let's focus on these basics.

Two Broad Classes of Federal Products

The General Services Administration (GSA) classifies federal purchases into two broad categories:

- General use.
- Mission-oriented applications.

The general-use category includes products and services that all agencies might need. They include office supplies and equipment, telephones, maintenance and janitorial services, and so on. Mission-oriented applications would include weapons systems for the Department of Defense, or new energy-saving inventions for the Department of Energy.

Six Important Government Business Opportunities

Within each of these two categories are levels of work, with each level representing a separate business opportunity. These six separate business opportunities are:

1. Major systems opportunities.
2. Major subsystems opportunities.
3. Major manufacturing opportunities.
4. Equipment and service opportunities.
5. Component opportunities.
6. Research opportunities.

The general-use category encompasses equipment and service opportunities. Mission-oriented applications encompass all six opportunities. Also, research opportunities are found within each of the other opportunities.

As conceptualized in Figure 1, the major systems opportunities are relatively few. These are the multibillion dollar operations in which major systems companies such as McDonnell Douglas, Boeing, and others develop and produce major weapon systems, space vehicles, and energy complexes. At the major subsystem level, a large company may develop and produce a significant portion of the overall system, as Pratt & Whitney produces the powerful F 100-PW-100 turbofan engines for the McDonnell Aircraft Company's F-15 Eagle fighter aircraft, which is made for the Air Force.

The next level of opportunity are major manufacturing contracts. Here the opportunity is not to develop a major system or subsystem, but to produce something in quantity that someone else has developed. The next Government opportunity is to produce equipment or supply services. The equipment or services may or may not be used in the major manufacturing, subsystem, or system opportunities. At the lowest level, there are component opportunities. These are items that go into making equipment, systems, or subsystems. Therefore, components may be used by firms taking advantage of any of the other Government business opportunities.

In general, proceeding from top to bottom of Figure 1, the size of individual companies going after each class of opportunities tends to become smaller, while the number of opportunities tends to increase. But, more important, each class of opportunities is distinct and has its own characteristics. Although all are in the Government market, each class of opportunity actually is a different subset of the overall market with different requirements, customers, and strategies for success. And while firms frequently can and do operate within more than one subset simultaneously, the apparent advantages of doing so often lead even major

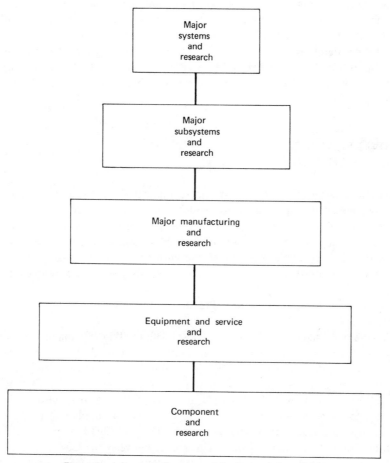

Figure 1. Important Government business opportunities.

companies into committing significant resources to a new market subset without having sufficiently analyzed the risks involved or even realized that a different market subset has been entered.

Two examples are worth relating here. A supplier of military body armor made from ceramic composite decided to go one step further and make the ceramic components as well. The company jumped in, bought the equipment, thought it bought the know-how, got a contract, and promptly found itself facing a major cost overrun. Why? Labor skills required for producing the ceramic composite had been significantly lower than those required for producing the body armor. When the company's higher labor rates (which supported the higher skills) were applied to the product and its material components, costs soared.

Example number two concerns a major systems company that decided that a major manufacturing opportunity was too good to pass up and bid against an old-line major manufacturer. Result? A million or so dollars to get the bid out, which had a price that was 30% higher than the winner.

Therefore, before rushing into more than one of these different levels of Government opportunities, you must define what opportunity subset you are currently in, what you have to do to get into the new subset, and what it will cost you to do so.

AN OVERVIEW OF THE PROCEDURES OF DOING BUSINESS WITH THE GOVERNMENT

Government business procedures are not complicated . . . once you know them. But you must know them in order to do business and in order to formulate the correct strategies and tactics to do business successfully. While later chapters will specify step by step the actions you must take in order to be successful, you should not skip this overview of the entire process. To do so gives you an overview of the forest, so that the individual trees will give you no trouble later.

General Use and Mission Application Procurement

Procurement of general-use items are consolidated within two major Government agencies: the GSA, or General Services Administration, and the Defense Logistics Agency (DLA). The GSA does the lion's share of the buying for civilian agencies, and it stores and distributes common-use items throughout the Government. The GSA also awards federal supply schedule contracts that allow individual agencies to order directly from you, the Government supplier. The DLA runs organizations called Defense Logistic Centers. These centers buy and supply commodities for military users. Under agreements between the GSA and DLA, the military makes purchases of some general-use items through GSA supply sources. Consolidated purchasing allows you to hit an estimated 90% of the general-use market through the GSA and DLA. But more on this later.

For the missions application items, including those used by the Department of Defense, you must approach each of the various units of the appropriate agency separately.

Government Procurement Regulations

As you might expect, the Government has developed several sets of regulations comprising thousands of pages, defining exactly how you and the Government must operate. As you also might expect, different regulations have been developed that are applicable to different Government departments and agencies. However, the basic sets of regulations are found in two publications:

- The Defense Acquisition Regulations (DAR), formerly called the Armed Services Procurement Regulations, are issued by the Department of Defense (DOD) and they establish uniform policies and procedures relating to doing business with that department of the Government.
- The Federal Procurement Regulations (FPR) define the policies and procedures pertaining to procurements by civilian executive agencies of personal property and nonpersonal services, such as construction. These regulations are issued by GSA; however, they may be further implemented by other Government agencies such as the National Aeronautical and Space Administration (NASA) Procurement Regulations and the GSA Procurement Regulations, implemented and issued by GSA.

Regardless of which of the Government regulations you are dealing with, the basic material on audits, termination, pricing, proposal preparation, property management, renegotiation, and so on, is almost the same in all incidences, and the contents of each set of regulations covers essentially the same material. To give you some idea of what this material is, here is the contents of the most extensive set of regulations, the DAR:

Section   I General Provisions
          II Procurement by Formal Advertising
        III Procurement by Negotiation
       IV Special Types and Methods
        V Interdepartmental Procurement
       VI Foreign Purchases
      VII Contract Clauses and Forms
     VIII Termination and Contracts
       IX Patents, Copyrights and Technical Data
        X Bonds and Insurance
       XI Federal, State and Local Taxes
      XII Labor
     XIII Government Property
     XIV Inspection and Acceptance
      XV Contract Cost Procedures
     XVI Procurement Forms
    XVII Extraordinary Actions to Facilitate the National Defense
   XVIII Procurement of Construction and Contracting for Architect-Engineer Services
     XIX Transportation
      XX Adminstrative Matters

Clearly there is a mountain of information here, and the DAR alone runs to 26 separate volumes plus appendices. To make the situation even more interesting, the regulations are constantly under revision. The question naturally arises, how important are the regulations, and what do you do about them?

The regulations are important. In fact, when you are confronted with a particular problem or situation, you should immediately consult the appropriate section. However, face it, not many specialist contract administrators, either Government or in industry, know all the regulations, or are able to keep up with all the changes, except as they require the information because of a contract they are involved in. It is unrealistic to imagine that you are going to become an instant expert in any of the regulations. But there is no need to. What you do require is access to an updated set of regulations when you need them. You can, of course, buy a set of any of the regulations from the Superintendent of Documents, U.S. Government Printing Office, Washington, D.C. 20402. Once your Government sales are well established, it isn't a bad idea to invest in a set of regulations applicable to the department or agency of the Government that you are doing business with. However, when you are first getting started you will probably be consulting them infrequently. Rather than invest several hundred dollars in the regulations plus a service to keep them updated, see if you can use someone else's. Your local Small Business Administration probably has a set, as do big university libraries and major Government contractors. None of these sources will mind your making an occasional visit to look something up if you approach them in the right way.

Equal Employment Opportunity Regulations

This worries many potential Government contractors. All contractors doing business with Uncle Sam must comply with all provisions of Executive Order 11246 of September 24, 1965 as amended by Executive Order 11375 of October 13, 1967, and with all rules, regultions, and relevant orders of the Secretary of Labor. Basically, you must not only comply with executive orders forbidding discrimination by Government contractors against any employee or applicant for employment because of race, color, religion, sex, or national origin, but you are also required to take affirmative action to ensure that employees are treated equally. You may be required to periodically report the racial composition of your work force. If there are an insufficient number of minority members in any job category, you will be required to specify the steps you will take to eliminate the imbalance.

Obviously, there are instances where the Equal Opportunity Regulations may not be totally applicable. For example, how do you adjust for racial imbalance if you are a one-man consultant firm? Usually the solicitation from the Government will carry a notice as to affirmative action requirements. For example, a recent request for proposal (RFP) from NASA's Marshall Space Flight Center carried the following:

"NOTE THE AFFIRMATIVE ACTION REQUIREMENT OF THE EQUAL OPPORTUNITY CLAUSE WHICH MAY APPLY TO THE CONTRACT RESULTING FROM THIS SOLICITATION." (NASA PR 3.501(b))

"NOTE THE CERTIFICATION OF NONSEGREGATED FACILITIES IN THIS SOLICITATION. Bidders, offerors, and applicants are cautioned to note the 'Certification of Nonsegregated Facilities' in the solicitation. Failure of a bidder/offeror to agree to the certification will render his bid or offer nonresponsive to the terms of solicitations involving awards of contracts exceeding $10,000 which are not exempt from the provisions of the Equal Opportunity clause" (October 1971) (NASA PR 3.501(b)).

Other Regulations and General Contract Provisions

In addition to the Equal Opportunity Regulations, Government contracts may contain other general provisions and cite other regulations that pertain to inspection requirements, disputes, patents, labor standards, and so on. For example, the Buy American Act limits use of articles, materials, and supplies to those that have been made or produced in the United States, unless justification for foreign purchase can be made in the public interest or the cost of the domestic product is unreasonable. The Walsh-Healey Act, which is applicable to contracts exceeding $10,000, provides for minimum wage rates, minimum ages of employees, maximum labor hours, safe and sanitary working conditions, and so on.

A recent U.S. Air Force RFP that resulted in a contract for several hundred thousand dollars included in the RFP the requirement for clean air and water certification, a Buy American Certificate, certification of nonsegregated facilities, an affirmative action program if the bidder had 50 employees or more, equal employment compliance in accordance with ASRP (now DAR) 7-2003.14(b) (3), and various cost-accounting standards.

Usually, exactly what is going to be required of you is spelled out in the RFP or the regulation or law referred to in the RFP. But if it is not, or you need help, you can get it from either the assigned Government contracting officer or the Small Business Administration. Copies of standard forms containing certain general provisions may be obtained from the nearest GSA Business Service Center, all of which are listed in Chapter 3.

HOW THE GOVERNMENT CLASSIFIES ITS PRODUCTS

In order to minimize the potential confusion that could arise from the fact that the Government buys so many different items, the federal catalogue system was developed. It lists a single name, description, and identification number for each supply item. This identification number, which contains 13 digits, is known as a National Stock Number (NSN), and it identifies a specific item in the Federal Supply System. For example, NSN 9515-00-230-6685 identifies steel plate, carbon (zinc coated), which fulfills all the requirements of a military specification, MIL-S-22698A.

Cataloging Handbook H2-1 published by the Defense Logistics Agency is the basic classification handbook for general use, but you can find a more comprehensive listing in the *Standard Industrial Classification Manual,* which is put out by the Office of Management and Budget of the Executive Office of the President. You can get both these publications from the Superintendent of Documents.

What Specifications and Standards Are and Where to Get Them

Federal Specifications and Standards (FED SPEC and FED STD) and military specifications and standards (MIL-SPEC and MIL-STD) are purchase descriptions of the supply items or services that are used in Government procurements. In general, they are based on actual performance criteria. Usually they describe products that are readily available; in fact, sometimes a brand name is used, with the requirement being "brand name or equal." However, occasionally the Government errs and the item specified is no longer obtainable anywhere at any price. Therefore, just because a federal or military specification is spelled out as required for a particular contract, don't automatically assume that the Government has checked the item out and that it is definitely obtainable. A few years ago, the Air Force advertised for several thousand navigation watches of a particular type in accordance with a certain established military specification, only to discover that the company that made a key component had gone out of business, and that there was no other source for that component in the world. I'll cover what to do in a situation like that in the next chapter, on special problems in bidding.

Federal or military standards aren't the same as federal or military specifications. The standards establish the technical limits that are referred to in the specifications, in RFPs or invitations for bid (IFBs), and in proposals and contracts. Standards may govern uniformity in materials, procedures for doing something, designs, processes, and even engineering practices. For example, MIL-A-43197(GL), a military specification for a fragmentation protective body armor, states that the testing of the armor end product will be accomplished in accordance with MIL-STD-662. MIL-STD-662 is entitled "Ballistic Acceptance Test Method for Personal Armor Material" and details exactly the testing procedure to be followed.

A complete list called *The Index of Federal Specifications and Standards* can be obtained from the Superintendent of Documents. You can also obtain a free booklet entitled *The Guide to Federal Specifications and Standards of the Federal Government* from field offices of the Department of Commerce, the SBA, and the GSA Business Service Centers. The latter are listed in Chapter 3. You can buy copies of federal specifications and standards from GSA Business Service Centers or from:

Specification Sales
GSA, Bldg. 197
Washington Navy Yard
Washington, D.C. 20407

To purchase military specifications and standards, write:

The Naval Publications and Forms Center
5801 Tabor Avenue
Philadelphia, PA 19120

The center will supply limited copies of specifications and standards without charge. Use a DD Form 1425 (Figure 2).

Qualified Products List (QPL) and What to Do About It

For many would-be Government contractors the QPL represents a source of considerable frustration, because for some products, if you are not on the QPL, you

NAVAL PUBLICATIONS AND FORMS CENTER
5801 TABOR AVENUE
PHILADELPHIA, PA. 19120
OFFICIAL BUSINESS
PENALTY FOR PRIVATE USE, $300

POSTAGE AND FEES PAID
DEPARTMENT OF DEFENSE
DOD-316

REQUISITION NUMBER *(For Local Convenience)*

Please self-address the above label. Forward this form to the address shown herein. A window envelope may be used. Your request submitted on this form will speed service. Reorder forms will be enclosed with each shipment.

SPECIFICATIONS AND STANDARDS REQUISITION	IFB, RFQ OR RFP CLOSING DATE

Send_____copies of the below listed documents which are listed in the DOD Index of Specifications and Standards.

STANDARDIZATION DOCUMENT SYMBOL	TITLE (From DOD Index of Specifications and Standards)
SIGNATURE	DATE

Fold

DD FORM 1425
1 OCT 72

PREVIOUS EDITIONS OF THIS FORM ARE OBSOLETE.
S/N 0102-LF-014 1701

TO: COMMANDING OFFICER
NAVAL PUBLICATIONS AND FORMS CENTER
5801 TABOR AVENUE
PHILADELPHIA, PA. 19120

Figure 2. Form DD 1425/Specifications and Standards Requisition.

won't be permitted to bid. To make matters more complicated, there can be some interesting problems in getting on the QPL. I'll discuss this in more detail in ways of doing business with the Government in Chapter 5. But for now, what is a QPL and what is it supposed to do?

The QPL is a list of manufacturers' products that have been found to be "qualified" by the U.S. Government. According to the GSA, certain specifications require qualification testing prior to the award of the contract (or, in most cases, even prior to the bid) because the period of testing would delay delivery of the product, or because the tests would require equipment not generally available, or because repetitive tests would be too costly, or, finally, because the Government requires assurance prior to contract award that the product is satisfactory for its intended use.

However, Jack W. Robertson, Washington editor of *Electronic News* and author of the book *Selling to the Federal Government*, says that the object of the QPL is to prevent incompetent firms from obtaining a contract through buying in, and then not delivering.

From my own experience in Government, I can say that all these explanations for the QPL have validity. But regardless of the reason, your problem is using the QPL to your own advantage. I'll get into that in Chapter 5.

You can find a list of federal specifications involving QPLs in the previously mentioned *Index of Federal Specifications and Standards*. You can find military specifications requiring QPL lsiting in *The Department of Defense Index of Specifications and Standards*, which you can also buy from the Superintendent of Documents.

Selling Old and New Items

To sell items currently procured by the Government through competitive bidding, most Government organizations use Standard Form 129, "Bidder's Mailing List Application" (See Appendix 2) to get you into the system, with some organizations using a supplemental form such as DD Form 558-1, "Bidder's Mailing List Application Supplement," used by the Department of Defense (Figure 3). You can also respond to a published advertisement appearing in the *Commerce Business Daily*, which I'll discuss in more detail a little later in this chapter, and then we'll really get down to how to use this publication to maximum advantage in Chapter 4.

If you want to sell a new item, or one that is an improvement over an item that the Government is currently buying, contact a GSA Business Service Center. They will have you complete a GSA Form 1171, "Application for Presenting New Articles" (Figure 4) and will also ask for explanatory data, sales literature, copies of printed commercial price lists, and a sales history, if any. However, the best way to introduce a new item is through a Government organization responsible for developing it through a so-called unsolicited proposal. This process, and the ways to make it pay off, will also be covered in a later chapter.

BIDDER'S MAILING LIST APPLICATION SUPPLEMENT

Form Approved
Budget Bureau No. 22-R091

IF ADDITIONAL SPACE IS REQUIRED, ATTACH SEPARATE SHEET AND REFER TO ITEM NUMBER

1.	OPERATIONS AT	ENGINEERING	PRODUCTION	OTHERS	TOTAL
NUMBER OF EMPLOYEES	MAXIMUM LEVEL				
	MINIMUM *(During last 2 yrs.)*				
	PRESENT LEVEL				

2. CONTRACTS HELD WITH ARMED SERVICES DURING PAST 3 YEARS *(List separately)*

CONTRACT NUMBER	DESCRIPTION OF ITEMS	DOLLAR VALUE

3. TYPES OF EQUIPMENT, COMPONENTS, MATERIAL OR SERVICES NOW BEING MANUFACTURED, PERFORMED, OR DEVELOPED *(Commercial and Military)*

4. FLOOR SPACE ENGINEERING (Sq. ft.)	LABORATORY	TOTAL FLOOR SPACE *(Including warehouse and manufacturing space)*

5. BRIEF DESCRIPTION OF BUILDINGS *(Type of construction and use)*

6. MACHINERY AND EQUIPMENT[1]

7. TESTING AND/OR LABORATORY FACILITIES[1]

8. ADDRESSES *(Including counties)* OF FACTORIES, FOUNDRIES, MINES, OR YARDS, IF ANY *(Specify)*

9. SECURITY CLEARANCE *(If applicable, check highest clearance authorized by clearing agency)*

FOR KEY PERSONNEL			FOR PLANT ONLY	
TOP SECRET	CONFIDENTIAL	SECRET	CONFIDENTIAL	
SECRET				

LIST DEPARTMENTS WHICH HAVE GRANTED SECURITY CLEARANCE AND DATES GRANTED

10. INCLOSURES *(Check)*
☐ FINANCIAL STATEMENTS, INCLUDING OPERATING STATEMENTS   ☐ DESCRIPTIVE LITERATURE
☐ ADDITIONAL INFORMATION ATTACHED   ☐ BROCHURE   ☐ CATALOG   ☐ PHOTOGRAPHS

11. I CERTIFY THAT THE INFORMATION SUPPLIED HEREIN *(Including any attachments)* IS CORRECT

DATE	NAME AND ADDRESS OF APPLICANT	SIGNATURE

[1]Give brief, representative outline of type and condition of machinery, equipment (6), and facilities (7) available; if not owned by firm, give status in detail.

Figure 3.   Form DD 558-1/Bidder's Mailing List Application Supplement.

Form approved OMB No. **29-R0071**

APPLICATION FOR PRESENTING NEW ARTICLES	Please read instructions on the back.	GSA CONTROL NUMBER

1. ARTICLE DESCRIPTION/IDENTIFICATION — *Only one product for each application.*

a. GENERIC NAME AND PLAIN WORD DESCRIPTION *(Attach detailed data concerning physical characteristics of the item; kind of material dimensions, and electrical data, where applicable; performance characteristics, component parts, packaging, technical specifications, and test data.)*

b. BASIC FUNCTIONAL PURPOSE(S) OF THE ARTICLE'S INTENDED USE *(If additional space is needed to answer this or any other questions, attach continuation sheet)*

c. BRAND NAME	d. CATALOG NUMBER	e. IS SAMPLE AVAILABLE ☐ YES ☐ NO
2. NAME OF MANUFACTURER'S MAIN OFFICE		4. APPROXIMATE UNIT (EACH) RETAIL PRICE
3. NAME AND ADDRESS OF FACTORY MANUFACTURING THE ARTICLE		$

5. ARTICLE SPECIFICATIONS AND RESTRICTIONS

If the article meets any of these specifications, show the specification number in the applicable block(s).	a. FEDERAL SPECIFICATION	b. MILITARY SPECIFICATIONS
	c. COMMERCIAL STANDARDS	d. OTHER *(Specify)*

e. LIST ANY RESTRICTIONS RECOMMENDED ON USE REGARDING HEALTH, SAFETY, OR OTHER HAZARDOUS OR ENVIRONMENTAL CONCERNS

6. HAS ARTICLE EVER BEEN REJECTED BY THE GOVERNMENT BECAUSE OF NONCOMPLIANCE WITH SPECIFICATIONS *If "Yes," explain.*
☐ YES ☐ NO

7. COMMERCIAL USERS OF ARTICLE — *Do not exceed five (List names, addresses, and telephone numbers)*

8. FEDERAL AGENCIES THAT HAVE PURCHASED THE ARTICLE *(List names, addresses, and telephone numbers)*

9. FEDERAL AGENCIES THAT HAVE EXPRESSED AN INTEREST IN THE ARTICLE OR MAY BE INTERESTED IN PURCHASING IT *(List names, addresses, and telephone numbers)*

10. APPLICANT'S BUSINESS IS	CATEGORY *(Mark applicable box(es))*
☐ MANUFACTURER ☐ DISTRIBUTOR ☐ JOBBER ☐ OTHER *(Specify):*	☐ WOMEN OWNED ☐ SMALL BUSINESS ☐ MINORITY OWNED ☐ LARGE BUSINESS

11. APPLICANT	a. TYPED (OR PRINTED) NAME AND ADDRESS	b. TELEPHONE NUMBER *(Include area code)*	c. DATE
		d. SIGNATURE	
		e. TITLE	

GENERAL SERVICES ADMINISTRATION

GSA FORM **1171** (REV. 10-78)

Figure 4. Form GSA 1171/Application for Presenting New Articles.

INSTRUCTIONS FOR PRESENTING NEW ARTICLES

Purpose. This form provides a uniform formal method for submission of new articles for GSA review. If sufficient demand can be anticipated and if the item presented is in a category for which the Federal Supply Service (FSS) has procurement responsibility, consideration will be given to including the new item in one of the FSS buying programs.

General. Prepare four copies of this application form for each new product to be presented. Retain one copy for your record. Send the original and two completed copies, with attachments affixed to each form, to the Business Service Center serving your state. Do not include samples of the article with this application. If required, they will be requested. If more space is required, use sheets of paper and indicate the item number to which comments apply.

Replies. Normally, applications are routed to the Federal Supply Service in the GSA Central Office, for technical evaluation and reply. Every effort is made to notify applicants of the status/disposition of an application within 60 days from the date of receipt by the Central Office. Formal written acceptance/rejection of your application will be made by FSS. All applications are processed as received. Requests for the status of this application should be directed to your regional Business Service Center.

Specific Item Instructions. Items not shown below are self-explanatory.

Item	
1	Give the generic name and describe the product in plain words (one product per application). *Detailed technical data must be attached.* Sales literature is rarely enough. If the product is made of plastic, for example, what kind of plastic - be completely specific. Summarize test data and laboratory reports available. This data will be requested if necessary. One application may cover different sizes, colors, etc. of the product.
4	Approximate retail price and unit of sale should be shown. Pricelists, e.g., retail, dealer, distributor, should be submitted with this application. (Special pricelists, printed just for the Government, are not acceptable.
5a thru e	Since evaluation of products offered requires knowledge in depth concerning kind of material, dimensions, formulations, electrical data, etc., all applicable Federal/Industry specifications and standards to which the product or components conform, must be cited in this item or data attached. *The Federal Supply Service must know what it is buying.* Where safety is a factor, UL approval will hasten processing.

Item	
	When a product is within the scope of Federal/Industry safety type standards, it must meet these standards. GSA will not contract for a product unless it meets the Department of Labor, Occupational Safety and Health Standards (OSHA).
7	Commercial users must be listed. The product must have an established catalog or market price and have been sold in substantial quantity to the general public.
9	In addition to listing sales to Government activities (item 8), it is helpful to list the Government people who have expressed interest in your product. Give each individual's name, address and, if known, telephone number. This will assist those conducting the evaluation to contact your reference for opinions and recommendations.
11	The name and address in this item should be the same as that which will appear on any subsequent contract. It is also the address to which all correspondence will be sent. Include telephone number(s).

Sign and date the original and two copies of this form and with all requested data attached to each copy, send them to the following GSA Business Service Center.

GSA FORM **1171 BACK** (REV. 10-78)

Figure 4 (*Continued*)

GOVERNMENT PROCUREMENT METHODS

Every document you will ever read about Government procurement that is published by the Government will tell you that the preferred method of Government contracting is by a method called "formal advertising." In theory, this method gives potential suppliers an equal chance to compete. The Government publicizes its need through:

- Formal advertisements in media such as the *Commerce Business Daily.*
- Invitations for bid (IFBs) sent to firms on established mailing lists.

A bid opening date is established, and on the appointed hour of that date all the bids are opened and the lowest responsible bidder meeting the terms and specifications is awarded the contract.

Well, formal advertising may be the preferred method, but it is definitely not the method most frequently used. Dr. J. Ronald Fox, a former Associate Professor of Business Administration at Harvard as well as an Assistant Secretary of the Army and author of the book *Arming America,* says that more than 80% of all military procurement dollars have been awarded through negotiation, which is the alternative procurement process permitted. Professor Fox goes on to say: "Senior officials in the Office of the Secretary of Defense believe that rapid changes in world events and available technology will continue to make negotiation the primary method of defense procurement." In fact, only 16% of all federal procurement dollars lumped together are awarded as a result of formally advertised bids.

In negotiated procurement, the rules are that the selection of a contractor will be made to the best advantage of the Government based not only on price but on other factors as well. The most common vehicle for securing bids in the negotiated procurement is the request for proposal (RFP) and sometimes the request for quotation, which I'll talk about in detail in Chapter 5.

Responsible Bidders and Offerors

As a Government contractor, you will soon discover that Uncle Sam has reserved several "catch-22s" that can be used to snatch your winning bid away from you. However, there is little to worry about if you understand what is expected of you ahead of time. The Government will only award contracts to responsible bidders or offerors. Now that's reasonable, isn't it? You are responsible, are you not? Well, unless you are prepared ahead of time, you may not be "responsible" by Government definition. It is the Government contracting officer who determines whether you are responsible or not according to guidance provided by the applicable procurement regulations. I emphasize the word "guidance" here. The contracting officer's appraisal of your bid includes what he thinks of your firm's plant, testing facilities, production capabilities, quality control, financial status, credit rating, and even your performance on previous Government contracts and, according to the General Services Administration, even your "overall integrity."

This means that you must practice some pre-bid salesmanship with respect to the contracting office of the agency you are planning to do business with.

Let me put this in perspective for you. By regulation, the Government is required to consider doing business with any potential bidder who meets the letter of the regulation, whether or not this agency knows you or has done business with you before. Now, with noting more than a written proposal and a bid price to go on, would you want to do business with someone whom you had never done business with before, and perhaps didn't even know? Well, the Government isn't wild about the idea either. So its authorized representative, in this case the contracting officer, wants to know more. And if he doesn't like what he is able to learn, he can legally dump you—even though you have otherwise "won" the contract by the nominal rules pertaining to the bid.

However, this is clearly a case in which an ounce of prevention is worth a ton of cure. You don't have to be General Motors. Just get in there before you even make a bid and explain what you have and where you're going. You can win huge Government contracts working out of your garage or an office in your home if you convince the contracting officer that you know your stuff and are "responsible," according to his definition. It's important to keep in mind the contracting officer's motivation here. He's not out to take you. But he is responsible for ensuring that the Government is not going to be taken in some way if he awards you the contract. If you are asked for additional information before the contract is awarded, don't shrug this off as being unimportant. This is an opportunity to really show off your company, the abilities of its management, and your capability for performing Government work. Really run with this opportunity.

If an offer from a small business is rejected on the grounds of insufficient capacity or inadequate credit, the contracting officer is required to notify the Small Business Administration (SBA). The SBA then looks into the situation. If the SBA feels you can perform the contract, they will issue a Certificate of Competency. If everything else is in order, the contracting officer will then award you the contract. But you will save time, money, and ulcer attacks by pre-bid marketing so that the Government buyers will get to know you and things never go this far.

Then, once you haver performed well on one government contract, you are in great shape to get future work with much less hassle. You are no longer an unknown with the folks you have done the work for. You are now accepted as a known quantity. And for Government work with new customers you can ask your old customers if you can use them as a reference. You will probably have to document and describe previous Government work anyway, but it never hurts to inform and alert your old customers. Then when you begin contacting potential new customers, you can give the name and telephone number of your current, satisfied, and forewarned Government customer as a reference.

Responsive Bids and Offers

Not only must you be responsible, but your bid or offer must be "responsive." Here again, you have to go by what the Government means by this, not what you or I or Noah Webster might mean. Government contracts are awarded on the basis of the lowest responsive and responsible offer.

According to the regulatons, your bid may be considered nonresponsive for several reasons.

One reason: if the offer doesn't conform to the essential requirements of the RFP or IFB. What are these "essential requirements"? They could be specifications, or delivery schedules, or the work itself as described in the RFP. For example, while in the Government, I once saw an offeror's proposal thrown out as non-responsive because it proposed to do more than the contract called for. The statement of work in the RFP said that the contractor must study one aircraft type from each of five different aircraft classes listed: fighters, bombers, helicopters, reconnaisance aircraft, and transports. The contractor proposed, within a fixed price bid, to study *four* different aircraft in each class.

Second, if you as bidder impose conditions that would modify requirements of the IFB or RFP or limit liability to the Government that would give you an advantage over other bidders, your offer can also be discarded as nonresponsive. Examples of this include a notice that the product is subject to prior sale; or that prices are subject to change without notice, if no definite price is given; or if your offer arrives late.

You won't do business with the Government for very long before you realize that, when it feels like, the Government accepts what could most certainly be called nonresponsive offers. A basic principle that you must understand is that the Government, as represented by its agents with whom you must deal, will do a lot of strange things when it feels it is in its best interests. This principle is so basic and so important that I'm going to restate it in capital letters.

THE GOVERNMENT WILL FREQUENTLY VIOLATE ITS OWN RULES IF GOVERNMENT REPRESENTATIVES FEEL THAT IT IS IN ITS BEST INTERESTS.

This does not however mean that you should intentionally violate the rules and regulations of Government procurement. Not at all. You should strive to obey each and every one. In general, this will maximize your winning of Government contracts. But when all else fails, keep the basic principle in mind, and if you believe what you propose is indeed in the best interests of Uncle Sam, work to convince the Government of this at all stages of doing business, both before the bid, during the bid, and afterward. But do *not* do it in your proposal.

Your proposal must be responsive to have any chance of winning. If some new, perhaps last-minute and therefore not presold idea occurs to you, and you are tempted to propose something different from what the Government asks for in the RFP or IFB, I recommend submitting both a responsive and an alternative proposal. I will tell you now, however, that for various reasons that we'll get into later in the book, this alternative proposal will probably not be accepted. But at least you will have documented your "better solution" while not ruining your chances at the contract with your responsive proposal.

To insure being responsive, the GSA recommends reviewing the following checklist before submitting an offer:

Has every question been fully and accurately answered and all requested information been furnished?

Are all the requirements of the basic specification understood? Have requirements of other referenced specifications in the invitation to bid been checked, including requirements for packaging and marking?

Have computations of the bid price been rechecked and has the price quoted been verified as accurate and complete?

Has due consideration been given to likely market conditions during the period in which performance will occur under the contract terms? Is the cost of raw materials rising? Are labor costs increasing? Are transportation costs a factor?

Can the delivery requirements of the invitation be met?

Has the offer been proofed after typing to be certain that no figures have been transposed or other typographical errors made?

Has the offer been signed?

Will the offer be mailed in time for receipt prior to the established deadline for opening?

The Government usually isn't totally hard-nosed about honest mistakes. For example, correction of responsive bids is permitted under Government regulations. Therefore, if the contracting officer suspects that you have made a pricing error, he will ask you to verify the offer before making the award. Similarly, if there is an obvious clerical error, your bid may be corrected and still considered if verification of your intended bid can be obtained. However, you should certainly not depend on someone else to catch and correct your blunders. You will lose both contracts and money if you are not careful.

Contract Termination

Contract termination may be initiated by the Government for two reasons: for default, or for the Government's convenience. While contract termination is obviously not very desirable for the contractor, there are basic differences between the two reasons for termination, and their effect on you as contractor.

Contract termination for default occurs when you fail or refuse to deliver the required supplies or perform the required services or otherwise perform as you agreed to do under the contract, or when in the Government's view you fail to make progress to such an extent as to endanger the performance of the contract. During performance of the contract, the Government will continually review that performance. If any of the above reasons for default are noted, the contracting officer will attempt to work out a mutually acceptable solution with you. However, if this can't be done, the Government can terminate your contract and find someone else to do the job. If the termination is for default, and the contract with the new supplier necessitates a higher cost to the Government, you may be held liable for the difference.

Termination for the Government's convenience is an entirely different matter. It carries no stigma and you are allowed to recover all "reasonable and allowable" costs that you have incurred up to the point of termination, as well as costs you incur in carrying out the termination with a reasonable profit. Why would the Government terminate "for convenience"? Sometimes an agency will simply run out of money for a project. For example, several small contracts were cancelled by the Army when the office's budget was thrown off by several million dollars following a contractor's successful suit. A NASA R&D contract got the axe when a better and cheaper solution to the original problem was found.

Many contracts that should be are never terminated simply because to terminate them is more expensive than carrying them out to completion.

We'll be getting deeper into termination tactics in a later chapter.

The Commerce Business Daily

The *Commerce Business Daily* (Figure 5) is so important to Government contracting that it deserves to be treated out of sequence as a part of this general overview of doing business with the Government. It is the Government's main method of making interested parties and potential bidders aware of proposed procurements, forthcoming bids, and contract awards. In addition, it includes subcontracting leads, sale of surplus property, and foreign business opportunities. With some few exceptions, the *Commerce Business Daily* is required by law to publish all procurement actions of $5000 or more by civilian agencies, and $10,000 or more by the military. This publication is a *must* if you are going to do business with the Government. Although many large libraries subscribe to the *Commerce Business Daily* and it is also available at GSA Business Service Centers, it is obviously much more convenient to get your own copy. You can subscribe for $105 per year delivered first class, or $80 per year, second class. Whether its worth the extra $25 to get it first class or not depends on how you are going to use it, since second class takes several days longer. If you are going to use it as a source for immediate bidding, then it's clearly in your interest to get it as soon as possible. Write to:

Superintendent of Documents
Government Printing Office
Washington, D.C. 20402

WEDNESDAY, MARCH 21, 1979

Commerce Business Daily

U. S. DEPARTMENT OF COMMERCE
Juanita M. Kreps, Secretary

A daily list of U.S. Government procurement invitations, contract awards, subcontracting leads, sales of surplus property and foreign business opportunities

U. S. GOVERNMENT PROCUREMENTS

Services

A Experimental, Developmental, Test and Research Work (includes both basic and applied research). [EDTR].

A--SITE PARTICIPATION IN AN EXPERIMENTAL ONE-MEGAWATT SOLAR THERMAL ELECTRIC POWER PLANT WITH A SMALL COMMUNITY APPLICATION. Program Research and Development Announcement (PRDA) for site participation in an experimental solar thermal electric power plant of approximately 1 MWe with startup scheduled for the end of CY 1982.

Participation requirements will be described in the PRDA. These are expected to include an available of approximately 10 unencumbered acres suitable for the plant together with transportation, utility and maintenance services and a suitable connection to a utility grid.

The site application for this first engineering experiment is to be a small community with an electric demand load of less than 100 MWe. Site participation teams are expected to include, as a minimum, a community agency and an electric utility with a distribution network. Evaluation criteria will be described in the PRDA. Additionally, the PRDA will include advisory qualification criteria to provide prospective proposers with a basis for making a decision as to whether or not to submit a proposal.

Potential site participants who wish to receive the PRDA, if and when issued, should provide a written expression of interest no later than March 30, 1979. This is not a request for proposal. The construction, installation and testing of the experimental solar thermal power plant is a separate but parallel action and is not a part of this PRDA. The plant design will be based on a point focusing solar thermal technology. The plant is intended to augment the existing utility system in meeting peak-to-intermediate load demands during a typical day. However, the primary purpose of the plant is the collection of experimental data.

It is anticipated that the PRDA will be released during April 1979. This is a request for expressions of interest to develop a source list. No additional information is available at this time. Parties interested in receiving the PRDA, if and when issued, should submit a written request and a self addressed mailing label. Telephone requests will not be accepted. (072)

U. S. Department of Energy, Albuquerque Operations Office, P.O. Box 5400, Contracts and Procurement Division, Albuquerque, NM 87115, Att: B. Bradley

★A--ADVERTISING SUPPORT FOR ECO PHASE II. This office intends to negotiate a contract with Evans & Bartholomew, 1430 Larimer Square, Denver, CO 80202. See Note 46.

★ A--QUICK RESPONSE POLICY, ECONOMIC AND TECHNICAL ANALYSIS SUPPORT. Negotiations are in process with Energy and Environmental Analysis, Inc., 1111 North 19th Street, Arlington, VA. 22209, on a non-competitive basis. See Note 46. (072)

Department of Energy, San Francisco Operations Office, 1333 Broadway, Oakland, CA 94612

★ A--MISSION APPLICATIONS OF LIMITED ENERGY VEHICLES. Negotiatins will be conducted with Sharwater, Inc., PO Bx 264, 8 Parl St., Stoningtn,' CT 06378 — o/a 19 Mar 79 — For he effrt described in Technical Rquirement N087, Amnd 2. See Noés 27 and 46. (073)

Hq, US Army Missile R&D Cmmand, Atn: DRDMI-ICBB/Robrts, 205/876-5474, Redstn Arsenl, AL 35809

A--ADDITIONAL SUPPORT FOR THE PHALANX CLOSE-IN-WEAPON SYSTEM (CIWS) PROGRAM — RFP N00024-79-R-7216 (S) will be issued to Tecolote Research Inc., 5276 Hollister Ave., Santa Barbara, CA 93111 since this is a continuation of work being performed under an existing contract. See Note 49.

A--SUPPORT SERVICES TO ASW — Modification to Contract N00024-77-C-6058 will be issued to TRW, Inc., TRW Defense and Space Systems Group, 7600 Colshire Drive, McLean, VA 22102 since this firm has performed precedent work and is the only firm which can meet the requirements.

A--SUPPORT OF THE AEGIS SHIPBUILDING PROJECT RELATED TO AN/SPY-1A RADAR. RFP N00024-79-R-5160 will be issued to Technology Service rCorporation, 8555 16th Street, Silve Spring, MD 20910 since that firm has the knowledge and experience required for this acquisition.

A--SUPPORT TO THE NAVSEA SURFACE EFFECT SHIP PROGRAM OFFICE BY EVALUATING THE LATEST DESIGN REQUIREMENTS AND SHIP DESIGN CONFIGURATIONS. RFP N00024-79-R-5384 will be issued to NORTHROP Services, Inc., 1700 North Lynn Street, Suite 1100, Arlington, VA 22209, because they have performed precedent work.

A--SYSTEMS ENGINEERING AND TECHNICAL SERVICES FOR THE SUBMARINE ASW STANDOFF WEAPON DEVELOPMENT PROGRAM. Due to program schedule requirements, a high level of performance shall be required immediately following contract award. Therefore, in order to be fully responsive, the offeror must have the demonstrated capabilities or ability to immediatelyobtain prior to award, the following disciplines: (1) ASW Operational Analysis; (2) Missile Systems Technology and Development; (3) Missile System Specification/Ulatform Constraints; (4) System Interface Definition; (5) Present and Planned Combat Systems (FCS, Weapon Launchers/Handling); (6) Cost/Effectiveness Analysis; (7) Life Cycle Cost; (8) Data Management;(9) Management Information Systems; (10) ILS Implementation Support; (11) Configuration Management; (12) Cost/Schedule Management. Offerors must have at least a secret facilities clearance. For information call M. Mancher, Code 0263, 202 692-7708. (073)

Naval Sea Systems Command, Washington, DC 20362

★ A--INVESTIGATION AND ANALYSIS OF RADIATION EFFECTS — NASA/GSFC intends to issue — (RFP) 5-32403/231 to Space Science Services. See Note 46.

★ A--GODDARD SPACE FLIGHT CENTER intends to negotiate a contract with Business and Technological Systems, Incorporated, for the program development, data management, ADN testing of software — (RFP) 5-48077/253. See Notes 27 and 46. (072)

NASA Goddard Space Flight Center (GSFC), Greenbelt Road, Greenbelt, MD 20771

A--CONTRACT DEFINITION (CD) STUDY FOR AN ACTIVE ELECTRONIC DECOY (AED) FULL SCALE ENGINEERING DEVELOPMENT. NAVELEX intends to award not more than four study contracts. Competitors for subsequent program phases will be selected from the CD Study Contractors. Small business firms and others interested in subcontracting opportunities should request the offerors list from Code 2042 and make direct contact with firms listed therein. To receive RFP, Secret facility clearance must be on file — RFP N00039-79-R-0142. Closing date 30 Apr 79. See Note 48.

★ A--TECHNICAL STUDIES ON HF SYSTEM ARCHITECTURE — Negotiations will be conducted with SRI International, Menlo Park, CA —RFP N00039-79-R-0168(S) — See Note 46.

★ A--TESTING MODIFICATIONS TO VLF/LF TRANSMITTER — Provide for approximately one man year of effort (on call basis) — Qty One man/year plus 3 one/year options — Negotiations will be conducted with Continental Electronics Mfg. Co., Dallas, TX — RFP N00039-79-R-0165 — See Note 46.

★ A--DESIGN, DEVELOP, FABRICATE, TEST AND DELIVER SWITCHING SET, MESSAGE, AUTOMATIC, AN/GYC-7, FULL SCALE DEVELOPMENT MODEL AND SUPPORT — Qty 16 — Negotiations will be conducted with offerors who have been qualified as a result of Synopsis 52 which was published 4 March 1977 — Offerors list may be obtained from Code 2042 — RFP N00039-79-R-0114 — Closing 16 Apr 79 — See Notes 26, 40 and 48.

★ A--ENGINEERING AND TECHNICAL SUPPORT OF THE CINCUSNAVEUR INTELLIGENCE SUPPORT SYSTEM — Negotiations will be conducted with PRC Information Sciences Co., McLean, VA — RFP N00039-79-R-0166(S) — See Note 46. (073)

J. Howard, Tel. 202/692-0489, Naval Electronic Systems Command, Washington, DC

★ A--AUTOMOTIVE GAS TURBINE PROGRAM — Consists of additional effort under an existnig contract for AGT powertrain predesign and system analysis and long-lead technology subtasks. RFP 3-858463Q will be issued to the Ford Motor Corp., Dearborn, MI 48121. Inquiries concerning this procurement should be diected to Mail Sop 500-305 or by calling 216/433-4000, Ext 709. See Notes 40 and 46. (073)

NASA, Lewis Research Center, Cleveland, OH 44135

A--CONDUCT LABORATORY MEASUREMENTS for Kinetics of the heterogeneous hydrolysis of Dinitrogen pentoxide under Stratospheric Conditions—RFP LGR-9-3694 — Anticipated date of issuance is o/a 19 Mar 79. Copies available after issuance until supply is exhausted after which a copy may be examined at below. (073)

Department of Transportation, FAA Procurement Information Office, ALG-380 800 Independence Ave., S.W., Rm. 406 (202/426-8231) Washington, DC 20591

Content

Figure 5. *Commerce Business Daily* (front page only), March 21, 1979.

Alternatively, you can send your money to the nearest Department of Commerce field office, listed in Appendix 2, and they'll take your order.

Successful Protesting

If you think you are being taken advantage of in dealing with the Government, you can protest to the General Accounting Office (GAO) for help. Before you do this, however, you should immediately declare your displeasure to the contracting office with which you are involved. What actions should you protest? Such actions as sole source awards to a competitor, RFP or IFB terms written in favor of competitors, inequitable treatment of your proposal or of your company during negotiation. If you have a good case and present it without delay and in a professional (rather than an emotional) manner, there is a fair chance that if the situation itself is not rectified, you will at least get an unwritten, unspoken acknowledgment that the Government owes you one. After all, the Government people are not out to be unfair. Primarily they want to do what is in the best interest of the Government. Occasionally, like everyone else, they make mistakes. Also, they are not wild about the idea of your going higher up with the protest, which makes more work for them and clearly does not make them look good. However, your chances if you do go to a higher authority or the GAO are not particularly good. You should never carry your protest to GAO without having a very strong case indeed. But even then don't expect to win. Currently, only about 20% of the cases or fewer are decided in favor of the contractor. Also, it would be foolish not to consider the long-range effect of your protest. Taking your protest to GAO is certain not to win you any friends with your immediate Government customer. One company bidding on a $2 million dollar research and development contract for ejection seats successfully protested the loss of the award to GAO. This forced the Air Force to award two $2 million contracts. However, when the big production contract for $40 million came along, you can guess which company didn't get it. In other cases, by the time GAO comes up with a favorable decision, the contract is already complete. No victory there.

Some companies make a policy of telling the Government that they do not and will never protest under any circumstances. This is wrong, too. For one thing, the time may come when they are left with no alternative but to protest. When that happens, those firms immediately lose all future credibility with their customer. Secondly, even if a company never does protest, the potential of taking a protest to the GAO provides some minimum clout. If nothing else, this can be traded in for good will as the occasion arises.

If you make a habit of protesting, either to the Government office you are dealing with or to the GAO, you will do yourself no good. You will soon wish you were being paid for the act of protesting, because you certainly won't be receiving any lucrative Government contracts.

In summary, being wronged should be only one factor in your decision to protest to the Government. The other two components that you must consider are your exact objectives and the long-range results of your protest actions.

HOW TO USE MARKETING THEORY TO HELP YOU WIN

Marketing theory has made millions of dollars for the companies that know how to use it to maximize their profits. However, marketing theory is so relatively new that many companies confuse marketing with sales and so don't do anything more than renew their emphasis on the work of selling. Central to marketing theory is the marketing concept that says that not only should your firm be built around the marketing function, but that marketing and selling are quite different. Selling focuses on the product or service. Marketing focuses on the customer. As Peter Drucker says in *The Practice of Management:* "Marketing is not only much broader than selling, it is not a specialized activity at all. It is the whole business seen from the point of view of its final result, that is, from the customer's point of view. Concern and responsibility for marketing must therefore permeate all areas of the enterprise."

If you want to win in the Government marketplace consistently, you must use marketing theory to help you. To do that, you must concentrate the resources of your company not on selling your product or service, but on fulfilling your potential customers' needs. The application of marketing theory in accomplishing this will be covered in Chapter 6, as we develop a marketing strategy and a marketing action plan.

Now you know where we are going and how we are going to get there. Let's continue by looking at the Government procurement programs available to us in Chapter 2.

Chapter 2

GOVERNMENT PROCUREMENT PROGRAMS: THOUSANDS OF GOVERNMENT CUSTOMERS AND SOURCES OF MILLIONS OF DOLLARS IN CONTRACTS FOR THE SMALL BUSINESSMAN

MAJOR GROUPINGS OF GOVERNMENT PROCUREMENT PROGRAMS

Government procurement programs can be broken down into three major groupings:

- *GSA procurement programs.*
- *Military procurement programs.*
- *Civilian agency procurement programs.*

The GSA buys, stores, snd disburses items that are used throughout the Government. The GSA will also make special purchases for an individual agency requesting it and award federal supply schedule contracts. Once awarded, these contracts enable agencies to order directly from you, the supplier, without continually renegotiating or checking back with the GSA.

Each of the military services has its own procurement programs, but there are also consolidated buying programs for all services, local purchasing programs, and procurement of goods and services by some civilian agencies for the military.

Civilian agencies also have their own programs that enable them to purchase directly from suppliers, as well as obtain many items from GSA.

All of these programs are sources of potential big dollars in sales to you as a Government contractor.

Let's look at each of these programs individually and see what is available and where we can best direct our interest for big profits.

General Services Administration Procurement Programs

GSA contracts for millions of dollars in goods and services mainly through three of its six major subdivisions. These subdivisions are: Automated Data and Tele-communications Service (ADTS), Public Building Service (PBS), and Federal Supply Service (FSS).

Automated Data and Telecommunications Service (ADTS)

This subdivision operates the Federal Telecommunications System and is also responsibile for coordinating and providing for the economic and efficient purchase, lease, and maintenance of automatic data processing equipment for use by the other federal agencies. There are clearly some big and unique opportunities here. These are a few:

- Leasing and purchasing of terminals for teletype, data, and facsimile trans-mission.
- Installation and maintenance of transmission services.
- Automatic data processing (ADP) schedules.
- Automatic data processing (ADP) equipment requirement contracts.
- Teleprocessing service schedules.

GSA negotiates schedules for most of the commercially available ADP equipment on a yearly basis. These are fixed-price contracts with the quantity unspecified. They are used for buying additional equipment, rental and maintenance of equip-ment already installed, and for modifying installed equipment through the addition of special features.

Requirements contracts are awarded for many different types of automatic data processing systems including memory units, terminals, disk packs, punched card machines, and disk and tape drives. You can, of course, also sell the same or similar equipment directly to other federal agencies. However, the federal agency is re-quired to use GSA contracts when the equipment supplied through the GSA will meet the other federal agency's requirement. It is therefore worthwhile contacting GSA even if you are already selling to other agencies, because of the potential for getting into additional Government markets.

In a very similar fashion, the GSA establishes teleprocessing schedules and basic agreements that may be used by other federal agencies to satisfy their individual teleprocessing requirements.

Public Buildings Service (PBS)

The Public Building Service of the GSA offers other unique opportunities. These include: design contracts, construction contracts, building maintenance and repair contracts, property appraisal service contracts, broker service contracts, surveying service contracts, and art work for public buildings.

The PBS lets contracts with architect-engineers for all types of Government buildings and building subsystems including office buildings, hospitals, courthouses, research centers, heating and air-conditioning systems, elevators, escalators, and even repair and building alterations.

A special form is used, Standard Form 254, Architect-Engineer and Related Services Questionnaire (Figure 6).

To get this work, you usually must be located in the geographic area of the project, although GSA will deviate from this rule on projects they consider to be of national significance.

Construction contracts are awarded by IFB and go to the lowest responsive and responsible bidder, as explained in the previous chapter. Notices of forthcoming bids are published in the *Commerce Business Daily*, trade journals, and other appropriate publications, but like any other Government business, if you really plan on winning you must get in before the bid is requested. In the case of construction contracts, each of the GSA's regional offices of the Public Building Service maintains mailing lists of prospective bidders. To get on these lists, contact your nearest GSA Service Center, listed in Chapter 3.

You should also know ahead of time that bid bonds will be required for construction contracts in excess of $2000. The PBS will accept Standard Form 24, Bid Bond (Figure 7), plus a certified cashier's check, a bank check, or a money order. If you are successful, you must also provide a performance bond for the total amount of the bid and a payment bond for half that amount. To get these bonds, you'll need to contact a surety or bonding company. The SBA will help you with this.

Building maintenance and repair is handled by a division of the PBS known as the Office of Building Management. This office operates all the buildings that are under GSA's authority. The building manager contracts for small items or services that do not exceed $2500 per contract. Small and large contracts are handled under this category, which may include products like office equipment and furniture, hardware, janitorial supplies, tools, and cafeteria equipment, and services like garbage collection, operating a cafeteria, window cleaning, and so on.

You may be surprised to learn that you may be in demand by the GSA if you are a professional appraiser or a real estate broker. GSA does a good deal of its own appraising. However, a not insignificant amount is done by independent appraisers and appraisal companies. These appraisers are selected from the GSA Register of Available Real Estate Appraisers. To get on this register, use GSA Form 1195, "Application for Placement on GSA Register of Available Real Estate Appraisers" (Figure 8). If you provide brokerage services to the GSA, you will be locating buyers and giving public notice of Government buildings under PBS's control that are for sale. Brokers are selected by GSA from among brokers who have expressed an interest to GSA in providing these services and are qualified

| STANDARD FORM (SF) 254 | Architect-Engineer and Related Services Questionnaire |

STANDARD FORM (SF) 254

Architect-Engineer and Related Services Questionnaire

Purpose:

The policy of the Federal Government, in procuring architectural, engineering, and related professional services, is to encourage firms lawfully engaged in the practice of those professions to submit annually a statement of qualifications and performance data. Standard Form 254, "Architect-Engineer and Related Services Questionnaire" is provided for that purpose. Interested A-E firms (including new, small, and/or minority firms) should complete and file SF 254's with each Federal agency and with appropriate regional or district offices for which the A-E is qualified to perform services. The agency head for each proposed project shall evaluate these qualification resumes, together with any other performance data on file or requested by the agency, in relation to the proposed project. The SF 254 may be used as a basis for selecting firms for discussions, or for screening firms preliminary to inviting submission of additional information.

Definitions:

"Architect-engineer and related services" are those professional services associated with research, development, design and construction, alteration, or repair of real property, as well as incidental services that members of these professions and those in their employ may logically or justifiably perform, including studies, investigations, surveys, evaluations, consultations, planning, programming, conceptual designs, plans and specifications, cost estimates, inspections, shop drawing reviews, sample recommendations, preparation of operating and maintenance manuals, and other related services.

"Parent Company" is that firm, company, corporation, association or conglomerate which is the major stockholder or highest tier owner of the firm completing this questionnaire; i.e. Firm A is owned by Firm B which is, in turn, a subsidiary of Corporation C. The "parent company" of Firm A is Corporation C.

"Principals" are those individuals in a firm who possess legal responsibility for its management. They may be owners, partners, corporate officers, associates, administrators, etc.

"Discipline", as used in this questionnaire, refers to the primary technological capability of individuals in the responding firm. Possession of an academic degree, professional registration, certification, or extensive experience in a particular field of practice normally reflects an individual's primary technical discipline.

"Joint Venture" is a collaborative undertaking by two or more firms or individuals for which the participants are both jointly and individually responsible.

"Consultant", as used in this questionnaire, is a highly specialized individual or firm having significant input and responsibility for certain aspects of a project and possessing unusual or unique capabilities for assuring success of the finished work.

"Prime" refers to that firm which may be coordinating the concerted and

Figure 6. Standard Form (SF) 254/Architect-Engineer and Related Services Questionnaire.

Standard Form 254
General Services Administration,
Washington, D. C. 20405
Fed. Proc. Reg. (41 CFR) 1-16.803
Armed Svc. Proc. Reg. 18-403

complementary inputs of several firms, individuals or related services to produce a completed study or facility. The "prime" would normally be regarded as having full responsibility and liability for quality of performance by itself as well as by subcontractor professionals under its jurisdiction.

"Branch Office" is a satellite, or subsidiary extension, of a headquarters office of a company, regardless of any differences in name or legal structure of such a branch due to local or state laws. "Branch offices" are normally subject to the management decisions, bookkeeping, and policies of the main office.

Instructions for Filing (Numbers below correspond to numbers contained in form):

1. Type accurate and complete name of submitting firm, its address, and zip code.

   1a. Indicate whether form is being submitted in behalf of a parent firm or a branch office. (Branch office submissions should list only personnel in, and experience of, that office.)

2. Provide date the firm was established under the name shown in question 1.

3. Show date upon which all submitted information is current and accurate.

4. Enter type of ownership, or legal structure, of firm (sole proprietor, partnership, corporation, joint venture, etc.)

   4a. Check appropriate box indicating if firm is minority-owned. (See 41 CFR 1-1.13 or ASPR 1-332.3(a) for definitions of minority ownership.)

5. Branches or subsidiaries of larger or parent companies, or conglomerates, should insert name and address of highest-tier owner.

   5a. If present firm is the successor to, or outgrowth of, one or more predecessor firms, show name(s) of former entity(ies) and the year(s) of their original establishment.

6. List not more than two principals from submitting firm who may be contacted by the agency receiving this form. (Different principals may be listed on forms going to another agency.) Listed principals must be empowered to speak for the firm on policy and contractual matters.

7. Beginning with the submitting office, list name, location, total number of personnel and telephone numbers for all associated or branch offices, (including any headquarters or foreign offices) which provide A-E and related services.

   7a. Show total personnel in all offices. (Should be sum of all personnel, all branches.)

8. Show total number of employees, by discipline, in submitting office. (If form is being submitted by main or headquarters office, firm should list total employees, by discipline, in **all** offices.) While some personnel may be qualified in several disciplines, each person should be counted only once in accord with his or her primary function. Include clerical personnel as "administrative."

Figure 6   (*Continued*)

STANDARD FORM (SF)
254

Architect-Engineer and Related Services Questionnaire

Write in any additional disciplines — sociologists, biologists, etc. — and number of people in each, in blank spaces.

9. Using chart (below) insert appropriate index number to indicate range of professional services fees received by submitting firm each calendar year for last five years, most recent year first. Fee summaries should be broken down to reflect the fees received each year for (a) work performed directly for the Federal Government (not including grant and loan projects) or as a sub to other professionals performing work directly for the Federal Government; (b) all other domestic work, U. S. and possessions, including Federally-assisted projects, and (c) all other foreign work.

Ranges of Professional Services Fees

INDEX		INDEX	
1.	Less than $100,000	5.	$1 million to $2 million
2.	$100,000 to $250,000	6.	$2 million to $5 million
3.	$250,000 to $500,000	7.	$5 million to $10 million
4.	$500,000 to $1 million	8.	$10 million or greater

10. Select and enter, in numerical sequence, **not more than thirty** (30) "Experience Profile Code" numbers from the listing (next page) which most accurately reflect submitting firm's demonstrated technical capabilities and project experience. **Carefully review list.** (It is recognized some profile codes may be part of other services or projects contained on list; firms are encouraged to select profile codes which best indicate type and scope of services provided on past projects.) For each code number, show total number of projects and gross fees (in thousands) received for profile projects performed by firm during past five years. If firm has one or more capabilities not included on list, insert same in blank spaces at end of list and show numbers in question 10 on the form. In such cases, the filled-in listing **must** accompany the complete SF 254 when submitted to the Federal agencies.

11. Using the "Experience Profile Code" numbers in the same sequence as entered in item 10, give details of at least one recent (within last five years) representative project for each code number, up to a **maximum** of thirty (30) separate projects, or portions of projects, for which firm was responsible. (Project examples may be used more than once to illustrate different services rendered on the same job. Example: a dining hall may be part of an auditorium or educational facility.) Firms which select less than thirty "profile codes" may list two or more project examples (to illustrate specialization) for each code number so long as total of all project examples does not exceed thirty (30). After each code number in question 11, show: (a) whether firm was "P," the prime professional, or "C," a consultant, or "JV," part of a joint venture on that particular project (New firms, in existence less than five (5) years may use the symbol "IE" to indicate "Individual Experience" as opposed to firm experience.); (b) provide name and location of the specific project which typifies firm's (or individual's) performance under that code category; (c) give name and address of the owner of that project (if government agency indicate responsible office); (d) show the estimated construction cost (or other applicable

Figure 6 *(Continued)*

38

cost) for that portion of the project for which the firm was primarily responsible. (Where no construction was involved, show approximate cost of firm's work); and (e) state year work on that particular project was, or will be, completed.

12. The completed SF 254 should be signed by a principal of the firm, preferably the chief executive officer.

13. Additional data, brochures, photos, etc. should not accompany this form unless specifically requested.

NEW FIRMS (not reorganized or recently-amalgamated firms) are eligible and encouraged to seek work from the Federal Government in connection with performance of projects for which they are qualified. Such firms are encouraged to complete and submit Standard Form 254 to appropriate agencies. Questions on the form dealing with personnel or experience may be answered by citing experience and capabilities of individuals in the firm, based on performance and responsibility while in the employ of others. In so doing, notation of this fact should be made on the form. In question 9, write in "N/A" to indicate "not applicable" for those years prior to firm's organization.

Figure 6   (*Continued*)

Experience Profile Code Numbers
for use with questions 10 and 11

001 Acoustics; Noise Abatement
002 Aerial Photogrammetry
003 Agricultural Development; Grain Storage; Farm Mechanization
004 Air Pollution Control
005 Airports; Navaids; Airport Lighting; Aircraft Fueling
006 Airports; Terminals & Hangars; Freight Handling
007 Arctic Facilities
008 Auditoriums & Theatres
009 Automation; Controls; Instrumentation
010 Barracks; Dormitories
011 Bridges
012 Cemeteries (Planning & Relocation)
013 Chemical Processing & Storage
014 Churches; Chapels
015 Codes; Standards; Ordinances
016 Cold Storage; Refrigeration; Fast Freeze
017 Commercial Buildings (low rise); Shopping Centers
018 Communications Systems; TV; Microwave
019 Computer Facilities; Computer Service
020 Conservation and Resource Management
021 Construction Management
022 Corrosion Control; Cathodic Protection; Electrolysis
023 Cost Estimating
024 Dams (Concrete; Arch)
025 Dams (Earth; Rock); Dikes; Levees
026 Desalinization (Process & Facilities)
027 Dining Halls; Clubs; Restaurants
028 Ecological & Archeological Investigations
029 Educational Facilities; Classrooms
030 Electronics
031 Elevators; Escalators; People-Movers
032 Energy Conservation; New Energy Sources
033 Environmental Impact Studies, Assessments or Statements
034 Fallout Shelters; Blast-Resistant Design
035 Field Houses; Gyms; Stadiums
036 Fire Protection
037 Fisheries; Fish Ladders
038 Forestry & Forest Products
039 Garages; Vehicle Maintenance Facilities; Parking Decks
040 Gas Systems (Propane; Natural, Etc.)
041 Graphic Design
042 Harbors; Jetties; Piers; Ship Terminal Facilities
043 Heating; Ventilating; Air Conditioning
044 Health Systems Planning
045 Highrise; Air-Rights-Type Buildings
046 Highways; Streets; Airfield Paving; Parking Lots
047 Historical Preservation
048 Hospitals & Medical Facilities
049 Hotels; Motels
050 Housing (Residential, Multi-Family; Apartments; Condominiums)
051 Hydraulics & Pneumatics
052 Industrial Buildings; Manufacturing Plants
053 Industrial Processes; Quality Control
054 Industrial Waste Treatment
055 Interior Design; Space Planning
056 Irrigation; Drainage
057 Judicial and Courtroom Facilities
058 Laboratories; Medical Research Facilities
059 Landscape Architecture
060 Libraries; Museums; Galleries
061 Lighting (Interiors; Display; Theatre, Etc.)
062 Lighting (Exteriors; Streets; Memorials; Athletic Fields, Etc.)
063 Materials Handling Systems; Conveyors; Sorters
064 Metallurgy
065 Microclimatology; Tropical Engineering
066 Military Design Standards
067 Mining & Mineralogy
068 Missile Facilities (Silos; Fuels; Transport)
069 Modular Systems Design; Pre-Fabricated Structures or Components
070 Naval Architecture; Off-Shore Platforms
071 Nuclear Facilities; Nuclear Shielding
072 Office Buildings; Industrial Parks
073 Oceanographic Engineering
074 Ordnance; Munitions; Special Weapons
075 Petroleum Exploration; Refining
076 Petroleum and Fuel (Storage and Distribution)
077 Pipelines (Cross-Country—Liquid & Gas)
078 Planning (Community, Regional, Areawide and State)
079 Planning (Site, Installation, and Project)
080 Plumbing & Piping Design
081 Pneumatic Structures; Air-Support Buildings
082 Postal Facilities

Figure 6   (Continued)

083 Power Generation, Transmission, Distribution
084 Prisons & Correctional Facilities
085 Product, Machine & Equipment Design
086 Radar; Sonar; Radio & Radar Telescopes
087 Railroad; Rapid Transit
088 Recreation Facilities *(Parks, Marinas, Etc.)*
089 Rehabilitation *(Buildings; Structures; Facilities)*
090 Resource Recovery; Recycling
091 Radio Frequency Systems & Shieldings
092 Rivers; Canals; Waterways; Flood Control
093 Safety Engineering; Accident Studies; OSHA Studies
094 Security Systems; Intruder & Smoke Detection
095 Seismic Designs & Studies
096 Sewage Collection, Treatment and Disposal
097 Soils & Geologic Studies; Foundations
098 Solar Energy Utilization
099 Solid Wastes; Incineration; Land Fill
100 Special Environments; Clean Rooms, Etc.
101 Structural Design; Special Structures
102 Surveying; Platting; Mapping; Flood Plain Studies
103 Swimming Pools
104 Storm Water Handling & Facilities
105 Telephone Systems *(Rural; Mobile; Intercom, Etc.)*
106 Testing & Inspection Services
107 Traffic & Transportation Engineering
108 Towers *(Self-Supporting & Guyed Systems)*
109 Tunnels & Subways
110 Urban Renewal; Community Development
111 Utilities *(Gas & Steam)*
112 Value Analysis; Life-Cycle Costing
113 Warehouses & Depots
114 Water Resources; Hydrology; Ground Water
115 Water Supply, Treatment and Distribution
116 Wind Tunnels; Research/Testing Facilities Design
117 Zoning; Land Use Studies
201 _____
202 _____
203 _____
204 _____
205 _____

Figure 6 *(Continued)*

STANDARD FORM (SF) **254** Architect-Engineer and Related Services Questionnaire	1. Firm Name / Business Address:
	1a. Submittal is for ☐ Parent Company ☐ Branch Office

5. Name of Parent Company, if any:	5a. Former Firm Name(s),

6. Names of not more than Two Principals to Contact: Title / Telephone

7. Present Offices: City / State / Telephone / No. Personnel Each Office

8. Personnel by Discipline:

____ Administrative	____ Electrical Engineers
____ Architects	____ Estimators
____ Chemical Engineers	____ Geologists
____ Civil Engineers	____ Hydrologists
____ Construction Inspectors	____ Interior Designers
____ Draftsmen	____ Landscape Architects
____ Ecologists	____ Mechanical Engineers
____ Economists	____ Mining Engineers

9. Summary of Professional Services Fees Received: (insert index number)

Last 5 Years (most

	19____	19____	19____
Direct Federal contract work, including overseas	____	____	____
All other domestic work	____	____	____
All other foreign work*	____	____	____

*Firms interested in foreign work, but without such experience, check here: ☐.

Figure 6 (*Continued*)

OMB Approval No. **29-RO234**

2. Year Present Firm Established:	3. Date Prepared:
4. Type of Ownership: 4a. Minority Owned ☐ yes ☐ no	

if any, and Year(s) Established:

7a. Total Personnel ____________

____ Oceanographers
____ Planners: Urban/Regional
____ Sanitary Engineers
____ Soils Engineers
____ Specification Writers
____ Structural Engineers
____ Surveyors
____ Transportation Engineers

recent year first)

____ 19______ 19______

Ranges of Professional Services Fees

INDEX

1. Less than $100,000
2. $100,000 to $250,000
3. $250,000 to $500,000
4. $500,000 to $1 million
5. $1 million to $2 million
6. $2 million to $5 million
7. $5 million to $10 million
8. $10 million or greater

Figure 6 (*Continued*)

10. Profile of Firm's Project Experience, Last 5 Years

Profile Code	Number of Projects	Total Gross Fees (in thousands)	Profile Code	Number of Projects
1)			11)	
2)			12)	
3)			13)	
4)			14)	
5)			15)	
6)			16)	
7)			17)	
8)			18)	
9)			19)	
10)			20)	

11. Project Examples, Last 5 Years

Profile Code	"P", "C", "JV", or "IE"	Project Name and Location	
		1	
		2	
		3	
		4	
		5	
		6	
		7	

Figure 6   (*Continued*)

44

Total Gross Fees (in thousands)	Profile Code	Number of Projects	Total Gross Fees (in thousands)
	21)		
	22)		
	23)		
	24)		
	25)		
	26)		
	27)		
	28)		
	29)		
	30)		

Owner Name and Address	Cost of Work (in thousands)	Completion Date (Actual or Estimated)

Figure 6 (*Continued*)

		8	
		9	
		10	
		11	
		12	
		13	
		14	
		15	
		16	
		17	
		18	
		19	

Figure 6 (*Continued*)

Figure 6 (*Continued*)

		20	
		21	
		22	
		23	
		24	
		25	
		26	
		27	
		28	
		29	
		30	

12. The foregoing is a statement of facts

Signature: _____ Typed Name and Title: _____

Figure 6 (*Continued*)

	Date:	

Figure 6   (*Continued*)

BID BOND

(See Instructions on reverse)

24-103

DATE BOND EXECUTED *(Must not be later than bid opening date)*

PRINCIPAL *(Legal name and business address)*

TYPE OF ORGANIZATION *("X" one)*

☐ INDIVIDUAL ☐ PARTNERSHIP
☐ JOINT VENTURE ☐ CORPORATION

STATE OF INCORPORATION

SURETY(IES) *(Name and business address)*

PENAL SUM OF BOND					BID IDENTIFICATION	
PERCENT OF BID PRICE	AMOUNT NOT TO EXCEED				BID DATE	INVITATION NO.
	MILLION(S)	THOUSAND(S)	HUNDRED(S)	CENTS		
					FOR *(Construction, Supplies or Services)*	

KNOW ALL MEN BY THESE PRESENTS, That we, the Principal and Surety(ies) hereto, are firmly bound to the United States of America (hereinafter called the Government) in the above penal sum for the payment of which we bind ourselves, our heirs, executors, administrators, and successors, jointly and severally: *Provided,* That, where the Sureties are corporations acting as co-sureties, we, the Sureties, bind ourselves in such sum "jointly and severally" as well as "severally" only for the purpose of allowing a joint action or actions against any or all of us, and for all other purposes each Surety binds itself, jointly and severally with the Principal, for the payment of such sum only as is set forth opposite the name of such Surety, but if no limit of liability is indicated, the limit of liability shall be the full amount of the penal sum.

THE CONDITION OF THIS OBLIGATION IS SUCH, that whereas the Principal has submitted the bid identified above.

NOW, THEREFORE, if the Principal, upon acceptance by the Government of his bid identified above, within the period specified therein for acceptance (sixty (60) days if no period is specified), shall execute such further contractual documents, if any, and give such bond(s) as may be required by the terms of the bid as accepted within the time specified (ten (10) days if no period is specified) after receipt of the forms by him, or in the event of failure so to execute such further contractual documents and give such bonds, if the Principal shall pay the Government for any cost of procuring the work which exceeds the amount of his bid, then the above obligation shall be void and of no effect.

Each Surety executing this instrument hereby agrees that its obligation shall not be impaired by any extension(s) of the time for acceptance of the bid that the Principal may grant to the Government, notice of which extension(s) to the Surety(ies) being hereby waived; provided that such waiver of notice shall apply only with respect to extensions aggregating not more than sixty (60) calendar days in addition to the period originally allowed for acceptance of the bid.

IN WITNESS WHEREOF, the Principal and Surety(ies) have executed this bid bond and have affixed their seals on the date set forth above.

PRINCIPAL			
Signature(s)	1.	2.	Corporate Seal
	(Seal)	*(Seal)*	
Name(s) & Title(s) *(Typed)*	1.	2.	

INDIVIDUAL SURETIES			
Signature(s)	1.	2.	*(Seal)*
	(Seal)		
Name(s) *(Typed)*	1.	2.	

CORPORATE SURETY(IES)					
SURETY A	Name & Address		STATE OF INC.	LIABILITY LIMIT	Corporate Seal
	Signature(s)	1.	2.		
	Name(s) & Title(s) *(Typed)*	1.	2.		

Figure 7. Standard Form 24/Bid Bond.

APPLICATION FOR PLACEMENT ON GSA REGISTER OF AVAILABLE REAL ESTATE APPRAISERS

INSTRUCTIONS. Type, or print clearly. WE MUST HAVE COMPLETE MAILING ADDRESSES WITH ZIP CODES IN ALL PLACES WHERE ADDRESSES ARE REQUESTED. Completed form should be mailed in duplicate to the Regional Office, General Services Administration, having supervision over the area in which you have your office.

THIS SPACE GENERAL SERVICES ADMINISTRATION USE ONLY

CODE RECOMMENDED	DATE	REGIONAL APPRAISER (Signature)
CODE ASSIGNED	DATE	DIRECTOR, APPRAISAL STAFF (Signature)
DATE REGION NOTIFIED		DATE APPLICANT NOTIFIED (For regional use only)

1. NAME OF APPLICANT (Last, first, middle)	2. BUSINESS ADDRESS (Number and street)	
3. CITY	4. STATE	5. ZIP CODE	6. AREA CODE & BUSINESS TELEPHONE NO.

7. PRESENT OCCUPATION	8. TITLE

9. HOME ADDRESS (No., Street, City, State and Zip Code)	10. AREA CODE & HOME TELEPHONE NO.

11. DATE OF BIRTH	12. PLACE OF BIRTH (City and State)

13. NAME AND ADDRESS OF PRESENT EMPLOYER (If not self-employed) (No., Street, City, State and Zip Code)

14. BUSINESS HISTORY DURING PAST TEN YEARS *

PERIOD		OCCUPATION	NAME AND ADDRESS OF EMPLOYER (Include Zip Code)
FROM	TO		

15. EDUCATION (Highest grade attained)	16. NAME OF COLLEGE OR UNIVERSITY	17. DEGREES AND DATES CONFERRED

18. PROFESSIONAL ORGANIZATION(S) OF WHICH YOU ARE A MEMBER (Indicate if membership is Associate, Affiliate, or Candidate)

19. REAL ESTATE BOARD(S) OF WHICH YOU ARE A MEMBER

20. STATE(S) IN WHICH YOU ARE LICENSED AS A REAL ESTATE BROKER

21. SPECIFY ANY OTHER SPECIAL QUALIFICATIONS YOU HAVE FOR APPRAISAL WORK, INCLUDING ANY APPRAISAL COURSES YOU HAVE COMPLETED *

GENERAL SERVICES ADMINISTRATION
*Use additional sheets (8"x10½") if necessary.

GSA DC 72-4436

GSA FORM 1195 (REV. 10-71)

Figure 8. GSA Form 1195/Application for Placement on GSA Register of Available Real Estate Appraisers.

according to GSA's standards. Here again, refer to your local GSA Business Service Center in Chapter 3.

The need for surveying services is limited, but it is sufficiently large that GSA still advertises their general requirements for this service. Regional offices of the PBS usually contract with local surveyors under a selective professional services contract. Like all GSA programs, make contact with your closest GSA Business Service Center.

If you have ever wondered where the beautiful murals, paintings, sculptures, and other works of art found in public buildings come from, I am happy to tell you that this is also commissioned and paid for by the PBS of the GSA. Artists are selected in cooperation with the National Endowment for the Arts. That organization appoints a special panel for each project. This panel consists of local civic and art-oriented representatives and the project architect. Because the panel recommends the artists to the GSA, it is essential to make contact and market your work not only to the GSA, which is paying the bill, but also to the project architect and other members of the National Endowment for the Arts panel.

Federal Supply Service (FSS)

The FSS has an incredible number of procurement requirements because it is responsible for supplying tens of thousands of different common-use items such as books, hardware, pencils, water coolers, automobiles, desks, chairs, tables, cameras, dictating machines, paper, and so on, without which the Government could not operate. The FSS is involved in the operation of six major programs:

- Stock program.
- Federal supply schedules.
- Consolidated purchase contracts.
- Direct-order purchasing.
- Specialized transportation services.
- Personal property.

The stock program includes approximately 31,000 everyday, common-use items that are stored by the FSS in Government facilities and are distributed through requisitions by other Government agencies. These requisitions are received by a GSA regional office that then directs a Government supply distribution facility to ship them from stock. If the order is large enough to make direct delivery more advantageous, the FSS will not only buy the item from you but will also have you deliver it directly to the Government agency that wants it.

The federal supply schedule program provides an alternative method of purchase by the requirement for indefinite quantities of any one of approximately 700,000 products or services can be anticipated. Typical of these products and services are audiovideo equipment, duplicating supplies, furniture, lamps, electrical appliances, and automatic parts and accessories.

Under the program, FSS provides other federal agencies with sources for products and services. The schedule, which is an indefinite quantity contract usually for a period of a year, is placed directly with the supplier or contractor. You are paid not by the GSA but by the federal agency having the requirement. The Government solicits for bids under this program in the *Commerce Business Daily*. Contracts may be of the negotiated type as well as those simply going to the lowest bidder, so it is essential that you make the necessary contacts before the soliciation is published.

Consolidated purchase contracts are let for items not suitable for inclusion in either the stock program or the supply schedules. The GSA consolidates all the requirements from the various agencies into one and solicits bids for definite quantities, in contrast with the indefinite quantity contracts negotiated under the federal supply schedule program. As with the supply schedule program, you will be making delivery directly to the Government agency that needs your product or service.

GSA does direct-order purchasing for other Government agencies when they lack technical expertise or the required personnel to make the procurement; when the federal agency with the requirement believes that GSA can make a better buy because it knows the market better; when the agency has special requirements that differ greatly from normal Governmental needs; when the quantity of an order for a federal supply schedule item exceeds a maximum order limitation; or because of other special circumstances.

FSS contracts for specialized transportation services when requested by other federal agencies. These services include:

- Overseas shipments.
- Parking, crating, and marking of Government property.
- Transport of substantially heavy loads through metropolitan areas.
- Use of an armored car.

Note that some other agency must request FSS to make these contracts. These services may also be contracted for by the agency needing the service. They are also obtained through both the advertised and negotiated method of procurement.

Both FSS and the various Government agencies contract for the maintenance, repair, rehabilitation, and reclamation of personal property. Such service contracts may be let for almost anything: electronic equipment, stoves and refrigeration, bedroom furniture, sprinkling equipment, or television sets. According to the GSA, contracts are currently in effect for the reclamation and recycling of platinum, iridium, and silver from used aircraft spark plugs and magneto points, and for the recovery of silver from used photographic solutions and scrap film.

Happily, this FSS program is an especially good market since most of the work is done by small businesses along with the workshops of federally run Prison Industries, Inc. and those workshops employing the blind and handicapped.

Two other programs of the GSA are of some interest because of the business opportunities they offer. Both are under the Office of Transportation and Public Utilities. The Motor Equipment Services Division operates 100 motor pools nationwide and in Puerto Rico. Every motor pool requires vehicles that must be bought or rented, in addition to parts, accessories, and other related services. The Office of Procurement handles these purchases and similar purchases for other agencies.

The Public Utilities Management Division of the Office of Transportation and Public Utilities contracts for utilities under an area-wide utility contract when available. When area-wide contracts are not available, individual utility contracts are executed. GSA is authorized to contract for utilities for up to a ten-year period, but usually lets contracts of a one-year duration. Purchases of more than $10,000 are made by contract, while the purchase order method is used for smaller dollar amounts.

For particular information about any of the GSA programs, you should contact a GSA Business Service Center. (See Chapter 3.)

Military Procurement Programs

Armed forces procurement programs include those by the separate departments (Army, Navy, and Air Force), those done on a consolidated basis, those done locally, and those done for the military by other Government agencies (mainly GSA).

The armed forces are under the Department of Defense (DOD), which essentially runs the entire U.S. defense effort including the three military departments and the Defense Logistics Agency (DLA). The DLA, by the way, was formerly known as the Defense Supply Agency (DAS), and you will see it referred to as such in the Lockridge case study that is the appendix of this book. However, the Office of the Secretary of Defense doesn't make procurements. The individual military departments and various defense agencies let the contracts, either for their own or combined DOD requirements when a single department or agency is designated as the lead agency or executive agent. One of the big guns in military procurements is the Assistant Secretary of Defense, Manpower, Reserve Affairs, and Logistics. This office formulates policy and procedures that direct and coordinate the procurement system and logistical relationship of the various military organizations as well as the procurement actions of major DOD supply efforts. The research and development efforts (and these can be extremely large in dollar amounts) are performed on contract to the Departments of the Army, Navy, or Air Force.

THE DEPARTMENT OF THE ARMY

In the Department of the Army, the U.S. Army Materiel Development and Readiness Command, known as DARCOM, is responsible for varied functions including procurement, research and development, testing and evaluation, production, storage and distribution, inventory management, maintenance, and dispersals. The two largest areas of responsibility are materiel readiness and research and development. The term "materiel readiness" refers to the fact that the command is responsible for the materiel even after it is issued and in the hands of the troops. Under materiel readiness are found such major subordinate commands as the U.S. Army Armament Materiel Readiness Command (ARRCOM) at Rock Island, Illinois; the U.S. Army Communications and Electronics Materiel Readiness Command (CERCOM) at Fort Monmouth, New Jersey; the U.S. Army Missile Materiel Readiness Command (MIRCOM) at Redstone Arsenal, Alabama; the U.S. Army Tank-Automotive Materiel Readiness Command (TARCOM) at Warren, Michigan; and the U.S. Army Troop Support and Aviation Materiel Readiness Command (TSARCOM) at St. Louis, Missouri. DARCOM's research and development function is accomplished by the U.S. Army Armament Research and Development Command (ARRADCOM) located at Dover, New Jersey; the U.S. Army Aviation Research and Development Command (AVRADCOM) located in St. Louis, Missouri; the U.S. Army Communications Research and Development (CORADCOM) at Fort Monmouth, New Jersey; the U.S. Army Electronics Research and Development Command (ERADCOM) at Adelphi, Maryland; the U.S. Army Mobility Equipment Research and Development Command (MERADCOM) at Fort Belvoir, Virginia; the U.S. Army Missile Research and Development Command (MIRADCOM) at Redstone Arsenal, Alabama; U.S. Army Natick Research and Development Command (NARADCOM) at Natick, Massachusetts; and the U.S. Army Tank-Automotive Research and Development Command (TARADCOM) at Warren, Michigan. In all, DARCOM consists of a nationwide network of 66 military installations and 73 major activities. These various customers can be found in Appendix 2. In every case, each major subordinate commodity command buys, develops, or maintains the types and categories of items that are assigned to it for management. The procurement function is performed by the Director of Procurement and Production for each subordinate command.

In general, the functions of DARCOM are paired, with one organization being responsible for research and development of a product area and another responsible for "materiel readiness," which includes follow-on procurement and maintenance.

U.S. Army Armament Research and Development Command (AARADCOM) and U.S. Army Materiel Readiness Command (ARRCOM)

The product responsibility of these commands include weapons and ammunition, both nuclear and nonnuclear munitions, weapons systems and support equipment, fire control equipment, practice and training munitions, rocket and missile warhead sections, demolition munitions, mines, bombs, grenades, flame and incendiary systems, pyrotechnics and munitions, offensive and defensive chemical material and riot control systems, biological and radiological material, as well as assigned and special tools and equipment that are a part of or must be used with any of these main procurement items. The command also does applied research and exploratory development that supports the major development efforts, such as Piccatinny Arsenal located at Dover, New Jersey, where research in the fields of explosives, propellants, and pyrotechnics is conducted.

U.S. Army Communications Research and Development Command (CORADCOM), the U.S. Army Electronics Research and Development Command (ERADCOM), and the U.S. Army Communications and Electronics Materiel Readiness Command (CERCOM)

These commands manage the produce area that includes communications, communications electronics, intelligence equipment, electronic warfare, aviation electronics, combat surveillance, target acquisition and night vision equipment, photographic and microfilming equipment, identification friend or foe systems, automatic data processing, radar, meterological and electronic radiological detection materiel, and batteries and electric power generation equipment. These commands also carry out various types of basic and applied research, such as at the Harry Diamond Laboratories in Washington, D.C., which perform basic and applied research in radiating and influence fusing, electronic timers for weapons, advanced energy transformation, command systems, basic research in the physical sciences, and so on.

U.S. Army Missile Research and Development Command (MIRADCOM)and the U.S. Army Missile Materiel Readiness Command (MIRCOM)

These commands handle guided and ballistic missiles; air defense systems, including fire control coordination, target missiles, and free rockets; and related commodities and equipment.

U.S. Army Tank-Automotive Research and Development Command (TARADCOM), and the U.S. Army Tank-Automotive Materiel Readiness Command (TARCOM)

These two commands together are responsible for the design, development, procurement, production, maintenance, supply, and repair of all U.S. Army ground vehicles; and combat, general purpose, construction, materiel handling, and tactical vehicles for DOD; and all the components, parts, engine accessories, transmission, fuel, wheels, tires, steering systems, and brakes associated with ground vehicles.

U.S. Army Aviation Research and Development Command (AVRADCOM)

These are the folks that deal with R&D for Army aviation items including aircraft, airframe structural components, ground support equipment, wheel and brake systems, gas turbines, jet engines, internal combustion radial and horizontally opposed aircraft engines, parachutes and accessories, hydraulic pumps and starters, and thousands of related research activities including aviation materiel development for extreme environments and fuel contamination. AVRADCOM is paired with the U.S. Army Troop Support and Aviation Materiel Readiness Command (TSARCOM) for materiel readiness support activities.

U.S. Army Mobility Equipment Research and Development Command (MERADCOM)

MERADCOM's commodity area includes countermine, camouflage, barriers, tactical sensors, fuels and lubricants, fuel handling equipment, tactical bridging and stream crossing equipment, construction equipment, marine and railway transportation equipment, electric power generation and distribution equipment, tactical environmental control equipment, supply distribution and materiel handling, water and waste management, physical security sensors, and engineer typographic systems. MERADCOM is also paired with TSARCOM for the materiel readiness function.

U.S. Army Natick Research and Development Command (NARADCOM).

This command conducts R&D in the physical and biological sciences and engineering to meet military requirements for textiles, clothing, body armor, footwear, insecticides and fungicides, subsistence, containers, food service, tentage and equipage, air delivery equipment, and other equipment as assigned. NARADCOM is the third major R&D command whose paired member on materiel readiness is TSARCOM.

How do Do Business with DARCOM

In doing business with DARCOM, the command itself recommends the following steps:

"Step 1. Call, write, or visit the Small Business and Economic Utilization Advisor at the agency with which you desire to do business." (See Chapter 3.)

"Step 2. Discuss your capabilities, interests and capacities with the Small Business and Economic Utilization Advisor."

"Step 3. Request that each Small Business and Economic Utilization Advisor furnish a copy of SF129, Bidder's Mailing List Application and DD 558-1, Bidder's Mailing List Application Supplement." (See Figure 2.)

"Step 4. Complete forms and return them to each appropriate Small Business Office."

Your forms will provide the information necessary for the buying agency to place your company on the Bidder's List for those items/services in which you indicated interest and capability.

Do not rely entirely on automatic receipt of IFB or other solicitations. Follow step 5, below, if possible and maintain contact with the Small Business and Economic Utilization Advisor and/or buyer at the installations concerned.

"Step 5. Subscribe to and read the *Commerce Business Daily*." All routine procurements proposed by the Army must be publicized by certain prescribed methods, and in most cases, the method is publication in the *Commerce Business Daily*. There you will find a public record of upcoming procurements, awards of contracts, and searches for research and development capabilities. On the first Tuesday of each month, you will also find a section devoted to the Advanced Procurement Planning Information—an Army effort to reveal to interested members of industry as much specific unclassified planning information as it has available about any given item. The *Commerce Business Daily* is an excellent source for possible subcontracting leads. The winners of major contract award competition are published there as well.

"Step 6. Be alert to announcements of Business Opportunity Conferences, Trade Fairs or other federally attended or sponsored industrial liaison meetings in your area. Make it a point to participate whenever possible."

A complete listing of all Department of the Army research and development procurement programs, along with names and telephone numbers, will be found in Appendix 2.

THE DEPARTMENT OF THE NAVY

The Navy Materiel Command, located in Arlington, Virginia, has chief responsibility for Navy procurement, but the Military Sealift Command, the Commandant of the Marine Corps, and the Office of Naval Research also conduct major procurement programs.

The Naval Materiel Command

This command functions in a manner similar to DARCOM in the Army. It is an integrated materiel support agency that has central responsibility and accountability in the Navy for total weapon/support systems development, procurement, production, and support. In order to fulfill this function, the command operates through five principal subordinate commands. These are: the Naval Air Systems Command, the Naval Electronics Systems Command, the Naval Facilities Engineering Command, the Naval Sea Systems Command, and the Naval Supply Systems Command.

The Naval Materiel Command also has a number of separately organized projected offices, research centers, and laboratories that conduct programs in support of the mission of the command and its five main subdivisions. Further, this command serves as the procurement manager for the Navy Field Purchase System, with major purchasing/procurement offices in Washington, D.C., Philadelphia, Pennsylvania, and Long Beach, California.

The Naval Air Systems Command

This organization, like the other four, is located in Washington, D.C. It is responsible for research and development and production of Navy and Marine Corps aircraft and associated equipment, including airborne deployed ordnance and weaponry, photographic equipment, meteorological equipment, and overhaul and modification of aircraft and aircraft-associated equipment.

The Naval Electronics Systems Command

This command develops and produces electronic systems of all types including shore based, ship based, and for aviation and ballistic missile systems.

The Naval Facilities Engineering Command

This is the Navy's construction engineering arm. It is responsible for construction projects and materials, permanent facilities, harbor construction and development, deep ocean engineering, and materials to defend against atomic, chemical, and biological warfare, corrosion prevention in marine structures, and similar work pertaining to facilities construction or engineering.

The Naval Sea Systems Command

Just as the Naval Air Systems Command looks after many air systems, this command handles the Navy's ships, their design and that of allied equipment, weaponry and ordnance, including not only their construction, but also overhaul, modernization, and conversion. This command handles just about anything that goes into the water that the Navy uses.

The Naval Supply Systems Command

This command performs research and development in supply, logistics, and fiscal matters. But its major function is technical control over the field purchasing activities at Washington, D.C., Philadelphia, Pennsylvania, and Long Beach, California.

The Washington Navy Yard in Washington, D.C. buys industrial plant equipment including metalworking, manually and numerically controlled; other miscellaneous industrial equipment such as furnaces, welders and flame cutters, electrical measuring equipment, power distribution equipment, laboratory equipment, ADP equipment and computer software services; engineering and other technical services; pollution abatement studies; and other research, development, and test services required by the Government in the Washington area.

The Naval Regional Procurement Office at the naval base in Philadelphia makes major procurements for research and development associated with launching, guidance, and recovery of Navy and Marine Corps aircraft weapon systems and for underwater sound systems. This office also contracts for services such as moving and storage of household goods, services, and materials in support of Naval Intelligence Processing Systems aboard ship, and many other areas including engineering support of weapons systems and avionics, and general supplies for base and shipboard support.

The procurement office on Terminal Island at Long Beach, California buys items of a technical nature and research and development supplies and services for support of naval research and development in southern California. This spans procurement requirements related to electronic communication systems, detection systems, guided missiles and subsystems, warheads, freezing devices, torpedo parts, computer systems, and aircraft and weapons.

Naval Research and Development Centers and Laboratories

As pointed out earlier, these laboratories and development centers perform a variety of research and other activities in support of the Navy mission in general, and the functions of the Naval Materiel Command. A complete list of the Navy's laboratories and development centers will be found in the Appendix.

The Military Sealift Command

This command, with headquarters in Washington, D.C., is a separate processing activity under the Secretary of the Navy. It has charge of procurement of ocean shipping transportation, including ship chartering and ocean tonnage, and repair of oceangoing ships. It also procures emergency supplies and services abroad and does repair, overhaul, and alteration relating to Military Sealift Command vehicles.

The Commandant of the Marine Corps

The Office of the Commandant of the Marine Corps, also located in Washington, has responsibility for electronics equipment, specialized vehicles, and other equipment peculiar to the Marine Corps.

The Office of Naval Research

This agency is primarily concerned with the support of basic research and technology. The Chief of Naval Research plans and coordinates research and exploratory development programs throughout the naval establishment. This requires close consultation and collaboration with both the Chief of Naval Operations and the Commandant of the Marine Corps and other Navy organizations. The major areas of interest of the Office of Naval Research are vehicle warfare technology, including aerodynamics, aircraft survivability, flight control, and missile guidance and control; undersea warfare technology, including acoustics, oceanography, and communications and data processing systems; physical sciences; including physics, electronics, and solid-state sciences; mathematical and information sciences, including logistics, mathematics, operations research, statistics and probability, information systems, and fluid dynamics; biological and medical sciences, including dental sciences, medicine, physiology, biochemistry and microbiology; psychological sciences, including organization effectiveness, engineering psychology, and personnel and training; earth sciences, including Arctic research, geography, earth physics, and atmospheric sciences; material sciences, including metallurgy, chemistry, power and structural mechanics; and finally, ocean science and technology, including physical and chemical oceanography, marine geology, geophysics, ocean biology, and environmental acoustics.

A more complete listing of all Navy procurement programs along with the responsible official, address, and telephone number will be found in Appendix 2.

THE DEPARTMENT OF THE AIR FORCE

Within this agency the Air Force Logistics Command buys all supplies and services for weapons support and other operational systems; the Air Force Systems Command procures all Air Force systems and makes initial purchase of related support equipment, as well as conducting all research and development activities; and all other Air Force commands purchase supplies and services needed to operate Air Force bases around the world.

The following commands also purchase supplies and service related to their missions: Military Airlift Command—airlift and taxi service; Air Training Command—flight training; Air Force Communication Service—operation and maintenance of ground communication service; Air Defense Command—analysis, operation, and maintenance of missile and aircraft-warning systems.

The Air Force Logistics Command (AFLC)

This command is responsible for worldwide logistical support of all major systems within the Air Force after they enter the operational inventory. Until that time, and including the initial buy of new equipment, the Air Force Systems Command has responsibility. This support includes maintenance, repair, modification, procurement of spare parts, and operational support. These functions are performed by five Air Logistic Centers (ALCs) located at Oklahoma City, Oklahoma; Sacramento, California; Ogden, Utah; Warner-Robins, Georgia; and San Antonio, Texas.

Each ALC handles hundreds of different supplies and services in support of operational weapons systems assigned to it. (For a detailed listing, see Appendix 2.)

The Procurement Source System at an ALC is based upon the use of detailed commodity lists that contain those items procured by that particular ALC. You can get these detailed commodity lists by writing or calling the Air Force Logistic Command Small Business Specialists listed in Chapter 3.

The Air Force Logistics Command requires completion of the following forms to establish yourself as a potential supplier: Standard Form 129, "Bidder's Mailing List Application" (See Appendix), DD Form 558-1, "Bidder's Mailing List Application Supplement" (Figure 2), and AFLC Form 210 "Bidder's List Data" (Figure 9). Completing these forms and sending them to the Small Business Specialist for the commodities that you are interested in supplying will establish your company in the Air Force Logistics Command Procurement Services System.

The Air Force Systems Command (AFSC)

This command is responsible for buying Air Force systems from their inception as aerospace technological innovations through their development, testing, initial production, installation, and check-out. To accomplish this, the procurement portion of this mission is carried out by three major divisions and a number of lesser laboratories and development centers. The major divisions are the Aeronautical Systems Division (ASD), the Electronic Systems Division (ESD), and Space and Missile Systems Organization (SAMSO).

Aeronautical Systems Division (ASD)

ASD is located at Wright-Patterson Air Force Base, Dayton, Ohio, and is responsible for the design, development, and acquisition of aeronautical systems and related equipment.

Electronic Systems Division (ESD)

ESD is located at L. G. Hanscom Air Force Base, Bedford, Massachusetts, and is responsible for everything having to do with Air Force electronic and electromagnetic information and communication systems and equipment for command and control, surveillance, tracking, and other functions not having directly to do with aircraft systems.

Space and Missile Systems Organization (SAMSO)

SAMSO is located near the airport at Los Angeles and also at Norton Air Force Base, San Bernardino, California. SAMSO's job is the development and acquisition of space and missile systems and all related equipment.

BIDDERS LIST DATA

FORM APPROVED
OMB NO. 21-RO272

INSTRUCTIONS:

1. Items below are procured by: _____ ALC

_____

(AFB, State, Zip Code)

2. In order for your firm to appear on the computer prepared Bidders Mailing List for a particular item, you must enter your selections below exactly as they are shown in the Bidders List Catalog (use reverse side if necessary). Submit this form to the Directorate of Procurement and Production (PPDA) of the ALC listed above.

1. NAME OF BUSINESS: (Must be same as Block 2 of SF 129, unless a change is made.)

2. ADDRESS OF COMPANY: (County, Zip Code, MFR TWX No.)

3. CLASS	STOCK NUMBER, COMMODITY GROUPING OR SERVICE CODE	3A. DESCRIPTION

FOR AIR FORCE USE ONLY:

MFR. CODE	COUNTY	CITY	STATE	TYPE CONCERN	NATURE OF BUSINESS	NO. OF EMPL	DOLLAR CATEGORY	

Figure 9. AFLC Form 210/Bidder's List Data.

63

3. CLASS	STOCK NUMBER, COMMODITY GROUPING OR SERVICE CODE	3A. DESCRIPTION

NO FURTHER ENTRIES REQUIRED WHEN THIS FORM IS BEING SUBMITTED WITH SF 129. If the form is submitted to make a change to an application previously submitted describe the change in Block 4 and complete Block 5. Additions of new items will be entered in Block 3 and 3A. If the change deletes items previously submitted, enter the letter "D" to the left of the class number.

4. ADMINISTRATIVE CHANGES:

5. CERTIFICATION: I certify that information supplied herein (including all pages attached) is correct and that neither the applicant nor any person (or concern) in any connection with the applicant as a principal or officer so far as is known, is now debarred or otherwise declared ineligible by any agency of the federal government from bidding for furnishing materials, supplies, or services to the government or any agency thereof.

SIGNATURE: (Name & Title of Person authorized to sign)	DATE

Figure 9 (*Continued*)

Laboratories and Development Centers within AFSC

Within AFSC are laboratories and development centers that represent thousands of research and development opportunities to small business contractors. The Aerospace Medical Division (AMD), located at Brooks Air Force Base, Texas, is responsible for research in the life sciences, human factors, aerospace medicine, biomedicine, behavioral sciences, space medicine, biotechnology, human engineering, human resources, aviation medicine, space biology, and medical equipment. The Armament Development and Test Center at Eglin Air Force Base, Florida procures research and development, and conducts tests related to the evaluation of guns and other weaponry, nonnuclear ordnance, and the testing of weapons, concepts, techniques, and tactics. The Arnold Engineering Development Center located at Arnold Air Force Station, Tennessee conducts tests and laboratory evaluations of aircraft, missile, satellite, and space components and systems. The Rome Air Development Center at Rome, New York is interested in the research and development of electronic intelligence, communications, countermeasures, computer and data processing, and similar systems. At Kirtland Air Force Base, New Mexico, the Air Force Special Weapons Center is responsible for research, development, and testing of nuclear weapons systems.

There are several laboratories at Wright-Patterson Air Force Base (Dayton, Ohio) that investigate and fund different areas in research and development of interest to the Air Force. One is the Air Force Aero Propulsion Laboratory, which is interested in exploratory and advanced development of air breathing, electric and advanced propulsion, fuels and lubricatns, power generation, and supporting areas. Another, the Air Force Avionics Laboratory, works on exploratory development programs in electromagnetic transmission and reception, molecular electronics, bionics, vehicle environment lasers, photo materials and optronics, position and motion sensing devices, navigation and guidance, reconnaissance and avionics communications, and electromagnetic warfare. A third, the 6570th Aerospace Medical Research Laboratory, conducts behavioral and biomedical research mainly pertaining to human characteristics relating to performance of machinery and life support. The Air Force Flight Dynamics Laboratory conducts exploration and advanced development programs in flight dynamics, structures, aerodynamics, aerothermodynamics, performance, stability and control, control displays at crew station, environmental control, aerodynamic deceleration and escape, and equipment simulation and flight-testing techniques.

The Air Force Materiels Laboratory in New Mexico will contract for programs relating to exploratory or advanced development materiels sciences, metals and ceramics, nonmetallic materiels, manufacturing technology, and materiels application. Like the Air Force Special Weapons Center, this laboratory is located at Kirtland Air Force Base. It researches weapons effects, radiation hazards, delivery techniques, nuclear weapon components, weapons training devices, and other weapon research.

The Air Force Human Resources Laboratory is located at Brooks Air Force

Base, near San Antonio, Texas. It is responsible for exploratory and advanced developments in methods, devices, and procedures for the education and training of Air Force personnel, simulation techniques for the development of training devices and other training environments, and personnel, training, and manning factors in the conception, design, and development and testing of aerospace systems.

Air Force Office of Scientific Research (AFOSR)

This office is part of the Air Force Systems Command and is located at Arlington, Virginia. This office encourages and supports applied research designed to increase the understanding of the natural sciences and stimulate the recognition of new scientific concepts. AFOSR is organized into six principal directorates: the Directorate of Aerospace Sciences, the Directorate of Chemical Sciences, the Directorate of Electronic and Solid State Sciences, the Directorate of Mathematical and Information Sciences, the Directorate of Life Science, the Directorate of Physics. You can write the Small Business Specialist at AFOSR for information describing specific scientific areas of interest.

THE DEFENSE LOGISTICS AGENCY (DLA)

This agency is responsible to the Secretary of Defense for providing supplies and services in common use by all the military services and certain other federal agencies.

DLA procures a vast number of products—about $6 billion in new supplies annually. In addition, many indefinite delivery contracts are awarded annually by DLA, with the growing military agencies placing orders directly for the delivery of their requirements.

The DLA buys just about everything, but here are some general commodities the DLA itself advertises as "what we buy":

- Construction and automotive equipment:
    plywood and veneer
    lumber and millwork
    pipe, conduit, and plumbing fixtures
    hose and tubing
    fuel-burning equipment
    power and hand pumps
    winches, cranes, and conveyors
    diesel and gasoline engines and components
    cabs, frames, and components
    transmissions, brakes, and steering
    truck and tractor attachments
    self-propelled trucks and tractors

- Electronics:
    resistors
    capacitors
    filters and networks
    fuses and arresters
    circuit breakers
    electronic tubes and transistors
    semiconductor devices
    synchros and resolvers
    test equipment
    switches
    connectors
    crystals
    relays and solenoids
    coils and transformers
    headsets and handsets
    antennas and wave guides
    communication equipment
- Fuel, petroleum products, and services:
    gasoline and jet fuel
    fuel oils
    coal
    oils and greases
    petrochemicals
    operation of government-owned terminals
    commercial storage
    aircraft, fuel-delivery services at military installations and commercial airports
- General:
    chemicals
    wood pallets
    sandbags
    electrical hardware
    electric motors and generators
    welding equipment and supplies
    scientific instruments
    service and trade equipment
    food preparation equipment
    plastic fabricated materials
    photographic supplies
    scales and balances
- Industrial:
    hardware
    metal bars, sheets, and shapes

blocks, tackle, and rigging
fiber rope, cordage, and twine
bearings
chain and wire rope
rope-cable fittings
electrical wire and cable
packing and gasket materials

- Medical, dental:
  drugs
  biologicals
  reagent grade chemicals
  surgical, dental, and optician's instruments, equipment, and supplies
  X-ray equipment and supplies
  hospital furniture, equipment, utensils, supplies, and clothing
  medical sets, kits, and outfits
  laboratory equipment and supplies
  opthalmic goods

- Subsistence:
  meat, poultry, and fish
  fruits and vegetables
  coffee, tea, and cocoa
  food oils and fats
  soups and bouillon
  composite food packages
  dairy foods and eggs
  bakery and cereal products
  nonalcoholic beverages
  sugar, confectionery, and nuts
  condiments

- Textiles and clothing
  men's and women's clothing
  wool, cotton, and synthetic fabrics
  boots and shoes
  canvas products, tents, and tarpaulins
  raincoats and other waterproof garments
  hats and caps
  flags and pennants
  sunglasses
  socks, undershirts, and other knitwear
  body armor
  dress and work gloves
  protective helmets and liners

embroidered and metal insignias
decorations and badges
blankets

The DLA buys through six Defense Supply Centers. Each supply center has a Small Business and Economic Utilization Specialist to assist you. Here are the addresses of each center and the telephone number of each specialist. Note that the type of goods or services that each center handles is incorporated in the name of the center.

Defense Construction Supply Center
3990 East Broad Street
Columbus, Ohio 43215
Tel: (614)   236-3541

Defense Electronics Supply Center
1507 Wilmington Pike
Dayton, Ohio 45444
Tel: (513)   296-5231

Defense Fuel Supply Center
Cameron Station, Bldg. 8
5010 Duke Street
Alexandria, Virginia 22314
Tel: (202)   274-7428

Defense General Supply Center
Bellwood, Petersburg Pike
Richmond, Virginia 23297
Tel: (804)   275-3617 or 275-3287

Defense Industrial Supply Center
700 Robbins Avenue
Philadelphia, Pennsylvania 19111
Tel: (215)   697-2747 or 697-2748

Defense Personnel Support Center
2800 South 20th Street
Philadelphia, Pennsylvania 19101
Tel: (215)   271-2321

The DLA buys through formal advertising (IFBs) and through negotiation (RFPs and RFQs), as noted in Chapters 1 and 5. The DLA also buys by a unique method called Automated Small Purchase System (ASPS), Phase I and Phase II.

ASPS Phase I

ASPS Phase I is a method that DLA uses to purchase supplies through the placement of a Blanket Purchase Agreement, which DLA naturally call a "BPA." The
BPA is nothing more than a schedule through which the government can negotiate
a single contract for repetitive orders, just as other Government units like GSA
do. During the BPA development process, potential suppliers are required to
identify the manufacturers whose products they will agree to furnish if an order is
received from the Government. These manufacturers are identified by a special
Federal Supply Code for Manufacturers documented in the BPA. A BPA supplier
may specify any number of manufacturers for which he wants to be considered as
a source of supply. A BPA supplier may be considered as a source of supply for
selected classes of products by manufacturers identified in the BPA by code, or
all the products of one or more coded manufacturers.

Once a BPA is set up, you as a supplier are recorded in ASPS Phase I computer
files as a valid source of supply for the products of the manufacturers identified
by the Federal Supply Code for Manufacturers and/or the products as identified by Federal Supply Classes as identified in the agreement. You will then receive
calls for supplies as they come in. Of course, there will probably be more than
one supplier listed in the BPA. In that case, the computer will rotate the ordering
on an equal basis among the list suppliers.

ASPS Phase II

What DLA calls ASPS Phase II is an automated RFQ system. If you are listed in
an ASPS Phase I program, you will be automatically included under Phase II. It
is an RFQ system and not RFP because the aggregate amount involved is not
more than $10,000.

Here is how it works. ASPS Phase II automatically solicits all Phase I listed
suppliers through the computer generation of RFQs to sources of supply. The
price quotations received are evaluated automatically, and the computer even
selects the winner and generates all the award documents necessary to finalize
the purchase. I suppose eventually this will be carried forward to a point at which
you as winner will receive a telephone call from a computerized voice that will
inform you of the award and congratulate you on winning. As of this writing,
however, the Phase II computer only does the paper work automatically.

How to Sell to DLA

DLA suggests the following steps under the formal advertising procedures in its
booklet "How to Do Business with the Defense Logistics Agency":

1. *Tell DLA what you sell.* From the listing of supply centers above, you can
   determine which DLA center buys what. Write the appropriate supply center

and request that Standard Form 129, Bidder's Mailing List Application (as shown in the appendix) be sent to you. Complete the form and return it to the supply center for evaluation.

2. *Find out what the DLA wants to buy.* Once you are on a bidder's list, you will receive a notice from the DLA whenever they are in the market to buy the types of products that you sell. (This notice is the IFB discussed in Chapter 1.) It will describe in detail what the DLA wants and include the forms on which you will submit your bids. It also lists the terms of the contracts that will be awarded to successful bidders.

3. *Quote your best price.* You do not have to bid on the entire quantity that the DLA wants. You can bid on the entire quantity or on only that portion for which your productive capacity and financial resources are adequate. According to the DLA, if the lowest bidder does not quote on the entire quantity required in the IFB, contracts are awarded to a sufficient number of low bidders whose combined offerings meet the full requirements, provided that their prices are reasonable. All deliveries must be made in accordance with the schedule listed in the IFB. Submit your bid in the number of copies required by the IFB, and send it early enough so that it will reach the appropriate supply center by the hour and date listed for bid opening in the IFB.

You can see all bids and awards made at the issuing office. Contracts in excess of $50,000 must be reported in the *Commerce Business Daily.*

DLA provides the following hints to bidders:

"Read the Invitation carefully. It means exactly what it says. You are expected to follow all instructions and specifications set forth in the Invitation. The Invitation will tell you where to obtain all necessary specifications. Don't assume anything. In case of doubt as to the meaning of any part of the Invitation or specifications, communicate immediately with issuing office before the bid opening. If you cannot meet the specifications, you should not submit a bid. If necessary, examine the samples at the issuing office. They are there for your use."

"Include all your costs. Be certain that all costs are included. Don't forget preservation, packaging, packing, and marking. Remember that many things can upset your cost estimates. It is important to take them into consideration when preparing your bid."

"Prepare your bid accurately. Your bid is your formal offer to supply the required items at the price you indicate and on the terms we specify. Don't promise deliveries you cannot fulfill. If your bid is accepted, your contract will hold you to all the terms of the Invitation. If you make an error, the Defense Logistics Agency may not be legally able to grant relief. Be accurate."

"Submit your bid on time. Your bid must be received by the Purchasing Office prior to the hour set for the opening of bids. Unless otherwise stated in the Invitation, telegraphic bids will not be accepted. Be sure to comply with all requirements relative to the submission of bids."

Civilian Agency Procurement Programs

This section discusses opportunities available through civilian agencies other than the GSA opportunities that were discussed earlier. All civilian agencies publicize proposed procurements by means of news releases, paid advertising, the *Commerce Business Daily,* and by mailing IFBs, RFPs, or RFQs to known suppliers. But the burden of gaining initial recognition is still on you, usually by mailing a Standard Form 129, "Bidder's Mailing List Application."

But before putting you on a bidder's list, any Government agency is going to want to know a great deal more about you. Don't think you can always accomplish this by simply mailing a Standard Form 129 and a company catalogue. Before giving you contracts worth thousands or millions of dollars, the Government, just like you as a good businessman, wants some assurance that you can and will deliver what you promise you will. Uncle Sam's own booklet, "Doing Business with the Federal Government," says:

Before placing a firm on its bidder's mailing list, an agency will often require additional information such as:

- Production capability.
- Description of items normally produced.
- Number of employees.
- Plant and transportation facilities.
- Government contract experience.
- Financial status.
- Scope of the firm's operations.

You should expect that doing business will not be automatic and that you will have to do some selling. Otherwise you might wonder whether the Government is giving the proper care and attention to spending our well-earned tax dollars . . . right?

Chapter 7 will tell you how to accomplish preproposal marketing successfully. But for the moment, you should understand that you must gain the prospective buying agency's confidence. If the agency offers written material to help you in selling to the agency in question (and many do), you should certainly order this material and study it.

The civilian Government agencies offering opportunities are the Department of Energy and the National Aeronautics and Space Administration, so we'll discuss them first.

Department of Energy (DOE)

NASA was once in second place behind DOD, with the second largest budget for procurements pertaining to research and development. Not so today. In the Government's 1979 fiscal year, DOE's research and development budget was almost twice that of NASA's ($7.5 billion vs. $3.6 billion).

DOE was formed in 1977 from what were formerly ERDA (Energy Research and Development Administration), FEA (Federal Energy Administration), FPC (Federal Power Commission), and parts of five other agencies.

DOE research and development projects have to do with fossil and nuclear fuels, solar and geothermal energy, other advanced energy systems, energy conservation technology, and energy-related programs affecting the environment, safety, and national security.

Supplies and services are obtained by contracting with small businesses, industry, universities, and nonprofit institutions. These procurements are usually coordinated by headquarters in Washington, D.C. or by one of the eight field offices located in Albuquerque, New Mexico; Idaho Falls, Idaho; Oak Ridge, Tennessee; Richland, Washington; San Francisco, California; or Aiken, South Carolina. However, other DOE buying offices may indicate procurements and will provide assistance. The addresses for DOE headquarters, field offices, and other major buying offices will be found in Appendix 2.

DOE procurement activities cover a wide variety of services and supplies. Here is how DOE itself categorizes and describes these requirements:

- Materials, equipment, and supplies. These constitute the great majority of purchases made by major DOE agencies. Large quantity requirements are not characteristic except for materials and equipment required for new Government-owned facilities, materials and equipment for construction, and materials and equipment to operate and maintain electrical transmission systems, substitutions, and switching stations.

- Construction and architect-engineering services. All types of construction and design services ranging from administrative and auxiliary-support buildings to complex industrial and research facilities are purchased by DOE.

- Management services. These include services for the operation of production and research facilities and supporting activities, including transportation.

- Fuel processing, fabrication, and recovery services. DOE buys processing services for uranium, thorium, or plutonium compounds and alloys, fabrication of fuel elements, and the recovery of special nuclear material from scrap.

- Basic research. DOE supports basic research in energy-related fields by universities, nonprofit organizations, and commercial concerns.

- Applied research and development. DOE contracts for applied research and development with private concerns to do work either in their own or in Government research facilities.

- Consultant and professional services and studies. These include computer data service, consultant, and professional services in environmental fields, and studies in various fields of energy.
- Demonstration projects. DOE supports demonstration projects to assist the private and public sector in demonstrating the feasibility of commercializing concepts, processes, equipment, materials, and other devices.

DOE publishes the following booklets, which can be of considerable assistance to you in obtaining contracts in the various categories of goods and services DOE requires:

1. "Doing Business with DOE"
2. "Guide for the Submission of Research and Development Proposals by Individuals and Organizations" (other than educational institutions).
3. "Guide for the Submission of Research and Development Proposals by Educational Institutions."
4. "Contracting for Construction and Architect-Engineering-Services."

You can obtain any of these booklets by writing:

Department of Energy
Office of Procurement
Washington, D.C. 20545

National Aeronautics and Space Administration (NASA)

As pointed out earlier, NASA was once second only to DOE in procurements. This is no longer so today, but NASA still has a budget for billions of dollars in procurements—certainly with enough opportunities for Government business to last even the most ambitious company into the foreseeable future.

NASA requirements range from highly complex research and development for aeronautics and space systems to basic supplies, support services, and construction.

You can get detailed information on business opportunities with NASA by writing:

The Office of Procurement
NASA Headquarters
Washington, D.C. 20546

or any of the following NASA offices or centers:

Ames Research Center
NASA
Moffett Field, CA 94035

Flight Research Center
NASA
Edwards Air Force Base, CA 93523

Goddard Space Flight Center
NASA
Greenbelt, MD 20771

Headquarters, Contracts Division
NASA
Washington, D.C. 20546

Johnson Space Center
NASA
Houston, TX 77058

Kennedy Space Center
NASA
Kennedy Space Center, FL 32899

Langley Research Center
NASA
Hampton, VA 23365

Lewis Research Center
NASA
Cleveland, OH 44135

Marshall Space Flight Center
NASA
Huntsville, AL 35812

Wallops Flight Center
NASA
Wallops Island, VA 23337

Jet Propulsion Laboratory
NASA
Pasadena, CA 91103

National Space Technology Labs
NASA
Bay St. Louis, MO 39520

You can obtain more detailed information on what and how the various agencies of NASA buy in the booklet, "Selling to NASA." You can obtain this publication by writing to:

Office of Public Affairs
NASA Headquarters
Washington, D.C. 20546

If you think these are all the opportunities available in dealing with other civilian Government agencies, you are wrong. There are still billions of dollars in other opportunities available to you. Here are those remaining civilian agencies that make substantial buys from American industry.

Department of Agriculture (USDA)

The Department of Agriculture buys supplies, services, and construction through more than 200 local offices in the United States. However, there are four Agriculture agencies that account for about 90% of the dollar value of all USDA purchases. These are the Agricultural Research Service (ARS), the Animal and Plant Health Inspection Service (APHIS), the Forest Service (FS), and the Soil Conservation Service (SCS).

Agricultural Research Service (ARS)

ARS buys laboratory, scientific and testing equipment, farm equipment and supplies, light trucks and trailers, refrigerating and dehumidifying equipment, and furniture. ARS also has construction requirements for animal pens, insectaries, greenhouses, storage sheds, laboratory buildings, prefabricated buildings, windmills, wells, dock and harbor facilities, soil moisture tanks, fences, roads, driveways, and parking areas.
    ARS buying is decentralized and on a regional level. If you want to do business with ARS, contact:

Agricultural Research Service
U.S. Department of Agriculture
General Services Division
6505 Belcrest Road
Hyattsville, MD 20782

Animal and Plant Health Inspection Service (APHIS)

APHIS buys mainly the same items as ARS with some additionals. These include laboratory supplies, vehicles, farm equipment, office supplies and equipment, radio transmitting and receiving equipment, insecticides, data processing, and construction services.
    If you want to do business with APHIS, contact either of these two offices:

Animal and Plant Health Inspection Service
U.S. Department of Agriculture
Administrative Services Division
Procurement and Property Branch
6505 Belcrest Road
Hyattsville, MD 20782

Animal and Plant Health Inspection Service
U.S. Department of Agriculture
Administrative Services Division
Administration Operations Branch
123 East Grant Street
Minneapolis, MN 55403

Forest Service (FS)

In keeping with its responsibility for fostering, maintaining, and protecting U.S. forests, FS buys lookout towers, binoculars, fire-fighting tools, petroleum products, building and construction supplies, transportation equipment, motor vehicles, aircraft, parachutes, boats, engineering and laboratory equipment, radio equipment, refrigerators, tractors, graders, compressors, concrete mixers, trailers, cranes, explosives, chemicals, insecticides, seeds, fertilizers, hardware supplies, hand tools, machine tools, barbed wire, and paints.

FS also uses construction and similar services for its public works projects, which include the construction of roads, bridges, and buildings as well as insect control, tree planting, range vegetation, and brush disposal.

FS buying is decentralized and handled by regional and national forest staffs.

To do business with FS, contact:

Director of Administrative Service
Forest Service, U.S. Department of Agriculture
1621 North Kent Street
Arlington, VA 22209

Soil Conservation Service (SCS)

With its soil conservation responsibilities, SCS is interested in buying all sorts of equipment for soil sampling including laboratory equipment, photographic and radio systems, office furniture and supplies, data processing equipment, office machinery and supplies, vehicles and other transportation equipment, farm equipment, drafting and engineering equipment, and animal feed, insecticides, and fertilizers. Construction equipment is generally rented.

SCS also buys architect, engineering, and construction services including core drilling, construction of small dams, reservoirs, channels, debris basins, and other water-use and control structures.

SCS buying is decentralized at the state level. Write:

Soil Conservation Service
U.S. Department of Agriculture
Administrative Services Division
Procurement Management Branch
Washington, D.C. 20250

You can obtain a free brochure, "Selling to the United States Department of Agriculture," by writing:

U.S. Department of Agriculture
Office of Operations (PGAMS)
Room 131-W
Administrative Building
Washington, D.C. 20250

Department of Commerce

The Department of Commerce does a great deal of centralized procurement of supplies, equipment, and services for the various organizations within the department. To get on the Bidder's Mailing List and obtain additional information about procurement policies, write:

The Office of Administrative Services and Procurement
U.S. Department of Commerce
Washington, D.C. 20230

If you are a minority business enterprise, there is a special address that you can write to for additional help:

Market Development
Office of Minority Business Enterprise
Washington, D.C. 20230

There are also additional opportunities in fulfilling the specialized needs of the Department of Commerce's subordinate organizations. These include the National Bureau of Standards, the Social and Economic Statistics Administration, the Maritime Administration, and the National Oceanic and Atmospheric Administration. For the addresses of these organizations, consult Appendix 2.

Department of Health, Education, and Welfare (DHEW)

As this is being written, this department is being reorganized. However, if this reorganization is like others in the Government, it will be some time before all the pieces get sorted out, and meanwhile the old sources of business are still good.

DHEW procures articles and services for staff and operational programs involving health, education, social security, and general welfare. Of all subordinate organizations, the Public Health Service claims the largest dollar volume.

Procurement in DHEW is decentralized, but you can get help from DHEW headquarters by writing:

Director of Business Affairs
U.S. Department of Health, Education, and Welfare
Washington, D.C. 20201

You can also sell special administrative items and services bought by DHEW headquarters by writing:

Procurement and Contracts Section
Supply Operations Branch
Division of Administrative Services
Office of the Secretary
U.S. Department of Health, Education, and Welfare
Washington, D.C. 20201

The subordinate organizations of DHEW, all of which purchase various types of administrative supplies and services, include the center for Disease Control in Atlanta, Georgia; the Food and Drug Administration, the Health Resources Administration, and Health Services Administration, all located in Rockville, Maryland; the Office of Human Development in Washingtin, D.C.; the National Institutes of Health in Bethesda, Maryland; the Public Health Service in Rockville, Maryland; the Social and Rehabilitation Service in Washington, D.C.; and the Social Security Administration in Baltimore, Maryland. The addresses of all of these organizations will be found in Appendix 2.

DHEW has prepared a pamphlet for your assistance, "How to Do Business with DHEW." You can get it free from any of DHEW regional offices, which are located in Atlanta, Georgia; Boston, Massachusetts; Chicago, Illinois; Dallas, Texas; Denver, Colorado; Kansas City, Missouri; New York, New York; Philadelphia, Pennsylvania; San Francisco, California; and Seattle, Washington; or by writing to the Director of Business Affairs at the address listed above.

Department of Housing and Urban Development (HUD)

HUD is the Government organization that administers programs relating to housing needs and community improvement and development.

HUD buys water and space heaters, electric ranges and refrigerators, lawn mowers, paint, screen wire, toilet seats, garbage cans, hot-air furnace filters, window shades, and furniture. Write:

Office of Procurement and Contracts
U.S. Department of Housing and Urban Development
451 7th Street, SW
Washington, D.C. 20410

Regional offices of HUD procure supplies and services for the rehabilitation, repair, management, maintenance, sale, or demolition of HUD properties. To get this business, you must contact the regional office, because bidder source lists are not maintained at the national level.

You can get a list of regional and area insuring offices of HUD by writing and asking for HUD Form 788, Field Office Jurisdiction. Write to:

Publications Services Center
U.S. Department of Housing and Urban Development
451 7th Street, S.W.
Washington, D.C. 20410

Flood Insurance Administration

If you are an architect-engineering firm, there may be opportunities for you with this relatively new agency.

This program was authorized by Congress in 1968 to protect property owners who couldn't get flood insurance protection from private industry. In return for the federal subsidy that permits the insurance, each community subject to flooding is required to adopt minimum flood plan measures to reduce or avoid flood damage.

Your job, if you are qualified, is to identify those areas within a community that are subject to flooding.

If you are interested, you should submit Standard Form 254, U.S. Government Architect-Engineer and Related Services Questionnaire (Figure 6) to:

Flood Insurance Administration
U.S. Department of Housing and Urban Development
Engineering and Hydrology Division
451 7th Street, S.W.
Washington, D.C. 20410

Department of the Interior

The bureaus that make up the Department of the Interior do most of the buying. Procurements that are made centrally are arranged by:

Division of Property and Records
U.S. Department of the Interior
Washington, D.C. 20240

Department bureaus include the National Park Service, the Geological Survey, the Bureau of Mines, the Mining Enforcement and Safety Administration, the Fish and Wildlife Service, the Bureau of Indian Affairs, the Bureau of Reclamation, the Bureau of Land Management, the Alaska Power Administration, the Bonneville Power Administration, the Southeastern Power Administration, and the Southwestern Administration.

National Park Service

This service contracts for physical improvements and concessions in our national parks. To receive the latest list of offices that issue IFBs, write:

Division of Contracting and Property Management
National Park Service
U.S. Department of the Interior
Washington, D.C. 20240

Geological Survey

This agency buys drafting, surveying, laboratory, office, and electronic equipment; special photographic supplies; metals, lumber, machine parts, and hand tools. It also buys services for core and test-hole drilling, aerial photographs, and helicopter flights. The address is:

Branch of Procurement and Contracts
U.S. Geological Survey
Department of the Interior
205 USGS National Center
12201 Sunrise Valley Drive
Reston, VA 22092

Bureau of Mines

This agency's purchases are generally related to laboratory needs and the production of helium. These procurements are made at field research centers, laboratories, area and district offices, and helium plants.

To do business with the Bureau of Mines, file Standard Form 129, Bidders' Mailing List Application (Figure 2) at a field office. A list of Bureau of Mines field offices can be found in Appendix 2.

Mining Enforcement and Safety Administration

This administration makes procurements from area and district offices. These procurements include protective clothing for mine inspections; mine safety equipment; furniture and office supplies; and services, including training, relating to health and safety.

To get on the Mining Enforcement and Safety Administration's mailing list, write:

Division of Management Services
Mining Enforcement and Safety Administration
U.S. Department of the Interior
4015 Wilson Boulevard
Arlington, VA 22203

Fish and Wildlife Service

Here's an opportunity to sell small boats, outboard motors, construction and farming equipment, two-way radio transmitters and receivers, and fish foods.
    Write to:

Procurement Offices
Fish and Wildlife Service
U.S. Department of the Interior
Washington, D.C. 20240

or to one of the six regional offices listed in Appendix 2.

Bureau of Indian Affairs

This agency is the buyer of supplies and eqipment for agriculture subsistence items, school supplies, building maintenance, and construction of roads and irrigation ditches.
    If you are interested, write to the nearest office listed in Appendix 2.

Bureau of Reclamation

The Office of the Chief Engineer of this bureau makes central procurements for electrical and mechanical equipment including generators, turbines, transformers, and circuit breakers. The address is:
Chief Engineer, Bureau of Reclamation
U.S. Department of the Interior
Building 67
Denver Federal Center
Denver, CO 80225

    The bureau also makes various purchases such as office supplies of a nonspecialized nature. Write the nearest Bureau office listed in Appendix 2.

Bureau of Land Management

The central office of the bureau in Washington, as well as state offices and service centers, purchase a variety of goods including fire-fighting equipment, survey instruments, range grass seed, brushland plows, range land drills, and heavy equipment. These varied offices also contract for plowing, seeding, aerial spraying, and for construction of earth-filled dams, fences, and roads.

You can find out about all the opportunities listed by contacting one of the offices or a service center, which are listed in Appendix 2.

Alaska Power Administration

If you are located in or near Alaska, or are willing to relocate for the business, the Alaska Power Administration makes procurements at its headquarters in Juneau, at the hydroelectric power facilities at the Eklutna Project near Anchorage, and at the Snettisham Project near Juneau. These purchases are mostly for the operation and maintenance of hydroelectric power plants and facilities.

Interested? Write:

Adminstrator, Alaska Power Administration
U.S. Department of the Interior
P.O. Box 50
Juneau, AK 99802

Bonneville, Southeastern and Southwestern Power Administrations

These administrations all make purchases relating to electric power operations. In Bonneville, these commodities are used in 115,000, 230,000, 345,000, and 500,000 volt lines and substations. The Southwestern Power Administration purchases materials and supplies for the construction, maintenance, and operation of a 1600 mile transmission system. However, the Southeastern Power Administration purchases are for administrative operations, since this administration does not operate or maintain power facilities.

If you want to do business with these organizations, here are the addresses to write:

Procurement Office
Bonneville Power Administration
U.S. Department of the Interior
Portland, OR 97208

Administrator
Southeastern Power Administration
U.S. Department of the Interior
Samuel Elbert Building
Elberton, GA 30635

Administrator
Southwestern Power Administration
U.S. Department of the Interior

P.O. Drawer 1619
Tulsa, OK 74101

The Department of Justice

Each bureau under the Department of Justice does its own buying, although the
department itself does the buying for the headquarters offices. The bureaus include the Bureau of Prisons; Federal Prison Industries, Inc.; the Drug Enforcement
Administration; the Federal Bureau of Investigation; and the United States Marshals Service.

Bureau of Prisons

Prisons, which are like self-contained cities, buy a wide variety of goods. These
purchases are made by the individual prisons from local sources, or from national
supply houses.

To do business with prisons and get on their mailing lists, you must contact each
institution separately. The GSA's booklet, "Doing Business with the Federal
Government," recommends personal contacts by company representatives.

You can also obtain additional information by writing:

Bureau of the Prisons
U.S. Department of Justice
Washington, D.C. 20537

Federal Prison Industries, Inc.

This sounds like a business itself, and it is. The Federal Prison Industries, Inc.
buys raw materials for use in prison workshops. Most procurements are by negotiated contract and include steel for steel furniture construction, wool and cotton
for textile production, textiles for clothing, leather for shoes, lumber for furniture,
bristles for brushes, broom corn for brooms, and so on.

To get more information about this program and get on the mailing list, write to:

Purchasing Division
Federal Prison Industries, Inc.
U.S. Department of Justice
Washington, D.C. 20537

Drug Enforcement Administration (DEA)

This administration buys communication equipment, laboratory equipment, guns,
ammunition, and automatic data processing applicable to law-enforcement activities. If you're interested in selling to DEA, you should write:

Drug Enforcement Administration
Administration Services Division
U.S. Department of Justice
Washington, D.C. 20537

Federal Bureau of Investigation (FBI)

As you might imagine, the FBI is interested mainly in law-enforcement supplies, including radio and electronic equipment, special laboratory equipment, guns and ammunitions, and similar items.

For additional information write to:

Procurement and Administrative Services Section
Federal Bureau of Investigation
U.S. Department of Justice
Washington, D.C. 20535

United States Marshals Service

Here again, these folks are interested in law-enforcement items: weapons, ammunition, communications equipment, and related services. If you are interested in leasing real estate, the U.S. Marshals Service also lease real estate for law-enforcement purposes. Write:

Administrative Services Division
United States Marshals Service
U.S. Department of Justice
Washington, D.C. 20530

Department of the Treasury

The Treasury buys supplies and services mostly through its twelve bureau head-quarters; office supplies are purchased through its field offices. The biggest Treasury buys are through five bureaus: the Bureau of Government Financial Operations, Mint, Engraving and Printing, Customs Service, and the Internal Revenue Service.

To investigate possible business opportunities with the Department of the Treasury, write to each of the 12 addresses listed below.

Chief, Procurement and Personal Property Branch (Operations)
Office of the Secretary of the Treasury
U.S. Department of the Treasury
Main Treasury Building
Washington, D.C. 20220

Assistant Comptroller for Facilities
Bureau of Government
Financial Operations
U.S. Department of the Treasury
Treasury Annex No. 1
Washington, D.C. 20226

Chief, Procurement and Property Branch
Bureau of Alcohol, Tobacco and Firearms
U.S. Department of the Treasury
Postal Service Building
Washington, D.C. 20226

Procurement Officer
Office of the Comptroller of the Currency
U.S. Department of the Treasury
Fifth Floor, East Building
L'Enfant Plaza
Washington, D.C. 20219

Administrative Officer
Federal Law Enforcement
Training Center
U.S. Department of the Treasury
Brunswick, GA 31520

Chief, Procurement and Property Services Branch
Logistics Management Division
U.S. Customs Service
U.S. Department of the Treasury
Washington, D.C. 20229

Superintendent, Materials
Management Division
Bureau of Engraving and Printing
U.S. Department of the Treasury
Engraving and Printing Annex
Washington, D.C. 20228

Chief, Contract and Procurement Section
Internal Revenue Service
U.S. Department of the Treasury
Washington, D.C. 20224

Chief, Procurement Division
Bureau of the Mint
U.S. Department of the Treasury
Washington, D.C. 20220

Chief, Procurement Section
Bureau of the Public Debt
U.S. Department of the Treasury
Engraving and Printing Annex
Washington, D.C. 20226

Chief, Office Services Section
United States Savings Bond Division
U.S. Department of the Treasury
Washington, D.C. 20226

Procurement Officer
United States Secret Service
U.S. Department of the Treasury
Washington, D.C. 20223

Department of Transportation (DOT)

DOT decentralizes most of its procurement. The exception is for management
consultant services for studies concerning DOT's programs. If you are interested
in this aspect, write:

Department of Transportation/OST
TAD–43
400 7th Street, S.W.
Washington, D.C. 20590

   Major agencies of DOT that you can find business opportunities in are the Federal
Aviation Administration, Federal Highway Administration, U.S. Coast Guard,
Federal Railroad Administration, Urban Mass Transportation Administration,
and the St. Lawrence Seaway Development Corporation.
   DOT also publishes a free pamphlet to assist you. Ask for DOT Pamphlet 4200.1,
"Contracting with the United States Department of Transportation" by writing to:

Consumer Affairs Offices
U.S. Department of Transportation
400 7th Street, S.W.
Washington, D.C. 20590

Federal Aviation Administration (FAA)

The FAA buys aircraft; communications; air navigation, and air traffic control
equipment are bought nationwide; while at headquarters, acquisitions are research
and development services and major electronic systems.
   You can get additional information by writing to any FAA regional office listed
in Appendix 2 or to:

Procurement Management and Services Branch
Contracts Division
Federal Aviation Administration
U.S. Department of Transportation
Washington, D.C. 20591

Federal Highway Administration

This administration purchases road construction equipment, vehicles, parts, and support materials, as well as buying research and development services for safety standards and tests.
    To be notified of opportunities, send your Standard Form 129 to:

Procurement Branch
Federal Highway Administration
U.S. Department of Transportation
1717 H Street, N.W.
Washington, D.C. 20591

U.S. Coast Guard

District offices and other units of the U.S. Coast Guard purchase ship repairs, ship replacement parts, aircraft replacement parts, buoys, and other materials and construction to support Coast Guard operations.
    The Washington, D.C. office procures ships, aircraft, electronics equipment, supplies for new ships, and research services.
    If you are interested, write:

Commandant (FS-1)
U.S. Coast Guard
U.S. Department of Transportation
1300 E Street, N.W.
Washington, D.C. 20591

Federal Railroad Administration

This administration buys research in a variety of areas having to do with transportation including high-speed ground transportation concerning aerodynamics, vehicle propulsion, vehicle control, communications, and guideways. Write:

Federal Railroad Administration
Room 211
Donohoe Building
400 6th Street, S.W.
Washington, D.C. 20591

Note: the Alaska Railroad, part of this administration, makes its own purchases. If you are interested in selling to it, the address is:

Procurement Offices
Alaska Railroad
U.S. Department of Transportation
P.O. Box 7-2111
Anchorage, AK 99510

Urban Mass Transportation Administration

The principal awards of this administration are research contracts. Contact:

Urban Mass Transportation Administration
U.S. Department of Transporation
Washington, D.C. 20591

St. Lawrence Seaway Development Corporation

This Government corporation buys navigational lock operating equipment, related maintenance parts and equipment, and heavy construction equipment and spare parts. Write:

Administrative Services Offices
St. Lawrence Seaway Development Corp.
U.S. Department of Transportation
P.O. Box 520
Massena, NY 13662

Environmental Protection Agency (EPA)

EPA is primarily a regulatory agency with responsibilities for establishing and enforcing environmental standards concerning air and water pollution, solid waste management, pesticides, radiation, noise, and toxic substances. With so many diversified programs, the EPA buys many different kinds of products and services. Common to all programs in order to develop effective standards is the need for data gathering, analysis, and data processing. The EPA also contracts for construction, alteration, and repair of buildings, structures, and other real property.

To get additional information about EPA procurements, write and request a copy of "Contracting with EPA—A Guide for Prospective Contractors."

You can get a copy from any of these addresses:

Headquarters Contract Operations (PM-214)
U.S. Environmental Protection Agency
Washington, D.C. 20460

Contracts Management Division
U.S. Environmental Protection Agency
Cincinnati, OH 45268

Contracts Management Division
U.S. Environmental Protection Agency
Research Triangle Park, NC 27711

Tennessee Valley Authority

TVA buys centrally through its Division of Purchasing. TVA's purchases are made primarily for the construction and operation of electric power plants and transmission systems, construction of dams and locks, and development and experimental production of fertilizers. The products purchased include turbogenerators, steam-generating units, nuclear plant equipment, hydraulic turbines and generators, transformers, boilers, piping systems, switchgears, coal, coke, nuclear fuel, electrical and electronic supplies, communications equipment, structural and milled steel, phosphate rock, chemicals, and items for medical, laboratory, and photographic uses.

To do business with TVA, write:

Division of Purchasing
Tennessee Valley Authority
Chattanooga, TN 37401

United States Postal Service

The Postal Service buys a variety of goods and services through five regional offices, two area supply centers, and a facilities procurement division.

Among its purchases are mail-processing and mail-handling equipment; material transport and delivery service equipment; customer service equipment; office supplies, furniture, and office machinery; building and vehicle maintenance and repair; architect-engineering services; and research and development services.

You can obtain information on regional office procurements by contacting the Contracts and Supply Management Branch at the appropriate regional office listed in Appendix 2.

The Eastern Area Supply Center purchases items on the open market such as wooden bulletin boards, mail chutes, scales, building supplies, cash boxes, carrier straps and accessories, conveyor belting, envelopes, impact cones, U.S. flags, office supplies, packing materials, postmarking materials, rubber bands, seals, twine, corrugated paper cases, and similar supplies. Write:

The Eastern Area Supply Center
U.S. Postal Service

VA Depot
Somerville, NJ 08877

The Western Area Supply Center buys spare parts for electrical, electronic, vehicular, and mechanical equipment and assemblers. Write:

The Western Area Supply Center
U.S. Postal Service
Topeka, KS 66624

If you want to do construction work for the Postal Service, or leasing, write:

General Manager
Facilities Procurement Division
U.S. Postal Service
475 L'Enfant Plaza, S.W.
Washington, D.C. 20260

or you can write to the Director, Real Estate and Buildings, at the appropriate regional office.

If you're interested in helping to transport the mail, you should write to:

Director, Transportation Services Office
Logistics Department
U.S. Postal Service
475 L'Enfant Plaza, S.W.
Washington, D.C. 20260

To get on the bidder's list for your product or service, complete a PS Form 7429, Bidder's Mailing List Application, and a Form 7429-A, Commodity and Geographic Location Check-off (see Appendix 2) and send to:

Data Automation Division
Bidder's Mailing Lists
Western Area Supply Center
U.S. Postal Service
Post Office Box 19065
Topeka, KS 66619

To get these forms and a free booklet, "Selling to the Postal Service, Publication 151," write to:

Office of Contracts
Documents Processing Branch

Procurement and Supply Department
U.S. Postal Service
475 L'Enfant Plaza, S.W.
Washington, D.C. 20260

Veteran's Administration (VA)

The VA buys centrally, locally, and through subordinate departments.

The central purchasing office buys medical supplies, textiles, food, paper products, prosthetics and orthopedic aids, and laundry equipment. Their address is:

Marketing Center
P.O. Box 76
Hines, IL 60141

Locally procured items include perishable foodstuffs, laundry and maintenance services, pest extermination, and books.

The Department of Medicine and Surgery Supply Service purchases management consultant services. Opportunities that are available are published in two information bulletins:

1B 13-4 "Could You Use a Multimillion Dollar Customer?"
1B 13-5 "Let's Do Business"

Both can be obtained by writing:

Department of Medicine and Surgery Supply Service
Veterans Administration
810 Vermont Avenue, N.W.
Washington, D.C. 20420

The Office of Construction awards contracts for design, construction, and building technology research including those activities pertaining to the National Cemetery System. Where possible, these awards are made to firms located in the geographical area of the project.

If you are interested, you should contact:

Assistance Administrator for Construction
Veterans Administration
810 Vermont Avenue, N.W.
Washington, D.C. 20420

The Agency for International Development (AID)

The Agency for International Development, AID, lies outside the usual Federal procurement programs. AID was established within the Department of State in 1961 to carry out U.S. overseas programs of economic and technical assistance to less developed countries and bring them to a level of self-sufficiency. Actually, AID does very little procurement on its own, but what it does do is finance the procurement of commodities by foreign governments or private importers. AID opportunities are published in the *AID Financed Export Opportunities Circular*. This circular is obtainable at no charge by writing to:

Office of Small Business
AID
Washington, D.C. 20523

Pretty good, eh? If that doesn't uncover enough Government buying programs to keep you busy for a while, I don't know what will. And don't forget, almost every buying unit has a special free booklet that gives you even more information about how and what they buy and how they will help you in doing business. But if you're impatient to do business, read on. In the next chapter we're going to see how you can go and visit Uncle Sam himself and get help.

Chapter 3

HOW TO GET HELP FROM UNCLE SAM HIMSELF

UNCLE SAM WANTS TO HELP YOU

It is an incredible fact that the Government spends literally millions of dollars on various programs to help you to find, bid on, and win Government contracts. But perhaps even more incredible is the fact that relatively few businessmen take advantage of this tremendous windfall, which, after all, is paid for out of your own tax dollars.

Why is this so? If the programs that Uncle Sam offers to help you out are so good, why don't more potential or current Government contractors take advantage of this big-dollar helping hand? As close as I can determine, these tremendous programs are not better utilized for three main reasons:

1. A suspicion that since these programs are Government sponsored, something must be wrong with them.
2. A lack of knowledge of which programs are available.
3. A lack of knowledge of how to go about getting help from these programs.

In this chapter, I hope to convince you that these programs are worthwhile. I will also tell you which programs are available, and how to use them to maximize your competitive advantage.

WHY DOES UNCLE SAM WANT TO HELP YOU?

You may wonder about Uncle Sam's motivation for spending so much money to help you do business with him. After all, not many nongovernment customers are going to spend money, direct resources, and keep hundreds, if not thousands of experts on tap to help you do business. Why does the Government do this?

Joseph J. Zemicki, Chief of the Government Contracts Division of the Office of Business Development of the Small Business Administration, writes in Herman Holtz's excellent book, *Government Contracts:*

"As a government contracting official, I welcome this book because I look for it to result eventually in better proposals crossing my desk, and every contracting officer looks for that."

In other words, it is good business for the Government to spend money to help you because eventually it should result in better proposals, and beyond that, better products, fewer cost overruns, fewer problems, and lower costs. Therefore, helping you is in itself good business for the Government.

But this isn't the only reason Uncle Sam wants to help. Small business has always been at the heart of the American economy, American ingenuity, and American inventiveness. Your products and services contribute directly to full employment, a high standard of living, the quality of life, and the freedom that has made our country great. The good that you do on contract for the Federal Government spills over into all other areas of American living.

Finally, let's face it, there is a very real dollars-and-cents reason why Uncle Sam is more than willing to help. The more successful you are, the more tax dollars he collects. Since most Government contractors do a great amount of business in the civilian economy as well as with the Government, the Government component of your business tends to help the nonGovernment component with taxable income from both, and, of course, small businesses grow into bigger businesses. It was Sam Colt's garage-developed pistol that the Government bought in quantity in 1836, which led to the 22-year-old entrepreneur building the mighty Colt Firearms Company that today manufactures guns not only for the military but for police and sporting activities as well. The Douglas Aircraft Company division of the McDonnell Douglas Corporation, builder of thousands of airliners as well as military planes, literally got off the ground with its first million-dollar order from the U.S. Army for 0–2H observation planes back in the early 1920s. And then there's DuPont, whose chemical products today range from glue to the miracle high-strength material "Kevlar" (which goes into tires), which got its start by making gun powder for the Government during the Revolutionary War.

Needless to say, these three companies, and thousands of others like them, are a continuous source of tax dollars that enable the U.S. Government to run. Understandably, Uncle Sam wants you to succeed and grow, and so the programs he offers you are a rare bargain. Now let's look at them and see how we can use them to help us in doing millions of dollars in business with the Government.

Small Business Administration (SBA) Programs

The SBA was created in 1953 and the enabling act specifically requires the SBA to assist small businesses in Government contracting. To quote from the Small Business Act:

"The government should aid, counsel, assist, and protect, insofar as is possible, the interests of small business concerns in order to . . . insure that a fair proportion of the total purchases and contracts or subcontracts for property and services for the government (including but not limited to contracts or subcontracts for maintenance, repair and construction) be placed with small business enterprises."

To carry out this mandate, the SBA provides a wide range of services that will help you to win and fulfill Government contracts and subcontracts. Here are the six ways that the SBA can help you get Government contracts:

1. Small Business Set-Asides.
2. The Subcontracting Assistance Program.
3. Procurement Automated Source System.
4. Certificates of Competency Program.
5. Technology Assistance.
6. Information of Government Buying.

Small Business Set-Asides

This is one SBA program that assists you in winning Government contracts over which you have no control. You see, Uncle Sam believes so strongly that it is to his advantage to help you succeed that he is willing to accept some higher costs in buying in order to do this. That's the thrust of the set-aside programs for small business. Some programs are singled out, and big business cannot win these contracts because only small businesses are permitted to bid on them.

The SBA has developed cooperative programs with all major Government purchasing agencies in order to do this. It works through having proposed purchases reviewed by the officials who are going to do the buying, and then certain items are identified in whole or in a part, for contracting by small businesses only. Further, purchases not reserved for small business are subject to review by SBA Procurement Center Representatives. These representatives may also initiate a set-aside if they can demonstrate that adequate small business competition is available. Of course, the purchasing agency must agree to the SBA-initiated set-aside. But even if they do not, the SBA representative can appeal all the way to the Government agency or department head. Clearly, you have a strong friend in the SBA.

How do you take advantage of the small business set-aside? You should take the necessary action to become listed on all appropriate bidders lists, and keep your eyes open for opportunities listed in the *Commerce Business Daily*. On purchases where additional competition is needed, the SBA may furnish contracting officials with the names of capable small firms interested in bidding on the particular purchase. It therefore makes sense to have your capabilities known to the SBA. Do this by contacting one of the SBA field offices listed in the Appendix and ask for additional information. You should also request listing in the register of *Small*

Business Facilities. This is the one place where the SBA maintains a list of small firms that are interested in selling goods or services to the Government and its prime contractors. You should also know that when the SBA is looking for firms that would be interested in doing business, its regional offices do not only look to firms from their own geographic areas but from other areas as well. Therefore, although you may be listed on only one SBA register, this will expose you to Government contracting opportunities for small businesses everywhere.

The Subcontracting Assistance Program

You may be surprised to learn that although major Government contractors, the Boeings, the McDonnell Douglases, the TRWs, and others, are awarded billions of dollars in major Government acquisition contracts every year, much of this work is subcontracted to smaller firms. The SBA assists smaller firms in these areas of contract acquisition through its Subcontracting Assistance Program. Here's how it works. All Federal Government contracts in excess of $500,000 require the prime contractor to designate a small business liaison officer within their organization to look after subcontracting opportunities for small business. The prime's small business liaison officer must assist small businesses to qualify on the company bid lists and assist the individual small business in meeting the Government buyers for the prime contractor's goods or services.

The SBA's Subcontracting Specialists review and evaluate the prime contractor's policies and procedures as they affect small business and often recommend potential small business sources that are capable of bidding on the prime's requirements. The Subcontracting Specialists also offer assistance and counseling in solving problems encountered in acquiring and performing subcontracts.

If you are interested in subcontracting opportunities, you should contact the nearest SBA office listed in Appendix 2.

Procurement Automated Source System (PASS)

PASS is a fairly recent addition to the SBA's services, which will permit you to register once to have access to over 300 major Government acquisition activities and 60 prime contractors that have in excess of 300 divisions located throughout the United States. Using PASS, Government requirements for goods and services are matched by key words against the capabilities of registered firms. According to the SBA, more than 10,000 firms registered during PASS's first year of operation. If you have capabilities that most closely match the requirements of that particular procurement, you are asked to submit an IFB or an RFP.

If you are interested in this program, contact your nearest SBA regional office or write:

PASS, Small Business Administration
1441 L Street, NW

Washington, D.C. 20416

A listing in PASS and use of this incredible service costs you absolutely nothing.

Certificate of Competency (COC) Program

What happens if the Government agency you propose to do business with rejects your bid because it questions your ability to perform the contract? Can the contracting agency do this? Unfortunately, it can.

Remember that in order to be eligible for a contract award your firm must be "responsible." According to Government procurement regulations, the elements of responsibility include your technical ability, credit, capacity, capability, integrity, perseverance, and tenacity. That's quite a tall order! How in the world can you prove yourself responsible in terms of a definition like that? Have no fear, the SBA stands ready, if necessary, to certify your competency under the Certificate of Competency Program.

Here's how this program is set up. When an element or elements of your responsibility are in doubt, regulations require that the challenge be referred to the SBA. The SBA will then contact you to inform you of what has happened. At the same time, you are offered the opportunity to apply to the SBA for a COC.

If you apply for a COC, the contracting officer of the purchasing agency is notified, and a team of financial and technical personnel is sent by the SBA to survey your potential. The SBA, of course, has access to the pre-award survey that was the basis of the contracting officer's decision to question your ability to perform the contract. However, the SBA now conducts a completely new survey that evaluates your capabilities in terms of the requirement of the specific acquisition in question. In the words of the SBA itself: "Credit ratings, past performance, management capabilities, production schedules, and the prospects for obtaining needed financial help or equipment are all considered."

If you get the COC, the contracting agency is directed to award you the contract in accordance with the Small Business Act. However, you should know that a COC is valid only for the specific contract for which it is issued. The theory here is that although you may be capable of handling one contract, you may not be qualified to handle another. Also, remember that the evaluation was made of your capabilities in terms of the requirement of the specific acquisition in question. Therefore, if you gain a COC for one contract, you may or may not be able to obtain one for another contract.

You cannot apply for a COC before a determination or bid acceptance is made by the contracting officer, and you can only apply for a COC after the contracting officer has made a negative determination of responsibility.

Technology Assistance

The SBA offers three separate technology assistance programs that you can use to great benefit to assist you in Government contracting. These are:

1. The *R and D Directory* Program.
2. The Technology Utilization Program.
3. The Experimental Technology Incentive Program (ETIP).

The *R and D Directory* Program is for you if you are interested in participating in Government research and development programs. Request your nearest SBA field office to survey your firm for inclusion in the agency's *R and D Directory*. The directory is made available to Government agencies and prime contractors with R&D requirements.

The Technology Utilization Program can assist you in making use of research and development already performed under Government contracts. The SBA will provide you with advice, counsel, and technology search and retrieval help for production techniques, modernization processes, and with new-product development. In cooperation with other Government agencies, SBA operates a technology information transfer service through brochures that describe technology that may be of use to small businesses.

Through the ETIP program, the SBA conducts a series of studies designed to evaluate modifications that could be made in Government acquisition policies and procedures to enhance Government contracting with small firms for research and development.

Information on Government Buying

The SBA maintains an active information program on Government buying by:

- Individual counseling with you as a small business owner.
- Arranging "contract opportunity meetings" for small businesses.
- Providing publications on various aspects of selling to the Government.

SBA's counseling service assists you in determining which of your products and services can be sold to the Government and which Government agencies and offices are potential customers. You can also get help in obtaining Government specifications for specific products or services and on getting on the appropriate bidders lists. You can also get assistance in resolving problems with Government contracting officers, in having your products listed on the qualified products list, or in getting financial help on Government contracts.

The contract opportunity meetings are given in cooperation with buying agencies, chambers of commerce, business associations, and so on. At SBA contract opportunity meetings you can hear Government buyers discuss current buying procedures and what they buy. You can see examples of IFBs and RFPs for various products and services, and can ask questions firsthand of both Government representatives and prime contractors who are seeing subcontracting assistance.

Perhaps the most important publication on selling to the Government is the *U.S. Government Purchasing and Sales Directory*, published by the Small Business

Administration. Important parts of this directory will be found in the Appendix. This SBA publication is a comprehensive guide to the Government's purchasing and sales activities. It lists products and services bought by the Government, and who buys them. A copy can be obtained from the U.S. Government Printing Office.

GSA Business Service Center (BSC) Program

The GSA itself says that the Business Service Center is the first step in Government business opportunity. This GSA claim is backed by the fact that BSCs exist primarily to serve the entrepreneur in his search for Government contracts.
   Here are some of the things the BSC will do for you:

- Provide information and guidance on all GSA programs and other agency buying programs.
- Furnish invitations for bidding and specifications having to do with GSA programs.
- Help introduce your new or improved items or services into the system.
- Provide a list of contracting offices in the area of the BSC.
- Have available current copies of the *Commerce Business Daily*.
- Help you locate Government consumer or user level offices for your product or service so that you may accomplish sales or marketing activities.
- Furnish information regarding the total dollar volume and quantity of the item or items that appear in the GSA Stores Stock Catalogue or Federal Supply Schedule.
- Furnish information about the prices on the last procurement of an item appearing in the GSA Stores Stock Catalogue or Federal Supply Schedule as well as the winning contractor.

   The GSA says: "A typical GSA Business Service Center is located in the main lobby of a Federal building. An attractive reception area is provided along with displays of current bidding opportunities and other informational material. Employees are fully trained to answer all but the more technical questions."

The ten BSCs of the GSA along with their addresses, phone numbers, and the service areas they cover are as follows:

REGION	MAILING ADDRESS	SERVICE AREA
1	Regional Director of Public Services (1F1) General Services Administration	Connecticut, Maine, Massachusetts, New Hampshire, Rhode

John W. McCormack Building
Post Office & Courthouse
Boston, MA 02109
617/223-2868

Island, and Vermont

2   Regional Director of Public
Services (2F1)
General Services Administration
26 Federal Plaza
New York, NY 10007
212/264-1234

New Jersey, New York,
Puerto Rico, and
Virgin Islands

3   Regional Director of Public
Services (3F1)
General Services Administration
7th and D Streets, SW
Washington, D.C. 20407
202/472-1804

District of Columbia,
Maryland, Virginia,
and West Virginia

3   Manager, Business Service Ctr
General Services Administration
600 Arch Street
Philadelphia, PA 19106
215/597-9613

Pennsylvania and
Delaware

4   Regional Director of Public
Services (4F1)
General Services Administration
1776 Peachtree Street
Atlanta, GA 30309
404/526-5661

Alabama, Florida,
Georgia, Kentucky,
Mississippi, North
Carolina, South
Carolina, and Tennessee

5   Regional Director of Public
Services (5F1)
General Services Administration
230 South Dearborn Street
Chicago, IL 60604
312/353-5383

Illinois, Indiana,
Michigan, Minnesota,
Ohio, and Wisconsin

6   Regional Director of Public
Services (6F1)
General Services Adminstration
1500 East Bannister Road
Kansas City, MO 64131
816/926-7203

Iowa, Kansas, Missouri,
and Nebraska

7   Regional Director of Public
Services (7F1)
General Services Administration
819 Taylor Street

Arkansas, Louisiana,
New Mexico, Okla-
homa, and Texas
(except below)

	Fort Worth, TX 76102 817/334–3284	
7	Manager, Business Service Ctr General Services Administration, FOB Courthouse, 515 Rusk Street Houston, TX 77002 713/226–5787	Gulf Coast Area from Brownsville, Texas to New Orleans, Louisiana
8	Regional Director of Public Services (8F1) General Services Administration Bldg. 41, Denver Federal Ctr. Denver, CO 80225 303/234–2216	Colorado, North Dakota, South, Dakota, Montana, Utah, and Wyoming
9	Regional Director of Public Services (9F1) General Services Administration 525 Market Street San Francisco, CA 94105 415/556–2122	Northern California, Hawaii, and Nevada (except Clark County)
9	Manager, Business Service Ctr. General Services Administration 300 North Los Angeles Los Angeles, CA 90012 213/688–3210	Los Angeles, Southern California Clark County, Nevada and Arizona
10	Regional Director of Public Services (10F1) General Services Adminstration 440 Federal Building 915 Second Avenue Seattle, WA 98174 206/442–5556	Alaska, Idaho, Oregon, and Washington

If you want a free copy of the booklet about BSCs put out by the GSA, write to one of the BSCs listed above, a Federal Information Center, a field office of the U.S. Department of Commerce, or the SBA. Ask for: "Government Business Opportunities Through Business Service Centers of the General Services Adminstration."

Department of Defense (DOD)

There are numerous programs conducted under the auspices of one or another of the organizations within DOD. These might range from a seminar on how to prepare bids to sophisticated technology transfer programs that will plug you into the very latest technology and developments within DOD. All of the military services have one type or another of potential contractor programs in order to get you and your product or service on the right bidders list and give you an opportunity to bid.

To assist you in locating these opportunities, obtain a copy of the booklet, "Selling to the Military," from the Superintendent of Documents, U.S. Government Printing Office, Washington, D.C. 20402. The price is only $1.80 and it is worth every penny.

DCAS Small Business Specialist Program

DCAS stands for Defense Contract Administration Services, and this is a great program to help you with Government contracting with DOD. The small business specialist serves as advisor to the commander of the region, destrict, or organization to which he is assigned on problems and subjects of interest to small business and the industrial community. He also will provide individual and group counseling and assistance to you on matters pertaining to military prime and subcontract opportunities. If you want help in doing business with DOD, call your nearest DCAS small business counselor at the following address and phone numbers:

DCAS Headquarters
Defense Supply Agency
Cameron Station
Alexandria, VA 22314
Tel: 202/274-7605

DCASR, Atlanta:
3100 Maple Drive NE
Atlanta, GA 30305
Tel: 404/261-7310, x231

DCASD, Birmingham:
908 South 20th Street
Birmingham, AL 35205
Tel: 205/254-1460

DCASD, Orlando:
3555 Maguire Blvd.
Orlando, FL 32803
Tel: 305/894-7711, x281

DCASR, Boston:
666 Summer Street
Boston, MA 02210
Tel: 617/542-6000, x886

DCASD, Hartford:
96 Murphy Road
Hartford, CT 06114
Tel: 203/244-3336

DCASD, Rochester:
U.S. Courthouse & Federal Office Building
100 State Street
Rochester, NY 14614
Tel: 716/263-6419

DCASR, Chicago:
O'Hare Int'l Airport
P.O. Box 66475
Chicago, IL 60666
Tel: 312/694-3031, x6390

DCASD, Indianapolis:
Finance Center, U.S. Army
Building 1
Ft. Benjamin Harrison, IN 46249
Tel: 317/542-3155

DCASD, Milwaukee:
744 North 4th Street
Milwaukee, WI 53203
Tel: 414/272-8180, x207

DCASR, Cleveland:
Room 1821, Federal Office Bldg.
1240 East Ninth Street
Cleveland, OH 44199
Tel: 216/522-5122

DCASD, Detroit:
1580 E. Grand Blvd.
Detroit, MI 48211
Tel: 313/226-0100, x265

DCASR, Dallas:
500 South Ervay Street
Dallas, TX 75201
Tel: 214/744-4581, x205

DCASD, Phoenix:
3800 N. Central Avenue
Phoenix, AZ 85012
Tel: 602/261-4467

DCASR, Los Angeles
11099 South LaCienega Blvd.
Los Angeles, CA 90045
Tel: 213/643-0620

DCASD, San Francisco
866 Malcolm Road
Burlingame, CA 94010
Tel: 415/692-0300, x 523

DCASD, Seattle:
Building 5D
U.S. Naval Air Station
Seattle, WA 98115
Tel: 206/527-3451

DCASR, New York:
60 Hudson Street
New York, NY 10013
Tel: 212/264-0833 or 0834

DCASD, Garden City:
605 Stewart Avenue
Garden City, NY 11533
Tel: 516/741-8000, x379

DCASD, Springfield:
240 Route 22
Springfield, NJ 07081
Tel: 201/379-7950, x374

DCASR, Philadelphia:
P.O. Box 7478
Philadelphia, PA 19101
Tel: 215/271-4006 or 4007

DCASD, Baltimore:
Building 22
Fort Holabird
Baltimore, MD 21219
Tel: 301/527-3149

DCASR, St. Louis:
1136 Washington Avenue
St. Louis, MO 63101
Tel: 314/268-6223

DCASD, Twin Cities:

Federal Building
Fort Snelling
Twin Cities, MN 55111
Tel: 612/725-3803

Other DOD Counseling Services

The DOD has decided that each and every one of its procurement offices has
the responsibility to counsel and assist small, minority, and labor surplus area
businesses with any problems they may have in understanding procurement regulations and practices; determining the appropriate buyer agency for their product;
acquiring pertinent data on present or future DOD procurements; and other similar
information, help, and advice. In order to perform this function, every DOD procurement office has appointed a Small Business Specialist. Figure 10 is a complete
listing of these by state and office as of June 1980. For additional information and
the most recent list of specialists, write to the Superintendent of Documents and
order the booklet, "Small Business and Labor Surplus Area Specialists," published by the Department of Defense, Office of Assistant Secretary of Defense
Installations and Logistics. The price is $1.10.

The Big Three Free Face-to-Face Sources of DOD
Research and Development Information

I just don't think you will find anything like the Army's TILO (Technical Industrial Liaison Office), the Navy's NARDIC (Navy Acquisition, Research and
Development Center), or the Air Force's Information for Industry Offices anywhere else in the world. These three programs are the focal point for giving you,
as a member of industry, research and development planning and requirements
information. And believe me, the information on military R&D that you get
can put you way ahead of the competition. What you can get differs slightly
depending on which service's office you are visiting, but to give you some idea of
what is available, some of the information you can get at the TILO includes: R&D
planning summaries, which include projects currently being funded, the name,
address, and phone number of the responsible Government individual, and the
objective and approach on the project; a project listing with a Five Year Development Plan; a U.S. Army Project Management List that lists the address and phone
number of every U.S. Army Project/Product Manager, his deputy, and both their
addresses and phone numbers; an abridged version of Descriptive Summaries of
the U.S. Army Research, Development, Test and Evaluation Program, which
provides a descriptive summary of each program element to be funded; Requirements Documents Testing of Department of Army approved materiels actions; a
catalogue of Approved Requirements Documents, which lists Operational Capabilities Objectives, Currently Approved Materiel Requirements, and Materiel Requirements deleted during the past 12 months. At NARDIC you will be able to

Letters in Parentheses ( )
Indicate Military Organizations

(A) Army   (AF) Air Force

(N) Navy   (USMC) Marine Corps

(DSA) Defense Supply Agency   (DOD) Department of Defense

ALABAMA

Anniston

US Army School/Training Center (A)   Mrs. Mary W. Kirk
Ft. McClellan 36201   AC 205/238-4838

Anniston Army Depot (A) 36202   Mr. Andrew W. Burgin
                                      AC 205/237-6611, Ex*. 5136/1811

Birmingham

DCASD BIRMINGHAM (DSA)   Mr. Nolan L. Shory
908 South 20th Street 35205   AC 205/254-1460

Childersburg

Alabama Army Ammunition   Captain Thomas L. Stark
    Plant (A) 35044   AC 205/378-2411, Ext. 21

Dothan

NAVPLANTREPO (N)   Mr. S. M. Hutchinson, Sr.
Hayes International Corporation   AC 205/ 983- 4537/4538
Napier Field 36301

Huntsville

U.S. Army Missile Command (A)   Mr. Jeff D. Darwin
Redstone Arsenal 35809   Mrs. Mildred Wilkins
                                      Mr. Charles R. Gannon
                                      AC 205/876-3567 or 876-2376

U.S. Army Ballistic Missiles   Mr. Robert D. Ivey
    System Command (A)   Mr. H. L. Jones
P.O. Box 1500 - 35807   AC 205/895-3977

U.S. Army Engineer Div.   Mr. Thor S. Anderson
Huntsville (A)   AC 205/895-5660
106 Wynn Dr. 35807

Figure 10. Complete list of DOD Small Business Specialists.

Mobile

U.S. Army Engineer District -
   Mobile (A)
2301 Airport Boulevard 36601

Mr. A. L. Cameron
AC 205/690-2545

Montgomery

Hq. Air University (AF)
Maxwell AFB 36112

Major David L. Muzio
AC 205/293-6549

3800 Air Base Wing
Maxwell AFB 36112

Mrs. Eileen H. Noe
AC 205/293-5457

Ozark

U.S. Army Aviation Center (A)
Fort Rucker 36362

Chief, Procurement Division, DIO
AC 205/255-3404

Selma

Base Procurement Office (AF)
Craig AFB 36701

Mr. Edward J. Revord
AC 205/874-7431, Ext. 5700

ALASKA

Anchorage

U.S Army Engineer District (A)
P.O. Box 7002 99501

Mr. Ron Miller
AC 907/862-8216

Hq. U.S. Army Alaska, Ft. Richardson
AC of S, G-4 (A)
Supply and Services Div. 99505

Mr. F. D. Eshenower
AC 907/863-7203

Purchasing and Contracting Office (A)
Ft. Richardson 99505

Mr. Burton R. Marsch
AC 907/863-2207

Hq. Alaskan Air Command (AF)
Elmendorf AFB
APO Seattle, Washington 98742

Lt. Col. William J. Kormos
AC 907/753-4217 or 753-5180

Base Procurement Office
Elmendorf AFB (AF)
APO Seattle, Washington 98742

Mr. Myron E. Elliot
AC 907/754-2209 or 752-5205

Fairbanks

Purchasing and Contracting Office (A)
Ft. Wain Wright 99703

Mrs. Annie M. Smith
AC 907/353-6106

Base Procurement Office
Eielson AFB (AF)
APO Seattle, Washington 98737

Capt. James W. Medford
AC 907/372-4230 or 372-1167

Figure 10 *(Continued)*

ARIZONA

Chandler

Base Procurement Office (AF)
Williams AFB 85224

Mr. William L. Snell
AC 602/988-2611, Ext. 6618 or 6619

Flagstaff

Navajo Army Depot 86003 (A)

Mr. Jess Yniquez
AC 602/774-7161

Fort Huachuca

HQ Fort Huachuca (A)
U.S. Army Communications
   Command 85613

Mr. John A. Maliniak
AC 602/538-6191

Sierra Vista

HQ Fort Huachuca (A)
Industrial Operations 85613

Mr. Robert F. O'Neal
AC 602/538-3131

Glendale

58 Tactical Fighter Training Wing (AF)
Luke AFB 85309

Mr. John J. Andersen
AC 602/935-7411, Ext. 7162

Phoenix

DCASD, Phoenix (DSA)
3800 North Central Avenue 85012

(Vacant)
AC 602/261-4467

Tucson

Base Procurement Office (AF)
Davis-Monthan AFB 85707

Mr. Eugene L. Sierras
AC 602/793-3131

Yuma

U.S. Army Proving Grounds (A)
   85364

Mr. Mitchell Mikols
AC 602/328-2623

ARKANSAS

Blytheville

Base Procurement Office (AF)
Blytheville AFB 72315

Mr. Francis M. Nordeen
AC 501/763-3931, Ext. 7150

Little Rock

314 Tactical Airlift Wing (AF)
Little Rock AFB 72076

Mr. James N. Hamric
AC 501/988-3301

USA Engineer District (A)
P.O. Box 867 72203

Mr. Harold E. Wilson
AC 501/378-5721

Figure 10 (*Continued*)

Pine Bluff

USA Pine Bluff Arsenal (A)
71603

Mr. Joseph L. Zornek
AC 501/534-4600, Ext. 2526

CALIFORNIA

Alameda

Defense Subsistence Region
Hq, DPSC (DSA)
2155 Webster Street 94501

Mr. Harold K. Sharp
AC 415/869-2051

Anaheim

Rockwell International Corp.
  (AFPRO) (AF)
Electronic Group
3370 Miraloma Avenue 92803

Mr. Joseph L. Pannone
AC 714/632-2224

Barstow

Marine Corps Supply Center (N)
Bldg. 236, 92311

Mrs. G. E. Sullivan
AC 714/577-6881

Burbank

NAVPLANTREPO (N)
Lockheed Aircraft Corp.
P.O. Box 551 91520

Mr. D. M. Thaw
AC 213/847-4577

Camp Pendleton

Marine Corps Base 92055 (N)

Mr. F. H. Saitta
AC 714/725-3233

Canoga Park

Rocketdyne Division (AFPRO)(AF)
Rockwell International Corp. 91304

Mr. Dominic L. Affatato
AC 213/884-3380

China Lake

Naval Weapons Center 93555 (N)

Ms. JoAnn Bell
AC 714/939-2001

Culver City

Hughes Aircraft Company (AFPRO) (AF)
90230

Mr. Alva D. Moore
AC 213/391-0711, Ext. 6627

Figure 10 (*Continued*)

U.S. Army Aviation (A)
Hughes Aircraft Plant Activity
90230

Mr. Harry P. Valaski
AC 213/870-3361, Ext. 7096

Edwards

Air Force Flight Test Center (AF)
Edwards AFB 93523

Mr. James A. Beucherie
AC 805/277-2012

Fairfield

60 Military Airlift Wing (AF)
Travis AFB 94535

Mr. Donald R. Bertholdi
AC 707/438-2982

Hawthorne

Northrop Corporation (AFPRO) (AF)
Norair Division 90250

Mr. Louis V. Engbarth, Jr.
AC 213/675-4611, Ext. 6494

Herlong

Sierra Army Depot (A)
96113

Mr. Cris Beaber
AC 916/827-2111, Ext. 2417

Huntington Beach

McDonnell Douglas Astronautics
Co. (AFPRO) (AF)
Western Division
5301 Bolsa Avenue
Huntington Beach 92647

Mr. A. L. Monteith
AC 714/896-4446

Lathrop

Sharpe Army Depot (A) 95330

Mr. John F. Martin
AC 209/982-2604

Lompoc

Space & Missile Test Center (AF)
Vandenberg AFB 93437

Miss Jan Berry
AC 805/866-1611

Base Procurement Office (AF)
Vandenberg AFB 93437

Mr. Joseph A. Zielinski
AC 805/866-5428

Long Beach

Naval Regional Procurement
Office (N) 90801

Mr. J. E. Cravens
AC 213/547-6628

Figure 10 (*Continued*)

NAVPLANTREPO (N)
McDonnell Douglas Corp.
Douglas Aircraft Co., 90846

Mr. W. J. Barnhart
AC 213/593-9693

SUPSHIP, CONVERSION &
REPAIR, USN (N)
Long Beach Naval Shipyard,
Bldg. 300, 90801

Mrs. B. A. Dill
AC 213/547-7325

Los Angeles

USA Engineer District (A)
P.O. Box 2711 90053

Mr. Alvin L. Smart
AC 213/688-5671

Space & Missile Systems Organization
AF Unit PO (AF)
Los Angeles 90045

Mr. Bruno Bornino
Mr. Lurman A. Neal
AC 213/643-2855 or 643-2856

Rockwell International Corp.
B-1 Division (AFPRO) (AF)
Los Angeles International Airport
90009

Major Ronald D. Patchett
AC 213/670-9151, Ext. 2148

DCASR, Los Angeles (DSA)
11099 South La Cienega Blvd.,
90045

Mr. Max M. Bennett
Mr. Robert L. Desmond
Mr. Edward O. Henry
AC 213/643-0620

Marysville

Base Procurement Office (AF)
Beale AFB 95903

Mr. Charles I. Johnston
AC 916/634-2951

Merced

Base Procurement Office (AF)
Castle AFB 95342

Mr. Gerald Summerskill
AC 209/726-2406

Monterey

U.S. Army Training Center (A)
Ft. Ord 93941

Mr. Charles L. Hopkins, Jr.
AC 408/242-2611

Novato

Base Procurement Office (AF)
Hamilton AFB 94934

Mr. Gerald J. Talmadge
AC 415/838-3751

Figure 10   (Continued)

Oakland

Military Traffic Management &
   Terminal
Western Service Western Area (A)
Oakland Army Base 94626

Mr. Edward J. Stapleton
Mr. Henry S. Kawakami
AC 415/466-3088

Naval Regional Procurement Dept. (N)
Naval Supply Center 94625

Mr. R. M. Gilbertson
AC 415/466-5037

Military Sealift Command,
   Pacific (N)
Naval Supply Center 94625

Mr. R. H. Sustarich
AC 415/466-5337

Petaluna

Purchasing and Contracting Office (A)
Two Rock Ranch Station 94952

Mr. Gerald J. Dignan
AC 415/PO 2-2751, Ext. 214

Pomona

NAVPLANTREPO (N)
General Dynamics, Pomona Div.
P.O. Box 2505, 91766

Mr. H. E. Edmonds
AC 714/629-5111, Ext. 3054

Port Hueneme

Naval Construction Battalion
   Center (N) 93043

Mr. M. J. Hugie
AC 805/982-5986

Riverside

Base Procurement Division (AF)
March AFB 92508

Mr. Donald A. Mantz
AC 714/655-1111, Ext. 2046

Riverbank Army Ammo Plant (A)
   95367

Mr. Eugene H. Johnson
AC 209/259-8100, Ext. 233

Sacramento

U.S. Army Engineer District (A)
650 Capital Mall 95814

Mr. Wesley R. Busby
AC 916/449-3400

Sacramento Army Depot 95801 (A)

Mr. Vernon J. Campbell
AC 916-388-2510

Sacramento Air Logistics Center (AF)
McClellan AFB 95652

Mr. John E. Lackey
Mrs. Kathryn C. Scheld
Mrs. Harriett E. Carpenter
AC 916/643-5070 or 643-2819

Figure 10   (*Continued*)

Base Procurement Office (AF)
Mather AFB 95655

Mrs. Laura T. Sambuceti
AC 916/364-2740 or 364-4263

Aerojet General Corporation
(AFPRO) (AF)
P.O. Box 15846
95813

Captain John W. Bandy
AC 916/355-2073

San Bernadino

Aerospace Audio-Visual Serv. (AF)
Norton AFB 92409

Mr. Llewellyn M. Lookingbill
AC 714/382-3313

63 Air Base Group (AF)
Base Procurement Office
Norton AFB 92409

Mr. Edward C. Williams
AC 714/382-7845

San Bruno

Western Division (N)
Naval Facilities Engineering Command
P.O. Box 727 94066

Mr. E. L. Fenn
Mr. T. J. Faltinon
AC 415/871-6600, Ext. 2751

San Diego

Naval Supply Center (N)
937 N. Harbor Drive 92132

LCdr. D. H. Giffin
AC 714/235-3312

Naval Undersea Center (N)
92132

Mrs. Eleanor Solan
AC 714/ 225-2423

SUPSHIP, CONVERSION & REPAIR,
USN (N)
Box 119, Naval Station 92136

Mr. G. J. Meade
AC 714/235-2428

Marine Corps Recruit Depot (N)
92140

Captain V. Whitehead
AC 714/225-4605

Naval Electronics Laboratory Center (N)
271 Catalina Boulevard 92152

LCDR J. D. Certain
AC 714/225-6760

San Francisco

U.S. Army Engineer Division (A)
South Pacific
630 San Some Street 94111

Mr. Morris Sheklow
AC 415/556-0579

Procurement Division, DCSLOG (A)
Presidio of San Francisco 94129

Mr. Jack Bowers
AC 415/561-4716

Figure 10 (*Continued*)

114

U.S. Army Engineer District (A)
100 McAlliston Street 94102

Mrs. Rose W. Tom
AC 415/556-3486

Letterman General Hospital (A)
Presidio of San Francisco 94129

Mr. Tetsuo Ihara
AC 415/561-5474

SUPSHIP, CONVERSION & REPAIR,
USN (N) 94135

Mr. E. J. Farley
AC 415/641-2546

DCASR San Francisco (DSA)
866 Malcolm Road
Burlingame, California 94010

Mr. R. R. Govea
Mr. Michael Tyson
Mr. Robert Lane
AC 415/692-0300, Ext. 523

San Pedro

Ft. MacArthur 90731 (A)

Chief, Purchasing Office
AC 213/831-7130

Sunnyvale

NAVPLANTREPO (SSPO) (N)
Lockheed Missile & Space Company, Inc.
P.O. Box 504 94088

Mr. D. C. Banovitz
AC 408/742-4093

(AFPRO) (AF)
Lockheed Missile & Space Company
94088

Major David T. Sakakida
AC 408/742-3996

United Technology Center (AFPRO) (AF)
P.O. Box 358 94088

Mr. Donald P. Krauhs
AC 408/739-4880, Ext. 2186

Tracy

Defense Depot Tracy 95376 (DSA)

Ms. Janet Drury
AC 209/ 835-0800, Ext. 205

Twentynine Palms

Marine Corps Base (N)
Bldg - 1525, 92278

Mr. G. T. Hyde
AC 714/367-9111, Ext. 6813

Vallejo

Mare Island Naval Shipyard (N)
94592

Mr. R. N. Carver
AC 707/646-3265/2262

Victorville

35 Tactical Fighter Wing (AF)
George AFB 92392

Mr. Paul Waas
AC 714/269-2310

Figure 10 (*Continued*)

115

Colorado Springs

Procurement and Production Office (AF) Box 7 USAF Academy 80840	Mr. A. A. Savage AC 303/472-4410
Hq. Aerospace Defense Command (AF) Ent AFB 80912	Mr. Willie B. Floyd AC 303/591-4926
4600 Air Base Wing (AF) Peterson AFB 80914	Mr. Willie B. Floyd AC 303/591-4926

Denver

Rocky Mountain Arsenal (A) 80240	Mr. Charles Leedholm AC 303/288-0711, Ext. 314
AF Accounting and Finance Center (AF) 3800 York Street 80205	Miss Peggy J. Barrett AC 303/825-1161, Ext. 6322
Base Procurement Office (AF) Lowry AFB 80230	Mr. Forest G. Morris AC 303/394-2871 or 394-2469
Martin-Marietta Corporation (AFPRO) (AF) 80201	Mr. Leon R. Salsman AC 303/794-5211, Ext. 2386
Fitzsimons General Hospital (A) 80240	LTC William B. Kerr AC 303/366-8758

Englewood

DCASD, Denver (DSA) 701 W. Hampden Ave. Suite E. 3210 80110	Mr. Earl Mossaman AC 303/837-4375

Ft. Carson

4th Infantry Div (Mech) (A) Ft. Carson 80913	Mr. Hazen C. Kramer AC 303/471-4080, Ext. 5524

Pueblo

Pueblo Army Depot (A) 81001	Mr. C. A. Burnett AC 303/549-4277

Groton

SUPSHIP, CONVERSION & REPAIR, USN (N) Electronic Boat Division General Dynamics Corporation 06340	Mr. E. J. Kagan AC 203/446-7475

Figure 10 (*Continued*)

Naval Submarine Base (N)   Mr. J. C. Sweeney
New London, Box 500 06340   AC 203/449-3735

Hartford

DCASD, Hartford (DSA)   Mr. John F. Seaver
96 Murphy Road 06114   AC 203/244-3336

East Hartford

NAVPLANTREPO (N)   Mrs. A. C. Moore
Pratt & Whitney Aircraft   AC 203/565-6971
   06108

Stratford

NAVPLANTREPO (N)   Mrs. C. I. Lamson
Sikorsky Aircraft   AC 203/378-6361, Ext. 620
North Main Street 06497

DELAWARE

Dover

436 Military Airlift Wing (AF)   Mr. Harold A. Smith
Dover AFB 19901   AC 302/734-8211, Ext. 6028 or 6029

DISTRICT OF COLUMBIA

Washington

Army Small Business Advisor (A)   Mr. Harold J. Margulis
Office of the Assistant Secretary   AC 202/OXford 78113, 72868
   of the Army (I&L)
Room 2E577 - Pentagon 20310

Office, Chief of Engineers (A)   Mr. Theo A. Henningsen
Room 4A233, Forrestal Bldg.   AC 202/ OXford 36635

U.S. Army Topographic Command (A)   Mrs. Angela A. Lyddane
6500 Brooks Lane 20315   AC 301/986-2821

Office of the Surgeon General (A)   Major Lowell McKinster
Room 2E 533, Pentagon 20310   AC 202/697-8286

Defense Nuclear Agency (DOD)   Mr. J. W. Watson
Washington, D.C. 20305   AC 202/325-8311

Defense Supply Service (A)   Mr. C. Leslie Walleigh
Room 1E234, Pentagon 20310   AC 202/OXford 52007

Figure 10   (*Continued*)

U.S. Army Medical R & D Command
Office of the Surgeon General (A)
Room 8F090, Forrestai Building 20314

LTC Floyd L. Coddington
AC 202/693-8360

Office, Chief, National Guard
   Bureau (A)
Room 2E379, Pentagon

Mr. J. Barry Cormany
AC 202/OXford 73895

Walter Reed Army Medical
   Center (A) 20012

Mrs. Leslie Sweeney
AC 202/427-5525

Walter Reed Institute of Research (A)
   20012

Major John K. Welton
AC 202/576-2039

Office of the Assistant Secretary
   of the Navy (INSLOG) (N)
Room 124, Crystal Plaza 5, 20360

Special Assistant for Small
   Business and Economic
   Utilization
      Mr. Morris Questal
      AC 202/692-7122
   Staff Assistant
      Mrs. L. M. Newton
      AC 202/692-7127

Headquarters, Naval Material
   Command (N)
Room 524, Crystal Plaza 5, 20360

Mr. D. J. Wolf
AC 202/692-3559

Naval Air Systems Command (N)
Room 150, Jefferson Plaza 1, 20360

Mr. J. F. Lenahan
AC 202/692-0935 or 692-0936

Naval Electronic Systems Command (N)
Room 3E10, National Center 1, 20360

Mr. Charles Fiedelman
Mrs. Ruth Day
AC 202/692-6091

Strategic Systems Project Office (N)
Room 1022A, Crystal Mall 3, 20376

Mr. M. C. Gibbons
AC 202/695-6208

Naval Sea Systems Command (N)
Room 4W10, National Center 3, 20360

Mr. C. C. Gruneberg
AC 202/692-3679
Mr. S. Tatigian
AC 202/692-3680

Naval Supply Systems Command (N)
Room 514, Crystal Mall 3, 20376

Mr. R. F. Quinn
AC 202/695-5954/5952

Headquarters, U.S. Marine Corps (N)
Mail: HQ., U.S. Marine Corp
(LBS) Washington, D.C. 20380
Physical Location: Room 646
   Commonwealth Bldg
1300 Wilson Blvd, Arlington Va.

Mr. W. R. Bray
AC 202/694-1939

Figure 10   (*Continued*)

118

Military Sealift Command (N)　　　　　Captain R. C. Van Osdol
Room 316, Tamol Bldg.　　　　　　　　AC 202/282-2600
4228 Wisconsin Ave., NW 20390

Chesapeake Division (N)　　　　　　　Mr. E. L. Bernhardt
Naval Facilities Engineering　　　　　AC 202/433-4151
　　Command
Washington Navy Yard, 20374

Naval Regional Procurement Office (N)　Mr. J. B. Jones
Washington Navy Yard　　　　　　　　Mr. P. S. Logan
Building 200, Room 400, 20374　　　　AC 202/433-2957

Naval Research Laboratory (N)　　　　Mrs. M. M. Best
　　20375　　　　　　　　　　　　　AC 202/767-3698

Naval Oceanographic Office (N)　　　　Mr. J. W. Johnson
　　20373　　　　　　　　　　　　　AC 202/763-1268

Air Force Small Business Advisor (AF)　Mr. Donald E. Rellins
Directorate of Procurement Policy　　　Mr. Marvin D. Stearn
　　DCS/S&L　　　　　　　　　　　　Mrs. Inis F. Millholland
Room 4C279, Pentagon 20330　　　　　AC 202/697-4126 or 697-5373

Air Force Systems Command (AF)　　　Mr. David H. Oswalt
Andrews AFB 20331　　　　　　　　　AC 301/981-6107

HQ Command USAF (AF)　　　　　　　Lt. Col. F. H. Coursen
Andrews AFB 20331　　　　　　　　　AC 301/981-2601

Washington Area Procurement　　　　Mr. Jack E. Bynane
　　Center (AF)　　　　　　　　　　　AC 301/981-2601
Andrews AFB, Washington 20331

Office of Scientific Research (AF)　　　Mrs. Corrine G. McDonald
Building 410　　　　　　　　　　　　AC 202/693-0164
Bolling AFB 20332

Defense Mapping Agency (DOD)　　　　Mr Constantine G. Pappas
Topographic Center　　　　　　　　　AC 202/227-2467
5600 Brooks Lane, NW
Washington, D.C. 20315

Publications Directorate, U.S. Army　　Mr. Buford B. Vogel
　　MDW (A)　　　　　　　　　　　　AC 202/693-7811
ATTN:DAAG-PAR-C, Forrestal Bldg 20314

Figure 10　(*Continued*)

Cocoa Beach

Air Force Eastern Test Range (AF)   Mr. Howard S. Gedeist
Patrick AFB 32925   Mr. Danuel R. Hoskins
     AC 305/494-2207

Homestead

31 Tactical Fighter Wing (AF)   Mr. D. K. Wilson
Homestead AFB 33030   AC 305/257-7327

Jacksonville

U.S. Army Engineer District (A)   Mr. Richard R. Allen
P.O. Box 4970 32201   AC 904/791-2735

Naval Air Station, Supply Dept. (N)   Mr A. V. Gagliardo
P. O. Box 21-A 32212   AC 904/772-2914

SUPSHIP, Conversion & Repair, USN (N)   Mr. E. T. Fisher
Drawer T, Mayport Naval Station   AC 904/246-5742
   32228

Mary Esther

1 Special Operations Wing (AF)   Mr. Pascal L. King
Hurlburt Field   AC 904/884-6216
Eglin AF Aux. Fld. 9, 32544

Orlando

Naval Training Equipment Center (N)   Mr. J. R. Haitz
   32813   AC 305/646-5515/5121

DCASD, Orlando (DSA)   Mr. DeFarest A. Long, Jr.
3555 Maguire Blvd.   AC 305/894-7711, Ext. 281
Orlando 32803

Panama City

Naval Coastal Systems (N)   Mr. O. R. Holley
   Laboratory 32401   AC 904/234-4308

4756 Air Base Group (AF)   Mr. Jerry A. Starr
Tyndall AFB 32401   AC 305/283-6266

Pensacola

Naval Air Station (N)   Mrs. M. W. Young
   32508   AC 904/452-2411

Figure 10 (*Continued*)

Tampa

56 Tactical Fighter Wing (AF) MacDill AFB 33608	Mr. Thomas L. Cummins AC 813/968-3815

Valparaiso

Armament Development & Test Center (AF) Eglin AFB 32542	Mr. J. V. Leftwich Mrs. Dorothy E. Anderson AC 904/882-2843

West Palm Beach

NAVPLANTREPO (N) Pratt & Whitney Aircraft Florida Research & Development Center, P.O. Box 2691 33402	Mr. G. R. Parks AC 305/844-7311, Ext. 2511

GEORGIA

Albany

Marine Corps Supply Center (N) P.O. Drawer 18, 31704	Mr. E. N. Henley AC 912/439-5825

Atlanta

U.S. Army Forces Command (A) Ft. McPherson 30330	Mr. Arnold M. Scherer AC 404/752-2512
U.S. Army Engineer Division (A) South Atlantic Title Building, 30 Pryor St., SW 30303	Mr. D. A. Barnes AC 404/526-6689
Fort McPherson 30330 (A)	Mr. Robert L. Ward AC 404/752-3316

Augusta

U.S. Army School/Training Center (A) Fort Gordon 30905	Mr. William A. Youngblood AC 404/791-2434

Columbus

Hq., U.S. Army Infantry Center (A) Fort Benning 31905	Mr. Donald E. Goodroe AC 404/545-5171

Forest Park

Atlanta Army Depot (A) 30050	Mr. Frank R. Hinkley AC 404/363-5411, 5412

Figure 10   (*Continued*)

GEORGIA – Cont'd

Hinesville

Hq., U.S. Army Flight Training
   Center (A)
Fort Stewart 31214

Mr. Noland E. Purcell
AC 912/876-3571, Ext. 3563

Marietta

94 Tactical Airlift Wing (AF)
Dobbins AFB 30060

Mr. H. G. Hillhouse
AC 404/424-8811

Lockheed Georgia Company
   (AFPRO) (AF) 30061

Mr. Milton K. Johnston, Jr.
AC 404/424-2016

DCASR, Atlanta (DSA)
805 Walker Street
   30060

Mr. Allen Trippeer
Mr. Riley H. Curtis, Jr.
AC 404/424-6000

Savannah

U.S. Army Engineer District (A)
200 E. St. Julian St.
P.O. Box 889 31402

Mr. Donald W. Murphy
AC 912/233-8822, Ext. 292

Valdosta

38 Flying Training Wing (AF)
Base Procurement Office
Moody AFB 31601

Mr. Thomas L. Toole
AC 912/333-4211, Ext. 3453 or 3535

Warner Robins

Hq. Air Force Reserve (AF)
Robins AFB 31093

Mr. John C. Jones
AC 912/926-5584 or 926-5585

Warner Robins Air Logistics
   Center (AF)
Robins AFB 31093

Mr. Robert F. Beckmann
Mr. Wade H. Jordan
Mrs. Geraldine Hogan
AC 912/926-5871 or 926-5873

GUAM

U.S. Naval Supply Depot, Purchase
   Div. (N)
FPO San Francisco 96630

Mr. F. C. Abraham
339-2114 /5188

43 Combat Support Group (AF)
Andersen AFB
APO San Francisco 96334

SMSgt Charles T. Scott
366-6214

Figure 10 (*Continued*)

HAWAII

Honolulu

Procurement Division -- DIRSS
USAR HAW (A)
P.O. Box 222 96810

Mr. Lawrence C. Au
AC 808/863-670

Hq. Pacific Air Forces (AF)
Hickam AFB
Mail: APO San Francisco 96553

Lt. Col. Lloyd A. Tholen
AC 808/430-0111, Ext. 4499680
   or 4499634

15 Air Base Wing
PACAF Procurement Center (AF)
Hickam AFB
Mail: APO San Francisco 96553

Mr. Edward P. Asmus
AC 315/430-0111, Ext. 4493860
   or 4495731

Pearl Harbor

Pacific Division (N)
Naval Facilities Engineering
   Command
FPO San Francisco 96610

Mr. T. H. Reid
AC 808/474-8194

SUPSHIP, Conversion & Repair, USN (N)
14th Naval District, Box 400
FPO San Francisco 96610

Mr. F. J. Aylett
AC 808/422-0544

Officer in Charge of Construction (N)
   Naval Facilities
Engineering Command, MIDPAC
FPO San Francisco 96610

Mr. Earl J. Ralph
AC 808/474-8194

Naval Supply Center Regional
   Procurement Dept. (N)
Box 300
FPO San Francisco 96610

Mr. E. A. Salomone
AC 808/471-0705

Pearl Harbor Naval Shipyard (N)
Box 400
FPO San Francisco 96610

LCDR D. T. Munro
AC 808/471-8220 or 474-1136

Fort Shafter

U.S. Army Engineer Division (A)
Pacific Ocean
APO, San Francisco 96558

Mr. Robert H. Stiver
AC 808/438-9700

IDAHO

Mountain Home

366 Tactical Fighter Wing (AF)
Mountain Home AFB 83648

Mrs. Peggy R. Thomas
AC 208/828-2749

Figure 10   (*Continued*)

Belleville

Hq. Military Airlift Command (AF)   Mr. Thomas E. Gonsalves
Scott AFB, 62225   AC 618/256-2123 or 256-2122

Contract Airlift Division (AF)   Mr. Gene E. Ohl
Military Airlift Command   AC 618/256-2294
Scott AFB, 62225

375 Aeromedical Airlift Wing (AF)   Mr. David W. Gabler
Scott AFB 62225   AC 618/256-3036

Chicago

U.S. Army Engineer Division,   Mr. J. M. Fears
   North Central (A)   AC 312/353-6397
536 S. Clark St. 60605

U.S. Army Engineer District (A)   Mr. Ernest Howard
219 S. Dearborn St. 60604   AC 312/353-7473

928 Tactical Airlift Group (AF)   Mrs. Ethel C. Tonkin
Chicago-O'Hare Int'l. Airport 60666   AC 312/694-3031, Ext. 2581

DCASR, Chicago (DSA)   Mr. George Podlesok
O'Hare Int'l Airport 60666   Mr. Victor J. Ripp
P.O. Box 66475   Ms. Rose Marie Cotton
      AC 312/694-3031, Ext. 2243

Defense Subsistence Region   Mr. Michael J. Popik
   Headquarters, DPSC (DSA)   AC 312/353-5006
536 S. Clark St. 60605

Fort Sheridan

Fort Sheridan (A)   Mr. Spencer
   60037   AC 312/926-3326

Granite City

U.S. Army Headquarters & Installations   Mr. Victor Murphy
   Support Activity (A) 62040   AC 618/263-5362

Great Lakes

Naval Administrative Command   Mrs. L. M. Boyer
   Supply Dept (N)   AC 312/688-6942
Naval Training Center Bldg. 3200 60088

Joliet

Joliet Army Ammunition Plant (A)   Mr. Douglas Thompson
   60436   AC 815/424-2514

Figure 10 (*Continued*)

Rantoul

Base Procurement Office (AF)
Chanute AFB 61868

Mr. John W. Eversole
AC 217/495-2112 or 495-3008

Rock Island

U.S. Army Engineer District (A)
Clock Tower Building 61201

Mr. G. R. Morrell
AC 309/788-6361, Ext. 312

U.S. Army Armament Command (A)
Rock Island Arsenal 61201

Mr. Woodson Ely
AC 309/794-5336

U.S. Army Rock Island Arsenal (A)
61201

Mr. Woodson Ely
AC 309/794-5336

Savanna

Savanna Army Depot (A)
61074

Mr. John A. Washburn
AC 815/273-2211, Ext. 4150

INDIANA

Charlestown

Indiana Army Ammunition
Plant (A) 47111

Mr. Keith Warren
AC 812/282-8961, Ext. 5122

Crane

Naval Weapons
Support Center (N) 47522

Mr. P. A. Anderson
AC 812/854-1542

Indianapolis

Fort Benjamin Harrison (A)
46216

Mr. Samuel E. Vaughn
AC 317/542-2783 or 542-2784

Naval Avionics Facility (N)
6000 E. 21st Street 46218

Mr. D. H. Batey
AC 317/353-3608

General Motors Corporation,
Detroit-Diesel-Allison (AFPRO) (AF)
2355 So. Tibbs Avenue 46241

Mr. Jack H. Marrion
AC 317/243-4961

DCASD, Indianapolis (DSA)
Finance Center, U.S. Army
Building 1
Fort Benjamin Harrison 46249

Mr. Charles F. Loch
AC 317/546-9211, Ext. 3155

Figure 10   (*Continued*)

INDIANA – Cont'd

Madison

Jefferson Proving Ground (A)   Ms. Ruby Reibel
47250   AC 812/273-1423, Ext. 3132

Newport

*Army Ammunition Plant (A)   Mr. Lawrence Kittell
47966   AC 812/245-4532

Peru

Base Procurement Office (AF)   Mr. Harold G. Robertson
Grissom AFB 46971   AC 317/689-2131

IOWA

Burlington

Iowa Army Ammunition Plant (A)   Mr. John J. Cechota
56201   AC 319/754-5731, Ext. 2209

KANSAS

Fort Leavenworth

Fort Leavenworth (A)   Mr. Donald C. Jewell
66027   AC 913/684-2532

Fort Riley

Fort Riley (A) 66442   Mr. Willard M. Lee
     AC 913/BE 9-3238

Lawrence

*Sunflower Army Ammunition Plant (A)   Mr. William G. Moorhead
66044   AC 816/471-6922, Ext. 4339

Parsons

Kansas Army Ammunition Plant   Mr. V. E. Sutton, ACTG
67357 (A)   AC 316/421-4000, Ext. 285

Wichita

Base Procurement Office (AF)   Mr. O. C. Burkes
McConnell AFB 67221   AC 316/685-1151, Ext. 6768

*Inactive

Figure 10   (*Continued*)

KENTUCKY

Hopkinsville

Fort Campbell (A) 42223

Mr. Richard Connor
AC 502/798-2325

Fort Knox

U.S. Army Armor Center (A)
40121

Mr. William Mahanna
AC 502/624-7152

Lexington

Lexington-Blue Grass Army Depot
40507 (A)

Mr. Wendell E. Cartmell
AC 606/293-3538

Louisville

U.S. Army Engineer District (A)
P.O. Box 59 40201

Mr. William H. Cheesman
AC 502/582-5706

Naval Ordnance Station (N)
40214

Mr. R. P. Ayo
AC 502/361-2641, Ext. 404

LOUISIANA

Alexandria

23 Tactical Fighter Wing (AF)
England AFB 71304

Mr. Willard H. Dunn
AC 318/865-2333

Fort Polk

Fort Polk (A)
71459

Chief, Procurement Div., DIO
AC 318/578-2833

New Orleans

U.S. Army Engineer District (A)
Foot of Prytania Street 70160

Mr. Douglas D. Goodman
AC 504/865-1121, Ext. 287

SUPSHIP, CONVERSION & REPAIR,
USN (N)
8th Naval District 71046

Mr. E. L. Beatty
AC 504/361-2548

Defense Subsistence Region
Headquarters, DPSC (DSA)
4400 Dauphine St. 70140

Mr. Alvin W. LaCoste
AC 504/948-1278

Figure 10   (*Continued*)

127

Shreveport

Louisiana Army Ammunition Plant
71102 (A)

Mr. Joseph L. Smith
AC 318/459-5107

Base Procurement Office (AF)
Barksdale AFB 71110

Mrs. Robbie S. Parker
AC 318/456-2113

MAINE

Bath

SUPSHIP, CONVERSION & REPAIR,
USN (N)
574 Washington Street 04530

Mr. A. E. Greenlaw
AC 207/443-3311, Ext. 2372

Limestone

Base Procurement Office (AF)
Loring AFB 04750

1st Lt. Charles R. Elliott
AC 207/999-2286

MARYLAND

Aberdeen Proving Ground

U.S. Army Aberdeen Proving Ground (A)
21005

Mr. Richard Hall
AC 301/278-3878

Hq. U.S. Army Test and
Evaluation Command (A) 21005

Mr. Paul Piako
AC 301/278-5184

Adelphi

Harry Diamond Laboratories (A)
2800 Power Mill Road 20783

Mr. Franklin Rainier
AC 202/394-1076

Annapolis

Naval Academy (N)
21402

Lt. R. D. Maas
AC 301/267-3498

Baltimore

U.S. Army Engineer District (A)
P.O. Box 1715 21203

Mr. C. J. Dow
AC 301/962-2196

NAVPLANTREPO (N)
Westinghouse Electric Corp
Defense and Electronic Systems Center
P.O. Box 746, 21203

Miss F. B. Armiger
AC 301/765-3479

Figure 10   (*Continued*)

Towson

DCASD, Baltimore (DSA)   Vacant
300 E. Jappa Road 21204   AC 301/828-1545

Bethesda

Naval Ship Research & Development   Mr. C. R. Slaton
    Center (N) 20084   AC 202/227-1214

Dundalk

U.S. Army Intelligence Center (A)   Miss Frances Rafferty
    and Fort Holabird 21219   AC 301/527-3220

Edgewood Arsenal

U.S. Army Edgewood Arsenal (A)   Mr. John J. Kaufman
    21010   AC 301/671-2309

Fort Ritchie

U.S. Army Communications Command   Mr. Martin I. Freeman, Jr.
Procurement Div., Industrial Opera- AC 301/878-5324
    tions Dir.
Hq, Fort Ritchie (A)
Fort Richie 21719

Frederick

U.S. Army Medical Material   Major Michael L. Johnson
    Agency (A)   AC 301/663-2242
Fort Detrick 21701

Fort George G. Meade

Maryland Procurement Office (A)   Mrs. Madeline Pyles
Directorate, Procurement and Production   Mrs. Charles Eckman
U.S. Army Electronics Command   AC 301/688-6974
9800 Savage Road 20755

Purchasing & Contracting Office (A) Mr. William Montgomery
Fort George G. Meade 20755   AC 301/677-3717

Indian Head

Naval Ordnance Station (N)   Mr. H. D. Coleman
    20640   AC 301/743-4342

Figure 10   (*Continued*)

Patuxent River

Naval Air Station, Purchase Div. (N)   Mr. M. F. Eckman
Supply Dept. 20670   AC 301/863-3783

Silver Spring

Naval Surface Weapons Center,   Mr. T. L. Debeck
White Oak Laboratory (N) 20910   AC 202/394-1477

NAVPLANTREPO (N)   Ms. M. R. Gill
8621 Georgia Avenue 20910   AC 301/589-7700, Ext. 350

MASSACHUSETTS

Bedford

Electronic Systems Division (AF)   Mr. John F. Condon
L. G. Hanscom Field   Mr. William Cabral
Bedford 01730   AC 617/861-4973

Boston

SUPSHIP, CONVERSION & REPAIR,   Mr. N. Lamberti
   USN   AC 617/542-6000, Ext. 126
Boston Naval Shipyard (N)
1st Naval District 02129

DCASR, Boston (DSA)   Mr. Edward J. Fitzgerald
666 Summer Street 02210   Mr. John E. McManus
     AC 617/542-6000, Ext. 886

Chicopee Falls

439 Tactical Airlift Wing (AF)   Mr. Edward T. Kennedy
Westover AFB 01022   AC 413/557-3508

Fort Devens

Fort Devens (A) 01433   Ms. Frances Rafferty
     AC 617/796-2430

Figure 10 *(Continued)*

Natick

U.S. Army Natick Development
   Center (A) 01760

Mr. James F. Kelly
AC 617/653-1000, Ext. 2328

Pittsfield

NAVPLANTREPO (SSPO) (N)
General Electric Ordnance Systems
100 Plastics Ave 01201

Mr. L. C. Herbs
AC 413/494-3262

Waltham

U.S. Army Engineer Division,
   New England (A)
424 Trapelo Road 02154

Mr. Stanley W. Kulik
AC 617/894-2400, Ext. 249

Watertown

U.S. Army Materials and Mechanics
   Research Center (A) 02172

Mr. Armando J. Constantino
AC 617/926-1900, Ext. 355

Wilmington

AVCO Corporation (AFPRO) (AF)
Systems Division
Wilmington 01887

Mr. Albert Weiskopf
AC 617/657-3177

MICHIGAN

Battle Creek

Defense Logistics Services Center (DSA)
Battle Creek Federal Center 49016

. . . . . .
AC 616/962-6511

Detroit

U.S. Army Engineer District (A)
150 Michigan Avenue 48226

Mr. E. Czarny
AC 313/226-6420

DCASR, Detroit (DSA)
1580 East Grand Boulevard 48211

Mr. John S. McCallum
Mr. Douglas Koster
AC 313/923-0100, Ext. 265

Marquette

Base Procurement Office (AF)
K I Sawyer AFB 40843

Mrs. Anita M. Hill
AC 906/346-6511, Ext. 2300

Figure 10 (*Continued*)

Oscoda

Base Procurement Office (AF)
Wurtsmith AFB 48753

Mr. Roy L. Lemons
AC 517/739-2011, Ext. 2482

Sault Ste. Marie

Base Procurement Office (AF)
Kincheloe AFB 49788

Mr. Gilbert F. Peterman
AC 906/495-2380

Warren

U.S. Army Tank-Automotive
   Command (A) 48090

Mr. Joseph Higuchi
Mr. Joseph Ardito
Mr. Lawrence Lennartz
AC 313/264-1100, Ext. 2341,
   or 2310, 2398

MINNESOTA

Duluth

4787 Air Base Group (AF)
Duluth International Airport 55814

Mr. Deward D. Retherford
AC 218/727-8211, Ext. 2240

New Brighton

Twin Cities Army Ammunition Plant (A)
P.O. Box 689, 55440

Mr. Owen O. Mobley
AC 612/612-3633, Ext. 750, 751

Minneapolis

934 Tactical Airlift Group (AF)
Minneapolis-St. Paul International
   Airport 55417

Mr. Floyd R. Olson
AC 612/725-5413

St. Paul

U.S. Army Engineer District (A)
1135 U.S. Post Office and
   Customhouse 55101

Mr. Eugene D. Korhonen
AC 612/725-7614

DCASD, Twin Cities (DSA)
Fort Snelling
Federal Building
Twin Cities, Minn. 55111

Mr. Roman T. Schumacher
AC 612/725-3808

Figure 10 (*Continued*)

MISSISSIPPI

Biloxi

Base Procurement Office (AF)
Keesler AFB 39534

Mr. Gordon E. Bishop
AC 601/377-3230 or 377-3232

Columbus

14 Flying Training Wing (AF)
Columbus AFB 39701

Mr. George W. Speed
AC 601/434-7322, Ext. 7517 or 7534

Pascagoula

SUPSHIP, CONVERSION & REPAIR,
USN (N) 39567

Mr. Doyle E. Turner
AC 601/769-0270

Vicksburg

U.S. Army Engineer District (A)
U.S.P.O. & Courthouse Bldg. 39180

Mr. Marion Metzger, Jr.
AC 601/636-1311, Ext; 435

U.S. Army Engineer Division
Lower Mississippi Valley (A)
P.O. Box 80 39180

Mr. Cecil B. Cooper, Jr.
AC 601/636-1311, Ext. 334

U.S. Army Engineer Waterways
Experimental Station (A)
Halls Ferry Road 39180

Mr. A. J. Breithaupt
AC 601/636-3111, Ext. 2423

MISSOURI

Fort Leonard Wood

Fort Leonard Wood (A)
65473

Mr. Daniel Jakovich, Jr.
AC 314/368-3914

Grandview

Hq. Air Force Communications
Service (AF)
Richards-Gebaur AFB 64030

Mr. Allan S. Weithman
AC 816/331-4400, Ext. 3475

Base Procurement Division (AF)
Richards-Gebaur AFB 64030

Mr. Robert M. Marler
AC 816/331-4400, Ext. 2837

Independence

Lake City Army Ammunition
Plant (A) 64056

Mr. Joseph F. Callahan
AC 816/796-3900, Ext. 8

Figure 10 (*Continued*)

Kansas City

U.S. Army Engineer District (A)
700 Federal Office Bldg. 64106

Mr. K. E. Salters
AC 816/374-5544

Kansas City Subsistence Regional
Headquarters, DPSC (DSA)
623 Hardesty Avenue 64124

Mr. Dallas C. Jaekels
AC 816/374-6273

Knob Noster

Base Procurement Office (AF)
Whiteman AFB 65301

Mrs. Nell E. Evans
AC 816/563-3641

St. Louis

U.S. Army Aviation Systems
Command (A)
12th & Spruce Streets 63166

Mr. Leonard H. Richman
Mr. Cleon Gilberg
Mr. Chas. Robinson
AC 314/268-3177

*Gateway Army Ammunition Plant (A)
63143

Mr. Alton D. Bain
AC 314/268-6344

U.S. Army Engineer District (A)
210 North 12th Street 63101

Mr. William O. Cauble
AC 314/268-2845

U.S. Army Troop Support
Command (A)
4300 Goodfellow Boulevard 63120

Mr. Harris E. Clark
Mr. Craig Rolen
AC 314/263-2222

McDonnell Douglas Corporation
(AFPRO) (AF) 63166

Mr. John King
AC 314/232-2503 or 232-2504

DCASR, St. Louis (DSA)
1136 Washington Avenue 63101

Mr. Walter Schrader
Mr. Thomas G. Moore
AC 314/268-6223

*St. Louis Army Ammunition Plant (A)
63120

Mr. Herman J. Hartmann
AC 314/263-3842

MONTANA

Great Falls

Base Procurement Office (AF)
Malmstrom AFB 59402

Mr. John M. Edwards
AC 406/731-3743

*Inactive

Figure 10 (*Continued*)

NEBRASKA

Grand Island

*Cornhusker Army Ammunition
  Plant (A) 68801

Mr. S. Charles Fisher
AC 308/382-4420, Ext. 421

Omaha

U.S. Army Engineer District (A)
215 North 17th Street 68102

Mr. W. G. Tracy
AC 402/221-4100

U.S. Army Engineer Division,
  Missouri River (A)
215 North 17th Street 68101

Mr. Hilbert Mitzel
AC 402/221-3010

Hqs. Strategic Air Command (AF)
Offutt AFB 68113

Mr. William T. Haneline
AC 402/294-4632

Base Procurement Office (AF)
Offutt AFB 68113

Mr. Harry G. Hall
AC 402/294-2611

NEVADA

Hawthorne

Naval Ammunition Depot (N) 89415

Mrs. Ruth Welsh
AC 702/945-2838

Las Vegas

57 Fighter Weapons Wing (AF)
Nellis AFB 89191

Mrs. Sylvia F. Hyer
AC 702/643-4003

NEW HAMPSHIRE

Portsmouth

Portsmouth Naval Shipyard (N)
  03801

Mr. A. J. Rodis
AC 207/439-1000, Ext. 233

Base Procurement Office (AF)
Pease AFB 03801

Mr. Ellsworth L. Shovan
AC 603/436-0100, Ext. 1337

NEW JERSEY

Burlington

*Burlington Army Ammunition
  Plant (A) 08016

Mr. Momert C. Oreszko
AC 609/386-4000, Ext. 331

*Inactive

Figure 10 (*Continued*)

Dover

Picatinny Arsenal (A)
  07801

Mr. Elton H. Holloway
AC 201/328-4106, 4104

Fort Dix

Fort Dix (A) 08640

Mr. John B. Townsend
Chief, Procurement Div., DIO
AC 609/562-4252

Fort Monmouth

Fort Monmouth Procurement
  Division (A)
P & P Directorate
U.S. Army Electronics Command
  07703

Mr. Gerald F. O'Connell
Mr. John Meschler
Mr. Robert J. Wright
Mrs. Diann E. Curry
AC 201/532-4511

Lakehurst

Naval Air Station (N)
Hangar #5, Building No. 194
  08733

Mr. R. G. Serra
AC 201/323-2744 or 657–4912

Springfield

DCASD, Springfield (DSA)
240 Route 22 07081

Mr. Peter P. Gitto
Mr. Charles P. Ferraro
AC 201/379-7950

Wrightstown

438 Air Base Group (AF)
McGuire AFB 08641

Mr. Edward Aja
AC 609/724-2100, Ext. 3604 or 2414

NEW MEXICO

Alamogordo

49 Tactical Fighter Wing (AF)
Holloman AFB 88330

Mr. Billy R. Fawvor
AC 505/473-6511, Ext. 3048

Albuquerque

U.S. Army Engineer District (A)
517 Gold Avenue, Southwest 87103

Mr. Max C. Apodaca
AC 505/766-2680

Figure 10   (*Continued*)

4900 Air Base Group   Mr. John A. Everts
   (AFSC) (AF)   AC 505/264-3819
Kirtland AFB 87117

AF Contract Management Division (AF)   Mr. Robert W. Kellhofer
Kirtland AFB 87117   AC 505/264-869ö

Defense Atomic Support Agency (A)   Mr. John W. Palmer
Field Command   AC 505/264-8241
Purchasing & Contracting Office
(SBSV-E)
Sandia Base 87115

Clovis

27 Tactical Fighter Wing (AF)   Mr. Dominic A. Schreiber
Cannon AFB 88101   AC 505/784-3311, Ext. 2941

White Sands

U.S. Army White Sands   Mr. Paul J. Burns
Missile Range (A) 88002   AC 915/678-1401

NEW YORK

Bethpage

NAVPLANTREPO (N)   Mr. S. S. Soskin
Grumman Aerospace Corp. 11714   AC 516/575-1557

Brooklyn

Fort Hamilton (A) 11252   Chief, Purchasing Office
                                        AC 212/836-4100, Ext. 4143

SUPSHIP, CONVERSION & REPAIR,   Mr. Tony Trozzo
   USN (N)   AC 212/965-5615
3rd Naval District, Federal Office
Bldg., 29th St. & 3rd Ave. 11232

Military Sealift Command, Atlantic (N)   Mr. G. W. Bayerle
58th Street & 1st Ave., 11250   AC 212/439-5400, Ext. 5270

Navy Resale System Office (N)   Mr. I. Gordon
29th St. & 3rd Ave., 11232   AC 212/965-5620

Figure 10   (*Continued*)

Military Traffic Management and
   Terminal Service - Eastern
   Area (A)
1st Avenue & 53rd St. 11250

Mr. Peter C. Belotte
AC 212/GE 9-5400

Buffalo

U.S. Army Engineer District (A)
1776 Niagara Street 14207

Mr. Roderick R. Madore
AC 716/876-2285

Farmingdale

AFPRO (AF)
Fairchild Republic Company
Farmingdale 11735

Mr. Robert O. Hall
AC 516/531-2434

Garden City (L.I.)

DCASD, Garden City (DSA)
605 Stewart Avenue 11533

Mr. Anthony R. Civello
Mr. Irving E. Adler
AC 516/741-8000, Ext. 379

Great Neck (L.I.)

NAVPLANTREPO (N)
Sperry Rand Corp.
c/o Sperry Div. 11020

Miss M. D. Seaman
AC 516/574-1641

NAVPLANTREPO (N)
Strategic Systems Div.
c/o Sperry Rand Corp. 11020

Mr. G. L. Kershow
AC 516/574-3464

New York City

U.S. Army Engineer District -
   New York (A)
26 Federal Plaza 10007

Mr. Bill Hallahan
AC 212/264-9012

U.S. Army Engineer Division
North Atlantic (A)
90 Church Street 10007

Mr. A. B. Kilarjian
AC 212/264-7532

DCASR New York (DSA)
60 Hudson Street
New York, N.Y. 10013

Mr. Carl Davis
Mr. Brian A. Bannon
Mr. Andrew J. Zuber
Mr. Michael Galatola
AC 212/264-0833, 0834

Figure 10 (*Continued*)

Niagara Falls

914 Tactical Airlift Group (AF)   Mr. Henry M. Blane, Jr.
Niagara Falls International   AC 716/297-4100, Ext. 307
   Airport 14306

Plattsburgh

Base Procurement Office (AF)   Mr. Paul R. Pierson
Plattsburgh AFB 12903   AC 518/565-7432

Rochester

DCASD, Rochester (DSA)   Mr. Henry J. Kohlmeir
US Courthouse & Federal Bldg.   AC 716/263-6419
100 State Street 14614

Rome

Rome Air Development Center (Ar) Mr. John J. Vella
Griffiss AFB 13440   AC 315/330-4020

Base Procurement Office (AF)   Mr. James B. Isom
Griffiss AFB 13440   AC 315/330-7783

Watertown

Camp Drum (A) 13603   Mr. Dewey Cocuzzoli
                                   AC 315/782-6900, Ext. 243

Watervliet

Watervliet Arsenal (A) 12189   Mr. A. V. Paparian
                                   AC 518/273-4610, Ext. 5005

West Point

U.S. Military Academy (A)   Mrs. Doris Schoellhorn
Purchasing & Contracting 10996   Major Darman Place
                                   AC 914/938-3417

NORTH CAROLINA

Camp Lejune

Marine Corps Base (N)   Mr. J. C. Crumley
   28542   AC 919/451-5520

Figure 10 (*Continued*)

Cherry Point

Marine Corps Air Station (N) Mr. P. B. Beachem
28522 AC 919/466-3446/2692

Fayetteville

Hqs. 18th Airborne Corps and Mr. Donald Y. McKay
Fort Bragg (A) 28307 AC 919/396-4111, Ext. 61105

317 Tactical Airlift Wing (AF) Mr. Linwood A. Matthews
Pope AFB 28390 AC 919/394-2161

Goldsboro

4 Tactical Fighter Wing (AF) Mr. William L. Page
Seymour-Johnson AFB 27530 AC 919/736-5714

Wilmington

U.S. Army Engineer District (A) Mr. R. C. Kirby
38401 PO Box 1890 AC 919/763-9971, Ext. 9458

NORTH DAKOTA

Grand Forks

Base Procurement Office (AF) Mr. Levon J. Bjertness
Grand Forks AFB 58201 AC 701/594-6571

Minot

Base Procurement Office (AF) Mr. Eugene R. Teeters
Minot AFB 58701 AC 701/727-4761, Ext. 3045

OHIO

Akron

NAVPLANTREPO (N) Mr. R. E. Livak
Goodyear Aerospace Corporation 44305 AC 216/794-2085

Cincinnati

U.S. Army Engineer Division Mr. Nelson W. Eisenacher
Ohio River (A) AC 513/684-3048
Federal Office Building
550 Main Street 45201

General Electric Company Mr. James W. Backscheider
(AFPRO) (AF) AC 513/243-6007
(Evendale) 45215

Figure 10 (*Continued*)

140

OHIO – Cont'd

Cleveland

DCASR, Cleveland (DSA)
Federal Office Building, Room 1821
1240 E. Ninth St. 44199

Mr. Joseph Donnelly
Mr. Clarke Reece
Mrs. Jean Spicer
AC 216/522-5122

Columbus

NAVPLANTREPO (N)
Rockwell International Corp.
4300 E. Fifth Avenue 43216

Mr. E. W. Roach
AC 614/239-3058

Base Procurement Office (AF)
Rickenbacker AFB 43217

Mr. Edwin M. Wilson
AC 614/492-4235

Defense Construction Supply
Center (DSA)
3990 East Broad Street 43215

Mr. Carl Peterson
AC 614/236-3541

Dayton

Hqs. Air Force Logistics Command (AF)
Wright-Patterson AFB 45433

Mr. Gale W. Farris
AC 513/257-3317 or
257-7632

Aeronautical Systems Division (AF)
Wright-Patterson AFB 45433

Mr. Thomas Dickman
Mr. James Beach
AC 513/255-5322

Research & Development (AF)
Aeronautical Systems Division
Wright-Patterson AFB 45433

Mr. Lawrence L. Grier
AC 513/255-3825

Base Procurement Office (AF)
2750th Air Base Wing
Wright-Patterson AFB 45433

Mr. Henry T. Brown, Jr.
AC 513/257-2324

Defense Electronics Supply Center (DSA)
1507 Wilmington Pike 45444

Mr. B. L. Castle
AC 513/252-6551, Ext. 5231

Newark

Aerospace Guidance & Metrology
Center (AF)
Newark Air Force Station 43055

Mr. Jimmy B. Spears
AC 614/522-5470

Figure 10   (*Continued*)

Ravenna

*Ravenna Army Ammunition Plant (A) Mr. Palmer P. Loro
   44266 (A)   AC 216/889-1661, Ext. 303

Vienna

910 Tactical Fighter Group (AF)   Mr. Philip Montmore
Youngstown Municipal Airport 44473   AC 216/358-7111,Ext. 326

OKLAHOMA

Altus

443 Military Airlift Wing (AF)   Mr. Paul E. Collins
Altus AFB 73521   AC 405/482-8100, Ext. 7320 or 7321

Enid

Base Procurement Office (AF)   Mr. Howard R. Hunter
Vance AFB 73701   AC 405/237-2121, Ext. 7565 or 7566

Fort Sill

U.S. Army Artillery Center (A)   Chief, Procurement Div. DIO
Fort Sill 73503   AC 405/351-1264 or 351-1267

McAlester

Naval Ammunition Depot (N)   Mr. R. D. Everett
   74501   AC 918/421-2011

Oklahoma City

Oklahoma City Air Logistics Center (AF) Mr. David W. Barghols
Tinker AFB 73145   Mr. Roy H. Sadler
                                         Mr. Joseph F. Scheller
                                         AC 405/732-7321, Ext. 2601

Tulsa

U.S. Army Engineer District (A)   Mr. Ival L. Sauter
P.O. Box 61 74102   AC 918/581-7318

OREGON

Hermiston

Umatilla Army Depot (A)   Mr. John Boyd
   97838   AC 503/567-6421, Ext. 2311 or 2091

*Inactive

Figure 10 (*Continued*)

Klamath Falls

827 Air Defense Group (AF)
Kingsley Field 97601

Mrs. Virginia A. Brower
AC 503/882-4411, Ext. 316

Portland

U.S. Army Engineer District (A)
P.O. Box 2946 97208

Mr. Adam B. Mello
AC 503/777-4225

U.S. Army Engineer Division,
    North Pacific (A)
210 Customs House 97209

Mr. Earl Redding
AC 503/221-3797

Wood Products Office,
    DCSC (DSA)
2850 S.E. 82nd Avenue 97266

Mr. Karl T. Lehmann
AC 503/777-4441, Ext. 315

PANAMA

Canal Zone

Base Procurement Office (AF)
24 Composite Group
Box 3037
Howard AFB
Mail: APO New York 09020

Captain Robert W. Menestrina
84-4330 or 4114

1930 INF BDE (Canal Zone) (A)
APO New York 09827

Major Charles Thompson
. . . .

PENNSYLVANIA

Annville

Hqs. XXI U.S. Army Corps (A)
Indiantown Gap Military
    Reservation 17003

Mr. James Cowhey
AC 717/273-2601, Ext. 214

Carlisle

Carlisle Barracks (A)
    17013

Chief, Procurement Div., DIO
AC 717/245-4816

Chambersburg

Letterkenny Army Depot (A)
    17201

Mr. Donald R. Gayman
AC 717/263-6386

Figure 10 (*Continued*)

Mechanicsburg

Navy Ships Parts Control Center (N) 17055	Mr. David L. Ro~~nds AC 717/766-8511, Ext. 3527

New Cumberland

New Cumberland Army Depot (A) 17070	Mr. Thomas Elhajj AC 717/782-6109

Philadelphia

Frankford Arsenal (A) Bridge-Tacony Streets 19137	Mr. William C. Burr AC 215/831-6328, Ext. 7220
General Electric Co. (AFPRO) (AF) (Valley Forge) P.O. Box 8555 19101	Mr. Simon J. Nagel AC 215/962-6434
U.S. Army Engineer District (A) 2nd & Chestnut Streets 19106	Mr. Albert P. McClain AC 215/597-4716
U.S. Army Boeing/Vertol Plant Activity (A) 19142	Mr. Robert Broadhurst AC 215/522-3021
Navy Aviation Supply Office (N) 700 Robbins Avenue 19111	Mr. L. M. Shapiro AC 215/697-2806
Northern Division-Naval Fac. (N) Engineering Command, Bldg. 77 19112	Mr. F. J. Chieffalo AC 215/755-4841
Naval Regional Procurement Office (N), U.S. Naval Base 19112	Miss Mary M. Maguire AC 215/755-4017
Marine Corps Supply Activity (N) 1100 South Broad Street 19146	Vacant AC 215/546-2000, Ext. 3780
Defense Industrial Supply Center (DSA) 700 Robbins Avenue 19111	Mr. Frank J. Clark AC 215/697-2747
Defense Personnel Support Center (DSA) 2800 South 20th Street 19101	Mr. Matthew E. Kryston Mr. Richard R. Husser Mrs. Rita A. Strassburg AC 215/271-2321
DCASR, Philadelphia (DSA) 2800 South 20th Street 19101 P.O. Box 7478	Mr. Nathan P. Dordick Mr. Frank R. Dearden AC215/271-4006 or 4007

Figure 10   (*Continued*)

Pittsburgh

U.S. Army Engineer District (A) 2032 Federal Building 1000 Liberty Avenue 15222	Mr. Nicholas B. Ives AC 412/644-691
911 Tactical Airlift Group (AF) Greater Pittsburg Airport 15231	Mr. John L. Chamblin AC 412/264-5000, Ext. 293
DCASD, Pittsburgh (DSA) 1610 S. Federal Building 1000 Liberty Avenue 15222	Mr. John Petro AC 412/644-5972
*Hays Army Ammunition Plant (A) 15207	Mr. Emery L. Leposky AC 412/262-8411

Scranton

Scranton Army Ammunition Plant (A) 156 Cedar Avenue 18501	Mr. Aldo A. Recife AC 717/342-7801, Ext. 203

Tobyhanna

Tobyhanna Army Depot (A) 18466	Mr. Joseph J. Perry AC 717/894-8301, Ext. 9234

Warminster

Naval Air Development Center (N) 18974	Ms. Rose G. Mandrack AC 215/672-9000, Ext. 2456

Willow Grove

913 Tactical Airlift Group (AF) Willow Grove Air Reserve Facility 19090	Mr. Robert J. O'Brien AC 215/672-4300, Ext. 57

PUERTO RICO

Aguadilla

1640 Air Base Wing (AF) Base Procurement Division	Mr. Arturo Mena AC 174/891-1510, Ext. 2571 or 2573

San Juan

U.S. Naval Station (N) FPO New York 09551	Mr. Mario Aponte AC 809/863-2000, Ext. 5432

*Inactive

Figure 10   (*Continued*)

145

RHODE ISLAND

Davisville

Officer in Charge of Construction (N)   Mr. J. T. Craffey
Naval Facilities Engineering Command,   AC 401/267-2447
   Contracts
Naval Construction Battalion Center 02854

Newport

Naval Underwater Systems Center (N)   Mr. P. G. David
  Bldg. 126T 02840   AC 401/841-4533

SOUTH CAROLINA

Charleston

U.S. Army Engineer District (A)   Mrs. Marieta H. Cade
P.O. Box 919 29402   AC 803/577-4321

Naval Supply Center (N)   Mr. B. A. Jamrogowicz
  29408   AC 803/743-2703

Southern Division (N)   Mr. R. G. Skaggs
Naval Facilities Engineering Command   AC 803/743-3995
2144 Melbourne Street 29411

437 Military Airlift Wing (AF)   Mr. Paul V. Crowe
Base Procurement Office   AC 803/747-4111, Ext. 2139
Charleston AFB 29404   or 2558

SUPSHIP, CONVERSION & REPAIR,   Mr. C. A. Stamp
  USN (N)   AC 803/743-2663
6th Naval District
U.S. Naval Base 29408

Columbia

U.S. Army Training Center and   Mr. Thomas J. Cooper
  Fort Jackson (A) 29207   AC 803/751-6918

Myrtle Beach

354 Tactical Fighter Wing (AF)   Mrs. Marie J. Repec
Myrtle Beach AFB 29577   AC 803/448-8311, Ext. 3849

Parris Island

Marine Corps Recruit Depot (N)   Mr. J. M. Lopatka
P.O. Box 34 29905   AC 803/524-3158

Figure 10 (*Continued*)

Sumter

363 Tactical Reconnaissance Wing (AF)   Mr. Luther A. Pack
Shaw AFB 29152   AC 803/775-1111, Ext. 2434

SOUTH DAKOTA

Rapid City

Base Procurement Office (AF)   Mr. Richard Q. Rasmussen
Ellsworth AFB 57706   AC 605/399-2721

TENNESSEE

Chattanooga

Volunteer Army Ammunition Plant (A)   Mrs. Katherine Dunn
P.O. Box 1748 37401   AC 615/892-0115, Ext. 4216

Kingsport

Holston Army Ammunition Plant (A)   Mr. Buford F. Elmore
    37662   AC 615/247-9111, Ext. 125

Memphis

U.S. Army Engineer District (A)   Mrs. Sibyl S. Edens
668 Federal Office Building 38103   AC 901/534-3116

Defense Depot Memphis (DSA)   Mrs. Grace M. Grimes
    38114   AC 901/744-5652

Defense Industrial Plant Equipment   Mr. David R. Potter
    Center (DSA)   AC 901/744-5671
Defense Depot Memphis 38114

Milan

Milan Army Ammunition Plant (A)   Mr. Elbert L. Parker
    38358   AC 901/686-1531, Ext. 124

Millington

Naval Air Station, Memphis (N)   Mr. W. H. Watson
    38054   AC 901/872-5271

Nashville

U.S. Army Engineer District (A)   Mr. Hobart D. Parish
P.O. Box 1070 37202   AC 615/749-7276

Figure 10   (*Continued*)

Tullahoma

Arnold Engineering Development
   Center (AF)
Arnold AF Station 37389

Captain Temple Bowling, IV
AC 615/455-2611, Ext. 7843

TEXAS

Abilene

Base Procurement Office (AF)
Dyess AFB 79607

Mr. William D. Banks
AC 915/696-2581

Austin

67 Tactical Reconnaissance
   Wing (AF)
Bergstrom AFB 78743

Mr. O. D. England
AC 512/385-3441

Big Spring

Base Procurement Office (AF)
Webb AFB 79720

Mr. Robert W. Campbell
AC 915/267-2511, Ext. 2605 or 2164

Corpus Christi

Naval Air Station, Purchase Div.,
   Supply Dept., (N)
Bldg. 10 78419

Mrs. C. E. Ray
AC 512/939-2400

Corpus Christi Army Depot (A)
   78419

Mr. John Allgood
AC 512/939-3131

Dallas

U.S. Army Engineer Div.
Southwestern (A)
Main Tower Building
1200 Main Street 75202

Mr. John A. Brigance
AC 214/749-3036

NAVPLANTREPO (N)
Ling-Temco-Vought Aerospace Corp
Vought Systems Div.
P.O. Box 5907 75222

Mr. R. B. Brown
Mr. R. D. Jenkins
AC 214/266-3911

DCASR, Dallas (DSA)
500 South Ervay Street
   75201

Mr. George R. Phillips
Mr. James L. Klechner
Mr. Larry F. Lytle
AC 214/744-4581, Ext. 205

Figure 10 (*Continued*)

Del Rio

Base Procurement Office (AF)   Mr. Rocque Medina
Laughlin AFB 78840   AC 512/298-3511, Ext. 2753 or 2439

El Paso

William Beaumont Army Medical   Major Robert S. Pearsall
  Center (A) 79920   AC 915/568-1701

U.S. Army Air Defense Center (A)   Major Clark
Fort Bliss 79916   AC 915/568-4201

Ft. Hood

III U.S. Army Corps and Ft. Hood (A) Mr. A. V. Juliano
  76544   AC 817/685-2711

Ft. Wolters

U.S. Army Primary Helicopter   Mr. Harry E. Cohen
  Center, Ft. Wolters (A) 76067   AC 817/325-2421

Ft. Worth

Base Procurement Office (AF)   Mr. James E. Underwood
Carswell AFB 76127   AC 817/738-3511, Ext. 5253

General Dynamics Corp. (AFPRO) (AF)   Major William Head
Convair Aerospace Division 76101   AC 817/732-4811, Ext. 2274

U.S. Army Engineer District   Mr. J. W. Titsworth
P.O. Box 17300 (A) 76102   AC 817/334-2128

U.S. Army Bell (A)   Mr. C. Larry Middleton
Plant Activity   AC 817/282-7111, Ext. 355
P.O. Box 1605, 76101

Galveston

U.S. Army Engineer District (A)   Mrs. Mabel B. Breen
606 Santa Fe Building 77550   AC 713/763-1401

Houston

2578 Air Base Group (AF)   Mrs. Bertha McNeill
Ellington AFB 77030   AC 713/487-1400, Ext. 2964

Lubbock

Base Procurement Office (AF)   Mr. William M. Weeks
Reese AFB 79489   AC 806/885-4511, Ext. 2449 or 2749

Figure 10 (*Continued*)

Marshall

Longhorn Army Ammunition Plant (A)
75670

Ms. Ellen M. Tillman
AC 214/697-3181, Ext. 2532

San Angelo

6940 Security Group (AF)
Goodfellow AFB 76904

Mr. Eugene A. West
AC 915/653-3231, Ext. 775

San Antonio

Hqs. U.S. Army Health Services
Command (A)
Procurement Office, DCSLOG 78234

Mr. Walter F. Glomb
AC 512/221-3568

Ft. Sam Houston (A) 78234

Mr. Donald M. Furru
AC 512/221-2930

Brooke Army Medical Center (A)
78234

Major Walter R. Hays
AC 512/221-5446

San Antonio Air Logistics
Center (AF)
Kelly AFB 78241

Vacant
Mr. James R. Thacker
Mr. Edward G. Cline
AC 512/925-6918 or 925-6919
or 925-6910

Base Procurement Office (AF)
Lackland AFB 78236

Mr. Dean C. Friestrom
AC 512/671-4195

Hqs. USAF
Cryptological Depot (AF)
78243

Mrs. Shirley R. Howard
AC 512/925-2821

12 Flying Training Wing (AF)
Randolph AFB 78148

Mr. Edwin J. Schneider
AC 512/652-4326 or 652-5261

Air Training Command (AF)
Randolph AFB 78148

Mr. Jimmie L. Neff
AC 512/652-5636 or 652-4402

3303 Procurement Squadron (AF)
Randolph AFB 78148

Mr. Bobby L. McCue
AC 512/652-3352 or 652-3660

Aerospace Medical Division (AF)
Brooks AFB 78235

Mr. James Chessher
AC 512/536-3351

USAF Security Service (AF)
78243

Mr. Thomas E. Englishbee
AC 512/925-2901 or 925-2334

Figure 10   (*Continued*)

Texarkana, Texas

Lone Star Army Ammunition
    Plant (A) 75501

Mr. John H. McFadden
AC 214/8ᴜo-1737

Red River Army Depot (A)
    75501

Mr. Earl J. Baker
AC 214/838-2656

Wichita Falls

Base Procurement Office (AF)
Sheppard AFB 73611

Mr. Glenn A. Ladd
AC 817/851-2663 or 851-2338

UTAH

Brigham City

Thiokol Chemical Corp. (AFPRO) (AF)
P.O. Box 524 84302

Mr. G. Wilford Koller
AC 801/863-3511, Ext. 32803

Magna

NAVPLANTBRREPO(SSPO) (N)
Hercules, Inc.
P.O. Box 157, 84044

Ms. M. C. Hansen
AC 801/250-5911, Ext. 3002

Ogden

Ogden Air Logistics Center (AF)
Hill AFB 84406

Mr. Thomas E. Lightfoot
Mr. Ralph Quarles
Mrs. Lola M. Phipps
AC 801/777-4145 or 777-4146

Defense Depot Ogden 84407 (DSA)

Mr. Julius L. Pretti
AC 801/399-7347

Dugway

U.S. Army Dugway Proving
    Grounds (A)
1750 S. Redwood Road 84022

Mr. Edward Coucher
AC 801/522-2102

Salt Lake City

U.S. Army Support Detachment (A)
Salt Lake, Ft. Douglas 84113

Miss Jacqueline D. Pehrson
AC 801/328-1384

Tooele

Tooele Army Depot (A)
    84074

Ms. Naomi R. Smith
AC 801/882-2550, Ext. 2607

Figure 10   (*Continued*)

Alexandria

Washington Procurement Office (A)
Directorate Procurement & Production
U.S. Army Electronics Command
5001 Eisenhower Avenue 22333

Ms. Ollie Dickens
Ms. Beverly Brueser
AC 202/274-8884

Military District of Washington (A)
Procurement Div., Bldg 15
Cameron Station 22314

Mrs. Geraldine Ude
LTC Frank W. Keel
Mr. James G. Richardson
AC 202/274-6592 or 274-6594
or 274-9172

Army Materiel Command (A)
5001 Eisenhower Avenue 22304

Mr. Jose A. Ramirez
Ms. Dolores Mahon
AC 202/274-8185 or 274-8186

U.S. Army Communications Command
CONUS (A)
Washinton Area Purchasing & Contracting
Hoffman Building
2461 Eisenhower Avenue 22331

Mr. T. Shea
AC 202/325-0530

Small Business & Economic & Utilization
Advisor's Office (DSA)
Hqs., Defense Supply Agency
Cameron Station, Room 4B 110
5010 Duke Street 22314

Mr. William C. Girard
Mr. George H. Fisher
Mr. Richard R. Stevens
Mr. Hubert L. Smoczynski
AC 202/274-6471

Defense Contract Administration
Services (DSA)
Cameron Station, Room 8B390
22314

Mr. George C. Tolton
Mr. Lloyd C. Alderman
AC 202/274-7605

Defense Documentation Center (DSA)
Cameron Station
5010 Duke Street, Bldg. 5 22314

Mr. Robert H. Rea
Mr. Robert B. Wrenn
AC 202/274-6881

Defense Fuel Supply Center (DSA)
Cameron Station
5010 Duke Street, Bldg. 8 22314

Mr. Robert J. Toporcer
AC 202/274-7428

Naval Facilities Engineering
Command (N)
Hoffman Bldg. 2, Room 11N57
200 Stovall Street 22332

Mr. Bernard Barston
AC 202/325-8550

Hqs., U.S. Army Military District
of Washington (A)
Special Asst. for Procurement
Cameron Station 22314

Mrs. Geraldine M. Ude
AC 202/274-9172

Figure 10 (*Continued*)

Arlington

Office of Naval Research (N)
Room 718 Ballston Center Towers 1
800 N. Quincy St., 22217

Mr. L. O. Lincoln
AC 202/692-4523

Office of Chief of Naval Operations (N)
Navy Department Procurement Branch
Room 772, Commonwealth Bldg.
1300 Wilson Boulevard 22209

Mr. D. H. Blankley
AC 202/694-5502

Charlottesville

The Judge Advocate General's School,
U.S. Army (A) 23901

Chief, Purchasing Office
AC 804/293-7460

Dahlgren

Naval Surface Weapons Center,
Dahlgren Laboratory (N)
Supply Dept. 22448

Mr. R. K. Payne
AC 703/663-8851

Falls Church

Military Traffic Management
Command, U.S. Army
Nassif Bldg.
5611 Columbia Pike 22041

Mr. Joseph W. Tabler
AC 202/756-2271 or 2272

Fort Belvoir

U.S. Army Engineer Center &
Fort Belvoir (A) 22060

Chief, Procurement Div., DIO
AC 703/664-3840 or 664-2234,
664-3291

U.S. Army Mobility Equipment (A)
Research and Development Center
22060

Mr. Emil Wilson
AC 703/664-5633

Figure 10 (*Continued*)

Fort Eustis

U.S. Army Air Mobility Research
& Development Laboratory (A)
23604

LTC William J. Quinn
AC 703/878-5003

U.S. Army Transportation Center (A)
Fort Eustis 23604

Chief, Procurement Div., DIO
AC 804/878-2808

Fort Lee

U.S. Army Quartermaster Center (A)
Lee 23801

Chief, Procurement Div., DIO
AC 804/734-4308

Fort Monroe

Procurement Office - DCSLOG
Hq. U.S. Army Training
& Doctrine Command (A) 23651

Mr. George O. Phillips
AC 804/727-3221

Fort Monroe 23651

Chief, Purchasing Office
AC 804/727-2630

Hampton

4500 Air Base Wing (AF)
Langley AFB 23365

Mr. William C. Cloyd
AC 703/764-3246

Tactical Air Command (AF)
Langley AFB 23365

1st Lt. Nancy L. Ladd
AC 804/764-5371 or 764-2617

Newport News

SUPSHIP, CONVERSION & REPAIR,
USN (N) 23607

Mr. K. R. Duffie
AC 804/247-4136

Norfolk

U.S. Army Engineer District,
Norfolk (A)
Fort Norfolk
803 Front Street 23510

Mr. Marvin E. Linville
AC 804/625-8201, Ext. 210

Atlantic Division (N)
Naval Facilities Engineering
Command, U.S. Naval Base, 23511

Mr. K. E. Godfrey
AC 804/444-7621

Naval Air Systems Command (N)
Representative, Atlantic
Naval Air Station 23511

Mr. G. M. Weeks
AC 804/444-4275

Figure 10 (*Continued*)

Naval Supply Center (N)
23512

Mr. K. A. Lettieri
AC 804/444-1309

Portsmouth

SUPSHIP, CONVERSION & REPAIR,
USN (N)
5th Naval District
P.O. Box 215 23705

Mr. J. P. Eastwood
AC 804/393-3269

Norfolk Naval Shipyard (N)
23709

Mr. J. P. Eastwood
AC 804/393-3269

Quantico

Marine Corps Base (N)
22134

Mrs. R. D. Patton
AC 703/640-2921

Radford

Radford Army Ammunition Plant (A)
24141

Mr. Carl R. Marple
AC 703/639-7631, Ext. 7185

Richmond

Defense General Supply Center (DSA)
Bellwood, Petersburg Pike 23297

Mr. Frank C. Paxton
AC 804/275-3617

Warrenton

Directorate for
    Procurement (IAMCPA)
USASA Materiel Support Command (A)
Vint Hill Farms Station 22186

Mrs. Barbara Stippich
AC 703/347-6272

WASHINGTON

Bremerton

Naval Supply Center (N)
Puget Sound 98314

Mr. N. W. Anderson
AC 206/478-2922

Officer In Charge of Construction (N)
Naval Facilities Engineering Command,
    Contracts - TRIDENT
5610 Kitsapway, P.O. Box UU
Wycoff Station 98310

Mr. W. N. Reichers
AC 206/478-3211

Keyport

Naval Torpedo Station 98345 (N)

Mr. R. E. Peterson
AC 206/396-2488

Figure 10 (*Continued*)

Seattle

U.S. Army Engineer District (A)
4735 East Marginal Way
  South 981?⁴

Mr. George R. Foss
AC 206/764-3773

SUPSHIP, CONVERSION & REPAIR,
  USN (N)
13th Naval District 98115

Mr. R. P. Tomkins
AC 206/527-3326

The Boeing Company (AFPRO) (AF)
  98124

Mr. Richard L. Bean
AC 206/655-3750 or 655-4086

DCASD, Seattle (DSA)
Building 5D
U.S. Naval Support Activity 98115

Mr. Oscar G. Peterson
AC 206/527-3451

Spokane

Base Procurement Office (AF)
Fairchild AFB 99011

Mr. Clayton S. Phelps
AC 509/247-2161

Tacoma

Fort Lewis 98433 (A)

Mr. August Rediske
AC 206/967-5103

Madigan Army Medical
  Center (A) 98431

Mr. William F. Clark
AC 206/967-6707

62 Military Airlift Wing BPO (AF)
McChord AFB 98436

Mr. Charles L. Wilk
AC 206/984-2531

Walla Walla

U.S. Army Engineer District (A)
Building 602, City-County Airport
  99362

Mr. Ronald G. Hallmark
AC 509/525-5174

WEST VIRGINIA

Huntington

U.S. Army Engineer District (A)
502 Eighth Street 25721

Mr. Lester L. Nida
AC 304/529-2619

Figure 10 *(Continued)*

156

WISCONSIN

Baraboo

Badger Army Ammunition Plant (A)
   53913

Mr. Jack H. Coyle
AC 608/356-5525, Ext. 543

Camp McCoy

Camp McCoy (A)
   54656

Mrs. Zelda M. Loomer
AC 608/555-1212, Ext. 3610

Milwaukee

440 Tactical Airlift Wing (AF)
General Billy Mitchell Field 53207

Ms. Elizabeth D. Parsons
AC 414/481-6400, Ext. 347

DCASD, Milwaukee (DSA)
744 North 4th Street 53203

Mr. John W. Shade
AC 414/272-8180, Ext. 207

Sturgeon Bay

SUPSHIP, CONVERSION & REPAIR,
   USN (N)
P.O. Box 26, 54235

Mr. W. J. Komorske
AC 414/743-4453

WYOMING

Cheyenne

Base Procurement Office (AF)
Francis E. Warren AFB 82001

Miss Lucille G. Keffer
AC 307/775-2964

Figure 10 (*Continued*)

review Science and Technology Objectives, Operational Requirements, Research
and Development Planning Summaries, Research and Technology Work Unit Summaries, Laboratory Program Summaries, Proceedings of Advanced Planning Briefings for Industry, and various other requirements and planning documents. At
the Air Force Information for Industry Offices, you will find Required Operational
Capability Statements used to identify operational needs and to request new or
improved capabilities; Program Management Directives that initiate, approve,
change, modify, or terminate a program; Planning Activity Reports that describe
development planning activities; Technology Needs that describe specific items
of research and technology required for the development of systems, subsystems,
or capabilities; Technical Objective Documents that describe each laboratory's
technology program; the Research Planning Guide, which describes research objectives categorized in seven technical areas and various subareas; and Program
Element Descriptive Summaries that are abridged versions of the Department
of the Air Force supporting data for RDT and E budget estimates. The Air Force
Information for Industry Offices will also supply you with information about
the Air Force Potential Contractor Program.

Do you think this information is worth anything if you want to do R&D business
with DOD? You better believe it!

Now the only question is, how do you plug into this incredible amount of market
research information? First, you must understand that much of this information
is sensitive to the defense of our country. Therefore, these services are only available to responsible U.S. citizens who have a demonstrable capability and the desire
to do R&D work for DOD. Also, you must register for access to DOD information
services through a DOD component based either on a current DOD contract or
participation in one of the military services potential contractor programs. Each
service may also have requirements peculiar to their program. For information on
how to visit these facilities, contact any of the offices at the address or telephone
number listed below.

TILO offices are:

U.S. Army Aviation Systems Command
ATTN: DRSAV-EXR
P.O. Box 209
St. Louis, MO 63166
Tel: 314/268-3821

U.S. Army Troop Support Command
ATTN: DRSTS-KT
St. Louis, MO 63120
Tel: 314/263-2346

U.S. Army Tank-Automotive Research
and Development Command

ATTN: DRDTA-REZ
Warren, MI 48090
Tel: 313/573-2372

DA/DARCOM
West Coast TILO
1030 East Green St.
Pasadena, CA 91106
Tel: 213/792-7146

U.S. Armament Research and
Development Command
ATTN: DRDAR-PMP
Dover, NJ 07801
Tel: 201/328-3047

U.S. Army Missile Research and
Development Command
ATTN: DRDMI-IBA
Redstone Arsenal, AL 35809
Tel: 205/876-2598

U.S. Army Electronics Command
ATTN: DRSEL-RD-S
Fort Monmouth, NJ 07703
Tel: 201/544-4341

U.S. Army Training Device Agency
ATTN: DRCPM-TND-SE
Orlando, FL 32813
Tel: 305/646-5761/5771

   NARDIC has three locations:

Headquarters Naval Material Command
Room 862, Crystal Plaza Building No. 5
2211 Jefferson Davis Highway (Route 1)
Arlington, VA 22202
Tel: 202/692-1113/1114

Headquarters, U.S. Army Materiel
Development and Readiness Command
Room 8S56
5001 Eisenhower Avenue
Alexandria, VA 22333
Tel: 202/274-9315

The mailing address for both of these NARDIC locations is:

Chief of Naval Material (MAT08T4)
Navy Department
Washington, D.C. 20360

NARDIC
Naval Ocean Systems Center
1030 E. Green Street
Pasadena, CA 91106
Tel: 213/792-5182

The Air Force Information for Industry Offices also have three locations:

Air Force Information for Industry Office
DRCDE-LO
5001 Eisenhower Avenue
Alexandria, VA 22333
Tel: 202/274-9305

Midwest Information for Industry
Office (MIFIO)
AFAL/TSR
Wright-Patterson AFB, OH 45433
Tel: 513/255-6731

Air Force Information for Industry Office
1030 East Green Street
Pasadena, CA 91106
Tel: 213/792-3192

If you live in Southern California, because the offices of all three military services are located in the same building in Pasadena, California, you can get free descriptive booklets of each service's program by writing to one of the offices listed.

Defense Documentation Center (DDC)

The DDC is the DOD's clearinghouse for research and development information in virtually all fields of science and technology involving subject categories from aeronautics to zoology. The DDC's mission is to exploit its immense collections of more than a million different titles to enable you to find the answer to three questions at any given time: What research is being planned? What research is currently being performed? What results were realized by completed research?
   How can this information help you? DDC information can:

• Tell you who in the DOD is interested in what
• Prevent your spending time and money doing what someone else has already done.

- Supply you with technical information that will help your own technical effort.
- Tell you what is going on in your technical area.

DDC's services include reports of completed R&D efforts; summaries of ongoing R&D projects; a referral service from a data bank of Government-sponsored activities specializing in scientific and technical information services not available in DDC; and an on-line retrieval system made up of a network of remote terminal stations linked to DDC's central computer for instant visual display of data from four major collections.

Like DOD's other R&D assistance programs, you must either be a current or potential R&D contractor. To register, write:

Defense Documentation Center
ATTN: DDC–TSR
Alexandria, VA 22314

Ask for an Information Kit. The kit will assist you in determining and/or becoming eligible for services, and contains the necessary forms and instruction for registering. In the kit you will find DD Form 1540, "Registration for Scientific and Technical Information Services," (Figure 11), and if you require access to classified data, DD Form 1541, "Facility Clearance Register" (Figure 12). Complete the appropriate form or forms, and send to the Government organization sponsoring you as a contractor or potential contractor. I will have more to say about these potential contractor programs later.

When DDC receives the completed and certified forms, a DOD User Code Number is assigned and a need-to-know profile established. You will get back from DDC a duplicate copy of DD Form 1540 along with a packet of materials that will help you get the maximum benefit from what DDC has to offer. The packet will include another form, DDC Form 256 (Figure 13), which is for ordering all the other forms for various DDC services. It may sound like a lot of paper work, but it's worth it for what DDC has to offer you if you are interested in its R&D business.

DOD's Potential Contractor Programs

The three services all maintain potential contractor programs under different names. In the Air Force and the Defense Advanced Research Projects Agency it is called the Potential Contractor Program (PCP). However, in the Navy it is the Navy/Industry Cooperative Research and Development Program (NICRAD), and in the Army it is called the Qualitative Requirements Information Program (QRI). The programs were established to assist contractors who may not have a current DOD contract, but have a demonstrable capability to do the work. It also provides a mechanism for the interchange of technical information between you and the Government, and for facilitating technology transfer. In other words, you can be plugged into Government data banks such as DDC and use TILO, NARDIC, or the

REGISTRATION FOR SCIENTIFIC AND TECHNICAL INFORMATION SERVICES
(No carbon paper is required in the completion of this form)

FOR DDC CENTRAL FILE USE

DOD USER CODE

APPROVING OFFICIAL FORWARD COMPLETED FORM TO:

DEFENSE DOCUMENTATION CENTER
ATTN: DDC-TSR-1
CAMERON STATION, BLDG. 5
ALEXANDRIA, VIRGINIA 22314

PART I - REQUESTER APPLICATION

CONTRACT TYPE

USER TYPE

FACILITY CLEARANCE

CONTRACT CLEARANCE

1. ORGANIZATION NAME

2. MAILING ADDRESS (Street, City, State, ZIP Code)

3. ATTENTION LINE (Name and Organizational Title of Requesting Official)

4. TELEPHONE NUMBER (Include Area Code)

5. SIGNATURE

6. DATE

7. PRIME CONTRACT/GRANT OR PROGRAM NO. (Enter one only)

8. EXPIRATION DATE OF ITEM 7

9. CLASSIFICATION REQUIRED
☐ UNCLASSIFIED ☐ NATO CLASSIFIED
☐ CONFIDENTIAL ☐ RESTRICTED DATA
☐ SECRET ☐ CNWDI

PART II - PRIME CONTRACTOR APPROVAL (If Part I is a Subcontractor)

10. ORGANIZATION NAME AND ADDRESS

11. SUB-CONTRACT NUMBER

12. EXPIRATION DATE OF ITEM 11

13. TYPED NAME AND SIGNATURE

14. DATE

PART III - CERTIFICATION AND APPROVAL

15. ORGANIZATION NAME AND ADDRESS

16. TELEPHONE NUMBER (Include Area Code)

17. DATE

18. TYPED NAME AND TITLE OF APPROVING OFFICIAL

19. SIGNATURE

THE DDC CENTRAL FILES MUST BE NOTIFIED IMMEDIATELY OF ANY CHANGES TO INFORMATION PROVIDED ON THIS FORM

(FOR DDC USE ONLY)

PART IV - SUBJECT FIELDS OF INTEREST

Circle required codes below. Mandatory only for Classified Services. First Number is the Subject Field; the second is the more specific group. See Subject Fields on Reverse.

01-01	06-12	11-01	15-05	19-04	
01-02	06-13	11-02	15-06	19-05	
01-03	06-14	11-03	15-07	19-06	
01-04	06-15	11-04	16-01	19-07	
01-05	06-16	11-05	16-02	19-08	
02-01	06-17	11-06	16-03	20-01	
02-02	06-18	11-07	16-04	20-02	
02-03	06-19	11-08	16-04.1	20-03	
02-04	06-20	11-09	16-04.2	20-04	
02-05	06-21	11-10	16-04.3	20-05	
02-06	07-01	11-11	17-01	20-06	
03-01	07-02	11-12	17-02	20-07	
03-02	07-03	12-01	17-02.1	20-08	
03-03	07-04	12-02	17-03	20-09	
04-01	07-05	13-01	17-04	20-10	
04-02	08-01	13-02	17-05	20-11	
05-01	08-02	13-03	17-06	20-12	
05-02	08-03	13-04	17-07	20-13	
05-03	08-04	13-05	17-08	20-14	
05-04	08-05	13-06	17-09	21-01	
05-05	08-06	13-07	17-10	21-02	
05-06	08-07	13-08	18-01	21-03	
05-07	08-08	13-09	18-02	21-04	
05-08	08-09	13-10	18-03	21-05	
05-09	08-10	13-10.1	18-04	21-06	
05-10	08-11	13-11	18-05	21-07	
05-11	08-12	13-12	18-06	21-08	
06-01	08-13	13-13	18-07	21-08.1	
06-02	08-14	14-01	18-08	21-08.2	
06-03	09-01	14-02	18-09	21-09	
06-04	09-02	14-03	18-10	21-09.1	
06-05	09-03	14-04	18-11	21-09.2	
06-06	09-04	14-05	18-12	22-01	
06-07	09-05	15-01	18-13	22-02	
06-08	09-06	15-02	18-14	22-03	
06-09	10-01	15-03	19-01	22-04	
06-10	10-02	15-03.1	19-02		
06-11	10-03	15-04	19-03		

Figure 11. Form DD 1540/Registration for Scientific and Technical Information Services.

FACILITY CLEARANCE REGISTER

INSTRUCTIONS

FOR CONTRACTOR:

1. Complete Part I in duplicate *(three copies if you desire a file copy).*

2. Forward two copies to the **Defense Contract Administration Services Region** *(DCASR)* having security cognizance over your company.

3. Separate facility clearance registers are required for each location to which classified material will be sent.

FOR COGNIZANT DCASR:

1. Complete Part II.

2. Forward one copy to DDC at the address given below.

3. If you have no record of facility clearance, return forms to contractor with appropriate explanation.

PART I

1. NAME AND MAILING ADDRESS OF FACILITY *(Classified material will be forwarded to this address)*	2. STREET ADDRESS *(Actual location if different from Item 1)*	
3. TYPED NAME AND TITLE OF REQUESTER	4. SIGNATURE	5. DATE

PART II

6. THE FACILITY LISTED IN PART I IS CLEARED TO RECEIVE AND STORE DEPARTMENT OF DEFENSE CLASSIFIED MATERIAL UP TO AND INCLUDING

☐ SECRET ☐ CONFIDENTIAL

(Any change affecting this facility clearance will be reported immediately to DDC.)

7. NAME AND ADDRESS OF THE DCASR	8. TYPED NAME AND TITLE OF CERTIFYING OFFICIAL	
	9. SIGNATURE	10. DATE

11. MAIL TO: Defense Documentation Center
Cameron Station
Alexandria, Virginia 22314

REMARKS

Figure 12. Form DD 1541/Facility Clearance Register.

163

FORMS REQUEST

INSTRUCTIONS: *Complete appropriate blocks and forward the original and one copy to the attention of* **DDC-TSR-1.** *Quantities requested should provide for three months supply. No carbon paper is required in the completion of this form.*

FORM NUMBER	TITLE	TITLE	UNIT	QUANTITY REQUIRED
DDC 1	DOCUMENT REQUEST	REQUEST COPIES OF REPORTS IN MICROFORM OR PAPER COPY (ESTABLISHED NTIS DEPOSIT ACCOUNT REQUIRED)	TAB CARD	
DDC 4	R&T WORK UNIT SYMMARY/ REPORT BIBLIOGRAPHY REQUEST	REQUEST REPORT BIBLIOGRAPHIES AND WORK UNIT SUMMARIES	4-PART SET CARBONLESS PAPER	
DDC 50	DDC ACCESSION NOTICE	PROVIDE CONTRIBUTING ORGANI- ZATION WITH AD NUMBER ASSIGNED TO REPORT	CARD	
DDC 55	REQUEST FOR LIMITED DOCUMENT	PROVIDE A MEANS OF OBTAINING RELEASE APPROVAL WHEN PRIOR RELEASE AUTHORIZATION IS REQUIRED	4-PART SET CARBONLESS PAPER	
DDC 64	RDT&E INFORMATION SYSTEMS REQUEST	PROVIDE FOR SPECIAL DISPLAYS WHEN REQUIRED IN A WUIS SUM- MARY. (FOR U. S. GOVERNMENT ORGANIZATIONS ONLY)	4-PART SET CARBONLESS PAPER	
DDC 256	FORMS REQUEST	PROVIDES A MEANS FOR ORDERING SUPPLIES OF FORMS	3-PART SET CARBONLESS PAPER	
DD 1540	REGISTRATION FOR SCIENTIFIC AND TECHNICAL INFORMATION	PROVIDE MEANS FOR REGISTERING WITH DDC FOR DEPT. OF DEFENSE SCIENTIFIC AND TECHNICAL INFORMATION	5-PART SET CARBONLESS PAPER	
DD 1541	FACILITY CLEARANCE REGISTER	REGISTER FACILITY CLEARANCE WITH DDC FOR CLASSIFIED SERVICE (NOT REQUIRED FOR U. S. GOVERNMENT ORGANIZATIONS)	3-PART SET CARBONLESS PAPER	

REMARKS

ORGANIZATION *(Complete name and address, including zip code)*	USER CODE
	NTIS DEPOSIT ACCOUNT NUMBER
	DATE REQUESTED
REQUESTER'S NAME AND TITLE	TELEPHONE NUMBER *(Include Area Code or Autovon No.)*

Figure 13. Form DDC 256/Defense Documentation Center/Forms Request.

164

Air Force Information Industry Office even though you may not have a current Government contract. To investigate these programs, make your initial contacts as follows:

Air Force Potential Contractor Program (PCP):

Headquarters, Air Force Systems Command
ATTN: DLXL
Andrews Air Force Base
Washington, D.C. 20331
Tel: 301/981–4632

Army Qualitative Requirements Information Program (QRI):

Commander
Armament Research and Development
Command (ARRADCOM)
ATTN: DRDAR-P-MP
Dover, NJ 07801
Tel: 201/328–3047

Department of the Navy/Industry Cooperative R and D Program (NICRAD):

(East Coast)
Chief of Navy Material (MAT03T2)
Navy Department
Washington, D.C. 20360
Tel: 202/692–0515

(West Coast)
Navy Research and Development
Information Center West
Naval Undersea Center
1030 East Green Street
Pasadena, CA 91106
Tel: 213/796–8898

DARPA Potential Contractor Program (DARPA/PC):

Defense Advanced Research Projects Agency
ATTN: TIO
1400 Wilson Blvd.
Arlington, VA 22209
Tel: 202/694–5919

Department of Commerce NTIS Program

The Department of Commerce does several nice things for the small businessman interested in doing business with Uncle Sam. One of these is publishing the *Commerce Business Daily*, which I will talk about in the next chanpter. The other is to run the NTIS. NTIS stands for National Technical Information Service, which is the central source of the public sale of U.S. and foreign Government-sponsored research, development, and engineering reports and other work prepared by Government agencies and/or funded by the national or local Government.

The NTIS ships no less than 20,000 information products daily and supplies its customers with about 4 million documents and microforms annually. The whole NTIS collection exceeds 1 million titles, about 105,000 of which are of foreign origin. All of these are for sale. NTIS's services include technical summaries of Government research published biweekly with an index; a bibliographical data file available on annual lease; *Tech Notes*, a biweekly publication that contains several one-page summaries of new applications for technology as developed by nine different federal agencies and their contractors; 26 different *Weekly Government Abstract* newsletters of research summaries on subjects ranging from administration to urban technology; custom data searches to meet special needs; completed data searches at $25 each; a list of Government inventions available for licensing; and much more. Clearly, NTIS can be a source of low-cost information on a wide variety of subjects. For a complete description of the services that NTIS offers, write:

U.S. Department of Commerce
National Technical Information Service
5285 Port Royal Road
Springfield, VA 22161

Ask for their free catalogue of information services. You will be amazed at what is available to you.

Government-Industry Data Exchange Program (GIDEP)

GIDEP is a cooperative Government-industry program that is managed and funded by the Government. The basic idea behind GIDEP is to reduce or eliminate expenditures of time and money by making maximum use of existing knowledge through Government-industry exchange. And there is certainly enough participating horsepower on the Government side. Participating agencies include DOD, NASA, the Federal Aviation Administration, the Department of Energy, the SBA, the National Security Agency, the GSA, and the Canadian Department of Defense.

Here is how it works. Each participant, Government or industry, submits test reports, calibration procedures, failure rate and mode data, and related technical information to the GIDEP operation center. The operations center reviews, processes, computerizes, indexes, and microfilms the documents involved for distribution to participants.

As a user, you have access to this data through two systems: the ALERT System in which you are notified of problem areas, and the Urgent Data Request (UDR) System in which you can question other participants about specific problems.

Participants are not assessed fees for this valuable service. However, you must provide an internal program in your firm to include someone to represent your firm with GIDEP (this can be you, yourself), a microfilm reader-printer, and adequate working area within your facility.

If you're interested in participating in GIDEP, the program is managed by the Navy. Write to:

GIDEP Operations Center
Naval Fleet Missile Systems Analysis
and Evaluation Group
Corona, CA 91720
Tel: 714/736-4677

Other Government Agency Programs

Many Government agencies, large and small, have developed their own programs to help the small businessman. To find out about these and get help, get a copy of The Complete U.S. Government Purchasing and Sales Directory from the Government Printing Office. You will find over 200 pages listing additional Government offices that are potentially interested in doing business with you.

You are now ready to make money doing business with Uncle Sam.

Up to know what we've done has been preparatory for what is coming in the following chapters. We're going to learn how to develop the Government customers we've found, the ways of doing business with the Government, how to develop a marketing strategy and a marketing action plan, and finally, how to bid, write, and win with your proposal.

Let's start with the next chapter and we'll learn how to develop the Government customers we've found.

Chapter 4

HOW TO GET GOVERNMENT CUSTOMERS TO BUY YOUR PRODUCT OR SERVICE

In Chapter 1, we learned how to get started in Government contracting. In Chapter 2, we explored the thousands of opportunities and millions of dollars in Government business potentially available to us. In the last chapter we found out how we get help from Uncle Sam in finding potential customers. In this chapter, we are going to learn how to get these potential customers to buy from us.

HOW TO READ THE *COMMERCE BUSINESS DAILY (CBD)* AND HOW TO USE IT

We talked about the *CBD* in Chapter 1. I have saved it for this chapter because it is a major tool in getting potential Government customers to buy from you.

Let's take a look at Figure 5, which is taken from the front page of a typical issue of the *CBD*. Under the general heading of "U.S. Government Procurement," you will see some typical notices of procurement invitations. These notices are listed under more than 100 different classifications, divided into two categories: "services" and "supplies." A complete list of *CBD* goods and services can be found in Figure 14a & b. For example, typical service classifications might be for "Experimental, Developmental, Test and Research Work," "Expert and Consultant Services," and "Maintenance and Repair of Equipment." Typical supplies classifications might be for "Weapons," "Metalworking Machinery," and "Pumps and Compressors." Most service classifications advertise RFPs, while most supplies classifications advertise IFBs. Remember, the RFPs require a price plus a proposal, while the IFB is awarded on bid price only.

A separate section for contract awards over $25,000 is classified in the same manner as the procurement invitations.

Reading the notices requires a little practice. The basics you already know. You must know the difference between RFP, RFQ, and IFB to know what is required. You will find a description of *CBD* legend in Figure 15 and a list of numbered notes in Figure 16. Using these as an aid, let's look at a couple of notices and see how you decipher them.

168

Services

A	Experimental, Developmental, Test, and Research Work	R	Architect-Engineer Service
H	Expert and Consultant Services	S	Housekeeping Services
J	Maintenance and Repair of Equipment	T	Photographic, Mapping, Printing, and Publication Services
K	Modification, Alteration, and Rebuilding of Equipment	U	Training Services
L	Technical Representative Services	V	Transportation Services
M	Operation and Maintenance of Government-Owned Facility	W	Lease or Rental, except Transportation Equipment
N	Installation of Equipment	X	Miscellaneous (Services)
O	Funeral and Chaplain Services	Y	Construction (Various)
P	Salvage Services	Z	Maintenance, Repair, and Alteration of Real Property
Q	Medical Services		

Figure 14a. Goods and Services Listed in the *Commerce Business Daily*.

Supplies, Equipment, and Materiel

10	Weapons	40	Rope, Cable, Chain, and Fittings
11	Nuclear Ordnance	41	Refrigeration and Air-Conditioning Equipment
12	Fire Control Equipment		
13	Ammunition and Explosives	42	Fire-Fighting, Rescue, and Safety Equipment
14	Guided Missiles		
15	Aircraft and Airframe Structural Components	43	Pumps and Compressors
16	Aircraft Components and Accessories	44	Furnace, Steam Plant, and Drying Equipment; Nuclear Reactors
17	Aircraft Launching, Landing, and Ground Handling Equipment	45	Plumbing, Heating, and Sanitation Equipment
18	Space Vehicles	46	Water Purification and Sewage Treatment Equipment
19	Ships, Small Craft, Pontoons, and Floating Docks	47	Pipe, Tubing, Hose, and Fittings
20	Ship and Marine Equipment	48	Valves
22	Railway Equipment	49	Maintenance and Repair Shop Equipment
23	Motor Vehicles, Trailers, and Cycles		
24	Tractors	51	Hand Tools
25	Vehicular Equipment Components	52	Measuring Tools
26	Tires and Tubes	53	Hardware and Abrasives
28	Engines, Turbines, and Components	54	Prefabricated Structures and Scaffolding
29	Engine Accessories	55	Lumber, Millwork, Plywood, and Veneer
30	Mechanical Power Transmission Equipment	56	Construction and Building Materials
31	Bearing	58	Communications Equipment
32	Woodworking Machinery and Equipment	59	Electrical and Electronic Equipment Components
34	Metalworking Machinery		
35	Service and Trade Equipment	61	Electric Wire; Power and Distribution Equipment
36	Special Industry Machinery		
37	Agricultural Machinery and Equipment	62	Lighting Fixtures and Lamps
38	Construction, Mining, Excavating, and Highway Maintenance Equipment	63	Alarm and Signal Systems
		65	Medical, Dental, and Veterinary Equipment and Supplies
39	Materials-Handling Equipment	66	Instruments and Laboratory Equipment

67 Photographic Equipment
68 Chemicals and Chemical Products
69 Training Aids and Devices
70 General Purpose ADP Equipment,
    Software, Supplies, and Support
    Equipment
71 Furniture
72 Household and Commercial Furnishings
    and Appliances
73 Food Preparation and Serving Equipment
74 Office Machines, Visible Record
    Equipment, and Data-Processing
    Equipment
75 Office Supplies and Devices
76 Books, Maps, and Other Publications
78 Recreational and Athletic Equipment
79 Cleaning Equipment and Supplies

80 Brushes, Paints, Sealers, and Supplies
81 Containers, Packaging, and Packing
    Supplies
83 Textiles, Leather, Furs, Apparel, and Shoe
    Findings; Tents and Flags
84 Clothing, Individual Equipment, and
    Insignia
85 Toiletries
87 Agricultural Supplies
89 Subsistence
91 Fuels, Lubricants, Oils, and Waxes
93 Nonmetallic Fabricated Materials
94 Nonmetallic Crude Materials
95 Metal Bars, Sheets, and Shapes
96 Ores, Minerals, and Their Primary Products
99 Miscellaneous

Figure 14b.   Supplies, Equipment, and Material.

Description of Legend

❶ The Procurement item is 100 percent set aside for small business concerns.

❷ A partial quantity or a portion of the procurement item is set aside for small business concerns.

❸ The contract is a labor surplus area set-aside under the provisions of Defense Manpower Policy No. 4A (DMP-4A).

❹ Notices of intention to purchase which are published before the IFB's are issued directly to those requesting the proposal.

❺ The procurement will be made in accordance with either ASPR part 5, paragraph 2-501 (Military agencies) or FPR part 1-2, paragraph 1, 2.501 (Civil agencies) and is the 1st step of a two step formally advertised procurement. Only those firms submitting qualified responses on the 1st step will receive notifications when the purchase is made.

★ This synopsis is published for informational purposes to alert potential subcontractors and/or suppliers of the proposed procurement. Additional proposals are not solicited.

NUMBERED NOTES are published only on the first working day of each week. The pages containing the "notes" should be retained for reference.

GPO 820—629

Figure 15.   *Commerce Business Daily* legend.

NUMBERED NOTE SYSTEM

If a "numbered note" is included in the item description of a proposed procurement, the note referred to must be read as part of the item.

1. This is the non-set-aside portion only. An additional quantity is reserved for award only to Labor Surplus Area Concerns under the procedures set forth in Department of Defense Armed Forces, Procurement Regulations, Section ASPR 1-804. A Company interested in becoming CERTIFIED ELIGIBLE Labor Surplus Area Concern, as that term is defined in ASPR 1-801, should contact the nearest local office of the appropriate State Employment Service for information and application forms. While certificates are issued only by local public employment offices, information may also be obtained from regional offices of the Manpower Administration of the U. S. Department of Labor in Atlanta (404/526-5411); Boston (617/223-6784); Chicago (312/353-4258); Dallas (214/749-2721); Denver (303/297-3091); Kansas City (861/374-3790); New York (212/971-5445); Philadelphia (215/438-5401); San Francisco (415/556-7414); and Seattle (206/583-7700). If regional offices are unable to supply the requested information business firms may write to the U.S. Training and Employment Service, Manpower Administration, U. S. Department of Labor, Washington, D.C. 20210 (ATTENTION: METTJ).

All bidders are cautioned that if eligibility for preference in award of set-aside portions is claimed, a certificate of eligibility must be furnished with the bid.

3. Solicitation Forms will be made available as soon as opening date is established.

4. Availability of Specifications, Drawings and Specification Exception. Specifications available at Commanding Officer, Naval Publications and Forms Center, 5801 Tabor Ave., Philadelphia, PA., 19120. Drawings and Spec., exceptions available at Defense Industrial Supply Center, Attn: Code PDA, Bldg., 36, 700 Robbins Avenue, Philadelphia PA., 19111.

5. The proposed procurement has been synopsized solely for the purpose of reflecting sub-contracting opportunities which may or may not be available. The firms listed in the Commerce Business Daily are the only firms known to the procuring activity which have the facilities, data and technical knowledge necessary to meet the procurement requirements. For those reasons, solicitation has been limited to those.

Any firm not listed in this published notice may obtain a bid set for direct bidding only by furnishing a written statement signed by a corporate official of the company, certifying that the company possesses the latest data and the facilities, equipment and technical know-how to perform as a prime contractor on the procurement concerned.

Requests for bid sets for this procurement will not be honored without the prescribed certificate from corporate level.

6. Copies of Invitation for Bids and Requests for Proposals may be examined at the following locations:

• Tobyhanna Army Depot, Tobyhanna, PA., 18466
• Fort Monmouth Procurement Division, Procurement and Production Directorate, U. S. Army Electronics Command, Fort Monmouth, N.J. 07703.
• Defense Contract Administration Services Region, 11099 South La Cienega Blvd., Los Angeles, CA., 90045.
• Defense Contract Administration Services Region, 666 Summer St., Boston, MA., 02210.

7. This is the second part of a two part solicitation. The first part is the Master Solicitation. Requests for copies of the solicitation Part II should request a copy of the Master Solicitation (Part 1) if the prospective bidder has not received a copy.

Figure 16. *CBD* numbered note system.

8. Qualified Products List Information, Services of Dept., of Defense and General Services Administration. To obtain products of requisite quality, certain government specifications call for qualification testing and approval of the products covered thereunder for listing on Qualified Products Lists. In such cases, qualification of specific products is required prior to the opening of bids or the award of negotiated contracts.

This publicizes the intention of the government to require qualification approval of and establish Qualified Products Lists on item covered by the specifications indicated. Suppliers are urged to write appropriate activities responsible for qualification as cited in the specification and to request information in the procedures for qualifying their products.

9. Copies of Military and Federal Specifications and Standards, Qualified Products Lists and Military Handbooks may be obtained from Commanding Officer, Naval Publications and Forms Center (NPFC), 5801 Tabor Ave., Philadelphia, PA., 19120. A request can be initiated by telephone (215/697-3321), telegraph, or mail in any form. However, it is preferred that private industry use a simplified order form, DD Form 1425, which includes a self-addressed label. Once a customer orders documents, NPFC will automatically provide the customer with sufficient blank forms to continually order in the preferred manner. Patterns, Drawings, Deviation Lists, Purchase Descriptions, etc., are not stocked at NPFC.

10. Interested firms may request copies of this proposed procurement from Commander, Naval Electronic Systems Command, Code ELEX 2042. Navy Department, Washington, D.C. 20360.

11. In connection with this proposed procurement, information as to whether your concern is considered small or large business is desired. For this item the general definition is to be used to determine whether your firm is either small or large, is as follows:

"A small business concern is a concern that is independently owned and operated is not dominant in the field of operation in which it is bidding on Government contracts and with its affiliates, the number of employees does not exceed 500 persons."

State in your response the size status of your concern utilizing the above definition.

12. This is a Small Business Set-Aside. Drawings and Specifications will be issued to the extent available, on a first received, first served basis.

13. This proposed procurement is under a 100 per cent small business set aside, the size standard for which is a concern, including its affiliates, having average annual sales or receipts for its preceding three fiscal years not in excess of $2,000,000.

14. This proposed procurement is under a 100 per cent small business set aside, the size standard for which is a concern, including its affiliates, having average annual sales or receipts for its preceding three fiscal years not in excess of $4,000,000.

16. Copies of Military and Federal Specifications, Standards and Qualified Products Lists May Be Examined at the Defense Personnel Support Center, or obtained from Commanding Officer, Naval Publications and Forms Centers, 5801 Tabor Avenue, Philadelphia PA., 19120. Such requests should be made on DD form 1425 (Specifications and Standards Requisition) indicating the specification title, number, date and any applicable amendment thereto. Requests may be made by letter if DD Form 1425 is not available or telegram in urgent situations. Telegrams should be addressed to Naval Publications and Forms Center, address above. All other specifications and Patterns, Drawings, Deviation Lists, Purchase Descriptions, Interim Purchase Descriptions and other documents referred to in specification may be obtained upon application to: Defense Personnel Support Center, Directorate of Clothing & Textiles, 2800 South 20th Street, Philadelphia PA., 19101, Attn: DPSC-TTFT or by calling 271-3230, Area Code. 215.

17. Sponsored by the Air Force Rocket Propulsion Laboratory, Research and Technology Division, Air Force Systems Command.

18. The proposed procurement is under a 100 per cent small business set aside, the size standard for which is a concern including its affiliates, having an average annual sale or receipts for its preceding three fiscal years not in excess of $4,500,000.

Figure 16   (*Continued*)

19. The proposed procurement is under a 100 per cent small business set aside, the size standard for which is a concern including its affiliates, having an average annual sale or receipts for its preceding three fiscal years not in excess of $7,000,000.

20. The proposed procurement is under a 100 per cent small business set aside, the size standard for which is a concern including its affiliates, having an average annual sale or receipts for its preceding three fiscal years not in excess of $5,000,000.

21. Requests for solicitation forms for the procurement of Clothing, Textiles and Equipment should be sent to the Defense Personnel Support Center, Procurement and Production Division, Directorate of Clothing and Textiles, 2800 South 20th Street, Philadelphia PA 19101. ATTN: DPSC-TPP, Procurement Processing Branch.

23. Copies of IFB's and RFP's may be obtained by applying to Bid Room (Code 205.4C) Bldg. 311-4E. Naval Regional Procurement Department, Naval Supply Center, Oakland, California 94625, or by calling Area Code 415/466-6220.

24. A request for copies for the proposal should be received by issuing office not later than ten days from the date of listing of this synopsis in the Commerce Business Daily.

Request for proposal (RFP) availability is limited and will be furnished to the requestor on a first received, first served basis until the supply is exhausted (which could be before the 10 day period has elapsed).

Telephone requests will not be honored.

25. Requests for copies of this solicitation must be postmarked not later than 10 days from the date of publication of this synopsis in the CBD. Requests postmarked later than that date will not be honored. Requests may be made by letter or telegram but telephone requests will not be honored. Availability of the solicitation is limited and will be furnished on a first received, first served basis. Please furnish a self-addressed stamped envelope for the solicitation requested or if a non-availability notice is desired.

26. Complete data not available. Available specifications, plans or drawings relating to the procurement described, do not fully provide all necessary manufacturing and construction detail.

27. It is suggested that small business firms or others interested in subcontracting opportunities in connection with the described procurement, make direct contact with the firm(s) listed.

28. Solicitations issued by the Defense Construction Supply Center, Columbus, OH 43215, are available for inspection at DCSC and the following DCASR Offices: New York, Atlanta, Dallas and Los Angeles.

29. Requests for copies of this solicitation should be received by Defense Construction Supply Center, Columbus, OH 43215, Attn: DCSC-POAB, not later than 10 days from the date of listing of this synopsis. Such requests may also be made by telephone (614/236-3446). Availability of the solicitation is limited and will be furnished on a first received, first served basis. If nonavailability notice is desired, furnish self-addressed, stamped envelope.

30. If drawings are cited in the solicitation, a written request for same may be submitted to Directorate of Technical Operations, Defense Construction Supply Center, Columbus, OH 43215, Attn.; DCSC-STR, or by calling 614/236-2344 or 236-2612. Requests should give the solicitation number and the bid opening date. Only drawings referenced in the solicitation will be furnished by DCSC. Copies of unclassified federal, military, and other specifications and standards (excluding commercial) may be obtained upon a written request using DD Forms 1425 to Commanding Officer, U. S. Naval Publications and Forms Center, 5801 Tabor Ave., Philadelphia, PA 19120, or by Telex 834295, Western Union 710-670-1685, or telephone (215/697-3321) in case of urgency. Commercial specifications, standards, and descriptions are not available from government sources, but must be obtained from the publishers.

31. Responses submitted should be in one copy only. Each response must be identified by the area number (reference) at the top (beginning) of each technical description. Responses should be sent to: Directorate of R&D Procurement, Attn.: ASD/PMR-1, Wright-Patterson AFB, OH 45433. Non-technical assistance may be secured by calling 513/255-3825.

Figure 16 *(Continued)*

32. When requesting bid set(s), provide information as to whether your organization (together with its affiliate) is a large or small business.

33. In accordance with the DOD High Dollar Spare Parts Breakout Program, only the firms who were identified during technical screening as either the prime equipment manufacturer or as the actual manufacturer of the part being procured have been solicited. Other offerors proposing to manufacture the part will not be considered for award under this solicitation UNLESS: (1) the offeror submits prior to or concurrent with his proposal evidence of having satisfactorily produced the required part(s) for the government or the prime equipment manufacturer(s); OR (2) the offeror submits prior to or concurrent with his proposal such complete and current engineering data for the part(s) (including manufacturing control drawings, qualification test reports, quality assurance procedures, etc.) as may be required for evaluation purposes to determine the acceptability of the part as supplied by your firm for government use.

A dealer offering newly manufactured items must submit concurrent with his proposal a certification specifying that the required part(s) will be obtained from one of the sources who has satisfactorily supplied the same part(s) to the government or the prime equipment manufacturer(s).

An offeror proposing to provide surplus parts manufactured by one of the sources identified during technical screening shall so notify the procuring contracting officer (PCO) at least ten days prior to the opening of bids or proposals. (See Note 36 below). The government will determine on a case-by-case basis, whether or not surplus parts can be considered in view of the criticality of the parts, and the impossibility of applying normal in-process inspection and quality assurance procedures to surplus parts. If it is determined that surplus parts can be considered, the solicitation will be amended to incorporate inspection criteria adequate to establish that the surplus parts conform to the applicable specifications.

If you desire to be solicited as a potential manufacturer for future procurements of this part(s), do not request the solicitation, but contact the procuring activity indicated in the synopsis for further information.

34. An additional approximate equal quantity being reserved for Labor Surplus Area Concerns under a partial determination, the procedures for which are outlined under ASPR 1-804.

35. Award will be made only for products which are qualified for inclusion in the Qualified Products List (QPL) at the time set for openings of bids, or award for negotiated contracts.

36. Concurrent with the notification of the PCO that surplus material is being offered, the offeror will provide the following certificate (If the material being offered is former government surplus, this certificate must be provided in addition to the information required by ASPR 1-1208 Government Surplus.)

The undersigned hereby certifies that the material to be furnished in response to solicitation (insert solicitation number) was manufactured by the original design manufacturer and/or his approved source. (Indicate quantities of each manufacturer). This material is new, unused, meets applicable specifications and is offered without rework or refurbishment of any kind. The undersigned further certifies that no changes have been made to the materials being offered. The quantities of material offered are available for shipment. The material (is/is not) in the original, unbroken container which is dated (show packaging date, if known, or indicate the type and condition of packaging). The offeror (does/does not) have in his possession the drawings/specifications applicable to the item(s) offered. (If drawings/specifications) are available indicate the issue letter and date of such drawings/specifications). The offeror (does/does not) agree to release drawings/specifications for Government quality assurance use upon request of the PCO.

37. Procurement is for a kit used in the overhaul or repair of government equipment. Kit consists of both competitive and source-directed items. Source-directed items are so designated to assure requisite interchangeability and reliability. Such parts must be furnished by USAF-approved sources shown herein, or at the discretion of the contracting officer, from a currently USAF approved source not shown, evidence of approval must accompany the offer; otherwise proposed substitute items will not be considered for award. Acceptance under previous awards of substitute items will not be considered to constitute prior approval. If you are interested in furnishing parts source-directed here, in future buys, contact OCAMA/PPDM, Tinker AFB, OK 73145, for specific information on how to be approved as a supplier, furnishing specific FSN and/or part numbers. Complete data (specifications, plans and drawings) for source-directed items are not available. Data for competitive items will be furnished with the solicitation.

Figure 16 *(Continued)*

38. The data applicable to this procurement does not describe the required unusual or unique manufacturing processes in sufficient detail to insure interpretation by industry as a whole. This solicitation is issued to firms known to this procuring activity which have the facilities and technical knowledge necessary to meet the procurement requirement. Any other firms possessing the capability of producing this item, should direct request for bid sets to Warner Robins ALC/PPDA, Robins Air Force Base, GA 31098 as appropriate.

39. Short-lead time for bidding necessary because of urgency of procurement.

40. This notice does not solicit additional proposals but is issued for the benefit of prospective subcontractors.

41. This notice does not solicit proposals but is issued for the benefit of prospective subcontractors with appropriate security clearance. Make direct contact with above firm(s) for subcontracting opportunities.

42. This proposed procurement is under a 100 percent small business set aside, the size standard for which is 500 employees.

43. This proposed procurement is under a 100 percent small business set aside, the size standard for which is 750 employees.

44. This proposed procurement is under a 100 percent small business set aside, the size standard for which is 1,000 employees.

45. This proposed procurement is under a 100 percent small business set aside, the size standard for which is 1,500 employees.

46. Synopsis published for informational purposes only. Solicitation documents are not available.

47. Availability of the solicitation is limited and will be furnished upon request on a first received, first served basis until supply is exhausted. If not received within a reasonable period of time, it will be understood the supply is exhausted. Copies of this solicitation may be viewed at the issuing office and at the followind DCASR Offices: New York, Atlanta, Dallas, and Los Angeles. Letter bids will be considered and must include as a minimum, a statement accepting all terms and conditions of the solicitation, item number, quantity, discount terms, delivery, F.O.B. point, and size of business. The outside of the envelope must be clearly identified as a letter bid giving solicitation number and opening date.

48. Security clearance will be required of all bidders or offerors.

49. Security clearance will be required of the successful bidder or offeror.

51. The General Provisions applicable to this solicitation will be either HEW Forms -313, -314, -315, -315A, -316 or SF-32. To conserve paper General Provisions will be mailed with solicitation only if specifically requested in writing at the time solicitation is requested. This office maintains a listing of offerors who have previously been provided copies of the General Provisions, so that no duplicate copies will be mailed. The information above apr'es only to those solicitations issued by the Department of Health, Education & Welfare, OS, Procurement and Contracts Section, Room 1741, HEW-N, 330 Independence Ave., SW, Washington, D.C. 20201.

52. An additional approximate equal quantity is being reserved for small business under a partial determination, the procedures for which are outlined under ASPR 1-706. The small business size standard for this procurement is 500 employees.

53. The proposed procurement is under a 100 per cent small business set aside, the size standard for which is a concern including its affiliates, having an average annual sale or receipts for its preceding three fiscal years not in excess of $12,000,000.

56. Requests for copies of this proposed procurement should be received not later than 10 days from the date of publication of this notice in order to facilitate mailing of same to the extent copies are available directly to the inquirer at time of issuance. Availability of the solicitation is limited and will be furnished on a first received, first served basis.

57. Requests for copies of this proposed procurement should be received as soon as possible in order to facilitate mailing of same to the extent copies are available, directly to the inquirer at time of issuance.

58. Bid sets may be obtained by applying to the Naval Regional Procurement Office, Bldg. 200, 4th Floor, Washington Navy Yard, Washington, DC 20374.

59. Interested firms may request copies of this proposed procurement from Commander, Naval Sea Systems Command, Code 0215, Washington, D.C. 20362, or by phone to AC 202/692-7508.

Figure 16 *(Continued)*

175

60. Request for unpriced technical proposals pursuant to Two-Step Formal Advertising procedures in Sect II, Part 5 of the ASPR or Part 1-2, Subpart 5 of the FPR. Under Step One, offerors are to submit only one technical proposal (unless multiple proposals are authorized by the request for technical proposal) in sufficient detail to enable engineering personnel to make a thorough evaluation and arrive at a sound determination as to whether or not the proposed product meets the requirements of the Government. Price or cost estimates are not to be included in this first step. Invitation for bids (Step 2) will be issued at a later date to those firms whose technical proposals are determined to be acceptable.

61. Requests for solicitation forms should be sent to Director, Procurement Directorate, US Army Armament Research and Development Command, Dover, NJ 07801, in sufficient time to be received not later than 10 days from date of publication of this notice. Requests will be furnished on a first received, first served basis until supply is exhausted. If nonavailability notice is requested, furnish self-addressed stamped envelope.

62. Architect-engineer firms which meet the requirements described in this announcement are invited to submit: (1) a Standard Form 254, Architect-Engineer and Related Services Questionnaire: (2) a Standard Form 255, Architect-Engineer and Related Services Questionnaire for Specific Project, when requested; and (3) any requested supplemental data to the procurement office shown. Firms having a current Standard Form 251 or 254 on file with the procurement office are not required to resubmit this form. Firms responding to this announcement before the closing date will be considered for selection, subject to any limitations indicated with respect to size and geographic location of firm, specialized technical expertise or other requirements as listed. Following an initial evaluation of the qualification and performance data submitted, three or more firms considered to be the most highly qualified to provide the services required will be chosen for interview.

The Department of Defense policy for selection of architect-engineer firms is not based upon competitive bidding procedures, but rather upon the professional qualifications necessary for the satisfactory performance of the professional services required, subject to the following additional considerations: (1) specialized experience of the firm in the type of work required; (2) capacity of the firm to accomplish the work in the required time; (3) past experience, if any, of the firm with respect to performance on Department of Defense contracts; (4) location of the firm in the general geographical area of the project, provided that there is an appropriate number of qualified firms therein for consideration; and (5) volume of work previously awarded to the firm by the Department of Defense, with the object of effecting an equitable distribution of contracts among qualified architect-engineer firms including minority-owned firms and firms that have not had prior Department of Defense contracts. Firms desiring to register for consideration for future projects administered by the procurement office (subject to specific requirements for individual projects) are encouraged to submit annually a statement of qualifications and performance data, utilizing Standard Form 254, Architect-Engineer and Related Services Questionnaire.

63. Architect-Engineer firms which meets the requirements described in this announcement are invited to submit: (1) a Standard Form 254, Architect-Engineer and Related Services Questionnaire, (2) a Standard Form 255, Architect-Engineer and Related Services Questionnaire for Specific Project, and (3) any requested supplemental data, to the procurement office shown. Firms having a current Standard Form 254 on file with the procurement office shown are not required to resubmit this form. Firms responding to this announcement before the closing date will be considered for selection, subject to any limitations indicated with respect to size and geographic location of firm, specialized technical expertise, or other requirements as listed. Following an initial evaluation of the qualification and performance data submitted, three or more firms considered to be the most highly qualified to provide the services required will be chosen for interview. The contract for architectural and-or engineering services will be negotiated. Selection of an architect-engineer firm for negotiation shall be based on demonstrated competence and qualifications necessary for the satisfactory performance of the type of professional services required, including any special qualifications required by the procuring agency. Firms desiring to register for consideration for future projects administered by the procurement office (subject to specific requirements for individual projects) are encouraged to submit annually a statement of qualifications and performance data utilizing Standard Form 254, Architect-Engineer and Related Services Questionnaire.

Figure 16 *(Continued)*

64. Requests for copies of this solicitation should be received by issuing office not later than 10 days from the date of listing of this Synopsis in the Commerce Business Daily. Availability of the solicitation is limited and will be furnished on a first received, first served basis. Telephone requests will not be honored. If nonavailability notice is desired, furnished self-addressed, stamped envelope.

66. This proposed procurement contains an option for increased quantity not to exceed 100%. The government may elect to exercise the option at time of award or after award for a specified time as stated in the solicitation.

67. Requests for copies of this solicitation should be made as soon as possible. The number of copies available are limited and additional copies will not be made once the initial supply is exhausted. Copies will be furnished on a first received, first served basis until the supply is exhausted. Only one copy will be sent to each firm. Requests must be in writing via letter and must include three self-addressed adhesive mailing labels. Telephone requests will not be honored.

68. Information submitted should be pertinent and specific, in the technical area under consideration, on each of the following qualifications: (1) Experience: An outline of previous projects, specific work previously performed or being performed and any in-house research and development effort (2) Personnel: Name, professional qualifications and specific experience of scientist, engineers, and technical personnel who may be assigned as principal investigator, and/or project officer, (3) Facilities: Availability and description of special facilities required to perform in the technical area under consideration. A statement regarding industrial security clearance. Any other specific and pertinent information as pertains to this particular area or procurement that would enhance our consideration and evaluation of the information submitted.

Organizations having information on file with this procurement office may make reference to such information. There is no need to duplicate such data. However, supplemental specific information regarding the above question must be submitted. Acknowledgement of receipt of response will not be made.

70. Copies of Specifications, Standards and Qualified Products List may be examined at the Defense General Supply Center, or obtained from Commanding Officer, Naval Publications and Forms Center, 5801 Tabor Avenue, Philadelphia, PA 19120. Area Code 215/697-3321.

71. Drawings Interim Purchase Descriptions and Deviation Lists may be examined or obtained at the Defense General Supply Center.

72. Copies of IFB's and RFP's issued by the Defense General Supply Center, Richmond, Virginia 23297, may be obtained by addressing the Directorate of Procurement and Production, ATTN: DGSC-PO, or by calling 804/275-3350. Requests for copies of IFB's and RFP's should refer to both the Pre-Invitation Number (PIN) and IFB/RFP Number when both numbers are cited in the synopsis. Requests will be furnished on a first received, first served basis until the supply is exhausted. Firms on established bidder's list for these items will be mailed bid sets when they are issued.

73. Specifications, plans, or drawings relating to the procurement described are not available and cannot be furnished by the Government.

74. A responsible bidder shall be considered eligible if the bidder has previously executed or agrees to execute prior to award of a Job Order, a Master contract for Repair and Alteration of Vessel (DD-ASPR For 731).

75. Written requests for solicitations shall be directed to the Naval Avionics Facility, 21st Street and Arlington Avenue, Indianapolis, IN 46218, Attention: Bid Preparation Section, D/634.2, Please furnish a self-addressed, gummed label for each solicitation requested.

76. The material being procured is for use within vital submarine pressure boundaries, commonly referred to as Level I/Sub-Safe systems. As a result, contracts will be made only with those contractors whose inspection system conforms to MIL-1-45208A as certified by a joint DCAS/SPCC survey team. Additionally, the offeror must demonstrate to the survey team his awareness of and ability to provide the special controls set forth in the "Additional Ordering Date."

Figure 16 (*Continued*)

77. Availability of the solicitation is limited and will be furnished upon request on a first received, first served basis until supply is exhausted. Requests may be made by letter, telegram or TWX. Telephone requests will not be honored. Requests must be accompanied by a self-addressed, stamped envelope if a notice of nonavailability is desired. Copies of this solicitation may be viewed at the issuing office. Letter bids will be considered, TWX bids will be considered only if permitted by the invitation for bids. Both must include, as a minimum a statement accepting all terms and conditions of the solicitation, item number, quantity, discount terms, delivery, FOB point and size of business. The outside of the envelope must be clearly identified as a letter bid giving solicitation number and opening date.

79. Proposed procurement is a 100 percent set-aside for Small Business Concerns whose average annual receipts of the concern and its affiliates for its preceding three fiscal years must not exceed $7,500,000.00.

80. To expedite requests for solicitation, please furnish self-addressed gummed label, including the full solicitation number at bottom edge of label, in addition, individual request should be submitted for each solicitation required.

81. Only those sources for this item previously approved by the Government have been solicited. The time required for approval of a new supplier is normally such that award cannot be delayed pending approval of the new source. If you have not been solicited and you can furnish either (i) proof of your prior approval as a supplier of this item, or similar items satisfactorily for the Government or a (ii) data showing you have produced the same or commericial source, or (iii) test data indicating your product can meet service operating reguirements, or (iv) other pertinent data concerning your qualifications to produce the required item, please notify the PCO in writing, furnishing said proof or data along with your request for a solicitation.

82. Copies of the solicitation documents of the proposed procurement listed in this issue of the Commerce Business Daily are available, through individual requests for each solicitation, after date of release from Betty Hall, Procurement Operations Office/BL5, NASA, Johnson Space Center, Houston, TX 77058, TELEX 762-931, when requested on letterhead, until supply is exhausted, on a first come, first served basis, after which a copy may be examined at the above address. Copies may also be examined, but are not available at the following: NASA Headquarters, Industry Assistance & Small Business Advisor, 600 Independence Ave., FOB No 10, Room B127, Washington, DC 20546.

85. The General Provisions applicable to this solicitation will be either HEW Forms -314, -315, -315A, -316, or SF-32. To conserve paper, General Provisions will be mailed with solicitation only if specifically requested in writing at the time solicitation is requested. Solicitations will contain specific information regarding the General Provisions to be incorporated in any resultant contract. The information above applies only to those solicitations issued by the Department of Health, Education, and Welfare's Public Health Service.

86. Copies of IFB's and RFP's may be obtained by addressing the Commanding General, US Army Tank-Automotive Command, Procurement and Production Directorate, Michigan Army Missile Plant, Warren, Michigan 48090, ATTN: DRSTA-IAC. To expedite requests firms should furnish self-addressed gummed labels with each request for solicitation.

87. Published GPO information is current but subject to change without notice. Requests for solicitation must be made 5 weeks prior to effective date of contract. Firms interested in solicitation must conform to all requirements; and must be in the file of eligible suppliers of the U. S. Government Printing Office. Written requests must contain the program number as stated in the synopsis and shall be submitted to:

U.S. Government Printing Office
Printing Procurement Division
Room A-843, PPC
Washington, DC 20401

Each proposal and each request must be made separately on firm's letterhead.

88. The estimated cost of the proposed construction is under $25,000.

89. The estimated cost of the proposed construction is between $25,000 and $100,000.

90. Requests should be postmarked not later than 15 days from the date of publication of this notice in the CBD.

91. Caution—The drawings which will be furnished under this RFP and any resultant contract are proprietary to The Boeing Company. Firms interested in proposing on this RFP must submit the following certificate signed by an individual authorized to bind your company, or the bid package will not be furnished.

Figure 16 (*Continued*)

CERTIFICATE REGARDING THE USE OF
DATA PROPRIETARY TO THE BOEING
COMPANY

The offeror hereby acknowledges that the data to be furnished by the Air Force in this solicitation and any resultant contract, is proprietary to The Boeing Company and contains the appropriate proprietary legend.

The offeror certifies that he will observe the following data use restrictions:

(1) The limited rights legend will be strictly observed.

(2) The offeror shall be prohibited from reproducing in whole or in part any drawing so restricted except as required to respond to the bid request or fulfill contract requirements.

(3) The offeror is to be prohibited from incorporating any information and features of the drawings into other documentation or otherwise utilizing such information except for the performance of the bid and/or contract.

(4) All drawings or copies thereof will be returned to the Government at the completion of the bid or contract period.

97. The Government's annual requirements for this item are not expected to exceed $10,000.

98. Offers from sources whose product does not have current approval as a result of (1) previously supplying the subject item(s) of the solicitation to the Government, (2) furnishing subject item(s) to the original equipment manufacturer, or (3) specifying that the subject item(s) will be supplied by firms identified in (1) or (2) above, will not be considered for award for this procurement.

99. Responses will be directed to: Air Force Space & Missile Systems Organization Contractor Relations Office (BC) 643-2855, PO Box 92960, Worldway Postal Center, Los Angeles, CA 90009.

Figure 16 (*Continued*)

HOW TO READ AN IFB, AN RFP, AND AN RFQ

Look at Figure 17. What does this announcement actually say? The U.S. Army wants to buy 58 externally threaded rings, part number 12252516, meeting all specifications on NSN 5365-01-043-6622. These externally threaded rings are for the 152 mm gun mounted in the M60A1/M60A1E1/M60A3/M60A1E1 combat tanks. Contract will prepay shipping charges to the destination. If you're interested write to: U.S. Army Armament Materiel Readiness Command, Attn. DRSAR-PCP, tel: 309/794-4664, Rock Island, IL 61299 and ask for IFB DAAA09-78-M-6928, which will be issued on or about 3 July 1978. Opening date of the bid will be 30 days after 3 July 78 (4 August 78).

At the upper left-hand corner of the announcement, you will see a symbol that appears to be a numeral 1 inside a black ball. Consult Figure 15, *Commerce Business Daily* legend, and you'll see that this procurement item is 100% set aside for small business concerns.

The last part of the notice says to see notes 42 and 57. Look at Figure 16, *Commerce Business Daily*, numbered notes. You will see that note 42 merely confirms that the proposed procurement must go to a small business with fewer than 500 employees. Note 57 tells the reader that requests for copies of the procurement should be made as soon as possible to facilitate your getting a copy at the time of issuance.

Figure 18 is an announcement of a procurement for leather lining for shoes. Note that it is a negotiated procurement through an RFP(RFP 3PI-0130).

Figure 19 is an RFQ procurement for irrigation equipment.

---

53 Hardware and Abrasives.

● 53 - - **RING, EXTERNALLY, THREADED**—P/N 12252516—NSN 5365-01-043-6622—end use: tank combat, 152MM gun, M60A1/M60A1E1/M60A3/M60A1E2—58 each—FOB Dest.—IFB DAAA09-78-M-6928—issue date o/a 3 Jul 78 with opening date 30 days from issue— See notes 42 and 57. (179)

 US Army Armament Materiel Readiness Command, Attn: DRSAR-PCP, Tel: 309/794-4664, Rock Island, IL 61299

Figure 17. *CBD* IFB procurement.

---

83 Textiles, Leather, Furs, Apparel and Shoe Findings, Tents and Flags.

---

83 - - **LEATHER, LINING:** Shoe, Vamp Lining, Full Grain, Soft Tannage, 2½ to 3½ ounce Light Brown or Cream Color. Of good cutting value, suitable for Orthopedic and Safety Shoe Linings. Tannery Run Grade. 30,000 feet. RFP 3PI-0130, opening 17 Jul 78. (179)

 Federal Prison Industries, Inc., US Penitentiary, Leavenworth, KS 66048

Figure 18. *CBD* RFP procurement.

---

37 Agricultural Machinery and Equipment.

---

37 - - **IRRIGATION EQUIPMENT**—Miscellaneous (parts) irrigation equipment—Quantity required is FOR THE LOT—Delivery F.O.B. Destination (Stoneville, Mississippi)—RFQ. SEA-5130/EMC—RFQ due date approximately 17 Jul 78. (179)

 U.S. Department of Agriculture, SEA, SRAO, Room T-12024, 701 Loyola Ave., New Orleans, LA 70153. Tel: 504/589-6761, E. Charlot.

Figure 19. *CBD* RFQ procurement.

Figure 20 is an example of an advertisement for procurement against a supply schedule.

Figure 21 is an announcement for interested subcontractors to furnish goods to Government prime contractors, in this case Electro-Methods, Inc.; Westfield Gage Company, Inc.; and Birhen Manufacturing Company.

This shows successful preproposal marketing . . .

---

70 General Purpose ADP Equipment Software, Supplies and Support Equipment.

---

70 - - CONTINUE MAINTENANCE OF THE GOVERNMENT-OWNED INTERDATA MODEL 8/32 COMPUTER, Graphic Display terminal, and programmable asynchronous single line adapter. Deliver to GSFC, Greenbelt, MD. Acquisition shall be offered through the issuance of a delivery order against the General Services Administration, Automatic Data Processing Schedule Contract GS-00C-01230. Any questions shall be directed to Brad Poston, Code 246, (179)

NASA, Goddard Space Flight Center, Greenbelt, MD 20771

Figure 20.   *CBD* procurement by supply schedule.

● **28 - - SPACER, TURBINE REAR BEARING**—NSN 2840-00-787-7807RU—P/N 415547—applicable to J57. engine—503 each—(Material: AMS 6322 or AMS 6323 Steel)—deliveries to Tinker AFB—RFP F34601-78-R-2994 is being issued for subcontracting purposes and will embody information that the procurement is restricted to only the approved sources—contact may be made with the following approved firms for copies of the solicitation: (1) Electro-Methods, Inc., P.O. Box 54, 330 Governors Hyw, South Windsor CT 06074; (2) Westfield Gage Company, Inc., Ponders Hollow Road, Westfield MA 010185, and (3) Birken Manufacturing Company, 3 Old Windsor Road, Bloomfield CT 06002—For copies of RFP Contact Attn: PPDAR Tel. 405/734-5732—closing date: 78 Jul 16. See Notes 5, 27, 33, 40 and 80. (179)

Directorate of Procurement & Production, Oklahoma City, ALC, Tinker AFB, OK 73145

Figure 21.   *CBD* advertisement for subcontractor.

The story of the four announcements contained in Figure 22 is that of successful marketing. All four announcements say the same thing in different ways:

"RFP issued to . . ."
"Negotiations will be conducted with . . ."
"Solicitation Restricted to . . ."
"RFP N00383-78-R-3007 . . . has been issued to . . ."

All of these will be sole source awards, with only one company submitting a proposal. A very nice situation to be in indeed!

RESEARCH AND DEVELOPMENT SOURCES SOUGHT— THE EXCEPTIONS TO A RULE

Figure 23 is an announcement for Research and Development Sources Sought, specifically for an investigation of new screening-smoke material for the Army. This announcement is not a request for proposal, a request for quotation, or an

---

13 Ammunition and Explosives.

---

13 - - MISSILE WARHEAD SHELL—NSN 1336-01-027-4439—APN 10677480—Quantity—135 each—RFP DAAH01-78-R-0872—Closing date 24 July 78—RFP issued to: Metal Masters Inc., 333 Hwy 45S Drawer ''E'', Balwyn, MS 38824. See notes 26 and 27. (179)

U.S. Army Missile Materiel Readiness Command, Directorate for Procurement and Production, Attn: DRSMI-IAS, Tel: 876-4692/2890, Redstone Arsenal, AL 35809

★ **13 - - UP-DATE HITPRO II COMPUTER CODE** to accommodate a subsystem of the HIMAG vehicle, 6 months. 201/328-5522. Negotiations will be conducted with General Electric Ordnance Systems, Pittsfield, MA, under RFQ-DAAK10-78-Q-0211.

US Army Armament Research and Development Command, Dover, NJ 07801

---

14 - - SQUIB, ELECTRIC, P/N: 10293273; LANCE Missile System—QUANTITY: 615 Each—PERIOD OF PERFORMANCE: Contract award through April 1979—REQUEST FOR PROPOSAL: DAAH01-79-R-0017—PROPOSAL DUE 1 Sep 78. SOLICITATION RESTRICTED TO: Special Devices, Inc., (S), 16830 West Placerita Canyon Road, Newhall, California 92321. (179)

Purchasing Office: Commander, U.S. Army Missile Materiel Readiness Command, Directorate for Procurement and Production, Attn: DRSMI-ICCB-L, Redstone Arsenal, AL 35809

★**10 - - PROBE ASSY:** Used on the various Acft.—NSN 2RH 1040-00-499-4424-SX—Washington Technological Assoc. P/N 2518760—2 ea—East and West Coast Destinations—R FP N00383-78-R-3007—Due date 27 Jul 78—has been issued to Quanta Systems Corp., Washington Technological Associates Div., Rockville Md—See notes 40 & 73. (178)

Navy Aviation Supply Office, 700 Robbins Ave., Philadelphia, PA 19111

Figure 22. *CBD* sole source procurement.

---

invitation to bid. If you are interested in responding to the RFP concerning this work once it is released, it is necessary that you respond to this announcement with information regarding the total number of your employees and the professional qualifications of acientists, engineers, and other personnel that are qualified in this technical area. In addition, you should include a description of your facilities, an outline of previous work including specific work previously performed or being performed in the area of screening-smoke material, a statement regarding your industrial security clearance, and other pertinent material. If you don't respond within 14 days of publication of the notice, you probably won't be permitted to bid on this project.

Although you must respond to qualify to bid, you should look on your response as an opportunity to sell your capabilities—part of the preproposal marketing activities that really count. Sources Sought represents one of the few situations

RESEARCH AND DEVELOPMENT
SOURCES SOUGHT

In order that potential sources may learn of research and development programs, advance notice of the Government's interest in a specific research field is published here. Firms having the research and development capabilities described are invited to submit complete information to the purchasing office listed. Information should include: the total number of employees and professional qualifications of scientists, engineers, and personal specially qualified in the R&D area outlined, and description of general and special facilities, an outline of previous projects including specific work previously performed or being performed in the listed R&D area; statement regarding industrial security clearance previously granted; and other available descriptive literature. Note that these are not requests for proposals. Respondents will not be notified of the results of the evaluation of the information submitted, but the sources deemed fully qualified will be considered when requests for proposals are solicited. Closing date for submission of responses is 14 days from publication of the notice, unless otherwise specified.

INVESTIGATION OF NEW SCREENING SMOKE MATERIAL (effective in visible to 14 micrometer wavelength region)—scope of work involves investigating classes of material with promise as screening aerosols, rating candidate materials, determining effective methods of dissemination and providing samples for Government evaluation—period of performance to be twelve months - performance will require expertise ION Electro-Magnetic Radiation Generation, detection and absorption in addition to competence with classes of materials and devices proposed: Additionally experience in IR Absorption, weapon/munition/dissemination device design is required—performance will require scientific/engineering, fabrication and test facilities—interested firms are invited to submit qualifications to the purchasing office listed below to be received within 10 days of this notice—information furnished should include evidence of organizational background in similar efforts, description of facilities, and personnel resumes—performance will require secret clearance—RFQ DAAK11-78-Q-0212—only those sources deemed fully qualified will be solicited upon RFQ issuance—this is not a request for quotation. (179)
US Army Armament Research and Development Command, Procurement Directorate, CML/Ballistics Procurement Directorate, Attn: DRDAR-PRB-S, Aberdeen Proving Ground (Edgewood Area) MD 21010

Figure 23.   *CBD* Research and Development Sources Sought.

when an announcement in the *CBD* represents a specific opportunity that you should actually pursue. All the other notices should be thought of as sources of *potential* future customers, not as a specific bidding opportunity. The reason is that once an advertisement for an actual RFP, RFQ, or IFB appears in the *CBD*, you have only a limited time to submit a bid or proposal, usually 30 days or less. The time for preproposal marketing activities is gone. In fact, the Government will severely limit or prohibit your contact with technical people who actually decide on the winner. One large Government contractor, with a win rate of better than 60% on research and development contracts under $2 million, wins less than 2% of those bid "cold" based only on a *CBD* notice. Another successful small company with annual R&D sales of $1 million plus says that it has never won *any* contracts bid that were based solely on a notice in the *CBD*. The reasons for these problems, and their solutions, I will get into later when I talk about the critical importance of preproposal marketing activities and how to do them, in Chapter 7. For the moment, you should recognize that *CBD* notices are for potential customer location only—except for Sources Sought.

Why does Sources Sought represent an exception to this rule? The answer is that the time between the Sources Sought notice and release of an RFP, RFQ, or IFB may be a year or longer. Thus if you're really interested in bidding on an opportunity described in Research and Development Sources Sought in *CBD*, you will have time to practice preproposal marketing. *Want competitive information? Want to know which prices win? Then read contract awards.*

Figure 24 shows the beginning of a Contract Awards column in the *CBD*. The Government publishes information on unclassified contract awards exceeding $25,000 in value for civil agencies and $50,000 for the military. Like notices of opportunities, this section is a source of potential customers. In addition, it also represents a source of information for you regarding competition and pricing. Want to know whether you can be competitive with your product or service in the Government marketplace? Read the Contract Awards section and if you want to get a copy of the contract awarded, contact the awarding agency. The contract is in the public domain and cannot be withheld from you except on security

CONTRACT AWARDS

It is the Government's policy to publish information on unclassified contract awards exceeding $25,000 in value for civil agencies and $50,000 for military agencies.

The letter or number preceding each item is the service or supplies classification code.

Services

A Experimental, Developmental, Test and Research Work (includes both basic and applied research).

A - - DEVELOPMENT OF A VARIABLE CAPACITY COMPRESSOR CONTROLLER FOR SOLAR HEATING AND COOLING APPLICATIONS, Contr EM-78-C-02-5224 (Unsolicited Proposal) for $40,000 awarded to RHO Sigma, Inc., No. Hollywood, CA 91605.

A - - DESIGN AND DEVELOPMENT OF AN EXTRUDATE BREAK UP DEVICE, Contr. EW-78-C-21-8441 (Unsolicited Proposal) for $183,413 awarded to Ingersoll Rand Research Inc., Princeton, N.J. 08540.

A - - FEASIBILITY STUDY OF ESTABLISHING A FEDERAL PUBLIC CORPORATION, Contr. ET-78-C-01-3254 (Unsolicited Proposal) for $28,980 awarded to TPI Associates, Washington, D.C. 20036.

A - - OPTIMIZATION OF DISTRIBUTION TRANSFORMER EFFICIENCY, Contr. ET-78-C-01-3022 (PRDA No. ET-78-D-01-3022) for $94,000 to Westinghouse Electric Corporation, Pittsburgh, PA and Athens, GA.

A - - SOLAR POWERED PULSEJET PUMP IRRIGATION SYSTEM, Contr. EG-77-C-01-4121/A002 (Modification to Contract) for $104,671 to Payne, Inc. Annapolis, MD 21401.

A - - MEASUREMENT AND CORRELATION OF CONDITIONS FOR ENTRAPMENT AND MOBILIZATION OF RESIDUAL OIL. Contr. ET-78-S-01-

Figure 24.   *CBD* Contract Awards column.

grounds. Many times the agency involved will honor a request by telephone, but sometimes they will insist that you write a letter and request the information under the Freedom of Information Act.

Other *CBD* Sections

You will find other sections of the *CBD* useful to your developing business with Uncle Sam. These include "Business News," which contains information pertaining to forthcoming meetings and symposia of interest to Government contractors; "Trade Leads," which have export opportunities; "Future Construction Abroad"; "Department of State Aid Financed," which are programs in which the Agency for International Development (AID) puts up the money; and "Direct Sales," which are actually notices of opportunities with foreign government agencies and firms. The *CBD* also carries notices of the intent to establish new Qualified Product Lists and additional sources added to existing lists. I'll discuss what this may mean to you below.

How to Get Your Product on Qualified Products Lists

I talked about the Qualified Products List (QPL) in Chapter 1. Most commodities and many other products that the Government buys are purchased on the basis of standard specifications. For many of these purchases Uncle Sam wants your product to pass certain tests to insure that your product meets these specifications before he'll let you bid. When you pass the test, your firm's product gets put on the QPL. The Government uses the QPL in their buying. As an added sweetener, Government prime contractors use the QPL also when they buy various components for Government contracts. But remember, you cannot bid in some cases if your product is not *already* on the QPL. Therefore if you plan on selling a certain product that is already on a QPL, you should have your product tested as soon as possible.

How Do You Know If Your Product Must Have a QPL Listing?

The Government activity involved is what decides whether a certain product requires qualification testing. If it is decided that it does, this fact is published in the specifications for the product. You will find this information in Sections 3, 4, and 6 of the product specifications form, including what must be accomplished for qualifications testing and the name of the Government agency that you should contact for information about getting your product qualified. Therefore your first step is to obtain a copy of the specification for your product to find out if it needs to be qualified, and if so which agency to contact.

If you recall, a complete list of specifications and standards can be found in *The Index of Federal Specifications and Standards*, and you can obtain any specification or standard from one of the addresses listed in Chapter 1, using the form contained in Figure 2. The Navy, which controls the specification and standards program for all Government agencies, also maintains a "hot line" for urgent requests only. Call area code (215) 697-3321, 8 A.M. to 4:30 P.M., Monday through Friday, Philadelphia time. The Navy also recommends Telex and Western Union messages. Use Telex number 834295 or Western Union number 710-670-1685.

How to Get Your Product Tested for QPL Listing

The first step in getting your product tested for listing in the QPL is to test the product yourself to see whether it meets the performance and/or design limitations of the specifications. If it does not meet the specifications, then you must make whatever changes are necessary to meet the specifications.

Once you are assured that your product will pass the Government's tests, make your application by letter to the Government activity indicated in the "notes," section 6 or H of the production specification in which you are interested.

According to the SBA, this is what your letter to the procuring activity should contain:

- Number and date of the specification under which tests are desired.
- Your brand designation for the product.
- Location of the plant at which the product is manufactured. (If you are a distributor, write the name and plant location of the actual manufacturer.)
- If you propose to have the tests conducted in a private laboratory, the location of the facility at which you propose to have the tests run, and a list and detailed description of testing equipment to be used.
- Certification that:

1. You agree to be bound by all the provisions and terms set forth in the "Provisions Governing Qualification." You can get a copy of this document from the Government activity involved.
2. You are the manufacturer of the product or are a distributor authorized by the manufacturer to rebrand and distribute the product under your own brand designation.
3. You have determined from actual tests that your product conforms to the specification. (You should send test reports and other pertinent data along with your letter.)
4. You will supply items representative of your production for the qualification test.
5. You will supply items for the Government's use that meet all requirements of the specification.

6. If you fail the qualification test, you will not apply for a retest until you can show that you have corrected all the defects that were disclosed by previous tests.

7. You will not use the fact that your product is on a QPL for promotional purposes. In other words, you can't use your notice of qualification or anything else connected with the QPL to indicate that the Government approves or recommends your product.

8. If you make any change after your product has been qualified, you will notify the responsible Government agency. At the time of this notification, you will be required to state whether you believe the change will or will not affect the product's ability to meet the qualification test requirements.

Should You Have Qualification Testing Done in a
Private Laboratory or a Government Laboratory?

There are advantages and disadvantages in using either private or Government laboratory facilities for qualification testing. Let's look at testing in a Government laboratory first.

If you have your product tested in a Government laboratory, the following conditions will apply:

1. You will supply samples for testing at no expense to the Government.

2. You will be notified of costs, if any, in the letter that you will receive authorizing the tests.

3. The Government won't be responsible for any expense resulting from shipping samples to or from the test, damage during the test, or damage or loss of the sample while at the laboratory.

4. You must furnish adequate operating instructions with your samples.

5. You must ship in accordance with shipping instructions furnished by the Government.

6. The time of the test will be set at the convenience of the Government. You can observe the test, but you must get permission beforehand from the laboratory doing the test.

7. If the samples are damaged in shipping, you are allowed to make repairs or replace them prior to the test.

8. You may be permitted to make minor modifications to the product on the test floor if the Government feels that these modifications will improve the product and enable you to meet specification requirements.

9. Except in unusual circumstances, you will not be permitted to make major modification, and then only after the laboratory has received permission from the responsible Government agency.

10. You are *not* permitted to take an active part in the test.

11. The testing laboratory can stop the qualification tests at any time if, in the opinion of the testers, the product fails to meet any of the requirements of the specification.

When testing is completed, you will get an official notification of approval or disapproval, along with the full test report or its pertinent parts. Although the test report may circulate within the Government, the agency is not permitted to furnish information from the test report outside the Government without your permission. If you want your sample returned, you must request it and it is returned at your own expense.

Now let's look at qualification testing done in private laboratories. First, you should know that you may do the testing in your own laboratory, if you desire, or you can do part of the testing in your laboratory and part in a laboratory under contract to you. Here again, the rules are that you must pay for the samples, and that the Government will not be responsible for any expense connected with the tests, including shipment of the samples to or from the testing place, damage during the test, or damage or loss of the product while at the testing place.

If you don't use Government testing facilities for your qualification testing, here is how it works. First, the Government determines whether the testing facilities you propose are suitable or not and whether other terms you propose, such as equipment, comply with other requirements of qualification. If all goes well with your proposal, you will receive written authorization to proceed.

If you receive authorization to do the tests, they will be monitored by a Government representative. When the tests are complete, an official laboratory test report must be forwarded to the Government. This report must include:

- A title page with the date of report and test report number assigned by the testing laboratory; specification title, number, and date, and if the specification has amendments, their sheet numbers and dates; the name of the manufacturer and address of the home and plant office; a reference to the letter that authorized the tests; the name and location of the testing laboratory, whether the test was for qualification or requalification; and specification type, grade, class, or other Government designation, along with your own designation for the product.
- A one-page abstract of the product's performance on the qualification test, including the number of samples that passed and failed the test.
- A technical section that includes:

1. A list and description of test equipment used, including specification paragraph calling for this equipment, if applicable; equipment name and manufacturer with model and serial number and date of calibration, if applicable.
2. Test data sheets indicating average results if required by the specification and whether each unit passed or failed.

3. A comparison of a summary of test data results with specification requirements.

4. Other recorded data such as curves, graphs, photographs, and so on as required by the Government.

The test report must be signed by an officer or other authorized agent of the testing laboratory. The Government's representative who witnessed the tests must certify each copy of the report as valid. His certification must indicate whether he monitored the entire test or only part of it. However, even if the tests are successful according to the testing laboratory, and the Government representative certifies them as valid, the results are *not* acceptable unless the responsible Government agency determines that the product meets the requirement of the specification. This determination is made on the basis of the test report and any other information that the Government may have.

It should be clear that the major difference between whether the Government tests your product or you test it is the control you have in doing your own testing or paying a laboratory to do it for you. If you do the testing:

1. You determine when the tests will be held. Leave it to the Government and you may find yourself with a serious conflict about time—and this is one test you can't afford to miss.

2. If the samples require a change or modification to pass the qualification test, you will have a greater say as to whether this change is "minor" or "major."

3. You will have a greater influence as to whether or not to continue testing. remember, at the Government facility, if the Government decides that's the end of the test, that's the end of the test. At your own facility, you will have a greater motivation to continue testing in a marginal situation.

4. In Government facilities, you won't be permitted to take an active part in the test. In your own facilities, obviously, or with someone under contract, it is up to you. Who best knows the idiosyncrasies of your product—you or a stranger?

My recommendation is, if at all possible, to test your own product with a Government representative monitoring you, rather than vice versa.

What Is on the QPL?

Once you've made the QPL, what will be listed about your product anyway? The QPL will contain the Government's designation for the product, your designation, the qualification test report number, the manufacturer's name, and the address of the plant from which the sample was submitted.

The QPL itself will carry the symbol "QPL," followed by one number pertaining to the associated specification and a second number to identify the particular issue of the QPL pertaining to the specification. A QPL for military specifications contains that number only. For example, the third issue of a QPL for Military Specification MIL-C-43635 would be QPL-43635-3. However, for Federal Specifications, the complete specification designation is used because the number alone could refer to a number of different Federal Specifications. For example, the second issue of QPL for Federal Specification 00-I-104 would be QPL-00-I-104-2.

How Your Product Can Be Removed from the QPL by the Government

The Government can remove your product from the QPL for violation of any of the eight points of your certification or provisions on which the qualification approval was granted. A publication of the SBA, "Getting Your Product on Qualified Products Lists," lists six typical reasons why the Government removes products from the QPL. These are:

1. The product offered under contract does not meet the requirements of the specifications.
2. The manufacturer has stopped making the product, or is delivering a different product than the one originally qualified.
3. The manufacturer or distributor asks that the product be removed from the list.
4. The conditions under which qualification was granted have been violated.
5. The requirements of a revised or amended specification are entirely different from the previous specification, so that the former tests no longer apply to the product.
6. The product is that of a contractor, firm, or individual whose name appears on the "Consolidated List of Debarred, Ineligible, and Suspended Contractors."

With the exceptions of reasons 1 and 6, you will be given advance notification, along with the reasons that your product is about to be removed from the QPL. For reasons 1, 4, and 6 you will be asked to comment. If removal is for reason 5, you will be given the changed specification along with an opportunity to submit additional test data or samples for a new qualification test. If a manufacturer's product is to be removed from the QPL and one or more of his distributors are on the same QPL, they will receive copies of the same notice sent to him.

If a production item is not meeting the requirements of the specification, removal action may be delayed pending the outcome of tests. Also, if a successful resubmission is made within the time specified by the Government under these circumstances, your product may not be removed. The key, of course, is to maintain quality control and not to violate the terms of your listing so that you don't get in trouble in the first place. Getting on the QPL along with pre-bid marketing will bring you Government customers. Getting dumped for causes puts you back to square one.

How and Why to Screen Your Customer List

From the sources discussed in this book, from the *CBD*, and from the *U.S. Government Purchasing and Sales Directory* and from the Appendix, you will find hundreds of potential Government customers for your particular product or service. These customers in turn represent thousands of opportunities for business. However, no company, not even the very largest, can take advantage of the total potential of the volume of business available. But that's okay, because even a very few of these opportunities represent millions of dollars in sales. The problem is, in order to capture these millions of dollars in sales, you must screen the number of opportunities down to a workable number. Here's why:

- You have a limited number of resources. By attempting to go after too many opportunities, you spread yourself too thin. You are able to concentrate too few resources against any one opportunity. As a result, a competitor who concentrates his resources against this opportunity will win.

- In some cases the opportunity is not a real one. It is a program without real backing within the Government, an although one or more Government customers may be interested in paying you to buy the product or service, they haven't the funds to do so.

- Some programs are much more worthwhile to win than others. Profitability may be greater, or you may achieve a certain prestige by providing a particular product or service. The makers of the orangelike drink called Tang won a Government contract and provided this drink through NASA to the astronauts. While it is unclear what profits, if any, they achieved in selling the small quantity needed, the promotional value of this contract in advertising, and the fact that it was chosen to be used in space was worth millions of dollars.

- Some contracts will be much easier for you to win than others. For example, if the Government procuring agency is close to your location, this provides an advantage—not in transportation costs of the goods, which under Government regulations are equalized but during preproposal marketing, because you can visit your potential customer easier and at less cost. Or perhaps you already have a successful ongoing contract with a Government agency. An additional contract would be easier for you to win with this organization than with another agency with which you have never done business before.

Paul R. McDonald, teacher of thousands of students of Government contracting, says this:

Principal programs should be selected based on an analysis of alternative possibilities in relation to the following criteria:

1. Firmness of customer requirement.
2. Amount of present and future funding.
3. Relationship to the firm's normal market area and product lines.
4. The firm's capability.
5. The firm's competitive position.
6. Anticipated profit and peripheral benefits.
7. Length of time before the program will mature to the RFP stage.
8. The resources to be available at the time of the award.

Dick Close of R. N. Close Associates says that an early decision about whether to bid or not must be carefully made based on:

*   Critical, objective self-analysis of our capabilities and chances of winning.
*   Objective analysis of the competitor's chances.
*   Teaming/subcontracting options that we may have.
*   Company-funded R&D needed to fill in gaps in our technical capability.
*   Profitability analysis: risk versus return.

Government marketing expert Jim Beveridge says that every winning program you go after must fit these criteria: that there is a real customer requirement; that there are funds available; and that if you are planning on doing subcontract work for a prime Government contractor, that the "prime" has definitely decided to buy from someone else rather than to do it themselves.

Jack Robertson, Washington Editor of *Electronic News*, cites nine criteria for screening the bid in his book *Selling to the Federal Government:*

1. Has your company done its homework prior to the bid?
2. Is this a real bid that is meeting an actual need?
3. How well does the customer know your company?
4. Is the RFP or IFB that is released written in such a way that it is not in the interest of your company to bid?
5. Is the customer asking bidders to assume too much risk?
6. Is the bid "wired" for a favored vendor?
7. Is your company willing to put in another $10,000 to $100,000 (on some proposals) for extra proposal efforts such as best and final analyses, meetings and negotiating with the Government, and so on?

8. Is the agency setting up a glorified price auction?
9. Does the project fit in with your company's plans?

When screening your potential opportunities, you should consider all of these criteria and prune the number of opportunities down to a workable number. You should continually review your list of opportunities, and as additional information becomes available and changes occur in the programs you are interested in, you should revise your test. There are no set periods for this ongoing analysis and pruning of your Government business opportunities. However you should as a minimum screen your programs:

* Initially.
* After further contact with the customer.
* At your final bid-no bid decision, after receipt of the RFP, RFQ, or IFB, but before starting to work on your proposal.

Initial screening is necessary because of the sheer magnitude of opportunities for Government business in your area. I have found that the best way to accomplish this initial screening is a two-step method. In step 1, you make your list of opportunities along with the potential customer's name and phone number. Step 2 is working your way down the list and talking to each one. You introduce yourself, explain why you are calling, and explain the type of work you do, and find out whether there is a match or not. In some areas, there will be no match. Despite how the customer may have described his interests through one of the sources or programs described above, what the customer is interested in and what you supply may not be the same. Or perhaps the customer temporarily has no need of your product or service. In any case, initial screening should serve to eliminate the more obvious noncustomer situation that would result in a waste of your time, money, and personal resources.

The second important screening is made after further contact with the customer. Perhaps you have a face-to-face meeting. Or the customer sends you detailed information about his requirements. You are now in a better position to fine-tune your portfolio of potential business opportunities, based on much more information about the opportunity than you gained on first contact. Analyze this information and use the criteria of the experts to continue concentrating your win resources against those opportunities that you want and can best obtain.

The final screening is just before you bid. You have received the IFB, RFP, or RFQ. Even at this stage, it is not too late. Any bid will cost you money. Some large Government contractors have spent millions of dollars on the bid and proposal alone—and lost. No need to lose any money at all, even if you have invested a significant amount in your preproposal marketing activities. You can't win all of the opportunities available, and if you know you are not going to win at this point, why bid at all? You can use those hundreds, thousands, or even millions of dollars to help you with the ones that you can win.

How to Plan for and Make Presentations to the Customer

Presentations are an important part of getting the customer to buy your product and service. If you make the right bid or presentation:

- You will inform the Government about your product or service.
- You will build credibility for what you are offering to sell.
- You will learn more about the potential opportunities for business with the Government, which will help you decide whether or not to continue to pursue the business, and to win the contract should you bid on it.
- You will build consumer acceptance and merchandise your product or service, as described in Chapter 7.

The key to making a good presentation is the planning you do ahead of time. A presentation is not a speech; it should not be written out word for word. But your presentation should be structured, and that is your first task.

To structure your presentation, you must first decide on an overall theme. Perhaps your theme is that your company makes the best microwave components in the world. Fine. Then everything you say must be in support of this main theme in your presentation. The history of your company, as important as it may be to you, is irrelevant except as it relates to your main theme. The fact that last year one of your engineers designed a dandy telephone that won first place in an industrial design competition is irrelevant to this particular main theme. Write down the important facts that support the theme that your company makes the best microwave components.

When you have completed your presentation structure, consider how you will illustrate your structure. Nothing could be duller than your standing up and announcing a collection of uninteresting facts. But if you have something to illustrate each point that you are talking about, your facts will come alive and be more readily understood by your audience. Each idea basic to your structure should be illustrated by a chart, graph, picture, drawing, photograph, or even just a summation of the essential point or points you are making. Put each idea or an illustration on a separate sheet of paper, as in Figure 25. These sheets become the basis of your presentation process.

The presentation process is regulated and controlled by using 35 mm slides, viewgraps, or a handout containing the ideas and illustrations coming from your presentation structure. These aids can be made professionally by a graphics art firm, which you can find in the yellow pages of your phone book. By using one or more of these aids, you will be able to control the length of time for your presentation and tailor it to your individual audience. Thus you can be certain not to omit any important points in support of your central theme. And finally, it will be much easier for your audience to take notes of what you consider to be the most important parts of your presentation.

You can make your presentation:

- On 35 mm slides
- On viewgraphs
- On handouts

Figure 25. Each idea or illustration of your presentation structure goes on a separate sheet of paper.

Each aid has different advantages. The 35 mm slides are more expensive, but they are also the most convenient to carry with you on trips, especially if you have a large number. Viewgraphs are less expensive and usually easy to change or correct, if necessary. Printed handouts can be reproductions of "camera ready" copy, which is used in making viewgraphs. They are cheap and this cuts down on the amount of note-taking necessary for your audience. However, using handouts is sometimes not suitable for presentations to large groups. Because handouts insure that your audience has a copy of your main points even after you leave, they are a good aid to use in conjunction with either 35 mm slides or viewgraphs.

There is one more aid you should consider that I have not mentioned. This is sometimes called a "feelie." A feelie is a prototype or mock-up or sample of your product, or any other representation that the audience not only views but can actually touch.

Once you have your structure and aids together, you are ready for the next part of your presentation: practice. To practice, you must first decide how long a presentation you are going to give. To some extent this will depend on the customer and how much time he can allow you on the date you mutually decide upon for the presentation. However, if the time available isn't suffcent for a particular date, you can change it. Don't accept an insufficient time period if you feel more time is necessary to get your message across. However, once you agree to give your presentation within a certain period of time, stick to it.

Now that you know how long your presentation is to be, we can begin our practice sessions. The first couple of times, walk your way through it, using your aids as a guide. If your timing doesn't match the time available you can either add or drop ideas from your presentation. Do not try to memorize what you are going to say. Remember, it is not a speech. You have your aids to guide you. There is no need to memorize anything. Because of this, every time you give your presentation, it will be a little bit different, and that's fine.

After working out the major bugs, give your presentation before a friendly audience: wife, husband, employees, friends, or whomever you can draft for the purpose. Using a live audience has two advantages. First, it takes the edge off absolute panic when you must give your "pitch" before real live customers. Second, your friendly audience can catch any major holes in your delivery or presentation and tell you whether your theme is getting through or not and what to do to make your presentation even better. And even though everything is running like clockwork, always give your presentation one more dry run the night before you must do the real thing.

One last, but not insignificant point. Before you start traveling with a set of 35 mm slides or viewgraphs, be certain your potential customers have the proper machine for showing them, and that it will be available when you show up to make your pitch.

How to Develop a Special Brochure to Help You Sell Your Product or Service

If you are serious about selling to the Government, a first-rate brochure describing your firm, yourself, your product or service, your facilities, your capabilities, and any other relevant aspect of your business can be of great assistance. Every time you contact a Government office, leave a couple of copies of your brochure. Now you may think this does no good at all because the Government customer won't read the brochure. But even if the customer doesn't read your brochure, it can have a big impact. Here's how. A large contractor had been trying to get a Government R&D contract for development of a new composite material for years with no success. At countless meetings with the customer this company's representatives expressed their interest, told of the backing of top management, and detailed their capabilities for doing the work. No luck. Finally, a new marketing manager decided to try something different. He spent $10,000 and developed the most beautiful, glossy, mutlicolored brochure describing new composite materials that you ever saw. Every potential Government customer got a copy. The first year, this company won $500,000 in Government contracts in this technical area. Strangely, the general feeling was that few if any of the customers actually "read" the brochure. But as one customer said, "When I saw that brochure, I knew that the ———company really meant business."

If you develop a brochure describing your R&D capabilities, here's what the Government's booklet, "Selling to the Military," suggests you include:

1. Name of organization, and address.
2. R&D work now being performed.
3. Major R&D work completed.
4. Type of work for which firm is especially qualified.
5. List Government contracts previously undertaken and show the technical service, contract number, and brief description of work done, both as prime and subcontractor.
6. (a) Names and qualifications of scientists and primary technical personnel employed full time. (Include information about education, professional

experience, and papers published.) (b) Names and business connections of consultants and other scientific personnel available to the company. (c) Names and qualifications of other key personnel to be used on R&D work.

7. (a) Description of plant. (b) List of production equipment. (c) Laboratory and test equipment. (d) Special R&D equipment.

8. Current financial statements.

9. Security clearance—if you have had a "Facility Clearance" from the Army, Navy, Air Force, or other Government agency, state which. Security regulations are important and should be studied and observed with utmost care. Procedures and requirements are explained in "Questions and Answers on the Defense Industrial Security Program." This document is available for 55 cents from the Superintendent of Documents, Government Printing Office, Washington, D.C. 20401.

In this chapter, we've talked about how to get Government customers to buy your product and service by using the *Commerce Business Daily*, getting on the QPL, screening your potential customers, making presentations, and developing a brochure. In the next chapter, we will explore this theme in more detail and learn about the request for proposal mechanism that Government uses to do business.

Chapter 5

HOW THE GOVERNMENT DOES BUSINESS

In this chapter I will go into depth about the ways in which the Government does business. I will discuss federal advertising through the IFB, negotiated procurements with the RFP, the requests for quotation known as the RFQ, the proposal, Government grants, Announcements of Opportunities, and other means the Government has of requesting preliminary information.

We first encountered formal advertising back in Chapter 1. This is the preferred method of Government contracting, and under this method all known responsible suppliers are given an equal cahnce to compete. Uncle Sam himself defines formal advertising as "the means of contracting through the use of a competitive procedure which includes solicitation of bids and the awarding of a contract to the lowest responsive bidder whose bid conforms to the invitation."

The Government has pushed the concept of formal advertising since 1809 when it was discovered that various contractors had secured favorable Government contracts during the Revolutionary War through their contacts with Congressmen. Since then Government agencies have been required by statute to formally advertise their needs, with certain special exceptions for the public good, such as in time of war when formal advertising might take too long. What the Government seeks in promoting formal advertising is the benefits of competition in the marketplace. The Government believes very strongly that this competition results in lower prices and higher quality. At the same time, it encourages adequate sources of supply through the elimination of favoritism. On the other hand, I should add that astronaut John Glenn, as he prepared to launch on what was the first manned-orbital mission for the United States, stated that his thoughts were about the millions and millions of components in his spacecraft, all of which had gone to the lowest bidder.

THE PROCESS OF FORMAL ADVERTISING

Formal advertising begins with a solicitation for bids in the form of the invitations that are circulated widely in order to obtain maximum competition. Once the

198

requested bids are received at the specified hour, all bids are publicly opened and read aloud. They are eventually evaluated for responsiveness, as pointed out in Chapter 1. Finally, the award is made to the lowest responsible bidder and notification of the award is made. Formalization of the contract constitutes the final step in the formal advertising process.

INVITATION FOR BID

The invitation for bid is legally not an offer. It is comparable to situations in the nongovernment marketplace in which a potential seller advertises in general circulation media for all those interested to submit offers. What this means is that when you respond to such a solicitation this does not constitute an acceptance, nor does it bind you and the Government to a contract. Rather, it is an offer that in turn must be accepted or rejected by the Government.

The Government's solicitation, offer, and award are all made on one form, Standard Form 33, which is shown in Figure 26. These invitations are circulated widely in order to obtain the competition that the Government desires. There are various methods that the Government uses in soliciting these bids with the IFB. The principal method, of course, is mailing or delivering the invitations to prospective bidders. For this purpose a mailing list and the QPL discussed earlier are maintained by various purchasing activities. Additional methods of soliciting the bids include displaying copies of the invitation at the purchasing office and other appropriate public places, publishing brief announcements of proposed purchases in trade journals, publishing the essential details of a proposed purchase in newspapers, and, of course, notices in the *Commerce Business Daily*. When Standard Form 33 is completed and filled in correctly, it constitutes a bid.

THE BID

The bid you submit is an offer in the legal sense; therefore, if accepted, it constitutes a contract. How does this procedure work? Once the bids that you submit on Standard Form 33 are received and opened at the specified time, they are read aloud publicly. In addition, they are recorded on a form called an abstract of bids. On the abstract is contained such information as the name of the bidder, the invitation number, the bid opening date, a description of the procurement item, prices bid, and other pertinent information. This abstract is completed as soon as possible after opening the bids and is certified by the bid-opening officer.

You may modify or withdraw your bid at any time prior to the time fixed for opening by written or telegraphic notice. This notice must be received prior to the time fixed for the opening. This is also the case for late bids when the modification or withdrawal of the bid is sent before the time that is specified for the

<table>
<tr><td colspan="2">STANDARD FORM 33, JULY 1966
GENERAL SERVICES ADMINISTRATION
FED. PROC. REG. (41 CFR) 1-16.101</td><td colspan="2">SOLICITATION, OFFER,
AND AWARD</td><td colspan="2">3. CERTIFIED FOR NATIONAL DEFENSE UNDER
BDSA REG. 2 AND/OR DMS REG. 1
RATING: DO-A2</td><td>4. PAGE
1</td><td>OF
8</td></tr>
</table>

1. CONTRACT (Proc. Inst. Ident.) NO.	2. SOLICITATION NO. 3-857216-B [X] ADVERTISED (IFB) [ ] NEGOTIATED (RFP)	5. DATE ISSUED 1-8-79	6. REQUISITION/PURCHASE REQUEST NO 857216

7. ISSUED BY CODE [ ]	8. ADDRESS OFFER TO (If other than block 7)
NASA - Lewis Research Center 21000 Brookpark Road Cleveland, Ohio 44135	NASA - Lewis Research Center 21000 Brookpark Road Cleveland, Ohio 44135 Mail Stop: 500-213

SOLICITATION

9. Sealed offers in original and __2__ copies for furnishing the supplies or services described in the Schedule will be received at the place specified in block 8, OR IF HAND-CARRIED, IN THE DEPOSITARY LOCATED IN __Room 1301, DEB__, until __3:00 PM 2-5-79__
(Time, Zone, and Date)

If this is an advertised solicitation, offers will be publicly opened at that time. CAUTION—LATE OFFERS. See par. 8 of Solicitation Instructions and Conditions. All offers are subject to the following:
1. The attached Solicitation Instructions and Conditions, SF 33A.
2. The General Provisions which are attached or incorporated herein by reference.
3. The Schedule included below and/or attached hereto.
4. Such other provisions, representations, certifications and specifications as are attached or incorporated herein by reference. (Attachments are listed in the Schedule.)

FOR INFORMATION CALL (Name and Telephone No.) (No collect calls.): Bruce Shuman, A/C 216 433-4000, Ext. 6630

SCHEDULE

The following are attached hereto and made a part hereof:
1. Schedule Continued (Standard Form 36) Pages 5 through 8
2. General Provisions for Fixed Price Supply or Fixed Price Services Contract, November 1978, 3 pages.
   (Continued on page 5)

FABRICATION OF TITANIUM, METALLIC-FLUID HEAT PIPES AND TITANIUM-ALLOY, METALLIC-FLUID HEAT PIPES

NOTE THE AFFIRMATIVE ACTION REQUIREMENT OF THE EQUAL OPPORTUNITY CLAUSE which may apply to the contract resulting from this solicitation.
NOTE THE CERTIFICATION OF NONSEGREGATED FACILITIES IN THIS SOLICITATION. Bidders, offerors and applicants are cautioned to note the "Certification of Nonsegregated Facilities" in the solicitation. Failure of a bidder or offeror to agree to the certification will render his bid or offer non-responsive to the terms of solicitations involving awards of contracts exceeding $10,000 which are not exempt from the provisions of the Equal Opportunity clause. (OCTOBER 1971)

OFFER (NOTE: Reverse Must Also Be Fully Completed By Offeror)   BS:sp

In compliance with the above, the undersigned offers and agrees, if this offer is accepted within _____ calendar days (60 calendar days unless a different period is inserted by the offeror) from the date for receipt of offers specified above, to furnish any or all items upon which prices are offered, at the price set opposite each item, delivered at the designated point(s), within the time specified in the Schedule.

16. DISCOUNT FOR PROMPT PAYMENT _____ % 10 CALENDAR DAYS, _____ % 20 CALENDAR DAYS, _____ % 30 CALENDAR DAYS, _____ % _____ CALENDAR DAYS

17. OFFEROR NAME & ADDRESS CODE [ ] FACILITY CODE [ ] (Street, city, county, state, & ZIP Code) Area Code and Telephone No [ ] Check If Remittance Address Is Different From Above—Enter Such Address In Schedule	18. NAME AND TITLE OF PERSON AUTHORIZED TO SIGN OFFER (Type or Print)
	19. SIGNATURE	20. OFFER DATE

AWARD (To Be Completed By Government)

21. ACCEPTED AS TO ITEMS NUMBERED	22. AMOUNT	23. ACCOUNTING AND APPROPRIATION DATA
24. SUBMIT INVOICES (4 copies unless otherwise specified) TO ADDRESS SHOWN IN BLOCK __27__	25. NEGOTIATED PURSUANT TO [ ] 10 U.S.C. 2304(a)( ) [ ] 41 U.S.C. 252(c)( )	
26. ADMINISTERED BY (If other than Block 7) CODE [ ]	27. Submit Payment Invoices in CODE [ ] 5 Copies to: Finance Division (500-303) NASA-Lewis Research Center 21000 Brookpark Road Cleveland, Ohio 44135
28. NAME OF CONTRACTING OFFICER (Type or Print)	29. UNITED STATES OF AMERICA BY _____ (Signature of Contracting Officer)	30. AWARD DATE

Figure 26.   Standard Form 33/Solicitation, Offer, and Award.

opening; it may even be upheld if it is late if the bidder is not responsible for the delay in transmission. In any event it must be clearly shown that the modification or withdrawal was not submitted with knowledge of the terms of other bids.

One company routinely made it its policy to transmit a lower bid by telegraph for every bid opening. This was done strictly for security reasons. The company was not afraid that the Government itself would leak the bid, since the bids were sealed until the opening time. However, the company was concerned that information about the bid price might be leaked from sources within its own ranks. On one occasion when the bid was sent prior to bid opening by telegraph, it was not delivered to the bid room by Government employees until 45 minutes after bid-opening time. It turned out that this "late bid" was in fact the lowest bid. The bid was awarded to the company since it had not been responsible for the delay in transmission and it was clearly shown that the modification had not been submitted with knowledge of the terms of other bids.

A bid may still be modified after the opening of bids when the modification is in the interest of the Government and is not prejudicial to other bidders. For example, let us assume in the case just cited that the company had already won the competition as low bidder with its original bid. Then its updated bid sent by telegraph arrives 45-minutes later through no fault of its own and the new bid is even lower than the one with which it had "won." According to Government regulations, its new and even lower bid may still be accepted. Since, as low bidder, it was already entitled to the award, obviously no valid complaint can be made by the other bidders.

All bids may be rejected when it is in the Government's interest to do so. However, the General Accounting Office, which is the watchdog agency for all Government contracting, is not wildly enthusiastic about the Government rejecting bids in a cavalier fashion. It feels that insufficient reason for rejection is an abuse of administrative discretion. An analysis of GAO decisions about rejection of bids appears to indicate that the decision rests on whether the Government feels that by advertising again it may reasonably expect to receive more advantageous bids. "Advantageous" usually means at a lower price.

After the bids are opened they are evaluated. During this process the contracting officer may be faced with the necessity of eliminating some bids from consideration or rejecting all of them and starting all over again. If your bid does not conform in every respect to the essential requirements of the IFB, you should know that you will not be permitted to alter the contracting officer's evaluation by correcting the error or otherwise bringing up the standard of the bid so that it meets all requirements of the IFB. Because of this, you should be very careful about putting time limits on your bid. If an offer made in response to an IFB lapses due to the passage of time and the time limitation you have placed, it may not be reinstated unless the Government wants to do so. If the Government does want to reinstate your bid, someone must contact you and then you must consent to this in writing. Therefore, when dealing with IFBs and advertised procurements, do not routinely put time limitations on your bid unless it is essential for your business or the production of the item in question to do so.

Also, remember what we said earlier about the responsiveness of bids. A bid that is not submitted in accordance with the invitation or that contains qualifying terms or language that the Government considers to be of an excessive nature is considered to be nonresponsive. The Government will reject such a bid. If you fail to sign your bid, this also places its acceptability in the hands of the Government and they may not consider it. From the Government's point of view even if everything else is correct, when the bid lacks a proper signature with no other indication in the bid submission that the purported bidder intended to submit the bid, the Government cannot be sure that the bid was submitted by someone in authority. If the IFB requires that you state opposite each part number that your product complies with specifications and you fail to do this, your bid may be rejected as nonresponsive. Remember, the only errors that may be corrected after the bid opening are those that do not affect responsiveness of the bid.

The Government has some judgment, but leaving judgment in the hands of the Government regarding the rejection or acceptance of your bid is definitely not a smart way to do business. The Government contracting officers may waive minor deviation in bids that don't affect the price, quality, or other specifications or features of the items that you are furnishing, and secondly, do not prejudice the rights of the other bidders. In those cases in which the Government decides that your bid falls under this authority, they will generally allow you to correct your irregularity prior to the award of the contract. But again, you are wise to make certain that everything is correct before you send in your bid.

Late Bids

It is your responsibility to insure that your bid arrives at the correct address and on the desk of the correct person by the time set forth in the invitation to bid. Bids that arrive after the exact time set for opening are late bids, even though they may be less than a minute late. Usually if your bid is late, you cannot win, but there are a few exceptions to this general rule.

First, if the bid was sent by registered or certified mail not later than the fifth calendar day prior to the date specified for the receipt of bids. For example, a bid submitted in response to a solicitation requiring receipt of bids by the 20th of the month must have been mailed by the 15th.

Secondly, if it was sent by mail or telegram and it is determined by the Government that the late receipt was due solely to mishandling after receipt at the Government installation. The only evidence that the Government will accept for either of these exceptions is the U.S. mail postmark on the wrapper or on the original receipt from the Postal Service. If neither postmark shows a legible date, the bid, the bid modification, or withdrawal is assumed by the government to have been mailed late. The time of receipt at the Government installation is the time/

date stamped by the installation on the bid wrapper, or it may be any other documentary evidence of receipt established by the installation.

A Responsible Bidder

You may recall that there is a distinction between a responsive bid" and a "responsible bidder." The responsible bidder involves the ability to perform the contract and the bidder's capacity, while the responsive bid involves only the bidder's willingness to perform according to the Government's request. In practice there are four principal criteria used to determine whether or not you as a bidder are responsible. These are: your status as a manufacturer, construction contractor, or regular dealer; your financial position; your skill and experience; and your prior conduct and performance of Government contracts. In addition, your integrity or the lack of it is a major consideration in the determination of your responsibility.

The Firm Bid Rule

The firm bid rule establishes that the bid in response to an IFB cannot be withdrawn after its official opening. It is important to you because it is contrary to the ordinary principles of commercial contract law. The commercial rule is that an offer may be withdrawn at any time prior to acceptance in the absence of an option based on a consideration that would make the offer irrevocable. The firm bid rule operates only after the opening of the bid, and it does not stop you from withdrawing your bid after it is submitted but before the official opening.

There are, however, exceptions to this rule. It does not apply to negotiated contracts, which I will talk about later in this chapter. It does not apply if there has been a mutual mistake of material fact. It also does not apply if the IFB doesn't say anything about the question of withdrawal. You may also withdraw if the Government feels that it is in its interest to allow you to do so. Finally, the Government states that exceptions to the rule are made in cases in which to require you to perform the bid as made would be inequitable, unconscionable, or unreasonable. Thus there is plenty of maneuvering room here if you have erred through a gross mistake in price, but not much if the Government decides that it is a fair deal.

Mistakes in Bids

There are two basic rules that you must go by here. One, if your mistake is such that it makes your bid unacceptable and not responsive, your bid is going to be rejected. Two, since you don't have the right to withdraw a bid after the opening, the bid is effective with the mistake included after the opening. Again I want to emphasize that if you discover a mistake, correct it prior to the bid opening or better still, go over your IFB carefully and be certain that you don't make any mistakes at all. Despite what I have said previously, the Government may allow you to withdraw your bid if it can be reasonably established that it involves an honest mistake, but here again it is not what you claim, it is what the contracting officer feels and is reasonably certain about. In certain other cases you may be permitted to correct the bid from the mistaken version to the actual bid intended. This is allowed in a very small percentage of the cases in which it happens. If the contracting officer suspects that your low bid contains a mistake, he may request you to verify your bid. This should always be a red flag for you to go back and recheck your pricing. Once your verification has been made and you confirm the price, the contracting officer is under no obligation to inquire further.

Two-step Formal Advertising

Two-step formal advertising is a variation on the standard form advertising theme. It is used when definitive design and/or performance specifications are not available, but maximum competition is still desired. The first of the two steps required is the request for submission, evaluation, and, if necessary, discussion of a technical proposal without pricing. This determines the acceptability of the supplies or services offered. Next, a formally advertised procurement is requested from those companies that have submitted acceptable proposals in step number one. Two-step formal advertising is limited as to its use by the government. It can only be used if: available specifications or purchase descriptions are not sufficient or complete to permit full and free competition without technical evaluation; definite criteria exist for evaluation of technical proposals; more than one technically qualified source is expected to submit a proposal; a firm, fixed-price contract will be used; and, finally, sufficient time will be available for use of the two-step method.

After the proposal is received, the technical evaluation of the proposal is made. If your technical proposal is acceptable, you are notified both that fact and in general terms of the basis for the determination. If your technical proposal was marginal, you may be given a special opportunity through discussion to bring it up to an acceptable status. The IFB is only sent to you if your technical proposal is determined to be acceptable under the step-one phase.

Two-step formal advertising could be confused with negotiated procurements. However, there is one fundamental difference. In step two of two-step formal advertising the low bid must be accepted even though another bidder's proposal may appear more desirable at a slightly higher bid price. In negotiated procurement, the low bid need not be accepted.

Procurement by Negotiation

Although as noted earlier formal advertising is the preferred method of procurement, the majority of procurements actually take place by negotiation. This is because formal advertising is inadequate in a number of significant procurement circumstances. For example, urgent requirements may override the delays normally associated with formal advertising. There may be no competitive pricing because only one company is capable of doing the work. In this case a formally advertised bid would only lead to senseless delay. Government regulations list exceptions for which formal adveritsing can be dispensed with and negotiated procurement made. These exceptions include: a national emergency, public exigency, purchases of not more than $10,000, purchases of personal professional services, purchases outside the United States, medicines or medical supplies, supplies purchased for authorized resale, perishable or nonperishable subsistence supplies, supplies or services for which it is impractical to secure competition by formal advertising, experimental development or research work, classified purchases, technical equipment requiring standardization and interchangeability of parts, technical or specialized supplies requiring substantial initial investment or extended period of preparation for manufacture, when formal advertising procedures have failed to produce desired results, purchases in the interest of national or industrial mobilization, and purchases otherwise authorized to be negotiated according to law.

As you can see from these exceptions, there are plenty of reasons for the Government to get into the negotiated procurement business. As to whether most of your Government business will be negotiated or formally advertised, depends on the type of business that you are in. If your area generally falls into one of the exceptions noted above, then you will be doing most of your business by negotiation. Otherwise most of your business may be through formal advertisement, or you may be using both methods. To get a general idea, look at some of the notices in the *Commerce Business Daily*. By noting the type of advertisements made, that is either for an RFP or IFB, you can see which way of doing business with the Government you can anticipate.

In formally advertised procurement, the Standard Form 33 is used. This is also true with procurement by negotiation. If you will look at the top of Figure 26, you will notice that there is a box available for checking whether the procurement is by IFB or by RFP.

Procurement by formal advertising is always by low bid. However, different criteria are used to evaluate proposals made in response to an RFP. Some of these considerations are listed in the Defense Acquisition Regulations as a guide for the use of contracting officers and their negotiators in the evaluation of proposals. They are:

1. Comparison of prices quoted and consideration of other prices for similar supplies or services with due regard to production cost including extra pay shift, multishift and overtime costs, and any other factors relating to price such as profits, cost of transportation, and cash discounts.
2. Comparison of the business reputations, capabilities, and responsibilities of the respective persons or firms that submit quotations.

3. Consideration of the quality of the supplies or the services offered or of the same or similar supplies or services previously furnished with due regard to the satisfaction of technical requirements.

4. Consideration of delivery requirements.

5. Discriminating use of price and cost analysis.

6. Investigation of price aspects of any important subcontract.

7. Individual bargaining by mail or by conference.

8. Consideration of the nature and extent of the prospective contractor's cost-reduction program.

9. Effective utilization in general of the most desirable type of contract and in particular of contract provisions relating to price redetermination.

10. Consideration of the size of the business concerned.

11. Consideration as to whether the prospective supplier is a capital planned, capital emergency, capital producer under the capital industrial, capital readiness, capital planning program.

12. Consideration as to whether the prospective supplier requires expansion or conversion of plant facilities.

13. Consideration as to whether the prospective supplier is located in a surplus or scarce labor area.

14. Consideration as to whether a prospective supplier will have an adequate supply of qualified labor.

15. Consideration of the soundness of prospective contractor's management of labor's resources including wage rates, number of workers, and total estimated labor hours, with particular attention to possible uneconomical practices found in labor management agreements or in company policies, especially in the selection of contractors for development and production of major weapon systems and subsystems.

16. Consideration of the extent of subcontracting.

17. Consideration of the existing or potential workload of the prospective supplier.

18. Consideration of broadening the industrial base by the development of additional suppliers.

19. Consideration of the Government research and production property that the contractor will require the Government to provide and the elimination of the competitive advantage that might otherwise result therefrom.

20. Consideration of contract performance of facilities located in dispersed sites.

21. Advantages or disadvantages to the Government that might result from making multiple awards.

22. Consideration of the rules for avoidance of organizational conflicts of interest.

Clearly there is a lot more to look at in a proposal responding to an RFP than one responding to an advertised bid.

The Tricky Request for Quotations (RFQ)

In theory the RFQ is not really a procurement solicitation, but is exactly what the letters stand for, a request for quotations. A request for quotations is made on Standard Form 18, as shown in Figure 27. Officially it is used for procurements not expected to exceed $10,000. However, the rapidity by which an RFQ can be awarded (as opposed to an RFP) has led many contracting officers in the Government to use this for far larger sums. For example, I have bid and won an RFQ in excess of $1 million. There is also a major difference between the RFQ as used on Standard Form 18 and the IFB or RFP Standard Form 33, and that is that use of the Standard Form 18 is not an offer that may be accepted by the Government without further negotiation to form a binding contract. Therefore the rules mentioned previously regarding withdrawal prior to bid do not apply. If an RFQ is sent to you, further negotiation must take place before a contract with the Government can result. The Government cannot accept your proposal as is.

Unsolicited Proposals

According to the Government, an unsolicited proposal is one that is generated by a company on its own initiative without a formal request from the customer. In theory it is submitted in anticipation of a customer's recognized need for a product or service. In practice it does not work this way. If you submit an un-solicited proposal without an informal, unwritten agreement from the Govern-ment, you are almost certainly wasting your time, and your proposal will not be accepted. No matter how real the need may be that you have identified— which was the motivation for your submitting an unsolicited proposal—it is abso-lutely essential that preproposal marketing (as outlined in Chapter 7) be accom-plished before you submit an unsolicited proposal in an attempt to fulfill that need. The reasons for this are several:

1. Although you may have identified a general need, the specifics of this need may not be known to you. For example, if you have developed a new energy system, the method in which you conceptualize this system may not be acceptable to the Government, whereas with a small modification it may be fully acceptable.

2. Your unsolicited proposal (if it is truly not requested in any shape by your Government customer) is injected into an environment for which the budget has been set for probably more than a year and a half, and all projects have already been established for some period of time under this budget.

3. The Government customer to whom you are attempting to market, whatever your unsolicited proposal proposes, has been directing his programs and

REQUEST FOR QUOTATIONS
(THIS IS NOT AN ORDER)

PAGE 1 OF

| 1. REQUEST NO. See Block #3 | 2. DATE ISSUED 1-27-78 | 3. REQUISITION/PURCHASE REQUEST NO. 8-1-8-ES-03945-AP29-D | 4. CERTIFIED FOR NATIONAL DEFENSE UNDER BDSA REG. 2 AND/OR DMS REG. 1 RATING: |

5. ISSUED BY

PROCUREMENT OFFICE
GEORGE C. MARSHALL SPACE FLIGHT CENTER
NATIONAL AERONAUTICS & SPACE ADMINISTRATION
MARSHALL SPACE FLIGHT CENTER, ALABAMA 35812
FOR INFORMATION CALL (Name and tel. no.) (No collect calls) O. L. Smith
205-453-0405

6. DELIVER BY (Date)

7. DELIVERY
[X] FOB DESTINATION
[ ] OTHER (See Schedule)

8. TO NAME AND ADDRESS

(Street, City, State and ZIP Code)

9. DESTINATION (Consignee and address including ZIP code)

10. PLEASE FURNISH QUOTATIONS TO THE ISSUING OFFICE ON OR BEFORE CLOSE OF BUSINESS **2-20-78** (Date) SUPPLIES ARE OF DOMESTIC ORIGIN UNLESS

OTHERWISE INDICATED BY QUOTER. THIS IS A REQUEST FOR INFORMATION, AND QUOTATIONS FURNISHED ARE NOT OFFERS. IF YOU ARE UNABLE TO QUOTE, PLEASE SO INDICATE ON THIS FORM AND RETURN IT. THIS REQUEST DOES NOT COMMIT THE GOVERNMENT TO PAY ANY COSTS INCURRED IN THE PREPARATION OR THE SUBMISSION OF THIS QUOTATION, OR TO PROCURE OR CONTRACT FOR SUPPLIES OR SERVICES.

SCHEDULE

11. ITEM NO.	12. SUPPLIES/SERVICES	13. QUANTITY	14. UNIT	15. UNIT PRICE	16. AMOUNT

QUOTATIONS MUST SET FORTH FULL, ACCURATE, AND COMPLETE INFORMATION AS REQUIRED BY THIS REQUEST FOR QUOTATION (INCLUDING ATTACHMENTS). THE PENALTY FOR MAKING FALSE STATEMENTS IN QUOTATIONS IS PRESCRIBED IN 18. U. S. C. 1001.
PROPOSER OPERATES AS AN INDIVIDUAL _____, PARTNERSHIP _____, CORPORATION _____.
INCORPORATED IN THE STATE OF _____.
THE APPLICABLE SIZE STANDARD AS TO NUMBER OF EMPLOYEES TO QUALIFY AS SMALL BUSINESS FOR THIS PROCUREMENT IS ( ) OR LESS EMPLOYEES.

SUBJECT: TECHNOLOGY DEMONSTRATION MEASUREMENTS   ESTIMATED COST: $_____
FOR THE MOLECULAR WAKE SHIELD.

THE UNDERSIGNED OFFERS AND AGREES, IF THIS QUOTATION IS ACCEPTED WITHIN ____
CALENDAR DAYS (90 UNLESS A DIFFERENT PERIOD IS INSERTED BY THE PROPOSER) AFTER THE
LAST DATE FOR RECEIPT OF QUOTATION, TO PERFORM THE SERVICES IN ACCORDANCE WITH THE
QUOTATION.

SPECIAL NOTICE: PROPOSER WILL COMPLETE AND RETURN ORIGINAL OF STANDARD FORM 18 AND
THE ATTACHED CERTIFICATIONS AND REPRESENTATIONS. DO NOT RETURN PART "A" AND "B" OF
REQUEST FOR QUOTATIONS.

17. PRICES QUOTED INCLUDE APPLICABLE FEDERAL, STATE, AND LOCAL TAXES.

DISCOUNT FOR PROMPT PAYMENT ____ % 10 CALENDAR DAYS; ____ % 20 CALENDAR DAYS; ____ % 30 CALENDAR DAYS; ____ % ____ CALENDAR DAYS.

NOTE: Reverse must also be completed by the quoter.

| 18. NAME AND ADDRESS OF QUOTER (Street, city, county, State, including ZIP Code) | 19. SIGNATURE OF PERSON AUTHORIZED TO SIGN QUOTATION | 20. DATE OF QUOTATION |
| | 21. SIGNER'S NAME AND TITLE (Type or print) | 22. TELEPHONE NO (Include area code) |

Figure 27. Standard Form 18/Request for Quotations.

endeavors in a certain direction and plans have been established based on the budget and the project established for some period of time. It is not known, nor do you know, how your new proposal affects his previously well-established plans.

4. Because of the above factors, additional monies will probably be needed if it develops that your idea is fantastically good. In order to get this money, even if you can convince the responsible Government technical adviser, time is needed to convince this individual's superiors to fund your proposed idea. Because of this, regardless of the time of year, it is always well to practice the principles and techniques outlined in Chapter 7 and market your idea for an unsolicited proposal well before you document it and submit it formally. Once you have done this and both you and your Government customer are in agreement that you should submit an "unsolicited proposal," your chances of having it accepted are probably enhanced by over 100%

You should be especially careful with unsolicited proposals in putting a time limit on their acceptance. Remember that the proposal must not only be formally evaluated after you have completed the preproposal marketing process, but funds must also be found for it. Therefore setting a time limit may eliminate any possibility of acceptance. The funding of a proposal often occurs because of the constant problem of juggling funds at the end of the year. When other programs that were planned are somehow delayed and held over for the following fiscal year, sometimes the money can be reallocated to fund your program. The mechanics of developing and structuring an unsolicited proposal will be covered in Chapters 9 and 10.

If your unsolicited proposal is accepted, the results will be a sole source RFP. This is an RFP that is directed only to you and you are the only one permitted to respond. Thus while you still bid a price, furnish a certain technical proposal, a delivery schedule, and so forth, you will have no competition in doing this, and unless you really foul things up, your succes is assured.

If you are unsuccessful in getting a sole source RFP from your unsolicited proposal and the Government still thinks that it is a great idea, you may find that you are in receipt of a competitive RFP in which your ideas have been lifted by the Government and sent out to competitors as well as to you. The Government, ethically and by regulation, tries to avoid doing this. On the other hand, some ideas received are so general in nature (great idea: "men can fly through the air in a machine") that the Government feels that it has no recourse but to allow you to bid competitively against other potential contractors. This can also happen, however, even if your ideas are very specific. Therefore you must use your own judgment during preproposal marketing as to how much you should tell the Government or state in an unsolicited proposal.

As a Government program manager in charge of the development of body armor, I once met a contractor's representative who came to see me with a large bag and began to describe a type of body armor that was so fantastic that it practically weighed nothing and protected against everything. When I asked if the armor was in the bag the contractor's representative nodded, but said he could not show it to me since it was proprietary. This individual got no contract. Clearly the Government is not willing to buy a pig in the poke. On the other hand, some prudence as to how much information you should leave with or divulge to the Government may encourage your Government customer to buy only from you rather than in a competitive situation in which you will be forced to bid against others for your own idea.

Government Grants

These are essentially a specialized type of unsolicited proposal in which the Government asks for your ideas but does not specify exactly what it will fund. In writing a proposal for a grant you should follow the same lines as those of a superior proposal, including preproposal marketing activities. In fact, most people who fail at what is known as "grantsmanship" do so because they write a proposal first and then attempt to find someone from the Government who is willing to buy it. If you are in the grants business, you should avoid this. The basic concept that you must understand is that a grant is like any other Government proposal and must be developed through merchandising so that it is accepted before the formal written proposal is submitted. You cannot even write the proposal until you understand what the Government representative's responsibilities are, what he is interested in, and what he is authorized to do with his grants money.

If there is a basic difference between grants and other types of business with the Government, it is the fact that much less control is exercised once the grant is made, whereas Government contracts are closely monitored. While grantsmanship is a subject for many books in itself, I can recommend the following to help you with grants.

Federal Grants Management Handbook
Grants Management Advisory Service
2120 L Street, NW Suite 210
Washington, D.C. 20037

The Grants Planner by Daniel Conrad
The Institute for Fund Raising
3333 Hayes Street
San Francisco, CA 94102

In seeking sources of Government grants, I would recommend the following documents:

Annual Register of Grant Support and
The Catalogue of Federal Domestic Assistance

Marquis Who's Who, Inc.
200 East Ohio Street
Chicago, IL 60611

The Foundation Directory, Marianna O. Lewis, editor, and
Foundation Grants Index
Columbia University Press
136 South Broadway
Irvington, NY 10533

Announcement of Opportunities

These are used by some Government agencies to announce a solicitation for proposals that are of a more general nature and for which the necessary sum of money
has been budgeted in order to accomplish a general task. For example, NASA
issued an announcement of opportunity in 1978 for life-science investigations
on space shuttle Skylab missions from 1981 to 1983. This announcement gave
the general objectives and encouraged the potential respondents to propose investigations that met one or more life-science objectives established for these
early life-science flights. In this way a potential contractor could propose any
investigation he desired to pursue as long as it met the objectives of the announcement and was in accordance with the investigations that NASA wished to conduct.
  A special section of the announcement of opportunities indicates the guidelines
for proposal preparation that the announcing agency desires. For example, in
the announcement for the life-science objectives just mentioned, the guidelines
for proposal preparations required a covering letter signed both by the investigator and by an official or company officer of the investigator's organization.
It also required that 25 copies of the proposal be submitted, divided into two
separate sections: first, the investigation and technical section; and second, the
management and cost section. It had information regarding proposal length, a
proposal abstract, and the proposal contents that should be included, as well as
similar suggestions for the management and cost plans. The announcement of
opportunity and its resulting contract is like doing business somewhere between a
grant and an RFP.

Requests for Various Types of Information

Frequently the Government will make a request either formally or informally
for various types of information that later may result in your receipt of an RFP.
The request for information may be in the form of a capabilities request, a request
for cost information, or a request for information for planning. The capabilities
request is a request concerning the interests and capabilities of your company.
Very frequently it is formally advertised in the *Commerce Business Daily.* Usually
the notice in the *CBD* will state the supplies or services that the agency requires
and request that companies having the capabilities and resources to supply these

requirements submit a letter of interest, which must include a description of their capabilities to produce whatever the Government desires. Based upon this information the agency then sends written requests for proposals to the firms that are qualified and responded to the advertisement.

If you decide to submit a capabilities statement in response to a request from the Government you should not take it lightly, but go all the way in your submission. While it is true that some Government agencies merely use the request for information as a square-filler and consider all those companies responding to be qualified, many Government agencies apply a definite screening process and will permit only companies that they consider qualified according to their bid standards. Therefore you should give the same consideration to your capabilities submission as you do to any other proposal that you make to the Government.

A request for cost information is a request by a Government agency for you to submit an estimate of the cost of producing certain supplies or services. The request is generally based on a relative order of magnitude, or ROM, and is used by the procuring activity to develop rough estimates of cost in their planning and budgeting activities. Even though the Government will tell you that you are not held to the estimates that you make, you should realize that they are making real use of your figures and won't be thrilled if they are grossly in error. With this in mind, you should take into consideration that by the time the Government's RFP and data package are completed and sent to you, the cost due to inflation alone has usually risen considerably over your estimate. Therefore if you give a ROM to the Government, be sure to include enough of a pad so that Uncle Sam does not go wrong because of the time delay that is built into his system of developing an RFP.

Other general information that the Government uses for planning may be requested with respect to prices, delivery schedules, state of the art, and so forth, to assist the Government in both planning and making decisions having to do with their procurements. Official solicitations for information are limited and restricted by the procurement regulations, and usually such official solicitations clearly state that the agency does not intend to award a contract based on the request. If you are requested by the Government to furnish various types of information, you should consider this a positive sign since it means that at least in someone's eyes you are a potential Government contractor for the particular product or service about which the request is being made.

In summary, in this chapter I discussed various ways the Government has of doing business. In the chapters that follow we will see how we can maximize our win rate of Government contracts while following Uncle Sam's rules and methodologies and using this information to best advantage.

Chapter 6

HOW TO DEVELOP A MARKETING STRATEGY AND A MARKETING ACTION PLAN

STRATEGY

Strategy is the planning and the managing of any endeavor. Its use implies the allocation of resources, because it doesn't make any difference what the size of your company is; whether it is a large one or a very small one, from gigantic General Motors to a one-man operation, no company has unlimited resources. Therefore, implicit in any planning and managing strategy is the proper allocation of resources to bring profits to your organization in an effective and efficient manner.

Last year in the *Wall Street Journal* I was amazed to find a long article about how many of today's large corporations are encouraging their executives to study military strategy. Now why in the world would a corporation want its managers to learn military strategy? I believe it is because military strategy explicity demonstrates and is a tremendous example of the proper allocation of resources. Look at Figure 28, illustrating the Battle of Cannae. This famous battle took place more than 2000 years ago. Yet even today it is studied at military academies worldwide because it was the most decisive battle in military history. This battle was fought by that great Carthaginian general, Hannibal, against his sworn enemy, ancient Rome. Rome was renowned as the military power of its time with its mighty legions feared throughout the known world. Hannibal fought the Romans at Cannae with an inferior number of troops. But Hannibal knew how the Romans were organized and how they used their forces in attack. He deployed his forces accordingly, with most of his troops at the flanks, firmly anchored on the Autidus River. He echeloned his outer units forward so that the apex presented an extremely weak front. He split his cavalry into two forces. On his right flank was a small cavalry force that was ordered to hold the Roman cavalry in place. However, most of Hannibal's cavalry was massed on the left flank.

As the battle opened, Hannibal sent his stronger cavalry force around and behind the entire Roman army. They fought and destroyed the Roman cavalry from the rear while his smaller cavalry force attacked from the front. Meanwhile the Roman legions, with their overpowering force, marched steadily forward and the Cartha-

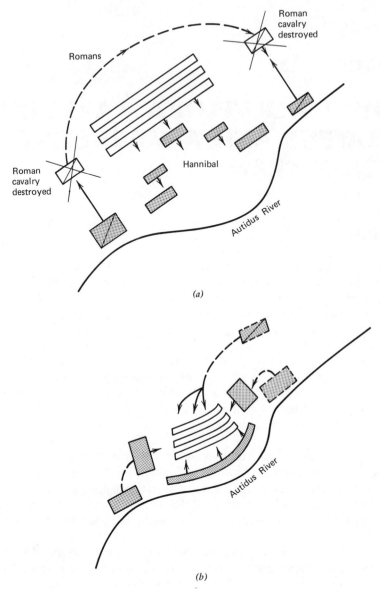

Figure 28. Battle of Cannae, 216 B.C. (a) Phase I. (b) Phase II.

ginians with their weakened apex fell back. By phase two of the battle the Roman legions were encircled in a canyon of massed Carthaginian infantry. At a signal, the two strong wings of Hannibal's forces fell in upon them and the Romans were annihilated.

In modern terms, this maneuver is called a double envelopment. As mentioned earlier, this was the most decisive engagement in military history and the Romans suffered more than 80% of their men killed in action. Hannibal's forces when he attacked were inferior in number to those of his powerful enemy. Yet he destroyed them. In business, strategy does not end with a double envelopment in which we destroy our competition as Hannibal did. But it is important to realize that the same principles apply to managing and planning in business in order to make the best use of the resources that are at our disposal.

There are many examples in business in which companies have inflicted "Cannaes" on their competition and gone on to business success. Did you know, for example, that Sears and Montgomery Ward were both about the same size in sales prior to World War II, and that after the war it was thought that Montgomery Ward would end up as the bigger company? But Sears developed a different marketing strategy that concentrated its resources and changed its old strategy from primarily mail-order sales to retail sales. It picked the best locations in every city to support the new strategy. And while Montgomery Ward, expecting a major depression after the war, sought to conserve its resources, Sears fearlessly invested its money in the new strategy. By the time Montgomery Ward could react, Sears was well entrenched in the best locations throughout the country. Today Sears is a business conglomerate that has entered many fields and whose sales far exceed Montgomery Ward's.

Another example is Minute Maid orange juice. Today Minute Maid makes other juices besides orange, but once orange juice was its sole product. If the orange crop failed in any given year, Minute Maid was in great danger of failing as well. On December 13, 1957, that is exactly what happened. A major Florida freeze destroyed much of the orange crop. Bigger competitors with more resources were able to purchase California oranges or those Florida oranges that had managed to survive by paying a premium price. Minute Maid was in great danger of bankruptcy. But the company came up with a superior strategy. Minute Maid engineers had been directed to develop machinery that would allow concentrated orange juice to be extracted from damaged oranges, something that had never before been done successfully in the industry. Minute Maid's allocation for resources and strategy was successful because their engineers succeeded in developing this process and introducing it at this critical time. The company was able to buy damaged oranges below the prices paid by its competitors and the net result was a tremendous success for Minute Maid. The rout of Minute Maid's competitors was like the rout at Cannae. A $2.4 million loss in 1957 was turned around, and earnings of almost $4.6 million were rolled up in 1958.

In 1973 Robert Ringer wrote his now famous book, *Winning Through Intimidation.* Ringer wrote to many publishers, seeking to get his book published. He was unsuccessful. So he also developed a superior strategy. This strategy was to publish the book himself. By this I do not mean subsidy publishing, whereby the author pays someone else to publish a book. No, Ringer found his own printer, designed his own book, and handled the distribution and marketing himself. He made speeches up and down the length of the country about his book and his philosophy. He took full-page ads out in magazines, inviting prospective customers to buy his book through mail order. So successful was his strategy that big publishers came to Ringer and offered him huge royalties in exchange for the publishing rights. The net result of Robert Ringer's successful strategy was a million-copy best seller. Today he has several other successful books on the market, each published by a major publisher.

STRATEGY IN GOVERNMENT MARKETING

I have talked about strategy in marketing of small and large businesses, but I have not mentioned Government marketing. What sort of strategy is possible in a marketplace that is largely controlled by the Government? Though this may have its limitations, a Hannibal-like strategy is still possible by manipulating the strategic variables over which we have control and adapting ourselves to those variables over which we have no control. In other words, we can still succeed by the proper allocation of resources. Which strategic variables do we have control over in the Government marketplace? We have control over the product itself, as well as its price, its distribution, and its promotion. Let's look at each in turn.

Developing a Strategy for the Product

What can we do with a product? For a product strategy we can add a new product, we can drop an old established product, we can find a new use for an old product, or we can modify a product in quality, size, shape, color, variety, and so forth. How can adding a new product be a successful marketing strategy in the Government marketplace?

Gentex is a successful Government contractor located near Carbondale, Pennsylvania. Today Gentex's sales are in the millions of dollars, but it was not so very long ago that this was not so. In the early 1960s Gentex was financially weakened from battles with its competitors. With some risk Gentex pursued an add-a-new product strategy that ultimately helped make it the vigorous company it is today. What Gentex found was that in the then-standard helicopter helmet worn by all crewmen in Vietnam, high levels of sound were not attenuated. In fact, sound levels reaching the helicopter crewman's ears were loud enough to produce deafness if sufficient exposure occurred. Gentex engineered and developed a new helmet that not only dramatically decreased noise but was far more comfortable than the helmet then in use. As the inventor of and holding the proprietary rights to this helmet, Gentex collected a royalty for every helmet produced whether by itself or by other helmet-producing companies for the Government.

Gentex then further exploited its successful strategy. It turned next to the protection of soldiers serving in armored vehicles. Similar problems with regard to sound and bump protection existed with the helmet then in use. This time in direct competition with competitors seeking to introduce other new helmets, Gentex developed a modified version of the sound-attentuaton system used in its helicopter helmets. Once again Gentex's helmet was adopted as standard by the U.S. Army, and Gentex sold millions of this proprietary product. What was the secret of Gentex's success? Gentex didn't just introduce a helmet. The helmet was part of an overall new-product strategy.

To simply drop a product made for Government use is not your decision. The Government makes this decision. However, you as a manufacturer can make a decision not to manufacture a certain Government product. Of what advantage is this? It frees resources otherwise committed to the manufacture of that product so that they can be used in new-product development, to buy new machinery, to introduce another product, and so forth. Therefore every decision to drop a product can be either in itself, or in conjunction with another action, a viable strategy to make your firm more profitable in the Government marketplace.

Gentex's great competitor was Sierra Engineering Company located in Sierra Madre, California. As Gentex had struggled in the 1960s for leadership in the field of helmets, so had Sierra succeeded in becoming preeminent in the field of oxygen masks. By the early 1970s Sierra Engineering Company was producing virtually every oxygen mask used by the three military services in the United States and in almost all Western countries with the exception of France and England. Sierra than discovered the need for a new product in American transport aircraft. In these airplanes an oxygen mask was not worn continuously or suspended from the helmet as in Air Force fighters or bombers. However, in case of an emergency, such as a fire or sudden decompression, immediate oxygen could be crucial to the crew's survival. Sierra succeededin modifying the oxygen mask that it was already producing as a sole-source product and designed a new framework for it. This new product was immediately adopted by the United States Air Force as standard, and Sierra's successful product strategy made it sole source as a producer of this mask for all the needs of the Air Force.

How to Develop a Price Strategy

There are three basic pricing strategies. We can either adopt a low price, we can go in with a high price, or we can use a meet-the-competition price. The low price is essentially a market penetration strategy. For example, for twenty years one company developed essentially all the parachutes used by the Government in parachute equipment for aircraft. A multimillion dollar research and development contract was advertised by the Air Force. It was assumed that this one company that had done all the business for the preceding 20 years would once again win the R&D contract. But a new and hungry company wanted this business and wanted to get into the parachute business very badly. This company spent considerable resources on learning the basics of the business and to insure winning the R&D contract that they felt was essential to penetrating this market, they bid an extremely low price for the development contract. Winning this initial contract led to other contracts in research and development and eventually to major production contracts. This is a low-price strategy.

At the opposite end of the spectrum is the high-price strategy. Once when I was a Government Program Manager I received six bids from six different companies to produce a certain product that we felt was essential to the war effort in Vietnam. One company's bid was 20% higher than all the rest, and yet it was this company that won this important multimillion dollar contract. How did this happen? They were able to do this by using a high-price strategy in which they portrayed themselves as the "top of the line," the Cadillac of the industry. The vigorous proof of the quality and superiority of the anticipated product convinced us that it was easily worth the additional 20% to the Government in order to get the best possible product that we could in this specific area. This is a sterling example of the high-price strategy.

The third price strategy that we might use is a meet-the-competition price strategy. If we choose to do this, this strategy implies that in some way other than price we are better than our competition. Otherwise why should the Government deal with us? In some fashion we must offer a better value. For example, the quality of our product may be higher, the scheduled delivery may be much better, the technical and performance properties of our product may be much greater, or something else beyond price must account for the superior value of our product. It should be noted when talking about price that our ability to manipulate this variable is extremely limited when responding to IFBs, since an IFB is a price competition alone. Therefore if we intend to bid competitively against other companies, we must have a low price in order to win. However, any of these pricing strategies is fully applicable when we are submitting a proposal in a response to an RFP or an RFQ or are introducing a new product through an unsolicited proposal.

How to Develop a Distribution Strategy

It is true that in Government marketing the distribution system is established by the Government. However, what you are able to control is the level in the system at which you wish to operate. For example, I showed you in an earlier chapter that you might function successfully as a Government contractor at either the highest level as a systems developer or at a lower level where you are doing, say, basic research or supplying components to someone else further up the ladder—for example, a subsystem or a systems manufacturer, who is in turn supplying to the Government. Which level you choose to operate at depends upon your individual situation and has been discussed previously. I won't repeat it here except to make you aware of the fact that at what level or levels you choose to operate is in fact a manipulation of the strategic variable of distribution. It is also a marketing strategy.

How to Develop a Promotional Strategy

The promotional variable actually has three components. These are personal selling, advertising, and promoting. Although it may not appear so at first glance, all three are fully applicable to the small businessman interested in selling to Uncle Sam. Personal selling is perhaps the most important component in the Government marketplace, and I will emphasize it throughout this book—especially in dealing with the Government for research and development and other types of proposals that must be made in response to an RFP or an RFQ.

Personal Selling

Personal selling and contact with the Government prior to receipt of the RFP or RFQ is absolutely essential. This is also true whenever you are attempting to introduce a new product into the Government marketplace. The amount of resources that you are able to put on personal selling in time, in salesmen, and in number of contacts that your salesmen or representatives make depends on whether you will be limited in doing business with the Government to a certain fixed geographic area or can call the whole country your territory, and whether in such contacts as research and development you are going to market to all levels of government including headquarters, the procuring agency, the user, and so forth, or limit yourself to just the procuring agency. These are all variables and constitute an allocation-of-resource problem to which you must give some thought.

Advertising

You may think when I mention the advertising component of the promotional variable that I am talking about the large institutional ads that appear in such magazines as *Aviation Week* and describe the outstanding accomplishments of some major Government contractor such as McDonnell Douglas, General Dynamics, and others. However, I am not talking about this at all because there are other types of advertisement that you can make as a Government contractor that can lead either directly or indirectly to additional Government business. Specifically, what I am talking about is writing articles, making speeches before audiences in which Government personnel are present, and otherwise getting yourself known and recognized as an expert in the particular field in which you are a Government contractor. Now you may not be able to write very well. If you can't write, you can hire someone else to do it for you. The point is that there are thousands of magazines that are published every year that are read by Government customers in your particular field. If you have a new product that you are trying to introduce, writing an article is one very good way of doing it. And as you probably recognize, an article that may run to four or five pages in a journal might cost up to $50,000 or $60,000, or even more if you had to pay for it as an advertisement.

In the same way, you can make speeches. The key here is to make speeches before the right organization. Every trade and professional association is continually looking for speechmakers; I don't care whether it is an association of attorneys or aeronautical engineers; if you have something to say, go to your library and look at a copy of the *Encyclopedia of Associations*, published by the Gale Research Company of Detroit, Michigan. Here you will find thousands of organizations listed, trade, business, and commercial organizations, agricultural organizations, technical organizations, and so forth. Write a short 30-to-45-minute speech about your product or service and then make a list of those organizations in your area whose members might include Government officials who might buy your product or service. Call each of these organizations in turn and tell them that you would very much like to speak before them on a subject of interest to them. You will find many organizations absolutely delighted to have you. In addition to free meals and good business contacts, you may even find yourself being paid for your speeches.

Another way in which you can manipulate the advertising component of the promotional variable is through the publicity release. A publicity release is simply a statement of fact about something that people would be interested in reading about. You write up a fact sheet entitled "Publicity Release," as in the example provided in Figure 29. Then go to a library and look up a reference book called *Standard Rate and Data*. In this publication you can locate magazines that are likely to be read by customers in the Government, and who are also likely to purchase your product or service. Make a photcopy of your release, enclose a 4 X 5 glossy photograph of your Product (if you have one), and include a covering letter in which you tell the editor about your product or service and why you are sending out the publicity release at this time. Use the sample covering letter in Figure 30, but adapt the style of writing to your particular situation. The U.S. Government's order for a particular protective device that I designed was directly attributable to the fact that I sent a publicity release to a number of magazines read by my Government customers. Figure 31 shows the result of a successful release.

Another part of your promotional variable is a capabilities brochure. I will discuss in a later chapter how to write a brochure about a product or a service on your capabilities, which should be attached to all proposals that you submit to the Government. But here I only want to mention that the resources that you spend on a brochure are part of this advertising component of the promotional strategic variable.

Promotionals

You may think promotionals are only for supermarkets and for companies using trading stamps, but this is not true. A standard tactic in the proposals of one

BUXTON ADVERTISING AGENCY

SIERRA ENGINEERING
News Release
For Immediate Release

NEWS RELEASE

NEW LIGHTWEIGHT BODY ARMOR
OFFERS INCREASED PROTECTION

SIERRA MADRE, CALIF. -- December 11, 1974 - The development of a new body armor that is only one-third the weight yet offers 28% more protection than current standard military models has been announced by Sierra Engineering Company.

The lightweight feature of the new Sierra Assault Body Armor Jacket, weighing only 3½ pounds (1.6 kilo), eliminates the problem of heat stress and combat fatigue caused by older designs.

A new high-strength flexible armor material, having five times the tensile strength of steel, provides fragmentation protection approximately 28% better than standard existing body armor.

The unique front closure system enables the armor to be worn like a jacket, permitting the wearer to don and doff the unit without removing the helmet.

This design also allows greater ventilation while wearing the armor with no degradation of protection where the two halves of armor are joined in front, in fact, at the overlap the protection is increased by an additional twenty-five percent.

The Sierra Assault Body Armor Jacket is available in three sizes, each of which is fully adjustable.

-30-

Editor Note: For additional information, contact William Cohen, Sierra Engineering Company, 123 Montecito Avenue, Sierra Madre, CA 91024   Phone: (213) 355-4281

Please reply to:

☐ *Union Bank Plaza/201 S. Lake Avenue/Pasadena, California 91101 (213) 795-5985/681-4993*
☐ *2101 East Fourth Street, Suite 215/Santa Ana, California 92705 (714) 836-6091/547-1691*
☐ *4341 Piedmont Ave/Oakland, California 94611 (415) 654-3526*

Figure 29.   News Release/New lightweight body armor offers increased protection.

```
Mr. A. B. Jones
Editor

_____
_____
_____

Dear Mr. Jones:

        Enclosed is a publicity release and glossy photograph

of our new product "Iron Coat."  "Iron Coat" is a non-toxic

chemical which can be used to treat any ordinary article

of clothing to increase its durability.  Tests have shown

that cloth sprayed with "Iron Coat" outlast non-treated

articles two to three times.  "Iron Coat" is currently

being submitted for test to various organizations of the

Department of Defense.

                              Sincerely,


                              John Smith
                              President
```

Figure 30.   Sample covering letter: Mr. A. B. Jones, Editor.

New Body Armor Developed

The development of a new body armor that is only one-third the weight yet offers 28% more protection than current standard military models has been announced by Sierra Engineering Company.

The lightweight feature of the new Sierra Assault Body Armor Jacket, weighing only 3½ pounds (1.6 kilo), elim-inates the problem of heat stress and combat fatigue caused by older designs.

A new high-strength flex-ible armor material, having five times the tensile str-ength of steel, provides frag-mentation protection ap-proximately 28% better than standard existing body ar-mor.

The unique front closure system enables the armor to be worn like a jacket, permit-ting the wearer to don and doff the unit without remov-ing the helmet.

This design also allows greater ventilation while we-aring the armor and no de-gradation of protection - where the two halves of armor are joined in front, in fact, at the overlap the protection is increased by an additional twenty-five per-cent.

The Sierra Assault Body Armor Jacket is available in three sizes, each of which is fully adjustable.

For information, contact William Cohen, Sierra En-gineering Company, 123 Montecito Avenue, Sierra Madre, Phone 355-4281.

Figure 31. New body armor developed.

company with whom I was employed was to offer a free set of reprocurement drawings, usually valued at about $20,000, coincident with the Government's order for a certain production quantity of the item once the research and development had been accomplished. Thus the offer to the Government might read, "Instead of pricing out Category E drawings required by the RFP, our company will offer a free set of reprocurement drawings to the Government coincident with an order of 20,000 widgets in any one year."

The net effect of this, of course, was to lower the price for the research and development bid by that $20,000. This meant our price was now $20,000 less than our competitors. The advanage to us was getting the contract and going through a learning process in making the first prototype or limited production items required, so that later items we made could be produced cheaper than our competition. The advantage to the Government was saving $20,000 in drawings until they were needed (if ever). The $20,000 for the drawings would be amortized over the cost of all of the units produced. A little risky? An investment? Yes, but so are all promotionals. This, then, is the Government marketing version of a promotional or sale, but don't think this is the only way of applying the principle. Use your imagination and you will find ways to beat the competition, satisfy the Government, make a profit, and at the same time stay within the rules of the Government procurement regulations.

Now let's look at the environmental variables, those variables over which we have little control. Now we'll see what we can do to adapt our strategy to them or to make them irrelevant to our winning.

These uncontrollable variables include demand, competition, the distribution structure, and legal constraints.

Demand

The demand for any product or service you should usually take as "given." Oh yes, you may be able to build demand for a product or service, but the cost may be so great that you yourself may never be able to make a profit from the demand that you were able to generate. Let me give you an example of this from my own experience in Government marketing.

After the 1973 war in the Middle East, one of my engineers read about dust being a problem in tanks. Thinking we had uncovered a real need in want of fulfilling, my engineer began making calls around the country to potential Government customers to see if he could interest someone in a program to develop a special anti-dust mask for tanks. Despite many phone calls, no one in the Government seemed interested. In the end it was decided to try to create our own demand through a concept proposal including pictures of the product and what it could do. This proposal was forwarded to the U.S. Army. In essence, we wanted to introduce our own idea of what we thought the U.S. Army needed. Despite considerable effort, a good proposal, and frequent contact we were unsuccessful in this endeavor. At the same time there were similar requirements in the Army for other products that we were capable of developing for which a demand was well established and that the Army definitely wanted. The lesson here is to always go after products for which a demand already exists in the Government. In these you will find your fortune. If you try to ram a product down the throat of a potential customer, you will spend time and money with no return on your investment.

Competition

You cannot control your competition. What you *can* do is learn what the competition is doing prior to establishing your strategy. You must also recognize and understand that after the introduction of your strategy, your competition will try to initiate a counterstrategy. For example, during the years of the Vietnam War personal armor was developed for soldiers. This armor, which weighed 30 pounds and covered both the front and back torso, could stop armor-piercing ammunition at muzzle velocity. One armor company exploited the product strategy and developed a new means of making the standard product and meeting the specifications of the Government at minimum cost. This company soon began winning the majority of armor contracts, which constituted millions of dollars in Government business during the height of the Vietnam conflict.

Its major competitor was in a quandary. It did not have the capability of developing this production process within a reasonable period of time. In the course of deciding what to do, the competition tested thousands of the new armor units made with this process against others made with the old process. It discovered that while the new product met the bare minimum specifications of the Government, it barely managed to do so. The competition discovered that armor made by the old process, although more expensive, was, in fact, testing approximately 20% better. This competitor then made this information available to the Government, along with a strong suggestion that different classes of armor be instituted so that the additional 20% protection offered could be ordered by those who needed it. The Government did so. This now presented the ordering customer with a choice, a lower-priced unit with less protection or a higher-priced one with more protection. Since the price normally is not specified in an IFB contract, many ordering customers specified the higher level of protection and the net result was that the determined competitor's counterstrategy was successful in winning a significant share of the armor contracts.

Regardless of which strategy you introduce, think one step ahead to what your competition is likely to do and be ready to counter this move as well.

The Distribution Structure

The distribution structure, as noted earlier, is established by the Government. It is fixed, but this does not mean that you should not spend time in learning how it operates and how to make best use of it. It has been said that knowledge is power, but only if you put it to use. Therefore, learn the distribution structure in Government contracting and then put this knowledge to use to make more profits for your company. The distribution structure and how to use it is discussed in Chapters 1, 3, 4, and 5 of this book.

Legal Constraints

The legal constraints define what you can and cannot do in Government contracting. Much of this information you can obtain from the Government itself, either through agencies such as the SBA and the GSA that are set up to help you, or through Government contracting officers who may help you if you ask, or through the various procurement regulations themselves, which you can purchase from the Superintendent of Documents in Washington, D.C. Of course for a legal problem you should go to an attorney familiar with Government contracting procedures. To find such an attorney call the local bar association listed in your phone book or contact the SBA. Though legal advice may not be cheap, it is worth it in many cases in order to enable you to adapt and initiate a winning strategy.

Other Strategic Marketing Concepts You Can Follow

There are three strategic marketing concepts that you should note that can help you win big Government contracts. The first is mass marketing, in which you attempt to sell to everyone. The second is market segmentation, in which you attempt to sell to a certain segment of the market. The third is product differentiation, in which you promote differences between your product or service and other competitive products or services.

You might think that mass marketing is always the correct strategy since it provides the biggest potential market for you. However, mass marketing can be a waste of resources if your product cannot be used or is not desirable for use by everyone who is in the mass market. For example, let's say body armor is your product. Body armor is used not only by the armed forces, but also by police departments, undercover agents such as the FBI, the CIA, and the Secret Service, and so forth. Mass Government marketing in this case would be attempting to sell one type of body armor to different agencies with different needs.

In market segmentation, on the other hand, you would take only a part of this market. For example, the armed forces is a segment of the body-armor market. The ground forces is an even more specific market. Market segmentation assumes that there is some common identifying characteristic shared by all parts of the market segment. In this case the identifiable segment would be the ground forces (the Army) as opposed to the Navy, Air Force, or police. Figure 32 is a brochure describing a product aimed at one segment of a market. The product, body armor, is clearly intended for infantry use and not for any other military or nonmilitary use. Can you imagine trying to mass-market the product described? This cumbersome armor would be very uncomfortable worn as a protective vest underneath street clothes.

A product differentiation strategy means that you must promote differences between your product and that of your competitors. However, there is the implicit assumption here that you have something different to promote. Clearly if your product is one used every day in a large quantity and is a fairly simple one such as a screw or a nail, there may be no such difference. Going back to the body-armor example, the armor illustrated has many features that can be used to promote a product differentiation strategy. You cannot do that for a product that is not demonstrably different.

If you are considering either market strategy, segmentation or product differentiation, in the Government marketplace, there are several factors that you should consider in making a decision. These factors are the size of the market; the sensitivity of your Government customer to product differences, real or imagined; the life cycle of your product; the type of product it is; the number of competitors

THE COMMANDO MK III ARMOR JACKET
WINS BATTLES!

74%
REDUCTION
IN
WOUNDS

83%
REDUCTION
IN
FATALITIES

♦ **PROTECTION**
  ■ High Level Fragmentation Protection of 564 meters per second (1850 feet per second).
  ■ Will Stop 9mm (USA) 124 gr. FMJ, .44 magnum 240 gr. (6″ bbl.), .357 magnum 158 gr. (6″ bbl.), .357 P magnum 90 gr. S and W (6″ bbl.), .357 magnum 125 gr. SJHP (6″ bbl.), .22 magnum (6″ bbl.), .41 magnum, .38 Caliber 125 gr., SJHP (6″ bbl.), .38 Caliber Special 158 gr., 00 Buckshot.

♦ **KPC ARMOR**
  ■ Flexible
  ■ Waterproof
  ■ Reduces or Eliminates Blunt Trauma
  ■ Will Not Spall

♦ **COMFORT**
  ■ Wt. 2.3 kilos (5 lbs.) size medium
  ■ Designed to Eliminate Heat Stress and Fatigue
  ■ 3 Sizes for Perfect Comfort and Fit
  ■ Fully Adjustable In Both Waist and Shoulders
  ■ Wear Like a Jacket With Full Protection In Front

♦ **DONNING AND DOFFING**
  ■ Without Removing Helmet
  ■ Emergency Doffing In 5 Seconds

GLOBAL ASSOCIATES
Protective Armor Systems
1556 N. SIERRA MADRE VILLA
PASADENA, CALIFORNIA 91107
U.S.A.

Figure 32. "The Commando MK III Armor Jacket Wins Battles!"

that you have; and, of course, the strategy or strategies that your competitors are using.

Let's look at each of these in turn. If the size of your market is very large, this suggests that a segmentation strategy may be advisable since you can break this very large market into two or more market segments. On the other hand, if the total market is too small then segmentation may not be feasible since the segment into which you break this small market may be too small to be sold to and still make a profit. Your customer's sensitivity to product differences are, of course, important and gets back to what kind of product or service you are attempting to sell. If you are selling screws and if you are able to convince your customers that there is a difference between your screws and those of your competitor, then a product differentiation strategy is possible. I emphasize this because it is the Government's sensitivity and perception that is important. Your screw may have twice the tensile strength of a competitor's screw. But if the Government doesn't see it or doesn't consider it important, then your product differentiation strategy will not be successful. Of course, the opposite can occur and the Government may think your product is great simply because it appears to be stronger.

The life cycle of the product may dictate that you should follow a segmentation strategy if you have entered into a fairly mature stage of the product's life cycle. In that case segmentation may provide an opportunity to go one up on your competitors by designing a special product for a specific market segment. For example, referring back to body armor, if the military and police markets became saturated, you might be able to gain both additional sales and profits by building special custom-fit body armor for heads of state. On the other hand, if the product is still in the introductory stage of its life cycle, then a product differentiation strategy that attempts to go after a major portion of the market may be more profitable. The type of product or service that you are selling has a significant effect upon which particular strategic concept to follow. If your product is a distinct item such as body armor then you can make significant changes in its design or performance as described above. This type of product lends itself readily to a market segmentation strategy. But if your product is a commodity, gasoline or a foodstuff, say, your Government customer is less likely to perceive differences among the different bids by various manufacturers; and if your product is truly unique, you may be able to initiate a product differentiation strategy and promote its differences in order to get your product demanded by the Government customer. Having a number of competitors is important because the more competitors there are the more difficult it is for you to get your particular product or service to stand out from the crowd. Thus the best strategy that you can employ is to identify with a certain market segment and leave the remainder of the field for your competitors to fight over.

On the other hand, if there are only a few firms in your industry, a strategy of product differentiation may be more effective and efficient since you can go after a bigger market and not have to split it with other contractors. As noted earlier, you must always consider beforehand what your competitor is likely to do after your introduce your strategy and you should also consider the strategy of your competitors at the time that you are developing yours. If you are entering a market in which the competitors are all using product differentiation strategies, then your counterstrategy should probably be to turn to market segmentation; that is, pick out a certain market segment for yourself and concentrate your resources there. Conversely, if there is currently an industry-wide segmentation strategy, it would probably be difficult for you to counter with product differentiation, in which you tried to sell one product to all segments. However, once again you can pick out one particular segment and within that segment use a product differentiation strategy to beat out your competitor.

Marketing Strategy Leads to a Marketing Action Plan

At this point, you have read the preceding chapters, you have located some potential customers for your product or service, you may even have had some face-to-face meetings, and having read the first portion of this chapter, you have an understanding of the various types of strategies that you may follow and the importance of each. You also have a general idea of which strategy you intend to follow in order to beat your competition with your product or service in the Government marketplace. Your problem now is how to develop a marketing action plan in order to win a Government contract. You may wonder why it is necessary to document your strategy in a marketing plan. Here is what a marketing action plan will do for you:

1. It will specify your overall marketing strategy and document it.
2. It will specify in detail which action steps you will take to implement your marketing strategy.
3. It will act as a road map to show you where you are going every step of the way in order to succeed.
4. It will bring together all the information needed so that other people on your team know what they must do and can act in a coordinated fashion.
5. It will allow you to conduct your own how-goes-it self-evaluation to see how you are doing as you progress to your first Government contract and those other Government contracts to follow that are a part of the plan.
6. It will provide a sales document that can be used, if necessary, to obtain additional funding from sources outside of your company.

The Three-Step Process of Accomplishing a Marketing Action Plan

The process of developing a marketing action plan is done in three steps: (1) in-depth screening of opportunities, (2) marketing analysis to decide a strategy, and (3) marketing plan development.

How to Do an In-Depth Screening of Opportunities

You will find that even after your preliminary screening of potential Government business, after talking with your prospective customers on the telephone, and after meeting them face to face, you will have more opportunities than you can possibly pursue. Similarly, since creation of each marketing action plan will require time and effort on your part, you will have more opportunities than you will have time to develop marketing action plans for them. Therefore an in-depth screening of opportunities to secure a workable number of opportunities with a high probability of winning is essential. In order to properly screen the opportunities available to you, you must consider the following factors:

1. What business are you in now, or do you want to be in?
2. Synergism between this opportunity and other opportunities already existing or that may exist in the future.
3. Company capabilities and limitations.
4. The strength of your customer's needs.
5. The profit potential, including return on investment.

Let's look at each in turn.

What Business Are You In?

The question of what business you are in or want to be in is the foundation of your planning and strategy and is crucial to it. Peter F. Drucker, the world's foremost management consultant and philosopher, a man who has devoted his entire life to the study and improvement of management, an author of numerous books and articles, a consultant, teacher, lecturer, and innovator, a man who has probably had more influence in the world of business and industry than any other, says that the question, "What is our business?" is the first responsibility of top management and that it is perhaps the most important single cause of business frustration and failure. Why is a seemingly simple question so crucial to success or failure?

If you haven't thought through the question of your company's business, your company is actually adrift. Here is why. Risk is inherent in business. You cannot afford risk. You can minimize it by making certain decisions and not making others. What's more, you can avoid certain risks while choosing to take others. In the Government contracting business the biggest risks come from uncertainties. Will Salt II pass the Congress or not? Will the MX funding be approved? Will we stress solar energy over the next 25 years? Will we build nuclear energy plants? Will we continue with fossil fuels? What will the new administration in Washington do, in the state capital, in our city? What is going to happen to the economy this year or next year? What is going to happen on the international scene? What will technology achieve or fail to achieve and how rapidly will this happen? Depending on the business we are in, we may respond differently. Therefore the question about what business our company is in is not an insignificant one, and in truth is the rudder that will direct our company either to success or to failure.

Synergism

If we already have a contract to produce 100 million widgets we can produce an additional 10 million at a greatly reduced cost. The same is true in research and development or in any product or service activity in dealing with the U.S. Government. If we already have some contracts in house or expect to get others, this synergism may not only help to reduce the cost of the present business but may actually help us to get future additional business in this area. All of this should be considered as either a positive or negative factor in evaluating a specific opportunity.

Capabilities and Limitations

Every company has certain capabilities and limitations that are unique to it. Just last week I was called by a small company that has been extremely successful in the marketing of medical products that it does not itself produce. It has grown over the past three years from start-up to sales of $3 million a year. At this point it wants to start producing the product itself, but it has absolutely no product capability or anyone within the company who is qualified to direct the start-up of production capabilities. Conversely, other companies may already be making a product that they are unable to market successfully or to its full potential. Some companies may be very strong in financial resources or financial know-how. Others will always suffer from a lack of financial resources; to them, money may always be a mystery for which outside expertise will be needed in order to insure the company's growth and survival. If your company has a very strong technical engineering team for a certain type of research and development, clearly this is an advantage for certain types of Government work. On the other hand, lack of this expertise may indicate that you should not pursue certain types of contracts or specialized opportunities that may be available to you.

The Strength of the Customer's Needs

The strength of the customer's needs is extremely important. During investigation of customer opportunities you will find these opportunities at various stages of completion and intensity. Some potential products will never come to the fore. They are simply dreams or imaginary visions of the particular Govenment customer that you have contacted. This is one of the reasons that you must contact various levels and different people in the customer's organization. Only in this way can you determine whether these potential programs are real or not. Only by discovering how strong the program's proponent in the Government actually is and how much power he actually has can you determine whether or not the program will actually go as far as being advertised for bid. In this manner, as well as in summing up various opportunities, you can determine for each opportunity the strength of the customer's need for a potential program. And the strength of this need should also have a major bearing on whether you should choose to pursue this opportunity or drop it.

Profit Potential

Profit potential may be listed last, but it is not least. Profit potential must always be considered. Clearly we desire to maximize the profit potential of our business consistent with individual ethics and the law. However, certain programs will be found to be more potentially profitable than others. In considering the profit potential we must not only consider the immediate contract, but potential contracts that may evolve in the future. For example, frequently the initial R&D contract breaks even or may even lose money for the company that undertakes it. However, this is acceptable if future contracts that the company will get as a result of this initial effort will have a big profit potential.

By means of the process just described, we should screen the opportunities into a workable number that we intend to pursue. Now that we have screened the opportunities the next step is a marketing analysis to decide which strategy to adopt in order to secure the objectives that we decide upon. This analysis is accomplished by deciding which marketing strategy concept we intend to adopt and which is better suited to our situation—mass marketing, market segmentation, or product differentiation—and which marketing variables we are going to manipulate while adapting to the environmental variables that we cannot control. Finally, we must proceed to develop our marketing action plan. This plan should be actually written down even if we are a one-man company, for the important and vital reasons that we have listed above.

Perhaps the first question about the marketing action plan that we must answer is what period do you do it for. In most cases I would suggest developing a marketing action plan for the length of the project. Thus if your project is for three years, then I would do a three-year marketing action plan. In other words, whatever length of time it takes in order to achieve the overall goals and objectives of the project, that is the period of time that you should allot to your marketing action plan. The overall marketing action plan outline, as shown in Figure 33, is broken down into four separate parts. The first is a situational analysis. The second part consists of problems and opportunities. The third concerns your marketing strategy, and the final part deals with action to be taken. Let's take each part individually.

Situation Analysis

This should be a general review of the situation regarding the product or service that you are offering and the environment into which you are introducing it. It should include product characteristics, price, distribution, and promotional activities. It should also include various environmental and other factors important to your marketing strategy, including demand and other important factors such

Marketing Action Plan Outline

I.   Situational Analysis

       (A general review of the situation regarding the
    product or the services that you are offering and the
    environment into which you are introducing it includ-
    ing product, price, distribution, promotional activi-
    ties, and environmental and other factors.)

II. Problems and Opportunities.

       (Summary of all factors in section are divided
    into the problem or opportunity category.)

III. Marketing Strategy

       1. Objectives

           (Target market segments, shares, sales
    volume and profits)

       2. Marketing Program

           (Product, price, distribution and promotion,
    and dollar amounts of each)

       3. Budget

           (Detailed breakdown of costs, sales, and
    profits for the duration of the project)

IV. Action Items

       (Who is going to do what, when, where, and how.)

Figure 33. Marketing action plan outline.

233

as who your potential customers are in the Government (by name), who makes the purchase decision, what market segments are available, what segments you are going after, and any data you have regarding sales to these segments currently, as well as what sales are forecast for the future. You should also discuss who your competition is, what resources they have, what types of programs they appear to be going after, and what retaliatory actions they are capable of taking depending on the strategy you employ. You should also discuss what is happening in the political and technological field that may affect demand for your product or service, the distribution structure that is available, how you plant to sell the product or service, what the cost/supply situation is, and how this cost varies with increased output of manufacture. You should also discuss any supply limitations. For example, if you are dealing with a product that has petroleum components, in light of the worldwide energy situation you should make some statement about the likelihood of a problem, and what you would do in the event of a petroleum shortage. You should discuss the resources of your firm, where your expertise lies (technology, research, marketing, etc.), as well as the limitations of your firm. Do you have financial limitations, for example, or are other resources limited? You should also discuss legal constraints that may affect your ability to sell this particular product or service to the Government. Finally, you should discuss anything else that you feel is appropriate to the situation and your analysis of it.

Problems and Opportunities

Sometimes a problem and an opportunity are the same thing, and each is just one side of the same coin. In this section you should summarize all the various factors in section I that are either likely to help your program succeed or hinder your program in accomplishing your objectives. This section should bring together everything from section I, subdivided into problems or opportunities.

Marketing Strategy

This is the actual marketing strategy that you have come up with. Basically it is divided into three main parts: the objectives, the marketing program that you are going to follow, and a budget. Let's look at each one.

The objectives are the precise goals for this program that you want to achieve. You should define the objectives specifically: target markets and target-market segments, what sales volume you anticipate and in what periods, and what profits you anticipate and are seeking during these periods. The second subsection is the marketing program. Here you should list the overall program for each element of the marketing mix: the product, the price, the distribution, and the promotion. You should also indicate why a particular action in each part of the marketing mix is proposed as well as the cost for each one of these substrategies that you are going to introduce. Further, you should indicate fail-safe points or controls as to when you will go back and check the progress you are making in each area of your program. You should also indicate what actions you will take if certain parts of your strategy do not work out as planned. You should always have at least one backup strategy planned if your primary strategy fails.

The third subsection of marketing strategy is your budget. Here you must have a detailed breakdown of your anticipated sales, anticipated expenses, and anticipated profits. You might include an income statement and a balance sheet for the project during the duration of the program. You might also include a project development schedule. This is much like the research schedule shown in Figure 40 except that the project development schedule should also show all your costs and your cost outflows and inflows during the anticipated period of development.

Action Items

The action items are a detailed list of the actions that must be taken by you to accomplish the marketing strategy that you have outlined in the preceding section. You should indicate not only that they will be done but when you will do them and, if others are involved, who will do them and who will be responsible. This action item section should answer questions such as who, what, where, when, and how things will be done.

Now I want to summarize this entire chapter by saying that you should have a completely documented strategy detailed as to the action items that you must take, what they will cost, and when you will do them in order to reach your objectives on a particular project with the Government that you want to go after. If you have done this and done it well, your chances of succeeding in the project and winning and doing big Government business will be greatly enhanced.

Chapter 7

THE CRITICAL IMPORTANCE OF PREPROPOSAL MARKETING ACTIVITIES AND HOW TO PERFORM THEM

IS THE EMPHASIS ON THE PROPOSAL MISPLACED?

Every Government marketing expert whom you may consult will mention the very heavy dependency on the proposal for selection of a winning contractor and will emphasize that you must have an outstanding technical proposal in order to win. The Government itself will tell you that the proposal is extremely important if you are to win Government contracts. Still another aspect may be of equal or even greater importance in winning Government contracts. Yet it is rarely discussed in depth by Government marketing consultants. This aspect is the preproposal marketing activites that go on long before you submit a proposal to the Government; in fact, even before you receive the RFP, RFQ, or IFB. Preproposal marketing activities include everything that you may do before you receive an official request for submitting a proposal to the Government.

Why do I feel that preproposal marketing activities are so important? Besides my personal experience as a Government marketer, I have done considerable research in this area. One extensive study showed that winning Government contracts was directly related to contacts with the Government customer regardless of either the price bid or the technical excellence of the proposal that was being submitted. In other words, as shown in Figure 34, as the number of contacts with the customer increases, the likelihood and probability of winning Government contracts also increases.

What kind of contacts am I speaking about here? Any type of contact with the customer including face-to-face visits at his facilities, telephone calls, visits of the customer to your plant or office, meeting the customer socially or professionally, such as at symposia, and so on. Why are customer contacts and preproposal marketing so important to winning? The theory that has evolved to date indicates that the reason that preproposal marketing activities are so important and so critical has to do with consumer acceptance theory and merchandising theory.

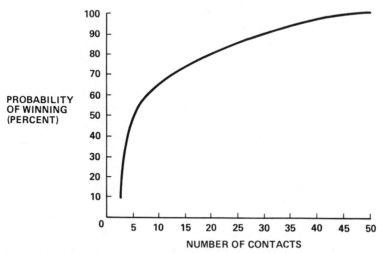

Figure 34. Probability of winning tends to increase with increased number of contacts.

Consumer acceptance theory has been known by marketing experts and acade-
micians since the mid 1930s, but it was first formulated in the form of a theory
in 1954. The basic thesis of consumer acceptance theory is that the obligation
of customer or consumer acceptance is the responsibility of the seller. According
to the theory, we can categorize three levels of intensity of consumer acceptance
that the consumer may achieve in relationship with the product or the service.
These three levels are: acceptance, preference, and insistence. To achieve acceptance, the very lowest level of intensity, the customer must have some positive
contact with the product or with the promotional effort that is promoting the
product. This minimal positive contact has resulted in the decision by the customer
to accept the product or service.

Preference, the second highest level of intensity, implies that the product will
be favored over its competition. To reach preference status means that a reaction
resulting from an even more satisfactory experience with this product or service
than with a competing one over a period of time has occurred. In other words,
the customer finds the product not only minimally acceptable but would rather
have it over someone else's product. The final and highest level of intensity of
consumer acceptance is insistence. This is the ultimate stage in which the customer
will take the product regardless of price or any other factor in order to obtain
this product or service. According to the theory, this stage can only be reached
by a full knowledge of the product. This knowledge must be very positive and

based upon considerable favorable experience with that product or service over all others.

Now let us consider this in terms of a proposal. A proposal alone does not really allow much time for much experience with the product or service. Even if we write a superior proposal to that of our competitors and our price is competitive, we risk coming up against a product or service that has succeeded in achieving insistence or preference through consumer acceptance theory. That is, the product or service has been "sold," not through the proposal alone (because the Government really has little time to spend evaluating proposals), but during the long period prior to the RFP being sent out. Under circumstances in which the Government customer has no opportunity to obtain satisfactory experience with a product prior to your submittal of a proposal (much less the opportunity of obtaining extensive experience in order to favor it over all others), it is inevitable that you will not win as frequently.

Consumer acceptance theory is the reason that many companies that bid for large numbers of Government proposals keep close records of them. They find that in bidding for contracts on which they have had no prior contact with the Government, they rarely win. On the other hand, their normal win rate for proposals on which they have had considerable contact with the customer may be quite high. One big Government contractor with which I was associated had a win rate of 76% under conditions of high preproposal contact. But when *no* preproposal marketing took place, their win rate dropped to 20% or lower.

The other theory that explains why preproposal marketing activities are crucial is called merchandising theory. Merchandising theory means fitting a product to a potential customer's needs. It is fitting what you can supply as a seller to what the customer can buy as a buyer, and acknowledging that when you start out, these two concepts of what you want to sell and what the buyer wants to buy may not fit together at all. This may occur because what you would like to sell to the Government customer may not be exactly what he wants to buy, or the price that you have in mind may be one that he cannot afford or does not feel that he should pay. Because of the enormous profit potential inherent in what the customer wants in the product or service, as well as the price itself, merchandising should be the central part of any marketing program.

Other major elements of the assumptions inherent in merchandising theory are that the market must be segmented in order to zero in on a specific customer and that this customer at any given moment has a number of conflicting wants and needs that he must satisfy. For example, he may feel that he needs a certain quality of product at the same time that he is considering the price that he can afford to pay for it. These wants and needs are influenced by the customer's physical or mental state, his previous conditioning, the immediate situation and environment that confront him, and most important, the products he knows about either directly through prior use or perhaps vicariously through communication with others. To complicate things more, these wants and needs and all the other factors I have mentioned are of different relative value and importance in satisfying the customer's desires. Furthermore, they have a great potential for changing and do in fact continually change. The customer's desire for a particular product or service may be influenced by your personal relationship with him, by how easy it is to obtain because of price and available funds, and other factors that affect the trouble and effort that the customer must go through to acquire a product.

Now you as a supplier may see the product in an entirely different light. Still there is a tremendous potential here. That potential is your ability to present the product and all its factors, including price and quality, in such a fashion that it can best satisfy the most important of the customer's wants and needs, or to alter the product within whatever limitations you are able to so that it best fits his wants and needs. In other words, you can either change what the customer wants or you can change what you have to offer. In order to do this you need to make presentations to the customer, to get feedback on these presentations, and to analyze the customer's wants and needs and the best ways to satisfy them. This must be done on a continuing basis right up to the time that you submit the proposal.

The concepts that I have just talked about are so important that I would like to restate them in bold print: **YOU CANNOT WIN GOVERNMENT CONTRACTS IF YOU DO NOT DO EFFECTIVE PREPROPOSAL MARKETING.**

Okay, we have covered why it is so important to do preproposal marketing. Now let's talk about how we can do it most effectively.

The first question about Government contacts and preproposal marketing is who should make these contacts. The general concept of interface with the Government customer is the concept of opposite numbers. This means that every individual in the Government should have an opposite number in your organization and should be identified as such. For example, if the Government's organization has a program manager then your program manager should deal with him. For the Government contracting officer, your contract administrator should be the contact. And if there is a project engineer in the Government organization, then your project engineer should deal with him. Now if you are a very small organization, you probably will be wearing three or more hats. You may be the contact in most cases, or even in every case. But if you have more than one individual on your staff then the concept of opposite numbers applies.

One question you might ask about the research performed on preproposal marketing is: Is the quality of the contact important? One of the things that I discovered in my research on preproposal marketing activities is, yes, the quality is very important. For this reason you must be quite sure that whoever the opposite number is, the contact must have rapport with that individual. Of course this will not be possible in every case. You will find individuals in the Government whom you like very much and vice versa. However, you will also meet people whom you can't get along with and who won't like you at all. Certain people *can* get along with these individuals though, and if there is more than one individual in your organization you should do your best to try to match up personalities so that people who can readily establish rapport are those making contact with one another. If you do this you will find that the quality of the contacts made will be better and the probability of your winning will increase. You will win more Government contracts as a result.

Now what kind of contacts should you be making? I already talked about initial contacts and presentations. Presentations should be an important part of the contact you make. A presentation need not be a formal one. An informal presentation, for example, can be made over the telephone. A presentation can also be made more formally at the customer's facilities, as outlined in an earlier chapter. When the customer comes to your facilities, you should take that opportunity to make a presentation. In fact, you should never make contact with the customer unless you have something planned to show him or to say. Now this something can be the so-called "feelie," that is, a tangible item that he can put his hands on and feel. It can also be a photograph. Or it can be written information or information that you relay verbally. But you should always have some sort of information to present at your meeting with Government customers.

Why should you do this? If you offer something of value to your Government customer, very frequently you will find that he offers something of value to you in return. In other words, it is a trade; you will give him information and he will give you information. What are you actually doing? You are putting merchandising theory into practice and merchandising your product or service to the Government customer.

The next question might be, how frequently should you make contact with the Government customer? The answer: as frequently as is necessary. Never make an unnecessary contact. You cannot profit from preproposal marketing theory by simply filling the square of making a phone call or making a face-to-face visit and doing or saying nothing meaningful. You must actually do something useful during a contact. Therefore whenever you have something to do that will help your marketing effort, you should make contact with the Government. Remember that the customer's requirements sometimes change rapidly, and at the same time that you are giving information to the Government and practicing merchandising theory, you are also obtaining intelligence about the program in which you are interested and on which you would like to bid, and altering your product or service to match what the customer wants.

When you are gathering information and merchandising you are also conducting marketing research. Market research is conducted by both primary and secondary means. Through primary means, you must actually gather the basic data yourself. Secondary data is information that someone else has gathered and published in some form. Both can be very useful to you in tracking a program, in merchandising, and in preparing yourself to bid a proposal that will win you the Government contract. In fact, you need this marketing information not only in the short range to bid a particular program or decide not to bid it, but also to obtain information on which you can base your long-range planning.

Where do you find this marketing information? I have already given you hundreds of sources of secondary information in earlier chapters. I have discussed how to make the initial direct contacts with the customer.

Let's talk now about these direct contacts. There are two concepts here that you must put to work for you during direct contacts. One is to ask questions and then listen, listening being of greater importance than asking the questions. The second concept is asking these questions of the right people. Some people in every organization will be very powerful and have a major impact on whether a certain program is funded by the Government and the scope of the program involved. Other officials who will talk as if they are very powerful may, in fact, have little impact on your program at all. Therefore, one of the major tasks that you have in marketing research is to find out which individuals are really the powerful ones and which ones are merely the talkers. Here again you must be careful, for frequently the talkers are the "good guys" with whom you get along with very well, and the ones that have the decision-making power may be harder to relate to. Don't kid yourself about this. Find the right individuals at every level, make contact with them, and merchandise your product or your service even if it is more difficult than talking to the less powerful talkers.

Here are some specific areas in which you should attempt to develop information about your program that will help you in winning.

1. Try to find out everything you can about your competitor, his capabilities in the technical, management, and financial area, and perhaps his plans, where he is, and what he is doing. This information can be of major importance to you on your proposal because a competitor is going to propose a certain solution to the Government's problem and your proposal should not only offer a better solution, but it should also show the Government why your competitor's solution is the wrong way to go.

2. Uncover as much information as you can about the customer's situation and his plans, how he buys, and his decision-making processes. Remember that every customer is different and though you may have dealt with one agency in the Government for some time, you will often have to adapt to new methods to work successfully with a new Government agency. It is worthwhile spending time conversing with various people in Government agencies that impact on your program to learn exactly how they operate and exactly what their desires and needs really are.

3. Get an organization chart of the customer's organization. For one thing, this will tell you who the key people are and the people to whom you should be talking. You will also get an idea of who reports to whom and who you should or should not spend time with. If you find that you are spending a great deal of time with an individual who is not in the line organization of the Government unit with which you are dealing, then you are probably wasting valuable time. As a consultant I once reviewed a manufacturer's

representative's letter to a major aerospace company. I found the entire letter was based on a full day's contact with one government official. I had dealt with this agency intimately, both when I was in the Government and when I was in industry. I was shocked to learn that the manufacturer's representative had spent the entire day dealing with an individual who had little knowledge of the program and was in a powerless position. I was also amazed to learn that he had no idea who was the manager of the program and thought that the project engineer was the program's manager's boss. Such basic mistakes are easily avoided. Ask for an organization chart or ask your contact to draw you a quick sketch of one. It is worth the time in order to find out your government customer's line of authority.

Once you really go to work, you should start thinking about what the probability of your obtaining a contract really is. This probability is based on two factors:

1. Will the program really get funding? Here again, you have to know who to ask and you shouldn't accept everything you hear without checking the facts.
2. How do you stack up against your competition? If the Government is going to fund the program and you are far ahead of your competition, you have a clear chance of winning. On the other hand, if the Government is going to fund it and you are lagging behind your competition, the situation is somewhat in doubt. If you are ahead of your competition and the probability of funding is not certain, the situation is also in doubt. You should always attempt to assess both of these factors on a continuing basis right up to the time that you receive the RFP.

HOW TO ASSESS YOUR COMPETITION

You can assess your competition by talking to your Government customer, keeping your eyes and ears open, and attending seminars or other meetings that have to do with your product or service area. For example, if you talk to a number of your Government customers in a single organization and they all seem to have a very positive and friendly attitude to a competitor, then you know that that competitor sits pretty high up in the eyes of the Government. On the other hand, if you sense a negative attitude toward your competition, you can assume the opposite. You can also draw conclusions about your competition by how the Government treats you. The only thing to be wary of here is that some Government customers tend to build you up and berate the competition when talking to you, and do the exact opposite when talking to your competition. You can minimize this risk of getting the wrong signal by talking to as many different people in the customer's organization as possible.

Along the same lines, you should attempt to assess what the customer's attitude is to the approach taken by your competitor. Is it positive or negative? You should also try to find out what importance the competitor attaches to the program, and here you might talk to the competitor himself. Sometimes you can get a tremendous amount of information in offhand discussions with your competition at technical or other meetings. You can also find out the amount of effort the competitor is spending in his marketing effort. How do you do this? Every time you see your customer you should casually ask about your competitors, those your customer has seen and those he has not seen. Most Government customers have a sign-in book. You should always look at the other signatures in the sign-in book when you sign in. Find out who has been there, who has been talking about the product or service you are interested in, who may be in competition with you. If this sounds like snooping, it is. But if the information is there in an open book, it is free information about your competition. Make use of it.

When doing market research, you should always attempt to assess the scope of the work that the Government wants done in a forthcoming program. Do this by keeping tabs on the program long before it officially starts. Try to get some idea how much money the Government has or wants to get for the program. Although the Government is usually secretive about this and similar information, you should nevertheless attempt to get this information. Never be afraid to at least ask the question. In many cases I got information right down to the last dollar as to how much the Government had for a particular program simply by asking.

Now why would the Government customer give me information like this even though it is strongly discouraged by his own regulations? For one thing, the Governmnet does not want a bid that is way out of line any more than you do. For example, I knew a fellow program manager in the Air Force who once received six bids ranging from $10,000 to $10 million—all for the same item! This was a clear indication that he had prepared a poor data package for the RFP and had not written it properly. But no one wants this to happen, certainly not in the Government. In this case, it was a guessing contest instead of a competition. He didn't have six competitors—he had only one real one. And that one, who ultimately got the contract, was the only bidder who had been bold enough to simply ask, "How much money do you have?" Thus it is in the Government's interest as well as your own to know the general scope of the work your customer wants done and how much he has to pay for it. Bear in mind that depending on how far in advance the customer sends out an RFP, you will have an opportunity to convince him that the money or the general work scope is insufficient for what his real needs are. There will also be a chance for you to go back and find out whether this is true or not or whether there is some way of doing what the customer wants within the scope and dollar figures he has indicated is possible.

As you progress in your preproposal marketing activities, some programs that you thought had a high probability of succeeding and that you were very much interested in doing for the Government will drop out. Far better to know this as soon as it happens than to go all the way down the line and still be spending money trying to develop a program that will never take place. Similarly, you will find that some programs will become much stronger than others. That's as it should be.

Remember that you cannot be strong everywhere, and it is for this reason that you must continually analyze the programs for which you are doing preproposal marketing and keep a portfolio of programs that you feel have a high probability of winning. Principal programs should be sleected based on an analysis of alternative situations in relation to criteria such as how firm a customer's requirement is, how strong you are compared with your competition, what is the present and future amount of the customer's funding, what are your capabilities to accomplish the proposal during the time frame in which the proposal is likely to be released, and what is your anticipated profit and other benefits from doing the program. You should also consider whether or not you should go after a particular program because of a synergistic effect on other products or services in your line.

Another method of contact that may be beneficial to you are symposia, especially if you make a presentation before an audience including members of the procuring organization in the Government you are dealing with. Making a technical presentation sets you up as an expert and gives you a stature and credibility that is above that of your competitors—unless they also make presentations.

The technical article serves the same purpose. Writing an article for a technical journal that is read by your Government customer can be extremely beneficial to you because it lends you the authority of an expert in your area. Full-page advertisements in magazines frequently go for $40,000 a page or more, so if you write a three-page technical article, you are getting $120,000 worth of free advertising. It costs you noting, and you may even be paid by the technical journal. Just bear in mind that the technical article has a long lead time, usually six months or more, and that in order to be effective on any one contract, it must be submitted early enough. Don't be discouraged if one journal rejects it. If you have several technical journals in your area, resubmit the same article. It may be accepted elsewhere.

Another technique that should be a part of your preproposal marketing activity is the press release, as already discussed. A press release factually describes a new product or service or something unusual that is of interest to the reader of the magazine or journal that publishes it. Every technical publication has need for hundreds of new product and service descriptions every year and they get them through press releases. A typical press release is shown in Figure 29. The article that resulted from this release is shown in Figure 31. It was subsequently published in many magazines that are read by Government customers. If you can write, you can write your own press release. Simply mail it, along with a covering letter and a 4 X 5 glossy photo, to the editors of magazines that service your product area and that are read by your Government customer. Again, you will end up with thousands of dollars worth of free advertising that is an important part of your preproposal marketing activities and will assist you in winning your contract long before you send your proposal to the Government.

Good preproposal marketing creates a favorable environment in which to submit an outstanding proposal. Preproposal marketing also gives you the ammunition so that you can prepare a superior proposal. By contrast, let's look at a company that does not do preproposal marketing. Such a company has no idea of what the customer really wants, except for what it says in the RFP. The RFP is limited to a certain number of pages. It is an abridgement of all that has gone before it. The company that has done no preproposal marketing has no idea what lies behind those written words. It has no idea what the scope of the work is. It has no idea of the relative importance of this program to other programs. It has no idea of the personalities involved, who will be evaluating the proposal, what their personal likes or dislikes are, or even who the managers are who will be managing the program. It has no idea of how much money is available. Does this give you a picture of the enormous value of preproposal marketing and why it is so crucial to winning?

One question frequently asked by the new or would-be Government contractor is: What about contact with the Government customer after the RFP, RFQ, or IFB is released? According to Government regulations, no regular contact is allowed from the time the RFP is released until the contract is awarded. Any contact that grows out of a question of a technical nature or a misunderstanding about the RFP, RFQ, or IFB is referred to the contracting officer, and then only with his permission is a technical adviser allowed to talk to you. Even so, any information that is given to you is usually also made available to your competitors. That is the only legitimate contact allowed under Government procurement regulations.

However, there is another type of contact, contrary to regulation, that is frequently made. This is a contact in which you talk to one of the technical personnel on the program without going through the contracting officer. When he receives your call he has two choices. If you really have something important to say he can decide to listen to you, or he may simply tell you he cannot speak with you and that you must ask your question through the contracting officer. This type of contact is sometimes important because RFPs are *not* written with perfect clarity and are frequently easy to misunderstand. If you can get through to your man without your competition doing the same thing and getting the same information, this is definitely an advantage.

In *Arming America*, H. Ronald Fox describes how Professor E. B. Roberts of the Massachusetts Institute of Technology did some interesting research 15 years ago on how industry does Government research and wins R&D contracts. Professor Roberts found that 50% of the contract winners and only 30% of the losers had been in contact with Government technical personnel during the period following receipt of the RFP but prior to submission of the proposal. (As you recall, this is the "illegal period" in which contact is not permitted.) Roberts also asked these contractors about whether the proposal was written to satisfy any known technical preferences of the customer. Sixty-eight percent of the winners said they knew and responded to technical preferences of the customer while only 33% of the losers did so. Roberts's in-depth studies led him to offer the following advice to Government contractors: "If you have not been on the pre-RFP phase of the procurement, begin by saying 'we should probably no-bid this RFP. . . .'" Roberts also said, ". . . you should expect to lose the award unless you have already been in close contact with the technical people of the customer's organization."

If you want to win Government contracts, the critical key is consumer acceptance, merchandising theory, and the tenacious practice of preproposal marketing activities.

Chapter 8

HOW TO ORGANIZE FOR DEVELOPING A PROPOSAL THAT WINS GOVERNMENT BUSINESS

WHY THE PROPOSAL IS CRITICAL FOR DOING BUSINESS WITH THE GOVERNMENT

The proposal is critical for doing business with the Government because even if you have done everything else right, you can still lose if you don't handle the proposal properly. On the other hand, it is still remotely possible (though this is rare), that you can make a mess of everything else but save the day by a brilliant, well-written, attractively priced proposal.

But this isn't the only reason that the proposal is so important to winning Government business. Paul R. McDonald, president of Procurement Associates and the American Graduate University, a man who has trained more than 20,000 men and women in how to do business with the Government, says that the importance of proposals in Government contracting cannot be overemphasized because the customer uses the proposal as the primary source of information upon which to base his selection of a contractor. This makes it a sales document as well as the actual point of sale.

Jim Beveridge is another expert who emphasizes just how crucial the proposal is for winning the contract. Beveridge has written two books on Government contracting and has conducted many successful seminars on the same subject. "No amount of marketing can bring about a win in a competitive world when the proposal is poor," declares Beveridge. In his book *Anatomy of a Win*, he goes on to state that the entire marketing effort should be focused around the submittal of a proposal and its acceptance by the customer.

If the proposal is really that important, you would think that agencies of the Government itself would recognize this fact, and they do. The U.S. Navy says: "The mission of the proposal is to convince the prospective customer that the company's solution is the best and that the company's personnel and facilities are eminently qualified to accomplish the technical and operational objectives." NASA adds, "The source evaluation process contemplates a thorough appraisal of contractors' proposals . . ." Finally, many Government agencies actually publish

247

information to assist you, as a prospective contractor, in proposal preparation. Here are just a few: "Guidelines for Preparing More Effective Engineering Proposals," (U.S. Navy Material Command); "Guide for Voluntary Unsolicited Proposals," (U.S. Army Material Command); "Guide for the Submission of Research and Development Proposals by Individuals and Organizations," (Department of Energy); "Guide for Unsolicited Proposals," (U.S. Air Force Systems Command).

Therefore, if you want to do millions of dollars in Government business, you must master the essential techniques of successful "proposalmanship." The basics that you must know are:

1. How to organize to win a proposal competition.
2. Your required actions when you receive a request for proposal from the Government.
3. How to write a proposal that will beat out your competition.

In this chapter, you will learn how to organize to win a proposal competition and what actions you should take when you receive the request. In the next chapter, you will learn how to write a proposal that will beat out your competition.

HOW TO ORGANIZE TO WIN A PROPOSAL COMPETITION

The key to winning a contract from an RFP or RFQ is in your basic organization for preparing the proposal, and this is true whether your company is large or small. However, you may organize differently depending upon the resources available to you and the frequency with which you respond to RFPs or RFQs or submit unsolicited proposals. One factor upon which this organization will depend however is on the size of your company.

The people you have working on any given proposal can be divided into three categories:

Category 1. People who do nothing but work on proposals.
Category 2. Technical personnel who are concerned only with the technical content and pricing of what you are bidding on.
Category 3. Personnel from other parts of the company whose input is needed.

Now if you are a small company, or have never bid on Government contracts before, you probably don't have personnel who do nothing but work on proposals. That's fine, and you should not let it worry you. You may never need personnel, full-time people, who work only on proposals. I knew a one-man company that worked out of a garage converted into an office. The owner did the basic proposal work himself and subcontracted the production. He won contract after contract over larger companies that had 100 or more people working on every proposal. It is not how many people you have working on every proposal, but rather how well the personnel resources you have are organized to do an effective and efficient job.

I'm going to start the discussion with the permanent proposal organization so that you will see some of the functions that must be performed in developing and producing a proposal. Remember, you may never need a permanent proposal organization. Only if you are submitting proposals so frequently that it would be cost effective to establish such a special proposal department should you consider doing so.

Here are the specific functions that a permanent proposal organization should fulfill:

1. Provide services common to the preparation of all proposals such as preparation of capabilities information, editing, preparation of illustrations, publication, and delivery of the proposal.
2. Serve as a focal point and coordinator of all requests for proposals received from the Government.
3. Maintain a file of past proposals, debriefings, resumes, facility descriptions and capabilities so that they will be readily available.
4. Develop standard operating procedures for the proposal preparation process.

Remember, we're talking about an organization that is not *ad hoc*, but is always in existence to work on proposals. Such an organization may develop and produce a hundred or more proposals in a single year. It smembers must be carefully selected, with assigned duties to carry out these important functions.

The Permanent Proposal Department and What They Do.

At the head of the Proposal Department, you need an overall manager. His basic function is to manage the Proposal Department, but if necessary he should be capable of working with the technical manager as a "proposal development manager." If your company has sufficient proposal activity to warrant a permanent proposal department but not so much that an additional individual to serve as proposal development manager is necessary, then the two can of course be the same person.

The proposal development manager works with the technical manager. He may or may not be subordinate to him. This is an important point, and somewhat controversial. Many companies have the proposal development manager reporting to the technical proposal manager. Perhaps an equal number have it the other way around. Those that have the proposal development manager in charge claim that he is the more logical choice because, despite the fact that the technical manager may know the technical end better than anyone else, that is but one aspect of the overall proposal. Also, the proposal development manager deals with proposals every day, whereas the technical manager does not. However, I believe the latter is a more logical choice to be held responsible for bidding the proposal. Why? What happens if the proposal is lost? The proposal development manager moves on to another program. But for the technical manager a loss may mean that he has no program, and consequently no work to do. He must either be reassigned to a new project or discharged. Then there is the Government customer himself to consider. He is generally very much against a proposal strategy in which the contractor's technical manager must take overall responsibility for what someone else took responsibility for in bidding and proposing. For these reasons, I believe it makes better sense to give the technical manager the responsibility for being the overall "proposal manager."

The proposal development manager is responsible for the production end of the proposal and for insuring that the standard operating procedures developed for the proposal process are implemented. He reports to the proposal manager for the purposes of the proposal, but to the manger of the Proposal Department on a full-time basis. Should he totally disagree with instructions regarding production that he receives from the proposal manager, he has the option of going up through his own chain of command so that the matter is thrashed out at a higher level. However, normally he acts as the proposal manager's right-hand man for production, and staff adviser regarding proposal preparation procedures and information.

Technical writers/editors may be part of the permanent proposal organization. Their function is to receive the first-draft material from technical people and polish it into a more effective presentation.

Draftsmen, illustrators, and photographers are essential members of the permanent staff. Their duties are to take rough sketches and turn them into professional-style art work or engineering drawings, and provide product photographs as requested by your technical people. They should also be expected to initiate suggestions pertaining to drawings, art work, and photography that would improve the quality of the proposal.

Perhaps the most essential part of the permanent proposal organization is a group of good typists. Not only will a good typing job improve the professional appearance of the proposal, but typists working only on proposals will insure that there is one consistent style of typing throughout.

What to Do If You Are Too Small for a
Permanent Proposal Organization

If you are too small for a permanent proposal organization, then the work must be split among other permanent divisions in the company, as well as the *ad hoc* technical proposal team. For example, one small company I know makes the drafting department responsible for proposal production, drawings, art work, and photography whenever a proposal must be submitted. The company's contract administrator serves as the focal point and coordinator of all requests for proposals from the Government. This office also assumes responsiblity for proposal delivery.

Meanwhile, the research and development department maintains its own files of past proposals, debriefings, resumes, facilities descriptions, and capabilities. The proposal development procedures to be followed are left pretty much to the proposal manager, with the unwirtten history of what has been done on prior proposals acting as a guide. The basic priniciple of this mode of proposal development operation is to assign each task to a logical office or individual in your company, and to do this well ahead of the time that the RFP is expected. In this way, who is going to do what and be responsible for what is not left as a last-minute emergency situation.

The Technical Proposal Team

Unless you are a very small company, the composition of the technical proposal team will change every time you respond to an RFP. Since the technical team is a temporary one, here again the key to getting the job done smoothly and maximizing your chances of winning is to do your planning and organizing early—well before receipt of the RFP.

Why Organizing Before Receipt of the RFP Is Important

For some strange reason, some companies will not begin to organize their technical team until the RFP actually arrives. It is as if the proposal development process were a race in which organizing ahead of time was prohibited or unfair. Time after time, I have watched such companies prior to receipt of an expected request for proposal. The normal daily work routine goes on. Then suddenly, the RFP arrives and pandemonium breaks loose and continues until the submitting of the proposal. Frequent overtime and frantic weekend work is typical. In the end, exhausted, the company submits the proposal at the very last minute with no time to go over the final draft thoroughly. This is the wrong way to do it. The first step in changing is to organize *before* the receipt of the RFP. This is one tactic that the Government neither penalizes nor looks upon with disfavor. And you will gain the following important advantages over your competition:

- You will have more time to develop a superior proposal after receipt of the RFP.
- Your team will be more psychologically prepared for their tasks in developing the proposal when it arrives.
- Your people will be more rested, make better decisions about proposal development, make fewer errors, and turn out a better proposal product.

You will have more time because you will not need to waste time organizing after the RFP comes in. Most RFPs will allow you only 15 to 60 days for a response, with 30 days being most common. It may take you three days to get the RFP from the Government. Under Government regulations, you must mail your proposal at least five days prior to the due date so that should some unforeseen act such as a blizzard come up that would delay your proposal, your bid would still be acceptable. Now that eliminates at least eight vital days, and you haven't done anything yet. This should make it clear that you will need every day allowed to do a good job.

Psychologists tell us that most people need a little time to get themselves ready for the responsibility you are going to assign them. But after receipt of the RFP it is too late for psychological preparation to be effective. Start psychological preparation before the RFP comes in. You will find that most of the members of your team have already planned out in their own minds what they are going to do when the RFP comes in. Some of the tasks you have assigned them will already be accomplished. This will result in more time saved.

If you organize and prepare before receipt of the RFP, there is no doubt that when it arrives you will have more time to do a good job. Instead of an endurance contest, your people can develop the proposal in an orderly manner. If they still have to work overtime and without sleep, at least you have taken action to minimize stressful conditions that lead to hasty decisions and mistakes.

You already have one key document to help you organize early and bring your proposal team up to speed: your marketing plan. Your marketing plan is your basic data source for getting your people ready before the RFP comes.

The Key Man on the Technical Team

The key man on the technical team is also the key man on the whole proposal. He is the technical manager, who from now on we will call the proposal manager. If the proposal manager wins, he should go on to be the project or program manager (or whatever title you use in your company), and if he loses, he doesn't have a program.

For the proposal manager, you need a real superman. First and foremost, he must be a leader and know how to manage. Second, he must be good technically. Don't make the mistake of putting the technical requirements first. The proposal manager's job is not for the faint-hearted. He must be strong enough technically to run his temporary technical staff, which may or may not normally report to him. In addition, this unique individual must also be strong enough and command sufficient respect to lead people from other divisions of the company that may not even be remotely associated with technical work. If the proposal manager is weak technically, you can always give him a strong technical assistant. But the reverse isn't true. No matter how good the man is technically, if he is not a good manager, don't make him responsible for managing a proposal.

I watched a company blow a million-dollar contract because the assigned proposal manager, a brilliant engineer, just wasn't the man to manage a proposal. Here's what happened. The company had done a study contract for NASA in which the flight hardware was projected to cost $350,000. Of these costs $50,000 was for two flight-qualified cooling fans that were to be procured from another firm that manufactured them. Two years later the company in question and two other companies received RFPs for the same flight hardware. The proposal manager saw his duties as restricted to finalizing the design and supervising the proposal's writing. He sent a note to his company's buyer to get each of the items listed in the quantities indicated by the study with no deviations. The buyer dutifully requested and received price quotes exactly as the proposal manager had instructed him to. The trouble came with the cooling fans. His contact at the manufacturer's told him that the fans were no longer being manufactured and that the tooling for them no longer existed. But the buyer nevertheless insisted on a quote on the fan as requested by the proposal manager. The buyer got his quote—based on having to construct new tooling for the fans. The total price came to $500,000.

So chaotic was the management of the proposal development that the proposal manager had no idea of any of his costs until two days before the proposal was due. The price tag on the proposal was in excess of $1 million, a big chunk of which was the $500,000 for the cooling fans. As a matter of interest, the contract was actually awarded at a price very close to the original $350,000 figure projected in the earlier study—but not to the company in question. This project went to one of its competitors. The moral? Get the best manager that you can find for your proposal manager.

If your company is a smaller one, your proposal manager will probably also have to write or supervise a good part of the actual writing of the proposal. So in addition to being able to manage and having a strong technical background, your proposal manager must also be able to write well. Some fellow, this proposal manager.

Additional Members of the Technical Proposal Team

The additional members will depend to some extent on how you decide to organize the team. In general, there are two possibilities.

- Organization by proposal area.
- Organization by technical area.

The first possibility is illustrated in Figure 35. This figure shows a management proposal manager, technical proposal manager, and cost proposal manager all subordinated to the overall proposal manager. The proposal manager should come from the permanent technical organization, and he should become the program manager or project manager after it is won. The management proposal manager and the cost proposal manager may come from the technical organization, or they could be assigned on a temporary basis from other divisions of the company. The technical proposal manager should come from the technical organization and will generally operate as the program manager's deputy. The management proposal manager is responsible for developing the management proposal, when a separate management proposal is required. The cost proposal manager develops the cost proposal in close coordination with the technical proposal manager, the buyer,

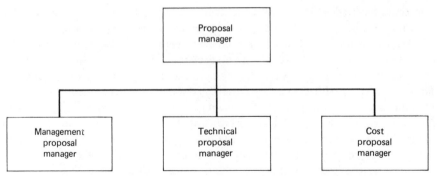

Figure 35. Technical proposal team organization by proposal area.

company finance, and the contract administrator. This organization emphasizes again the proposal manager's responsibility for the overall success or failure of the proposal.

Organization by technical area is shown in Figure 36. Each area manager is responsible for writing his own part of the proposal and cost-estimating his cut of the pie. The proposal manager puts the cost proposal together himself from the inputs from each separate area manager. Similarly, if a management proposal is required, he develops this also.

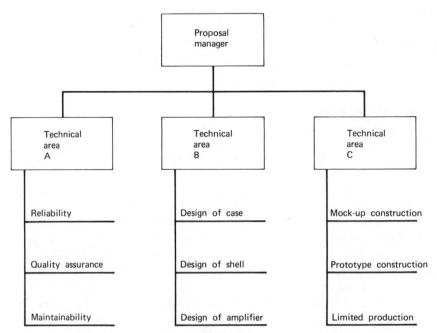

Figure 36. Technical proposal team organization by technical area.

Which type of technical proposal organization is used depends on the size of your company, the size of the proposal, the requirements specified in the RFP, and the relative strengths and weaknesses of the members of the technical organization and other divisions within your company. Select the organization that seems most relevant to your situation in the light of these factors.

Gold Team Operation—The Only Part of the Proposal Team that May Not Report to the Proposal Manager

The function of the Gold Team is to play "devil's advocate" and to review and criticize all aspects of the proposal from the veiwpoint of the Government as it is being written. As such, the Gold Team leader should report to the same individual as the proposal manager and he should be of approximately equal rank in the company. The individuals assigned to the Gold Team should be from the same special areas as those selected for the proposal. In keeping with the principle of giving the final authority and responsibility for the proposal to the proposal manager, the Gold Team's comments are recommendations and not directions. However, these recommendations should be documented and presented publically, with members of both the Gold Team and the Proposal Team in attendance. In this way, it can be assured that these recommendations are understood by all and seriously considered for implementation by the program manager.

The obvious alternative to the Gold Team system is to allow the program manager himself, or his superior in the organizational structure, to review, rule on, and pass judgment on the proposal. This is a mistake and should be avoided. Here is why. The program manager is just too close to the problem. He is involved in the proposal development on a continuous basis and the entire team is under his direction. He will be reviewing the proposal anyway. Asking him to step back and review it from the Government's viewpoint is asking him to grade his own work. It just can't be done very well.

On the other hand, using the proposal manager's hierarchical superior or supervisor presents a different problem. They are simply too far away from the problem. Their input will be resisted and resented as arbitrary. Also, because they are the proposal manager's bosses, their review carries too much strength; it comes down to direction rather than recommendation. For these reasons, organizational superiors should not constitute the Gold Team. Of course this is not to say that the proposal manager's boss does not have the right to direct a change and assume responsibility for it if he feels it is essential. Only that this is to be avoided 9 times out of 10.

Personnel from Other Parts of the Company Whose Input Is Needed

The third category of personnel concerned with the proposal are usually not considered members of the proposal team per se. However, their input is frequently vital to success of the proposal, and they too should be identified before the

RFP comes from the Government. In fact, they should meet with the proposal manager and be briefed well in advance regarding the background and other important aspects of the proposal. Such personnel include the assigned buyer, estimators, contracts administrator, financial specialist, and so on.

Here again, within established company regulations and policies, the proposal manager should be able to direct these specialists with regard to the proposal that he is responsible for bidding. The big problem is that these functions involve pricing, specifically such factors as overhead rate, profit, and so on. While we'll get into pricing and pricing strategies in some detail later on in the book, the proposal manager must to the maximum extent possible be able to price the proposal in terms of what he knows about the contract, what it takes to win, and special or additional benefits of the contract to the company. A pricing decision often and correctly is made at the top echelons of the company, with the financial vice-president demanding one overhead rate and the proposal manager arguing that if he is forced to use that overhead rate that they will lose the contract. Such arguments between the proposal manager and various specialist managers are normal, proper, and perhaps even desirable, since they air crucial questions with all supporting arguments out in the open so that a decision can be made with all the facts known. Under no circumstance, however, should a proposal manager abdicate his responsibility for pricing by indicating that it is some other department's responsibility. The confrontation of the Financial Department with the proposal manager and with other top management serving as judge and/or referee is essential where there is major disagreement. The same principle applies in other areas, in which the specialist involved disagrees strongly enough with the proposal manager's intentions that he feels that the decision should be carried up the chain of command and made at the top. Fortunately, in practice the proposal manager and the supporting specialist usually negotiate, so that generally only the tough ones that should go to the top actually do so.

What to Do When the Request for Proposal Finally Arrives

You have expected the RFP for some time, you have organized for it, you have done all the preproposal marketing that you were supposed to do, and sure enough, one day it happens. The RFP is actually handed to you.

Your first inclination may be to panic. Fortunately, you've read this book and know what to do. You have a plan. Here it is . . . the required actions you must take when you receive the RFP from the Government.

- Make the final bid/no-bid decision.
- Complete the planning package.
- Hold a kickoff meeting.
- Complete the first draft.
- Have a Gold Team review and presentation.

- Have top management review the plan, status and critical issues.
- Complete the second draft.
- Have another Gold Team review and presentation.
- Complete the costing.
- Have top management review and establish price.
- Complete the final draft.
- Have the final Gold Team review and presentation.
- Complete the printing.
- Deliver to the customer.

The Final Bid/No-bid Decision

Since you have already had one bid/no-bid decision, you may wonder why you need another. Remember, proposals are not cheap. You're going to invest a lot of man-hours in writing and producing a proposal. This costs lots of money for development and more money for production. You are not going to do this unless you intend to win. Therefore it makes sense to take one last look, using the techniques and form discussed earlier, to conform that you still want to go through with it, based on the latest information and the RFP itself. If you're bidding a big one, it's better to cut your losses and save up to $1 million or more in company resources and have them available to fight another day than to squander them on a proposal that you should perhaps have realized just wasn't for you. You should do this last bid/no-bid analysis within a day of receipt of the RFP.

How to Develop the Planning Package

Congratulations. So far, so good. You're still going to bid. Now you must develop your planning package. Actually, like the proposal organization, you should have done this some time prior to receipt of the RFP. At this point you are only finalizing your plan based on what actually appeared in the RFP as opposed to what you thought would be there. Here is what your plan should contain:

1. Background information. Note the customer's objectives and how the RFP fits into the customer's plans and what he is trying to do. Also write down company objectives and why this proposal is important to you.
2. The proposal team organization, including a proposal outline and personal writing assignments for each section. Don't forget to include the office and phone numbers of each participant. Even in a small company, it is nice to have all of this information together when you're in a hurry and need it.
3. The proposal preparation schedule. People work best against known due dates, so you should describe all major milestones, when they are due, and precisely who is responsible for accomplishing each one. Don't forget to allow time for mailing the proposal, getting art work done, production,

photography, Gold Team review and presentation, and so on. A chart is effective for showing an overview of the entire proposal timing. A typical proposal preparation schedule is shown in Figure 37.

4. Preliminary work statement. Get this out of the RFP. Rewrite it to make it more simple and more easily understandable. Your rewritten preliminary work statement should include if necessary: what tasks are to be accomplished, and what goods or services are to be provided.

5. Potential problem areas. List the known problems and tentative solutions that you have been able to develop so far.

6. Security information. If the RFP and the proposal are security classified, write down how security is to be handled in formulating the proposal. Note what information is considered proprietary by the company and how it is to be guarded.

7. Costing. Indicate the target price and target man-hours for each area.

8. Type of contract anticipated. Write down the type of contract the Government wants, what kind you want, and what your chances are of getting what you want.

9. Competitive information. List your competition and their strengths and weaknesses. Document how their approaches differ from yours and why your approach is better.

10. Potential subcontractors and vendors. Write down which major services and/or products are to be purchased, and from whom you anticipate they will be purchased.

11. Government-furnished equipment. Write down which supplies are to be furnished by the Government at no cost to the contractor.

12. Teaming arrangements. If your company is teamed with another company for this proposal, list what your responsibilities and the other company's are in relation to each other. Also note who is going to do what and how the other company's efforts are going to be directed for the proposal.

13. List special facilities or equipment to be utilized for the proposal effort.

14. Evaluation factors. Copy the factors listed in the RFP as to how the award is to be made, including special emphasis on items that are especially pertinent to what the Government wants.

The Kickoff Meeting

Now that your plan has been updated and is complete, you hold the kickoff meeting to bring everyone up to date and get the entire effort rolling. By "you" of course I mean the proposal manager; he should hold this meeting within two days of receipt of the RFP.

If possible, the planning package should be distributed prior to the meeting so that the participants will be familiar with it.

Proposal _____
Title _____
Proposal _____
Manager _____

Task or Milestone Responsibility

1. Planning package complete

2. Kickoff meeting

3. Design freeze

4. Make or buy decisions complete

5. Master parts list complete

6. Sketches complete

7. Preliminary pricing complete

8. Subcontract work statements complete

9. All work statement inputs complete

10. Subcontract bids received and evaluated

Figure 37. Proposal preparation schedule.

11. Proposal inputs complete												
12. First draft complete												
13. First draft review complete												
14. Final pricing complete												
15. All illustrations complete												
16. All photography complete												
17. All revisions complete												
18. Final typing complete												
19. Final review and proof complete												
20. All corrections complete												
21. Proposal reproduction complete												
22. Covering letter complete												
23. Delivery to customer												

△ Schedule date   − − −   △ New or slipped date   ▲ Actual completion

Figure 37 (Continued)

260

The purpose of the kickoff meeting is to insure that everyone knows what he is going to do, why he must do it, when it must be done, and how it fits into the overall plan. It also permits questions to be answered, and changes, where appropriate, to be made.

The Draft Completion-Gold Team Review Cycle

Time will always be critical in responding to a proposal. At the same time, if a Gold Team is going to be effective, they need something to review. Therefore it is essential that draft completion dates be met either through working overtime, night work, or whatever it takes. The same holds true for the Gold Team review and presentation. When a presentation of the review is scheduled, it must be made with the appropriate individuals in attendance. A form such as the one shown in Figure 38 can be used to document Gold Team review comments and as a basis for their presentation to the proposal team. If possible, you should schedule three Gold Team reviews and presentations, but two should be considered the minimum acceptable.

Costing

This is always a critical item, so don't let it get out of hand. Here again, much of the costing can be done in anticipation of receipt of an RFP, which will save time later when you are working on the proposal against a delivery date. But there should be constant feedback and monitoring as cost data becomes available and more exact man-hours are known. The proposal manager must spend as much time controlling the cost, and continually guiding it so that the target price can be arrived at, as he does on the technical and management aspects of the proposal combined.

Production

Finally, we come to this important milestone, producing the final proposal. This is the responsibility of the permanent proposal organization, or perhaps you must send the proposal outside of your organization to be reproduced. Either way, the entire production process is not easy, it cannot be done in one day, and sufficient time must be budgeted for it. To give you some idea of the magnitude of the task and the resulting time, here is what one leading Government contractor lists as the required production steps to be accomplished by its permanent proposal organization:

- Edit text.
- Compile master text.
- Complete final art.
- Start final typing.

Gold Team Review Comments

Volume # _____   Page # _____

Section # _____

Problem:

Suggested solution(s):

Volume # _____   Page # _____

Section # _____

Problem:

Suggested solution(s):

Volume # _____   Page # _____

Section # _____

Problem:

Suggested solution(s):

_____

Reviewer

_____

Date

Figure 38. Gold Team review comments.

- Complete final typing.
- Review and proof copy.
- Send copy to contract administrator.
- Complete review and proof of text.
- Complete corrections.
- Assemble and lay out proposal pages.
- Send pages to be photographed.
- Send pages to be lithographed.
- Collate pages and bind proposal.

Delivery to Customer

If you have planned and scheduled your proposal work well, you should not have much difficulty mailing the completed package to the Government five days prior to the due date. In this way, you will meet the Government's criteria for being on time, even if something unexpected occurred that would cause your proposal to arrive late. If you are unable to mail five days prior to the due date, you still have some options left.

1. You can use the Post Office's new 24-hour delivery service.
2. You can pay an airlines to deliver your proposal to your representative at the airport. They will hand-carry the proposal to its destination.
3. You can go yourself, or send someone you trust, with the proposal in hand.

Use the option you feel is appropriate. Don't be afraid of option three. If the proposal was important enough for you to put in so much effort, there is no sense in losing it in order to save several hundred dollars for an airline ticket, or several hours of your time, no matter how valuable.

In summary, the bottom line of this whole chapter is that in Government contracting the proposal is the name of the game. The first two steps toward winning with your proposal are to organize and plan well ahead of receipt of the RFP, and then to carry out the actions covered in this chapter once the RFP arrives.

Now you are ready for that third essential step—writing the proposal.

Chapter 9

WRITING THE PROPOSAL IS CRITICAL TO WINNING

We are now down to the "nitty-gritty" of Government contracting, the "point of the sword," or whatever else you want to call it. You win or lose depending on how well you write the proposal. How to write a superior proposal, one that wins the contracts and brings you tons of Government business, is the focus of this chapter. We begin by examining the components of a proposal—what should go into every proposal you write. How these components can be used for maximum impact on the customer—resulting in high scores on technical evaluations by the Government's source selection evaluation team—concludes the chapter.

THE COMPONENTS OF A PROPOSAL TO THE GOVERNMENT

Although every proposal is different, and different proposals may vary slightly in content, certain major components are common to every proposal you write to the U.S. Government. These elements are: the executive summary, the technical proposal, the management proposal, and the cost proposal.

The Executive Summary

The executive summary is a very important part of the proposal: it is read by almost everyone in the customer's organization who is interested in the contract you are bidding. Many of these individuals may not be technically familiar with the product or service desired and especially not with your company's approach to the problem. This is because:

- They are at high management levels within the customer's organization.
- They were brought to the program after the release of the RFP or RFQ.
- They somehow slipped through your preproposal marketing campaign, and were never the target of your preproposal marketing.

264

These individuals amount to a last-minute "curveball" by the customer because they may have a major impact on judging your proposal and selecting the winner of the proposal competition.

You therefore must write the executive summary so that an outsider can understand the exact need of the customer you are proposing to fill, and exactly how you are proposing to fill it.

In the executive summary:

- Briefly state the problem or what the Government wants.
- Give an overview of the main features of your solution or what you are proposing to provide.
- Stress your prior work in this field.
- State strong positive reasons why you should be awarded the contract.

You briefly state the problem in order to orient the reader to the situation that makes the Government need the proposed program. Identify both the immediate requirements of the customer and his long-term goals. Show that you understand exactly what the customer wants.

Your solution is the equivalent of selling benefits to a commercial or industrial customer. Give a brief description of how you propose to solve the customer's problem. Make it a synthesis of your entire proprosal, but subtly (or not so subtly) indicate why the features of your proposed solution are of benefit to the customer.

Stressing your prior work in the field establishes your qualifications not only as a bidder but as an expert, the most qualified bidder who is seeking the award for this contract.

Finally, the executive summary should conclude on a high note: everyone in your company is eager to begin and committed to do an outstanding job in performance of this contract.

The executive summary may vary in length from one or two paragraphs to 20 pages or more, depending on the size and scope of the proposal. But no matter how long or short in length, the trick is to write it so that it will be read and understood by any Government reader who reads it.

Sometimes the executive summary is combined with the technical proposal, as part of the introduction section. Sometimes it is completely separate. Regardless of how it is included in the proposal, this component always fulfills an identical function.

Here is an example of a successful executive summary.

EXECUTIVE SUMMARY

Development of Protective Aircrew Helmets

The expanded role of aircrew personnel in tactical support missions has made them particularly vulnerable to small arms projectiles and fragmentation hazards. During the past several years, armor technology has progressed substantially in the effectiveness of available ballistic materials to defeat these threats. Similarly, the design of helmet configurations and new concepts in head suspension systems have clearly enhanced the functional value of armor protection to the aircrewman.

Super-Tech Engineering, Inc. has been in the forefront of this advancing technology. Working under contract to the U.S. Air Force System Command since 1974, we have evolved many of the unique conceptual approaches in the design of aircrew helmet systems. Coupled with the design responsibility, we have developed a close involvement with the applicable manufacturing technology in the protective fiber industry. This has permitted us to generate designs within the growing capabilities of this industry, keeping pace with their progress, yet not compromising the functional qualities of our protective helmet system.

We hope to apply this cumulative experience in the proposed program, and recognize the importance of an effective systems approach in pursuing the objectives outlined. A fully coordinated effort is required to integrate the design and human engineering investigations with the fabrication of prototypes and final helmet assemblies. An efficient management plan has been developed for this purpose, and is structured about a team effort between Super-Tech Engineering and the Fiber Strong Company. Working cooperatively, we can provide the most advanced engineering and design capabilities, coupled with the significant expertise in producing ballistic nylon fiber armor, which will be necessary for the prototypes and the operational items.

To assure proper surveillance, within the Fiber Strong Company organization, their General Manager, Mr. William Dax, Jr., and their Director of Engineering, Mr. John Allen, will be personally responsible for the conduct of the final prototype fabrication effort and the ballistic integrity of the items which they will furnish. It is notable that the Fiber Strong Company is currently manufacturing ballistic nylon armor in substantial quantities for the U.S. Army, using a modified (reduced area) version of Super-Tech Engineering's 3-size helmet system. Their familiarity, therefore, with Super-Tech Engineering's advanced helmet configurations, and production experience with these new configurations, will help to reduce lead times and improve the reliability of the deliverable items.

Both Super-Tech Engineering, Inc. and the Fiber Strong Company are totally committed to the success of the proposed program, and we can assure the Air Force of our interest and initiative in producing a useful end product. We are pleased to respond to the subject RFP, and trust that the following sections of this proposal will fully amplify our approach to the problem, and demonstrate our capability to fulfill the important need expressed in this program.

The Technical Proposal

The technical proposal tells the customer the actual and explicit details of what you are proposing to do: provide a service, perform a study, develop components, or whatever. The three basic elements of the technical proposal are the introduction, technical approach or discussion, and program plan.

Introduction

An introduction is added even if you have already supplied an executive summary to your overall proposal. The introduction should be a relatively nontechnical abstract of the contents of your technical proposal. If the executive summary and introduction are combined, it should be done just as in the executive summary example above. In any case, include a clear statement of the problem in this section. The purpose of this statement is to demonstrate to the Government that you know precisely what they want. It is here that your preproposal marketing activities and research can really pay off, because not infrequently, the customer fails to state his real needs accurately in his RFP. You can really look good if you know their needs from prior contact and can put them down explicitly. But you must be careful with this. I am not advising you to write anything other than what the customer is asking for in the RFP. But let's say that you know from prior contact that it is important that a component that the customer wants to develop have an extended shelf life and he forgets to mention it in the RFP. You can look head and shoulders above your competition if you add a sentence like "An extended shelf life is an important consideration for this component."

Also, do not simply copy words from the RFP here. If you use the customer's exact words to demonstrate your understanding of the problem, he may think that you don't understand his problem at all—otherwise why would you copy his words directly from the RFP?

The Technical Approach or Discussion

The technical approach or discussion should be keyed paragraph by paragraph with each applicable approach in the RFP. Thus in an evaluation of your proposal, each approach can be located readily. If a Government evaluator fails to find your proposed solution to a particular problem, you get zero points for that particular portion of the evaluation even if your solution is buried somewhere within your technical discussion or approach. Even if the evaluator doesn't like your solution to his requirement, as long as he can find it you will get more than zero points. Do not make the mistake of thinking that the evaluator is going to spend a lot of time chasing down each one of your solutions. Frequently if he can't find it at once, you get the zero.

Here is an example of what I am talking about, taken from an actual RFP and the proposal used in response to it. The RFP stated under paragraph 4.0, technical requirements:

> The contractor shall be responsible for all the requirements presented below, shall provide the necessary materials, and shall provide and operate all necessary facilities. The program shall be divided into eight tasks divided

into two parts. Part 1 containing tasks A through C shall be process develop-
ment and qualification. Part 2 containing tasks D through H shall be demon-
stration components. The tasks shall be: (A) Quality Assurance Program,
(B) Process Development, (C) Qualification of Processes for Fabrication of
Demonstration Components, (D) Large Laminate Fabrication, (E) Fab-
rication of the I–Stiffened Type Skin Stringer Panel, (F) Fabrication of
Honeycomb Core Panels, (G) Fabrication of Chopped Fiber Moldings, (H)
Fabrication of a Representative Component of the Shuttle Aft Body Flap.

The RFP went on to describe each task in more detail. Part 1 was assigned paragraph number 4.1, and the A, B, and C tasks under Part 1 paragraph numbers
4.1.1, 4.1.2, and 4.1.3, respectively. Part 2 was assigned paragraph number 4.2
and tasks D through H paragraph numbers beginning with 4.2.1, and so forth.

The proposal submitted in response to this RFP carried the same organization,
even as to paragraph numbers, as shown in Figure 39.

You see how easy it was for the evaluator to follow each solution to each task
required. This simple technique in itself will put you ahead of your competition
in many proposals.

The technical approach or discussion really gives you your chance to resell the
solution you have been selling to the customer all along during your preproposal
marketing activities, and to demolish your competition. Here's how you can do it
in six easy steps:

1. Identify your customer's requirements as listed in the RFP.
2. Restate his basic problem clearly.
3. List alternative solutions to the problem.
4. Discuss the relative merits of the alternative solutions.
5. State the best solution (your solution).
6. Show how you will implement your solution.

Let's look at each step in turn. By following the exact outline of the RFP as I have
suggested earlier, you will assure that you identify each and every customer requirement, and that your solutions will be easy to find by the evaluator.

Next, for every requirement you should restate the basic problem concisely.
Here's where your preproposal marketing will pay off again, because while you
will know the full story and background behind every requirement that is stated
in the RFP, your competition who has not done his preproposal marketing properly
will not. Your concise statement of the problem will reflect not only what is
written in the RFP, but also what thought has gone into your words.

For every problem or task, you should list alternative approaches that might
reasonably constitute a solution. Do not neglect the solutions you know your
competition may offer. These should especially be listed, because examining them
presents you with an opportunity to demonstrate all their disadvantages and why
the customer should not adopt them.

For each alternative solution, you should discuss the advantages and disadvantages, the relative merits, and necessary tradeoffs. You should pay particular attention to the solution you have decided is best. Although this discussion should be done in an unbiased fashion, you should leave no room for doubt in the mind of your reader as to which solution is the best and should be adopted. It should be absolutely clear that none of the other potential solutions are as suitable as the best solution, and any potential solutions that can be totally demolished should get the full treatment.

The key here is not the use of many adjectives but the statement and documentation of hard-facts and figures that support the evidence cited. For example, if one solution is the use of a material that cannot always be obtained, it is insufficient to merely say that delivery of this material is unreliable. State facts and figures and give examples. For instance: "In 1980, fully 50% of deliveries of this material were late by one-to-two months, causing concurrent slippages in programs using this material." Or: "The Society of Material Engineers says, 'Due to the extreme difficulty of obtaining this material, its use should be avoided whenever possible.'"

Figure 39. Paragraph numbering and organization in a proposal.

Discuss and build up (or kill) potential solutions in terms the customer under-stands—the very factors that he has indicated during preproposal marketing and in the RFP are important to him. This may include cost, performance, delivery, quality, assurance, and so on.

Your relative merit section should be so strong and clear that after the customer has read it, he should be able to guess what your recommended solution is going to be. And then you confirm his thoughts by stating the best solution to his problem, which is of course the technical approach you intend to offer him.

The sixth and last step in the process of confirming the sale of your technical approach in the proposal is done by showing how you will implement your solution. You should not side-step any issues here. You may have listed disadvantages earlier, and in a general way stated how you were going to overcome them. Now you must be both accurate and precise, not only stating potential problem areas but showing exactly how you are going to overcome these areas, supporting your plans with facts, figures, and estimates. If your estimate should somehow be wrong, you should also indicate what you would then plan to do. Every possible question about your best solution should be answered here, and it should be answered so that hard facts are available that the evaluator can use to justify his support of your technical approach.

The program plan is the last part of the technical approach or discussion portion of your proposal. This plan covers how you intend to carry out your technical approach, including the sequence of events and when you plan to start and finish each technical task and requirement of the program. You should always include a graphic representation of your program plan, laid out in the same manner as the research schedule shown in Figure 40. Cost estimates are usually not shown here, and manpower estimates may or may not be.

Depending on the type and size of the potential contract and the requirements contained in the RFP, the technical proposal may also include systems engineering concepts; subsystem analyses; risk assessment; manpower considerations; reliability and maintainability; quality assurance; cost, time, and performance tradeoffs; related past experiences; separate engineering, fabrication and manufacturing plans; a technical data plan; configuration management; a make-or-buy analysis; and subcontracts.

The Management Proposal

The management proposal is the third major component of the proposal. Smaller proposals may have this section integrated with the technical proposal. You should use the Government's RFP as a guide on this. If the Government wants a separate management proposal, you should definitely provide one. If a separate management proposal is not mentioned in the RFP, then you can use your own judgment as to whether you should combine the information with that of the technical proposal in one section or supply it separately.

Basically the management part of your proposal tells how you intend to manage

Research Schedule
Preproposal Marketing Research

Months After Award of Contract

Task	1	2	3	4	5	6	7	8	9	10	11	12
Development of research tool												
Secondary data collection												
Interviewing												
Data recording												
Data analysis and computations												
Follow-up interviews												
Development of conclusion and recommendation												
Final report preparation												

Figure 40. Research schedule/Preproposal marketing research.

the proposed project, but it usually includes much more: a history of your company; a description of its structure, policies, and procedures as they relate to your ability to manage the program; project organization; key personnel; related past experience; and a description of your facilities.

One way of organizing the material that must be included in the management proposal is to break it down into five subsections: organization, program control, key personnel, subcontract and team management and control, and capabilities.

Organization

In the organization section, you start with your overall company organization and work down until you can show exactly where the project organization is going to fit it. Include charts that show the exact position and relationship of the program you are proposing. Show the detailed organization of the project on a separate chart. Include lines of communication, functional relationships, and divisions of responsibility.

In every organizational box, include the name of the individual you plan to assign to the duties indicated. You may wonder about your commitment to use a certain key individual in the position indicated. What if he resigns from your company? Remember, this proposal is your plan. Certain items you will have complete control over. If you include them in your proposal and then fail to do them, depending on their nature and importance the Government may or may not insist on compliance. But your control over the plan contained in your proposal can never be perfect, and one of these areas where you lack perfect control is in personnel. You cannot completely control either their health or their desire to remain with your company. Therefore you shouldn't be overly concerned about this aspect of your plan.

In order to maintain maximum flexibility, some companies name only the key managers and then include a statement prior to the resumes of other personnel that the actual individuals assigned will be selected from among the resumes included. Usually this is a poor practice, because:

- It gives the impression that your proposal plan hasn't been completely thought out.
- It fails to recognize the important and developing relationship with Government customers made during preproposal marketing by some of the "working level" people from your company. Frequently the Government customer will want very much to see these people assigned to the project. Indicating only a "maybe" on someone who has played an important early role does not help the cause.

Program Control

In this section you discuss your basic approach to providing sound planning, giving strong direction, and maintaining control over the main tasks required by the program. Orient your discussion around the individual named to head the project.

What sort of authority and support will he or she get from top management? Be explicit. List everything that will assist the top man in completing the program successfully.

For example: "The project manager of this program will report directly to the president of the company. This will give him ready access to top management and additional authority. Also, the company has a number of management tools that will assist the project manager in controlling the program. These include:

- Program Development Schedule.
- PERT
- Computerized cost and accounting system."

You would then describe each of these systems in more detail—why they are important, and how they will allow the project head to maintain complete control.

Outline other procedures and methods that will give assurance to your customer that you will be able to maintain complete control over the project. You should include discussions on your systems of scheduling and budgeting and how they are implemented, your procedures for reporting, and auditing techniques that you will use to ensure immediate problem detection and correction. Include samples of forms you may use in these procedures as well.

After discussing your approach to control, discuss the planning function and how you plan on organizing, staffing, and scheduling the project. Cover how top management will enter into the picture to review the planning, and if subcontractors or other companies are teamed up with you, how their preparation and review of the overall program plan will be accomplished.

Key Personnel

In this section, you will include biographical sketches of approximately one page in length (say 250–400 words) on each key individual assigned to the program. (Sometimes the RFP will specify that key personnel biographies be included in the capabilities section. Of course you should always comply with the requirements as stated in the RFP.)

The first item in this section is a short introduction as to what the section is. For instance: "The following are biographical sketches of key personnel to be assigned to this program."

Include in this section all individuals who have made contact with the Government during the preproposal marketing period, whether they are really "key personnel" according to a strict definition or not. The reason for doing this relates back to the relationship that they may have developed during this critical period. Omit someone who the customer feels should be "key" and you may give the impression that the company is misusing him. If this individual has developed a friendly relationship with one of the Government evaluators, it sets up a negative feeling with the evaluator at a crucial time—during the evaluation, when it is extremely difficult for a Government customer to ask a question pertaining to a subject like this, or for you to explain the actual situation. Even if the individual hasn't made friends with anyone in the Government, it may raise the question: "If the individual wasn't important in your organization, why did you send him out to waste my (the Government's) time?"

It is really critical that you develop a special resume for every type of contract that you bid. If the individual's background as shown doesn't support the particular work required by the contract, the Government is going to wonder what he is doing on the proposal. Are you short of people? Don't you give any thought to good qualified staffing? Is this contract really your top priority? When I was in the Government, one company submitting a proposal for an armor contract described a key designer's background as having been in design work in the recreational boating field—and didn't mention armor at all. We all wondered about that one, and you can bet it did not help the firm's case.

The format of the biographical sketch should be standardized for all of the key personnel whose sketches are included in this section. Typical information to include is:

1. Full name.
2. The proposed project assignment.
3. Special qualifications and background related to the project and/or the assignment.
4. Education and training.
5. Work experience in reverse chronological order, beginning with the current assignment and working back. Stress only the experience relating to and supporting this specific project.
6. Professional activities and honors, including publications and patents pertinent to the project.

Subcontract and Team Management and Control

This is a very difficult section, and contracts have been won or lost depending on how it is handled. Not infrequently you will need to work with someone else, some other company in order to accomplish all the tasks of the program. For example, perhaps your firm has an engineering capability but no means of production. Or maybe you have extensive manufacturing capabilities with a very limited ability in design. The other firms that you need will either work for you in some sort of teaming arrangement in which one member of the team is designated as the senior partner.

It is crucial that you explain why using your subcontractors is the most sensible arrangement, or if you have a teaming arrangement with another company, why your team is the best combination available. But beyond this, it is essential to describe how you are going to work together. And this is essential even if the subcontracting or teaming is between two different divisions of the same corporation.

In fact, this illustrates one of the major problems. Very frequently, the firm to which you plan to subcontract work or are teaming with is not located close to you. It may not only not be in the same city, it may not be in the same state. It is therefore essential that you explain in detail why this will prove to be no problem. Here are some of the ways in which you can do this:

1. If you have had past successful experience in a subcontracting or teaming relationship, describe this in detail and emphasize why control proved to be no problem.
2. Discuss the kinds of formal and informal controls to be implemented.
3. State specifically the reports required for control.
4. Tell what immediate actions you are prepared to take if things don't go as they should.
5. Explain why disadvantages, such as distances between you and your subcontractors or teammates, are really no trouble.
6. List the planned reviews with your subcontractors or teammates when you are going to get together face to face.

Always bear in mind that while there may be absolutely no problem in working with someone else at the other end of the country in completing a Government program, you must justify this to the Government. You only get one real chance to do this, and this is it.

Capabilities

This section contains your related experience, a description of your facilities, and key personnel if you didn't have a special section for that.

Let's talk about related experience first. The emphasis is on *related*. The experience that you include should convince your customer that your prior experience makes you uniquely qualified to do the job.

The top priority in related experience is, of course, related *Government* experience. Include which Government agency the work was done for, the contract number, the title of the program, and the approximate value in dollars. Include the name and telephone number of someone in the Government who will give you a good reference for your performance.

Many companies do more than this for each contract they have completed for the Government. They include not only the above information but also the objective of the contract, a short discussion about some of the things that happened during performance, and most important, a list of specific beneficial results that came out of the contract. Photographs of end-items developed or production are sometimes included. I recommend this approach. If you have numerous past Government contracts, then pick out the most outstanding that are in some way related to the contract you are bidding and discuss them fully. List the others in tabular form and for these you need provide only the basic information.

What if you have not done any previous Government contracts? In this case, you can discuss projects done for other companies, or even development programs accomplished and funded internally by your company. The basic reason for this section is the same—to stress that your experience in related work puts you well ahead of the competition for doing this program.

Facilities

The facilities section shows all the facilities that you have available and that you are going to use in accomplishing the proposed program. You may already have a special facilities brochure describing some of the outstanding features of your plant and its equipment. You should include the brochure as part of your facilities equipment. But you shouldn't stop there. For every major piece of equipment, discuss exactly how it's going to be used and why it specifically is needed for this program. Always highlight unique or superior facilities that you own and how their use will insure the program of an even bigger success.

The Cost Proposal

The cost proposal is the final major component of your proposal. This is the proposal that tells the price that the customer must pay, or at least the starting point for negotiation if he accepts or buys your proposal. Because of the Government's desire to evaluate the technical and management elements separate from the cost, the cost proposal is almost always packaged separately from the first two major proposal components.

In some cases, the Government will tell you exactly what form to use for your cost proposal, and will include them in the RFP. In others, your cost proposal is simply a price stated in your letter.

I'm going to go into detail regarding the techniques for arriving at that price in the next chapter.

TECHNIQUES OF WRITING THE PROPOSAL

The basic secret of success in writing a proposal is in having a *method* and this is true whether you are going to write the entire proposal or only one section. The steps are research, organize, and write.

Doing Research

Research is basic to your proposal. Of course, much of your research should have been done long before you started writing your proposal, during your preproposal marketing activities. However, additional research for your proposal is frequently required. There are two main points to remember. First, do your research in an organized fashion. Second, since you are usually working against a time deadline when writing a proposal, do not get so involved in research that you don't get started in the actual writing. Carry out your research in three steps:

1. Write down your objective and questions that must be answered in order to write the proposal.
2. Prepare a bibliography.
3. Scan, read, and take notes.

Let's say your objective is a study for the Small Business Administration about why more small companies don't export. First we'll write that down:

Objective: To determine why more small companies don't export.

Now let's think of some questions we need answered. These might include the following:

How many small companies are exporting compared to the total number of small companies that could export?
Has anyone ever looked into this problem before?
What advantages are there for a small company to export?
What disadvantages are there?
Does the Government help out in any way?

The next step is to prepare a bibliography. There are several sources for your bibliography:

• Books.
• Magazines and newspapers.
• Reports from other research.

Depending on your subject, you might start with the card catalogue of a technical library at the most convenient college or university. Start with the subject index, and note the title, author, and file number of books likely to contain the information you are after.

For magazine and newspaper articles, specialized books containing listings of articles are available. For example, the following general indexes are available at most libraries:

The Reader's Guide to Periodical Literature. This list contains thousands of articles published in general magazines.

The Industrial Index. This index lists articles published in industrial and trade journals.

The International Index.   This list contains articles published in foreign magazines.

The New York Times Index. As indicated, this index covers articles published in *The New York Times.*

There are, of course, more specialized books of magazine articles that may be useful, depending on the proposal you are putting together. When in doubt, tell the librarian what you are interested in and get help.

Write down the following information on articles:

1.   The author's full name.
2.   The title of the article.
3.   The name of the periodical in which the article appears.
4.   The volume and date of issue of the periodical.
5.   The inclusive pages of the article.

Technical reports represent an outstanding source of information for doing proposals. Refer to Chapter 3.

When you have assembled all possible sources of information, you are ready to begin your research by looking up each possible source of information, scanning the contents, reading what is pertinent, and taking notes.

Your note-taking need not be detailed so long as you can easily find the source from which the notes came. The following methodology should help you find this original source easily and conduct research efficiently:

Step 1.   Number each of your sources of information. That is, each magazine article, technical report, book, or whatever should be given a number.

Step 2.   Purchase some 5 X 8 inch file cards.

Step 3.   Write the title of the proposal in the upper left-hand corner of the card. This will keep this stack of cards from getting mixed up with another stack of cards if you are doing research on more than one proposal at the same time.

Step 4.   Write each separate subject concerning the proposal in the upper right-hand corner of a different 5 X 8 inch card.

Step 5.   As you go through your possible sources of information, you will find facts, quotes, and other information pertaining to each subject. Now instead of writing the complete book, article, or report title, you may write only the number you have assigned to that particular source of information.

This method has several advantages. First, you will save time in writing. You will always be able to find out where you obtained a particular bit of information.

You can easily keep all the subjects on one proposal together, and you will have all your notes and ideas pertaining to one subject together. Finally, you can re-arrange your card file of information as you work, or even as you write. This means you can easily revise the organization of your proposal without losing time re-arranging the research material you have gathered.

One word of caution when doing your research. Remember, this is only one step. You've got a long way to go to get the proposal out, so don't overresearch your proposal.

The second method step in writing your proposal is to organize it. I have already advised you to follow the same overall organization that the Government does in its RFP or RFQ. However, within this overall organization, you need to con-struct an organizational road map to write effective paragraphs that will have maximum impact within the overall organizational structure and win the contract.

Here's how you construct an organizational road map:

1. Select your message for that paragraph.
2. Write down specific ideas in support of this message.
3. Check your ideas.
4. Group your ideas.
5. Select a pattern.
6. Finalize your organization.

Selecting Your Message for That Paragraph

Let's say that one of the paragraphs under the general section called Technical Approach is entitled "Safety." The message that you decide that you want the customer to receive is "The system we will develop will be 100% safe in use." Write that message down. We will refer to the basic method through all of the following five steps.

Writing Down Specific Ideas

You have already written down many ideas on your 5 X 8 inch cards when you conducted your research. Now I want you to go through these cards and look at the subject areas and ideas you have written down. Safety may be one of your subject areas, and you may already have many ideas written down on the card. But in addition, you now have a specific message that you didn't have when you were doing your research. So look at the other cards as well, and write down all the ideas that support your message.

Checking Your Ideas

After you have written down all possible ideas that might be used in support of your basic message, you must check them carefully against that message. Satisfy yourself that each idea really fits within the scope of the topic you have selected. Delete those ideas that don't directly support your message. For example, maybe one idea that you wrote down was some information you found that the system you are going to propose is also safe in storage. If this doesn't support your basic message that the system is 100% safe in use, you might want to drop it, even though it's favorable.

While checking your ideas, you may think of some new ones, or come across some additional material that might be useful. Those that support your basic message, you can incorporate right away. Those that do not, you should discard.

Grouping Your Ideas

Now I want you to look at your ideas from a different viewpoint. I want you to notice that certain of your ideas under "Safety" and supporting your basic message can be grouped under more narrow definitions of your overall subject area. For example, under "Safety" and in accordance with our message "The system we develop will be 100% safe in use," we may find that "use" can be grouped under various phases: prelaunch, launch, gravity escape, flight, reentry, and impact. These then become our subparagraphs, each of which will still support our overall message. Of course, if the Government gives us the subparagraphs, then this grouping is done for us. We must only be careful that what we write supports our basic message or theme.

At this point, we should run a "how goes it?" check to see how our organizational road map is doing. There are two potential problem areas to look for: not enough ideas to support our message, and too many ideas to get across to the reader.

The first problem will leave our reader not fully convinced that the system we develop will be 100% safe in use. The second problem will confuse the reader and leave him unsure of exactly what our message is.

If either of these problems exists, fix your organizational road map now. If not, press on.

Selecting a Pattern

Most of your readers in the Government are thinking people who expect your ideas to be presented to them in a logical fashion. However, at the same time you must write in such a way as to persuade your reader that your offer is the best. This in turn will depend on the situation into which you are submitting your proposal, the individuals who will be evaluating your proposal, the amount and quality of preproposal marketing that you did, and other factors. Select the pattern that best satisfies the purpose of your writing, supports your basic message, and at the same time will offer the greatest appeal to your reader.

Here are some examples of writing patterns that can be used in writing your proposal.

- Topical pattern.
- Reason pattern.
- Time pattern.
- Space pattern.
- Narrative pattern.
- Problem-solution pattern.

The topical pattern is useful if you have a listing of a number of items. For example, listing 10 reasons why the safety system you selected is best could easily make use of the topical pattern. All you do is arrange your ideas in a natural sequence, one that will permit you to move smoothly from one idea to the next. List and discuss one reason why your safety system is best, move on to the second reason, and so on until you have discussed all 10 ways.

The reason pattern is a good one to use when you are trying to persuade. To use it, you first write your basic message. Then write your reasons for believing your basic message. These reasons are the main points of the paragraph you are working on. You support each reason by some kind of concrete proof such as a fact or statistics. For example:

Message: The system we develop will be 100% safe in use.

Reason 1:   Similar systems are fully developed, tested, and in use.

You can then prove Reason 1 as follows:

1. NASA has used the system on 100 successful flights since 1971 without a single failure.
2. The system has been used in aircraft since 1967. More than 10 million hours of flight have occurred with no failure of the system.

You would then go on to reasons 2, 3, 4, and so forth.

The time pattern is used primarily to give a historical perspective. Start with the first point in time. Continue point by point in chronological order until the present time. For example:

Our first safety system was developed for Project Mercury back in 1958. Successful use led to similar safety systems for Gemini, Apollo, and Skylab. Most recently, we have designed the safety system for NASA's shuttlecraft.

The space pattern doesn't have anything to do with outer space. This space refers to location. In fact, the space pattern is sometimes called the geographical approach.

If you wanted to write your paragraph on safety using the space pattern, here is one way you might do it.

The system we develop will be 100% safe in use.
Our safety systems which we have developed for use under sea._____

_____

_____

Our safety systems which we have developed for atmospheric vehicles.___

_____

_____

Our safety systems which we have developed for space vehicles._____

_____

_____

The narrative pattern is used to tell a story. After an introduction to get the reader in the mood, just tell your story as you would face to face. Add a conclusion to tie everything together and to insure that your reader understands the point. Don't think that the narrative pattern is out of place in a proposal. It has an important advantage, in that if it is well written the customer will be interested and read and follow your story closely. The narrative pattern represents a very sophisticated selling technique and method of subtly informing your reader and persuading him or her to your way of thinking.

The problem-solution pattern is a variation of the reason pattern, but there is an important difference. The difference is that you lead off with the message phrased as a problem, rather than a positive statement. To accomplish the problem-solution pattern effectively, you:

1. State the problem.
2. Discuss facts that affect the problem.
3. Propose solutions, stating each solution's advantages and disadvantages.
4. Draw conclusions and recommend your solution, which you propose as the best solution.

To state the safety system message as a problem you would say something like this: "How can we develop a system that will be 100% safe in use?"

The problem-solution pattern can be extremely effective in persuading the reader to accept your conclusion and your recommended solution because you appear to be impartially weighing the facts and can knock the competition without appearing to be biased. As pointed out earlier, you will find much of your preproposal writing extremely useful.

Give a lot of thought to which pattern to use. You can sometimes use a combination of patterns for maximum impact. The main thing is that you should use the pattern or combinations of patterns that will best get your message and your ideas across to your reader.

Finalizing Your Organization

All the previous work you have accomplished in organizing your material to support your message has caused you to make a lot of notes, some outlining, and do a lot of thinking. Now your task is to take everything you have done up to now and build a firm, detailed structure for the part of the proposal you are working on. This detailed structure is done in outline form. At this point you may be tempted to skip to the final organizing and go on to write your proposal immediately. Don't do it. A good outline will save you time in writing your proposal. Here's why:

- An outline will help you to concentrate on one point at a time. You won't need to waste time deciding whether you should be concentrating on some specific idea—you will know.
- An outline will help you to keep you on course on the subject about which you are writing. If you feel yourself straying from your subject, you won't have to reread everything you wrote to get back on track. Just look at your outline.
- An outline makes your writing almost interruption proof. Sometimes despite your best plans for uninterrupted work, you will be disturbed and distracted from your proposal. With a written outline, it is very easy to pick up where you left off.

You will find that the time you spend in preparing your outline is more than paid back through the time you'll save when you begin to write. Words will really flow because you will already have thought your ideas through.

It is easy to construct your detailed outline. You have already determined your basic message, collected the ideas from your research, formed these into idea groups, and selected a pattern to use. Now all you do is put your main idea groups, with the specific ideas under each main idea group, into the format of the pattern you have selected.

Good organization is the key to good proposal writing. It will not only save you time in doing your proposal, but will help you to write the kind of proposals that confirm and even enhance your preproposal marketing effort and win Government contracts.

WRITING

Writing is the last of the three major steps in getting your proposal done properly. If you do the first two steps as I have shown above, this step will be anticlimactic. After all, the hard work is done. All you do in the "writing" phase is to flesh out your detailed organization structure that has already been well thought out from research, integrate it with your selection of main messages for each major heading given to you by the government, collect and group your ideas, and select the writing patterns you plan to use. Here is what you do to fill out your organization structure with words.

State every main idea in your outline clearly and emphatically to your reader. For each main idea, you will write at least one paragraph. Every paragraph will have a relationship with every other paragraph, and with your basic messages.

Here is how this is done. Every good paragraph has three essential characteristics:

- A main idea.
- Support for that idea.
- Transition to help the reader follow the idea.

The main idea is the point you want to make. Technically it is called the topic sentence in the paragraph, and because it contains the main idea, it is the most important sentence in the paragraph.

Since the topic sentence is the most important sentence in the paragraph, we've got to be awfully careful where we put it. Usually the best place is at the beginning of the paragraph. Why?

- It makes it easy for the reader to find.
- This is the position in the paragraph where the reader's interest is greatest.

However, you can also put the topic sentence at the end of the paragraph. Putting your main-idea sentence at the end of the paragraph has its advantages, too:

- It's a good place if you are using inductive reasoning, in which you write about specific things that lead up to a general conclusion.
- If your paragraph is a long one, it's a safe place to put your topic sentence in order to be absolutely certain that your reader won't forget your main idea.

This gives you two choices

1. Put your topic sentence at the beginning of the paragraph.
2. Put your topic sentence at the end of the paragraph.

However, never bury your main idea somewhere in the middle of your paragraph.

To be certain that your reader understands your main idea, you must explain, reinforce, or emphasize it. You must always *support* your main idea. Here are some ways to do this:

- Use an example.
- Use an analogy.
- Quote statistics.
- State reasons.

The most important thing to consider in selecting the way to support your main idea is your reader. Select a way that you think will appeal to your reader, and that is within his background and experience.

Now let's look at some examples of main ideas and their support.

Remember that a main idea can be placed at the beginning or the end of the paragraph. Here's one at the beginning. It is italicized for emphasis.

> *Hiking is a healthy exercise.* The fresh air is good for development of the lungs. Leg muscles are hardened and grow larger. Strength and endurance increase with longer hikes.

Here is how you can place the same main idea at the end of the paragraph.

> When hiking, the hiker gets a lot of fresh air. Also, the leg muscles are hardened and grow larger. Strength and endurance increase with longer hikes. Clearly, *hiking is a healthy exercise.*

Note that support for the main idea in both of these paragraphs comes from reasons why hiking is a healthy exercise. Here are some other ways of supporting the same main idea.

An Example.

Hiking is a healthy exercise. A very sick man was advised by his doctor to hike. He began taking short hikes, which soon grew longer and longer. In the end he became well and very healthy.

An Analogy

Hiking is a healthy exercise. Just as a soldier hikes to keep in shape and stay in the best of health, the average man or woman can hike to stay healthy.

Statistics

Hiking is a healthy exercise. Those who hike regularly as compared with those who do not, suffer 30% fewer heart attacks, are 74% less overweight, and live an average of 12 years longer.

Now let's look at that third important characteristic of the good paragraph, transition. Transition will help the reader follow your idea.

When you have stated your main idea and supported it, you have expressed your main idea completely. But this is not enough. You are writing for your reader, and until you make certain that your reader can follow your main idea, your work is not finished. Transitions are used to make sure that your main ideas can be followed easily. Here are some transitional devices that you can use:

- A paragraph.
- A sentence.
- A phrase.
- A word.
- GOOD ORGANIZATION.

These transitional tools can be used:

- To tie new material with what has gone before.
- To preview to the reader what is coming next.
- To orient the reader so he will know exactly where he is.

Let's look at some examples. Let's say you are writing a long article and want to talk first about different species of animals, and then about what to feed them and how to care for them. You could organize your article into three sections:

1. Species.
2. Feeding.
3. Care.

Now you could go from one section to the next—species to feeding to care—without pause and still state your ideas completely. However, if you do this it is entirely possible that your reader will have difficulty following you.

One way to make it easier for your reader to follow what you have written is to insert a short *transitional paragraph* between each of the three sections. This will allow your reader a chance to stop, catch a breath, and get ready for the next idea to come.

Here is a transitional paragraph:

"We've examined many different laboratory species of animals. Now let's consider how to feed and care for them in space. First, we'll take a look at the feeding, then we'll consider general care."

Look at this transitional paragraph in closer detail. Note that:

1. The paragraph is short.
2. The first sentence ties in with what you have already written.

3. The second sentence lets your reader know what is to come.
4. The last sentence tells your reader in what order he will receive this information.

Instead of using a whole paragraph as a transitional device, you can also use a single *transitional sentence.* In order that you will be able to use the first sentence of the new paragraph for your main idea, put your transitional sentence *at the end* of the old paragraph.

". . . completes your organization. *However, even after organization is complete, there is one more item to take care of before you begin to write."*

"Documenting an outline of your article is very important. Today . . ."

The transitional sentence above is italicized. Note that this transitional device is short and to the point. It gives the reader an opportunity to orient himself before going on.

Transitional phrases are more common than either transitional paragraphs or transitional sentences. Use them whenever you think you need them. They will usually fit into most sentences either at the beginning or the end.

Here are some examples, with the transitional phrases italicized:

"On the other hand, you don't have to use transitional devices."

"At the same time, you needn't be afraid of using them if they make your writing clearer."

The list I gave you of transitional devices says that a single word can be used for this purpose. I am now going to prove it.

There are many *transitional words.* The ordinal numbers, *first, second, third,* and so on, are frequently used. Words like *therefore, accordingly,* and *however* are perfectly acceptable to do the job. *First,* you should decide on your purpose. *Next,* select a transitional word to make things easier for your reader.

Did you notice that "first" and "next" are both transitional words in the last two sentences? "First" is used to show that some kind of order is important. "Next" emphasizes the importance of a certain order again. *Therefore,* we should always write for our reader. The "therefore," another transitional word, alerts the reader for a conclusion or summary.

Of all the transitional devices, the best one is your own *organization.* Organize your writing so well that the reader will have no trouble understanding what you have written.

When rereading what you have written, be alert for segments that are difficult to understand. If you have problems in understanding, your reader will also. You should consider using transitional devices to make your writing clearer. But follow this principle whenever you are going to use a transitional device:

NEVER use a transitional paragraph IF you can use a transitional sentence. NEVER use a transitional sentence IF you can use a phrase. NEVER use a phrase IF you can use a word. IF THE ORGANIZATION OF YOUR ARTICLE DOESN'T REQUIRE IT, DON'T USE A TRANSITIONAL DEVICE AT ALL.

I have written a great deal about writing paragraphs without actually telling you how to break your material into paragraphs.

Think back to the three essential characteristics of a good paragraph:

1. Main idea.
2. Support for that idea.
3. Transition.

To break your material into paragraphs, just follow the steps defined by the three essential characteristics:

1. Take your main idea from your outline.
2. Support that idea as I've shown.
3. Use organization and transitional devices to make it easy for your reader to go from one main idea to the next.

That's all there is to it.

The Two Most Important Paragraphs

The two most important paragraphs are your introductory paragraph and the conclusion for a section of your proposal. We''ll look at each in turn.

The introductory paragraph has the three essential characteristics of a good paragraph as described in the preceding section. But in addition, the introductory paragraph is something special. It must introduce your entire article. Your title and your first paragraph will often determine whether your article will be read or not. Therefore, like the title (which we'll cover later), put a lot of effort on that first, oh so important opening paragraph. And that effort should be directed at attracting and holding your reader's attention.

You should:

- Put an eyeopener right at the beginning.
- Do something to make your reader sit up as if you had just rung a bell.
- Be dramatic.

For example, remember the safety message we looked at earlier? Would this get your attention?

"Our system has flown 50 million miles without one safety problem."

Or how about this for the first sentence of a paragraph in a proposal by a prison psychologist?

"I've been sent to prison more than 50 times."

Even the most ordinary things can be made exciting for your introductory sentence if you stop to think about it. Here is one by a person who simply likes to read.

"I have read more than 1 million printed pages."

And you don't have to use numbers:

"I taught karate at Vassar."

Rember this one?

"I was a Communist for the FBI."

You can see how easy it is once you really get going. Just remember that your introductory paragraph not only has the standard requirement of a main idea, support, and transition, it must also be a real attention-getter and immediately capture and hold your reader's interest. Then sit down and work out exactly how you will wow your reader in that very first sentence.

The Conclusion

The conclusion is your last paragraph. It has the very important function of bringing everything together. The rule is *never* leave your reader up in the air, dangling, with nothing to tie your story together. Always think of your conclusion as the final packaging. Package each section with a short summary of everything that went before. That summary is your concluding paragraph.

Your final paragraph can be long or short. It can go over, point by point, every main idea you covered in the section, or it can summarize everything in one sentence. But long or short, don't forget it. Without a conclusion, that section of your proposal is not complete.

In this chapter we've covered a lot of ground, but believe me when I tell you that spending your time going over this material until you've mastered all the principles and techniques covered it well worth your effort. Study this chapter and you will learn how to write superior proposals that will win Government contracts that others cannot win.

Chapter 10

HOW TO PRICE
YOUR PROPOSAL TO WIN

Pricing is an art, not a science. In this chapter we are going to learn the principles of that art so that you can price your proposal successfully and win Government contracts. Basically, the price of the product should be equal to the cost of material plus the cost of labor plus the profit. Having said this, I will spend the better part of the rest of the chapter explaining why this is not always so. In order to do this, first we have to know a little bit about price theory.

Where competition is important (and believe me, competition is always important), the Government buyer has the option of securing the supply or service from a number of different sources. According to the theory, the greater the number of sources that are available, the more the competition. Since there is so much competition, normally the price will be lower than it would be if there were no competition at all. This is the most desirable condition for the Government, which wants market conditions that permit full and free competition so that it can buy the item at the lowest price possible. The Government's definition of free competition is as follows: First, that there are a large number of competitors who bid against each other. Second, that there are also a large number of buyers to prevent any one buyer from controlling the market. (In this case, the buyer would be the Government itself.) Third, that the product or service itself must be a standard item, so that it would make little difference from which competitor the buyer made the purchase. Fourth, that there should be a complete and accurate knowledge of the conditions of supply and demand, and all the buyers and sellers must be aware of these conditions. Fifth, that the buyers must invite bids or quotations, that is, RFPs and/or IFBs and RFQs, and all the sellers must submit their responses under the same conditions and offer the same terms as to quality; performance, and delivery, so that the variable is the price. Sixth, that under these ideal conditions it is assumed that both the buyer and the seller will act in a completely rational manner. Seventh, that there must be flexibility in volume in the industry so that entry into the field and exit from it is relatively easy. Once again, these are ideal conditions. It is questionable that they ever exist.

PRICING UNDER CONDITIONS OF COMPETITION

There are a number of conditions that prevail under normal competition. Most products on the market differ from one another to some degree. Different brands of beer or wine don't taste the same. Different brands of toothpaste differ from one another. Even certain standardized screws or nails may differ in the composition of the material that is used in making them. This differentiation between different types of products and services is evident mostly in terms of brand names and through commercial advertising. Each manufacturer or supplier of the product endeavors to make potential buyers perceive his product as superior in quality to all competing brands. It is a fact, however, that a product bearing a specific label need not actually be different. It is the perceived difference that is important.

Next, circumstances under which a certain product is bought or sold make up another condition of normal competition. For example, a seller who is near his buyers has an advtange over his competitors who are farther away. This is because of transportation costs or it may be due simply to proximity. This advantage may be reflected in an overall lower price. Another competitive advantage occurs when a supplier has a product or service or can buy a product for resale in greater volume than his competitors. In this situation, this would allow him to sell at lower prices than his competitors. By a continual process of underselling the competition, such a supplier could eventually restrict if not eliminate his competition.

Product differentiation is often determined by style or design. For example, differences in automobile design are important in the buyer's choice of a car. In fact, an automobile manufacturer can suffer heavy loss when one of his body styles fails to appeal to potential buyers for whom it is intended. A good example of this was the Edsel, introduced in 1958 by the Ford Motor Company. On the other hand, the Mustang is a tremendously successful car introduced by the same company.

Obviously, a promotional campaign including heavy advertising can assist a company in dominating its competition.

Finally, you as a supplier of a product or service can get and keep competitive advantage over your competition if you can offer a better warranty or give better service than your competitors. An automobile dealer who is able to offer better maintenance will sell more automobiles than another dealer who is unable to do so. An appliance dealer who can provide more efficient service may sell more refrigerators and electrical appliances if he is able to offer better repair service. The various facets of pricing under "pure" competitive conditions affect the ultimate purchase price; however, if we consider these conditions in the setting of a Government marketplace, there are some differences in the price that you are able to charge the Government customer.

In addition to differences in pricing, depending upon various competitive conditions, there is the effect of costs on competitive bidding. Costs play an extremely important role in price determination, and this is especially true of standardized commodities for which units are relatively interchangeable. This is true in the case of raw materials such as steel, wood, or plastic and manufactured items that have not yet reached their final state.

Costs affect price in terms of the quantities that are produced. This is not as true where there is product differentiation, as in manufactured items. Unless for strategic reasons you are willing to take a contract at break-even or even at a loss, you must quote a price that will be low enough to place you in a price category that the Government will consider and at the same time a price that is high enough to allow you a profit when you win the contract.

Accordingly, the prices that are quoted to the Government cannot be based simply on what it costs to produce the item in question. They must also be based on what you think your competitors' price quotations will be.

Now, as noted earlier, under some conditions you should be willing to forego all profit and perhaps even some of your costs in order to win a certain contract. In such a case, you would quote a price so low that you undercut all competition. In the Government marketplace, this is called "buying in." The Government does not like this practice for several reasons. First, the Government feels that buying in might eventually result in a contractual default because of your inability to perform under conditions in which you may not be making any money. Secondly, the Government is concerned that this practice may lead to very high price quotations on subsequent contracts on which you may be awarded sole source.

There are additional advantages for you. You will have a difinite advantage over your competition in many situations even if you are not awarded a sole source contract. For one thing, you will have already paid for the tooling required to make a certain item under an initial contract. Since you will be the only supplier so far with the tooling, the production experience, and know-how, you would be able to outdistance your competition for any follow-up businesss. You might even recover your earlier profit loss on the buying in bid through contract changes or amendments that you can initiate after securing the contract.

OBJECT: TO PUT YOURSELF IN A SOLE SOURCE POSITION

Being in a sole source position is having a monopoly in dealing with the Government. Under these conditions you are the only supplier for any given product or service. To a certain extent, you can name your own price and since you are the only one supplying the item, you are able to totally control the market. Clearly the Government's objective is to keep you from getting into a sole source position. Much of the reason for going over this basic theory before entering into various techniques and methods and processes used in pricing is for you to understand this one basic objective. It is to your advantage to be in a sole source position. It is generally to the Government's price disadvantage. The Government has said this over the years, and has found that it incurs roughly 15% higher costs when dealing with a sole source contractor than when dealing with two or more competitive suppliers. Of course, there are also numerous advantages to the Government even if we are willing to accept the 15% higher figure claimed by Government analysts. A sole source may be more reliable, provide a much better product or service, and so on, so that the true costs to the Government may actually be lower in the end.

Methods of Pricing

While there are many methods that you may use in pricing a contract, there are two basic methods that are used most frequently. These are the market or competitive approach and the cost-plus approach.

The Competitive Approach

You may adapt your product to established prices or fix your price to overcome your competition. Or if you are a major producer of a certain item, you may determine the price on the basis of leadership and you may charge what the traffic will bear if you are in a sole source position.

Adaptation to Established Prices

When there is prevailing market price that is competititve, you must be able to produce and market the product within that established price. If you couldn't do this, you would be producing an item that is essentially unmarketable. No one would buy it. Let's look again at the auto industry. Every car manufacturer tries to bring out new models that will be attractive to the buying public and that will compete with competitors' models. A close examination will show that these prices are closely clustered around the different types of models available. Customers are certainly reluctant to buy a car if the price is way out of line with competitive prices charged for a similar style or model. When outlandish pricing does occur, frequently the customers will switch from one make of automobile to another in the same category. Setting price lines in this fashion to adapt to established prices in your market is clearly risky unless you can control your production costs and other potential manufacturing problems.

Pricing to Overcome Your Competition

Competitive conditions are of course critical to you are a supplier. Every product must be able to compete with similar products in the marketplace. Not only must you be able to compete with similar products, but also with replacement products. That is, if your product is made of one material (let's say steel or aluminum), it may be competing with other products made of plastic or some other composite material. That would be competing with similar products. But if you make missiles, your product may compete with airplanes, artillery, or tanks, because the final end is the objective intended for the product. If a tank can do a similar job to a missile, airplane, or artillery, then the tank's price must be considered along with the other similar-use products.

Price Determination on the Basis of Price Leadership

If yours is a relatively large firm, you can perhaps set market price by taking the initiative and setting these prices on your own. Such a price could be either lower or higher than the prevailing price. If it is higher, and you control a dominant share of the market, your competitors who are smaller will increase their prices in order to increase their profits. Price leaders in the United States are companies such as United States Steel, Standard Oil, and so forth. They are very carefully watched by other firms in the industry as well as by the Federal Trade Commission (FTC), because whenever these giants set a certain price, the other small firms in the industry set their prices to conform with the prices of the large companies.

Pricing by Charging Whatever the Traffic Will Bear

This concept reflects the fact that a price charge may be based on what you as a supplier believe the Government will be willing to pay. This is the exact opposite of pricing according to cost, and is illustrated by one Government contractor who noted that the value was in the eye of the beholder and that the price should be set accordingly.

Customary or Convenient Prices

Small commodity items, cigarettes, chewing gum, Cokes, sell for a certain fixed price. Such a price is termed a convenience price. These types of products are selected and purchased according to the consumer's taste and appetite and sometimes the availability of the product. Their prices tend to stay the same for long periods of time regardless of price fluctuation in raw materials, unless the fluctuations are severe. For example, for years the cost of a chocolate bar stayed at 5¢ and then 10¢ until the price of chocolate itself as a raw material began to increase enormously. With such common items it is very difficult to increase prices unless everyone in the industry does. In fact, it is well known that some producers will stop supplying a certain item rather than cut the price below a satisfactory profit margin. Other indirect attempts to change price have been done by cutting back on quality or size of the item. In this way, the product can be maintained at the convenient price. Here again, we might consider the candy bar, which shrank in size before it increased in price.

Cost-Plus Approach

The cost-plus approach to pricing is favored by the Government. It is found on all Government forms that you must use to document your pricing while bidding on a Government contract. It is very familiar to Government procurement people. Under this system you price the item on the basis of cost plus whatever the Government considers is a reasonable addition for profit. Your costs include both the cost to manufacture and distribute the product. Studies show that many Government contractors and manufacturers use the cost-plus method of pricing.

The costs used in cost plus may be direct or indirect depending upon the accounting system used. As a general rule, costs that can be directly charged to a unit of production are termed direct costs. These costs are associated with the purchase of manpower or material. Costs that cannot be identified with specific units of production are charged to an overhead account and termed indirect costs.

Although you will be required to substantiate your price to the Government through a cost-plus approach, it is the competitive or market approach that should decide your price. The cost-plus approach should only be used as a basis for developing your basement or bottom price, below which you cannot go without losing money on a particular contract.

Price and Cost Analysis

The Government contracting people use price and cost analysis for several purposes. First, they use it to forecast what a proposed procurement will probably cost in order to budget and obtain funding for a particular program. Second, they use it in evaluating bids, quotations, or proposals that you as a potential contractor have submitted for a certain procurement. Third, they use it in selecting the contractor who may be expected to perform the contract most efficiently. And finally, they use it in preparing for negotiations with you. For procurements that will exceed $100,000—except when competition is considered adequate by the Government or when certain other conditions specified by law are present—cost or pricing data are required from you and cost analysis is performed by the Government. This analysis will require you to organize your price presentation on a cost basis. Accordingly, you must understand price and cost analysis from the Government's viewpont.

The Government recognizes the role of competition in arriving at a price for a given contract. In a competitive market the Government knows that the price is generally closer to what the competition is bidding than to the cost of manufacture. From the Government's point of view if you are to make a profit, your performance on the contract must be at least as efficient as that of your most efficient competitor. Therefore if there is effective price competition, this will insure the reasonableness of a prospective price, according to the Government. Thus when the Government feels that enough competition is present, it will appraise only your total price and will not analyze your cost and profits separately.

However, one of your basic objectives is to eliminate competition and get yourself into a sole source position. Also, in many situations competition may be absent. You may be bidding a research and development contract in which the award may be based on technical proficiency rather than price. Under all of these circumstances the Government takes another approach. The Government is aware that your estimates of probable costs may include some padding, and also that your price may be geared to cover your estimated costs plus as much profit as you believe the Government will pay. Again, this is not unreasonable. It is just that the Government recognizes the fluidity of the negotiating position you are both in. Therefore whether you are in fact charging what the market will bear or whether you have closely estimated your probable costs with no padding, the Government will turn to cost analysis to ensure that it is paying what it considers a fair and reasonable price for what it is buying.

Now price analysis as a method is different from cost analysis. A correct and sound price decision can be made after price analysis without the use of cost analysis techniques at all. But conversely, such a decision cannot be made on the basis of cost analysis alone. In fact, price analysis is used in the price decision process by the Government on just about every procurement it makes, not only those that are required to be analyzed according to cost. In general the Government feels that if price analysis can do the job on relatively small procurements (that is, small in the dollar sense), there is no need to use cost analysis. On large procurements, however, you can be expected to have your bid analyzed very closely for both price and cost analysis. Obviously, it is in your interest that only price analysis be made since cost analysis is both more time-consuming (since you must supply additional figures and other data) and involves a more complicated negotiation process with the Government. Realistically, this usually means that you will end up reducing your price to some extent.

HOW THE GOVERNMENT BUYER FITS IN

In many situations the Government buyer knows the product or service sought as well as the market, the sources, and the prevailing prices. This is because of his acquaintance with past prices, quantities, schedules, discounts, and other terms of sale. He also knows the acceptability of past purchases to technical users within the Government. However, this presumption of knowledge is not always true. Many Government buyers will be new and lack background and experience in the particular area in which they are working. Many of the technical people will also be new and have limited experience. Further, in some complex research and development projects the Government will have little basis on which to make a decision about how much a certain development might cost or even a clear picture of the quantities, delivery schedules, specifications, and other factors involved. To some degree you will be able to help out and your suggestions will influence Government thinking through your preproposal marketing activities. In many cases you will be requested by the Government customer to supply information that he will be able to use in arriving at what he thinks will be the approximate price of a forthcoming procurement. But whether or not you assist the Government in arriving at a ball-park price for the procurement, you should keep in mind that the Government is always aiming for what it feels is a "fair and reasonable price." According to the Government a fair and reasonable price is one that is fair to both parties in the transaction with regard to quality, delivery, and the probability of the seller producing as promised. However, in real bottom-line terms what "fair and reasonable" really means is simply a price that is acceptable to both the Government and to you.

According to the Government, in most procurements made by formal advertising, in which the award is made to the lowest responsible bidder who conforms to requirements of the IFB, it is presumed that the price is fair and reasonable unless there is only on bid received. If there is only one bid received, the Government feels that it is necessary to determine whether this bid is reasonable or not. This is done through price analysis.

However, there is a different approach if the procurement is by negotiation through the use of RFQs or RFPs. Then the Government does not make the automatic assumption that the lowest offer is fair and reasonable. The thinking is that in negotiated procurement there are other factors to be considered in addition to price, including technical quality, ability to deliver on time, performance, and ultimate cost to the taxpayer. Cost ot the taxpayer itself may then be measured by factors such as ease of maintenance, transportation costs, service life, time between overhaul, and so on. Since the Government wants to insure that the final price arrived at by negotiation is fair and reasonable by its standards, this price will be subjected to some form of analysis: either price analysis by itself or frequently a combination of both cost and price analysis.

Price analysis is very simple. It can be done by a straight comparison of prices or by a comparison with an engineering estimate. Price analysis may also include estimating the ultimate cost to the taxpayer. But price analysis does not include evaluation of elements of the contractor's detailed estimate of the cost to perform the contract. That gets you into the area of cost analysis. Since an analysis based on cost elements does not primarily recognize other important factors in your business or in the marketplace, from your point of view price analysis alone is desirable. However, you can expect to be involved with cost analysis as well at some time during your career as a Government contractor.

How Price Analysis is Accomplished

Price analysis techniques are basically done through comparison. It is a comparison process of examining and evaluating the total price without including either separate cost elements or the proposed profit. Uncle Sam has identified five different methods of price analysis that may be accomplished. The first is simply a comparison of the price quotations that were submitted. The second is a comparison of current proposed prices with prices that have been paid in the past for the item or service. The third is the use of a rough yardstick to detect inconsistencies in price that should be subjected to a more intensive pricing inquiry. These yardsticks relate to quality and performance characteristics that can be equated to dollar value. For example, dollars per pound in hardware items or dollars per horsepower in machinery. Fourth, the comparison of published price lists, published market prices, or similar published data. In other words, the Government will look at catalogue prices versus the price you have quoted. Fifth, comparison of the proposed price with an independent estimate developed by price analysis of the procurement situation.

You should always be aware that the Government will do a price analysis of every contract that you bid. You should be sure that your price is generally in line with the prices that may be quoted or arrived at through any of these other sources.

Now let's look at cost analysis.

Methods of Contract Cost Analysis

You may recall that cost analysis is used to establish a basis for negotiation of contract prices where price competition is not adequate according to the Government, or when Uncle Sam feels that price competition is lacking altogether, or when price analysis by itself does not ensure what the Government believes is a reasonable price. Basically, costs are analyzed to determine if the total cost estimate approximates the dollars that it should cost to perform the contract if your company operates with reasonable economy and efficiency.

When costs and pricing data are required you will submit this data with the price proposal. You will be required to submit your data for analysis on a DD Form 633 (shown in Figure 41a) when dealing with the Department of Defense, and on a similar form when dealing with other departments or agencies of the U.S. Government. Once again, I want to emphasize that you will only be required to submit this data or use this form when the Government feels that price competition is ineffective and a full price or cost analysis is required.

You should know that the information that you supply the Government will be compared against data that the Government keeps in its own files listing past prices for certain products used as a rough gauge; audit reports that have been done on your company that are on file with various comptrollers of the different Government agencies that you might be dealing with; and other data including financial statements and annual reports, reports that have been prepared by you, records of previously negotiated contracts, renegotiation reports and subsequent board investigation reports, applicable Government estimates as well as industrywide rules of thumb or other estimating practices, indices of the Bureau of Labor Statistics (such as the cost-of-living index), daily newspaper commodity and market indexes and price lists, textbooks, handbooks, trade journal and catalogue information, findings of plant representatives and inspectors, price and cost information submitted by competing contractors, and in-house estimates developed by other Government personnel.

I mention these not to frighten you, but only to indicate that Uncle Sam does have a considerable amount of data available to him. The basic costs that you

This form is for use when submission of cost or pricing data (see ASPR 3-807.3) is required

PAGE NO.	NO. OF PAGES

NAME OF OFFEROR	SUPPLIES AND/OR SERVICES TO BE FURNISHED	
HOME OFFICE ADDRESS (Include ZIP Code)		
	QUANTITY	TOTAL AMOUNT OF PROPOSAL $
DIVISION(S) AND LOCATION(S) WHERE WORK IS TO BE PERFORMED		GOVERNMENT SOLICITATION NO.

COST ELEMENTS			PROPOSED CONTRACT ESTIMATE		
			TOTAL COST[1]	UNIT COST[2]	REFERENCE[3]
1. DIRECT MATERIAL[4]	a. PURCHASED PARTS[5]				
	b. SUBCONTRACTED ITEMS[6]				
	c. OTHER MATERIAL	(1) RAW MATERIAL[7]			
		(2) STANDARD COMMERCIAL ITEMS[8]			
		(3) INTERDIVISIONAL TRANSFERS (at other than cost)[9]			
2. MATERIAL OVERHEAD[10]					
3. INTERDIVISIONAL TRANSFERS AT COST[11]					
4. DIRECT ENGINEERING LABOR[12]					
5. ENGINEERING OVERHEAD[10]					
6. DIRECT MANUFACTURING LABOR[12]					
7. MANUFACTURING OVERHEAD[10]					
8. OTHER COSTS[13]					
9. SUBTOTALS					
10. GENERAL AND ADMINISTRATIVE EXPENSES[10]					
11. ROYALTIES[14]					
12. FEDERAL EXCISE TAX[15]					
13. SUBTOTALS					
14. PROFIT OR FEE					
15. TOTAL PRICE (Amount)					

I. HAVE THE DEPARTMENT OF DEFENSE, NATIONAL AERONAUTICS AND SPACE ADMINISTRATION, OR THE ATOMIC ENERGY COMMISSION PERFORMED ANY REVIEW OF YOUR ACCOUNTS OR RECORDS IN CONNECTION WITH ANY OTHER GOVERNMENT PRIME CONTRACT OR SUBCONTRACT WITHIN THE PAST TWELVE MONTHS?

☐ YES ☐ NO IF YES, IDENTIFY BELOW.

NAME AND ADDRESS OF REVIEWING OFFICE (Include ZIP Code)	TELEPHONE NUMBER

II. WILL YOU REQUIRE THE USE OF ANY GOVERNMENT PROPERTY IN THE PERFORMANCE OF THIS PROPOSED CONTRACT?

☐ YES ☐ NO IF YES, IDENTIFY ON A SEPARATE PAGE.

III. DO YOU REQUIRE GOVERNMENT CONTRACT FINANCING TO PERFORM THIS PROPOSED CONTRACT?

☐ YES ☐ NO IF YES, IDENTIFY: ☐ ADVANCE PAYMENTS ☐ PROGRESS PAYMENTS OR ☐ GUARANTEED LOANS

IV. HAVE YOU BEEN AWARDED ANY CONTRACTS OR SUBCONTRACTS FOR SIMILAR ITEMS WITHIN THE PAST THREE YEARS?

☐ YES ☐ NO IF YES, SHOW CUSTOMER(S) AND CONTRACT NUMBERS BELOW OR ON A SEPARATE PAGE.

V. DOES THIS COST SUMMARY CONFORM WITH THE COST PRINCIPLES SET FORTH IN ASPR, SECTION XV (see 3-807.3(c)(2))?

☐ YES ☐ NO IF NO, EXPLAIN ON A SEPARATE PAGE

This proposal is submitted for use in connection with and in response to _____

_____ * and reflects our best estimates as of this date,

in accordance with the instructions to offerors and the footnotes which follow:

*DESCRIBE RFP, ETC.

TYPED NAME AND TITLE	SIGNATURE
NAME OF FIRM	DATE OF SUBMISSION

Figure 41a. Form DD 633/Dept. of Defense/Contract Pricing Proposal.

1. The purpose of this form is to provide a standard format by which the offeror submits to the Government a summary of incurred and estimated costs *(and attached supporting information)* suitable for detailed review and analysis. Prior to the award of a contract resulting from this proposal, the offeror shall, under the conditions stated in ASPR 3-807.3, be required to submit a Certificate of Current Cost or Pricing Data *(see ASPR 3-807.3(e) and 3-807.4)*.

2. As part of the specific information required by this form, the offeror must submit with this form, and clearly identify as such, cost or pricing data *(that is, data which is verifiable and factual and otherwise as defined in ASPR 3-807.3(e))*. In addition, he must submit with this form any information reasonably required to explain the offeror's estimating process, including:

    a. The judgmental factors applied and the mathematical or other methods used in the estimate including those used in projecting from known data, and

    b. The contingencies used by the offeror in his proposed price.

3. When attachment of supporting cost or pricing data to this form is impracticable, the data will be specifically identified and described *(with schedules as appropriate)*, and made available to the contracting officer or his representative upon request.

4. The formats for the "Cost Elements" and the "Proposed Contract Estimate" are not intended as rigid requirements. These may be presented in different format with the prior approval of the contracting officer if required for more effective and efficient presentation. In all other respects this form will be completed and submitted without change.

5. By submission of this proposals offeror, if selected for negotiation, grants to the contracting officer, or his authorized representative, the right to examine for the purpose of verifying the cost or pricing data submitted, those books, records, documents and other supporting data which will permit adequate evaluation of such cost or pricing data, along with the computation and projections used therein. This right may be exercised in connection with any negotiations prior to contract award.

FOOTNOTES

NOTE 1. Enter in this column those necessary and reasonable costs which in the judgment of the offeror will properly be incurred in the efficient performance of the contract. When any of the costs in this column have already been incurred *(e.g., on a letter contract or change order)*, describe them on an attached supporting schedule. When "preproduction" or "startup" costs are significant or when specifically requested in detail by the contracting officer, provide a full identification and explanation of same.

NOTE 2. The use of this column is optional for multiple line item proposals, except where the contracting officer determines that a separate DD Form 633 is required for selected line items.

NOTE 3. Attach separate pages as necessary and identify in this column the attachment in which the information supporting the specific cost element may be found. No standard format is prescribed; however, the cost or pricing data must be accurate, complete and current, and the judgment factors used in projecting from the data to the estimates must be stated in sufficient detail to enable the contracting officer to evaluate the proposal. For example, provide the basis used for pricing the bill of materials such as by vendor quotations, shop estimates, or invoice prices; the reason for use of overhead rates which depart significantly from experienced rates *(reduced volume, a planned major rearrangement, etc.)*; or justification for an increase in labor rates *(anticipated wage and salary increases, etc.)*. Identify and explain any contingencies which are included in the proposed price, such as anticipated costs of rejects and defective work, anticipated costs of engineering redesign and retesting, or anticipated technical difficulties in designing high-risk components.

NOTE 4. Provide a list of principal items within each category of material indicating known or anticipated source, quantity, unit price, competition obtained, and basis of establishing source and reasonableness of cost.

NOTE 5. Include material for the proposed contract other than material described in the other footnotes under the cost element entitled "Direct Material."

NOTE 6. Include parts, components, assemblies, and services to be produced or performed by other than you in accordance with your designs, specifications, or directions and applicable only to the prime contract.

NOTE 7. Include raw and processed material for the proposed contract in a form or state which requires further processing.

NOTE 8. Include standard commercial items normally fabricated in whole or in part by you which are generally stocked in inventory. Provide explanation for inclusion at other than the lower of cost or current market price.

NOTE 9. Include all materials sold or transferred between your plants, divisions or organizations under a common control at other than cost to the original transferror and provide explanation of pricing method used.

NOTE 10. Indicate the rates used and provide an appropriate explanation. Where agreement has been reached with Government representatives on the use of forward pricing rates, describe the nature of the agreement. Provide the method of computation and application of your overhead expense, including cost breakdown and showing trends and budgetary data as necessary to provide a basis for evaluation of the reasonableness of proposed rates.

NOTE 11. Include separate breakdown of costs.

NOTE 12. Provide a separate breakdown of labor by appropriate category and furnish basis for cost estimates.

NOTE 13. Include all other estimated costs *(e.g., special tooling, facilities, special test equipment, special plant rearrangement, preservation packaging and packing, spoilage and rework, and warranty)* which are not otherwise included. Identify separately each category of cost and provide supporting details. If the proposal is based on a F.O.B. destination price, indicate separately all outbound transportation costs included in total amount.

NOTE 14. If the total cost entered here is in excess of $250, provide on a separate page *(or on DD Form 783, Royalty Report)* the following information on each separate item of royalty or license fee: name and address of licensor; date of license agreement; patent numbers, patent application serial numbers, or other basis on which the royalty is payable; brief description, including any part or model numbers of each contract item or component on which the royalty is payable; percentage or dollar rate of royalty per unit; unit price of contract item; number of units; and total dollar amount of royalties. In addition, if specifically requested by the contracting officer, a copy of the current license agreement and identification of applicable claims of specific patents shall be provided.

NOTE 15. Selling price must include any applicable Federal excise tax on finished articles.

Figure 41b. Instructions to Offeror.

submit on the DD 633 must be substantiated so that if, during negotiation, the Government quotes from any of the sources of information mentioned above that you have your own sources of information from which you can quote to back up your cost information.

As a matter of interest, until 1962 potential contractors were not required to submit their cost data in any standard fashion to the Government. However, to prevent deceptive pricing and the paying of unearned profits to contractors, Congress passed the Truth in Negotiation Act (PL 87-653). This act was designed to provide the Government with all the information it could obtain so that negotiations would result in what the Government feels is a fair and reasonable price according to its definition. In conjunction with the requirement to submit certified cost or price data, the Government will also require you to agree to the inclusion of a contract or procedure for adjusting the price in the event that the data proves to be misleading.

It is the Truth in Negotiation Act that requires you to submit your costs on the DD Form 633 or similar forms for other Government agencies. As shown, the DD Form 633 requires a breakdown of cost elements, profit, and total price. It also requires that explanatory submissions be included in the form of attachments. You must certify at the time of completion of negotiation or shortly thereafter that the data that you supplied is accurate, complete, and current. Though the DD Form 633 establishes a specific format for presenting the data, your cost elements and estimates may be presented in a different format as long as they are acceptable to the Government contracting officer. This deviation is acceptable to the Government under circumstances in which your particular accounting system makes the DD Form 633 impractical. However, the basic idea must be submitted in some fashion regardless of what form you may use.

If the Government audits you during or after performance and it is found that the data that you submitted earlier was not accurate, current, or complete, the Government contracting officer is empowered to reduce the contracting price by the amount of the overstatement. Of course you can appeal the contracting officer's determination if you do not agree with the ruling, through an appeals clause that will be in the contract.

You should also know that the DD 633 series includes not just the single form shown but also a series of forms that may be used and similar forms that are available for negotiation with other Government agencies such as NASA, the DOE, and so on. In the Department of Defense, these forms consist of DD Form 633-1 for technical services, DD Form 633-2 for technical publications, DD Form 633-3 for motion pictures, DD Form 633-4 for research and development, DD Form 633-5 for change orders, DD Form 633-6 for price redetermination, and DD Form 633-7 for a claim for exemption from certified cost or pricing data.

In cost analysis of the data that you provide to the Government, Uncle Sam classifies costs into three different groups: variable costs, fixed costs, and semivariable costs. Variable costs are costs that fluctuate directly and proportionally on a total basis with changes in volume of production or your business activity. Direct material and direct labor are both variable costs; as the volume increases, the costs of these materials and labor goes up as well. Fixed costs are those that remain relatively constant regardless of the volume of production or the business activity. Here the Government considers rent, depreciation, property insurance, and property taxes to be normal fixed costs. Finally, semivariable costs are costs that vary on a total basis with changes in volume, production, and business activity, but not necessarily in direct proportion to these changes. Some examples would be maintenance, heat, light, or power. A semivariable cost is one that is both variable and fixed. The variable and fixed parts of a semivariable cost can be separated and treated according to their own makeup.

The analysis technique that the Government calls CVP (for "Cost, Volume, Profit Analysis") involves first isolating the variable portion of the total cost under study. Once the fixed and variable costs are identified, the Government makes projections for production quantities other than that for which the analysis has been performed. By comparing the isolated costs with expected revenue and expected volume of production, the effect on fixed cost and profit is calculated and provides the basis that the Government uses as a negotiating position, linked to an incremental pricing concept.

Direct costs usually account for the largest part of the total cost of any contract that you may be negotiating with the Government and the Government recognizes this. Therefore you can expect the Government negotiators to concentrate on reducing direct costs in order to cut back the total price of the contract that you have bid. For example, you can expect the Government to look very closely at the amount of material that you say is required for the contract as well as the price of the material. You will, of course, include wastage of material and I would advise you to have detailed figures to show why this wastage percentage is what it is and supporting data for it. In analyzing the price of material you can expect the Government to make comparisons with prices from several different sources. Therefore if you wish to use a higher priced material, you should be ready to justify why it is absolutely necessary for the contract, and why you can't use a cheaper material.

You can also expect the Government to look very closely into labor and its allocation to direct or indirect costs. Direct labor will also account for a significant portion of the total contract cost. Obviously the Government would prefer you to charge labor to indirect costs rather than to direct since this will make possible a lower price for the specific contract under negotiation. So let's look at how the Government categorizes work and how it divides labor into direct or indirect categories.

The Government describes the characteristics of direct labor as follows: first, work directly associated with the project that usually produces a change in raw material; second, labor that is readily identified with the product. For example, if there is a worker whose sole function is to squirt oil on a part as it is being manufactured and he works on this component and no other, then it is direct labor. However, if this same employee squirts oil on many types of products or components, then this is indirect labor.

The third characteristic of direct labor is that it is important enough to merit special identification and measurement. If a worker's job is painting missiles olive drab and the missile itself is the product, then this is direct labor. If the worker's job is merely touching up those few spots that were missed and that is all, then his work is not important enough to justify charging his labor directly to that particular product. But remember that whether labor is considered direct or indirect is negotiable. So if you want the individual who is doing the touch up to be charged against direct labor, then you must justify it during negotiations with the Government.

Indirect labor differs primarily from direct labor in this manner: although it contributes to the production of the end-item, its results cannot be conveniently allocated into quantities that can be associated with individual end-items. A book by the U.S Air Force on negotiation and contract administration gives the following illustration: Suppose that a foreman is responsible for the supervision of 10 men operating machine tools. His work cannot be evenly divided among the 10. For example, one day he may be faced with a batch of components that have progressed as far as the assembly line and then found to be undersized. The foreman may spend the whole day at one machine solving this problem. At the same time, the other nine machines for which he is responsible are still turning out components. Moreover, the components that they are producing may be for work charged against a dozen different contracts. Under these conditions it would take a very complicated and cumbersome accounting system to allow the foreman's time to be charged to the individual end-items to which his labor contributes. Therefore, according to the Air Force, this foreman is performing indirect labor. However, if the shop for which he is responsible is working on a single contract, his labor can still be divided among the end-items and charged as direct labor against this single contract.

Now you should know that in general the Government is willing to let you make the decision as to whether a given labor is direct or indirect—subject to only one condition. That condition is that whatever decision you make must be applied consistenly within the life of the contract and among other contracts that are ongoing at the same time. The Government is not at all agreeable to your choosing one particular method that is advantageous to you at one point in time or phase of a contract and then switching to another method as that method becomes more advantageous.

The rates at which overhead costs for indirect labor are added to the charges for direct manufacturing are also settled through negotiation between you and the Government. Naturally, the Government wants these overhead rates as low as possible, so you can expect some tough negotiating on this item. One way that you can keep your overhead rates down of course is by charging everything you possibly can directly to the contract. Therefore as you negotiate these rates you will be continuously balancing off one type of charge against another. Preparation and prior planning are the answers to how you can do this effectively.

Analysis of Man-Hours

You can also expect to negotiate man-hours with the Government for many types of contracts. Basically, there are three procedures that are used: the normal estimating procedure, standard time studies, and the use of a learning curve. In the normal estimating procedure the estimator examines engineering drawings, schedules, specifications, and other descriptive materials in which the item is to be produced is described and defined as precisely as possible. From this examination he determines as accurately as possible how many man-hours of direct manufacturing labor should be required to produce the item. What results is a guess; but it is an educated guess. Standard time studies and tables of times are alternate methods of estimating direct labor hours based on the same basic idea: observing work and measuring time. In standard time studies each worker is timed with a stopwatch on his performance of a given operation. After all the workers have been timed, the operations that are needed to manufacture a product are adjusted for average work or or efficiency and added to established worker allowances. This gives a total manufacturing time for the product. Of course, to be realistic, the product should already be in production and a certain degree of proficiency already attained. Tables of times for performing such motions as reach, move, turn, grasp, position, disengage, and so on, under different conditions or varying distances, have been worked out and standardized.

Through the use of this information the standard unit production time can also be determined. The unit production time depends on the production method employed, as it does in a regular time study. An improvement in the production method should result in a lower production time. This system is useful for estimating direct labor costs when a regular time study would be impossible or when the production process is of a relatively simple nature. Learning curves are based on the theory that many types of production activities are subject to a learning process as production increases, causing the production time for any given units to decrease. In other words, as additional units are produced, the man-hours required for the production of a unit grows less. It was found during World War II that in airplane production this reduction of man-hours required took place in a more or less predictable manner, and that it was constant over a certain number of units manufactured. So that if the man-hours required for the production of units at one stage of manufacturing is known, man-hours required at a later stage can be predicted with some degree of confidence.

This learning curve, or improvement curve, has been found to apply to many types of mass production industries characterized by short production runs and a large amount of labor associated with manufacture. The basic reason that the learning curve works is simply that a constant predictable rate of improvement in the number of hours required to produce an item will occur under certain common manufacturing conditions. For example, to produce the first unit of any given item might take you 2000 production hours. To produce the second unit might take only 800. The third unit may take 500. To produce unit 10 may take only 300. By the time you get to unit 10,000, the time may have leveled off and may take about 200 hours. This learning curve is illustrated in Figure 42. Note that the steepness of the curve depends upon whether the curve is drawn at 95%, 85%, 80%, and so on. These different steepnesses describe different levels of learning improvement. You can expect to negotiate the steepness of the curve with the Government on many contracts in which large amounts of over $100,000 are involved and in which high production runs are called for.

Government Negotiation with Wage Rates

You can expect that the Government will also want to look at your wage rates on certain contracts where costing data will be required. The various rates of wages paid will vary with geographical location, total time of contract performance, and variations with labor mix; that is, variation of labor wage rates depending upon the type of labor force employed in your plant. If you decide to use an average wage rate, you will have considerable negotiating to do. The Government recognizes that a cutback during a recession will probably affect those men that are of least value to the contract and also at the lowest skill levels. Therefore the ones that are retained will probably be making uniformly higher salaries. As a result, the average wage rate of the remaining work force will be higher than it was prior to such a layoff. On the other hand, the hiring of more men as you get additional contracts may affect your average wage rate in the opposite direction. You can expect the Government to look at your wage rates under these conditions and negotiate which "average" wage rate you will use in your contract. You will be expected to substantiate any changes from your previous levels of pay.

Negotiating Indirect Costs

The Government will negotiate with you to establish the exact figures for all types of indirect costs including manufacturing overhead costs and other costs that are incurred in the operation of your plant but that can't be assigned to the specific manufacture of units related to the contract. You can expect negotiation regarding general administrative expenses incurred in the operation of your company's general offices and the management, supervision, and conduct of your business as a whole, including administrative and office salaries and other compensation related to personal services, rent, depreciation, auditing, supplies, utilities, postage, and so on. You can expect under indirect costs to negotiate selling expenses including salesmen's salaries and commissions, sales promotion, negotiation

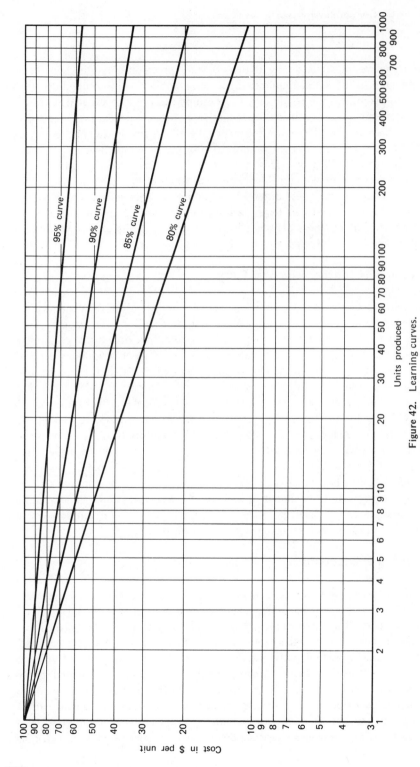

Figure 42. Learning curves.

306

liaison between your personnel and the Government, preparation of costs, engineering and bidding data, the providing of technical and demonstration services, and other related activities.

In order to project reasonable indirect costs, you would normally project your overhead costs and volume of business for each period of operation so that a fair share of the overhead costs are applied to each unit of production and sale during the particular period you are analyzing. This means estimating overhead costs, the production level, and the volume of business in terms of a base that is used for deriving an overhead application rate. Of course, actual indirect costs cannot be determined until the end of the accounting period, usually a year or more after the work has been accomplished, but you must do your estimate at the beginning of the period, prior to performing the contract and incurring either direct or indirect costs. Government procurement regulations provide for four different methods of establishing indirect costs chargeable to a Government contract. These are:

1. Negotiated overhead rates.
2. Forward pricing rate agreements, known as FPRAs.
3. Advanced understandings.
4. After-the-fact audit determination.

Negotiated Overhead Rate

Negotiated overhead rate envisions a policy and procedure governing the negotiation of final overhead rates for use in cost reimbursement contracts, as discussed in an earlier chapter. The purpose of a negotiated final overhead rate is to provide for a uniform approval covering a number of government procuring activities having contracts with a single contractor in order to reduce the administrative work on both sides and bring about a timely settlement of reimbursement claims. Typically, the procedure for the establishment and use of a negotiated overhead rate generally is set in motion when you as a contractor submit a proposal for a certain overhead rate and following an advisory audit report accomplished by the Government. The appropriate contracting officer who is negotiating with you reviews these documents, conducts the negotiation, obtains a cost and pricing data certificate, and prepares both a buying written agreement to be signed by both you and the Government and a detailed negotiation memorandum. The agreement includes a list of expected contracts that identifies any contract with advanced agreements or special provisions and their applicable overhead rates. The negotiation memorandum must also document the rates negotiated, reasons for any variation from the audit report, the period of rate applicability, the basis for determining the rates, the specific items treated as direct cost, and, when applicable, the billing rate agreed upon for the succeeding period.

Forward Pricing Rate Agreements (FPRAs)

The forward pricing rate agreements are written agreements that are negotiated with the Government to ensure that certain rates are available for use during a specific period in the pricing of contracts or contract modification. The rates that you negotiate should represent a reasonable projection of costs that may be incurred in future periods that are not easily estimated for or identified with the specific contract. These costs are not limited to overhead but may also include such things as labor rates, material handling costs, and so on.

Advanced Understandings

Advanced understandings are used on specific cost items. If advanced understandings can be negotiated to cover some elements of the overhead costs, the task of agreeing upon appropriate overhead application is simplified.

After-the-Fact Audit Determination

When final overhead rates have not been negotiated previously, the contracting officer directs an after-the-fact audit to decide which overhead rate will be applied to the contract.

Weighted Guidelines for Establishing a Profit or Fee Objective

Because of Congressional interest in excessive Government contractor profits and the inability of Government analysts to apply realistic cost and price techniques to more complex items, the weighted guideline system was developed as a basis for profit or fee negotiation.

Under this system, an initial dollar amount of profit or fee is calculated based on a percentage of the various elements of cost, your assumption of contract cost risk, your past performance and other selected factors such as source of resources and special achievement, if any that is required by the contract.

The objective of the weighted guidelines is to tie your performance more directly to profits.

In this chapter we have been concerned with the ramifications of pricing and negotiating Government contracts. The basic message here is that you should be prepared for negotiation by gathering as many facts as possible that you can bring to bear in face-to-face meetings with the Government contracting officer. A great help in developing a price for Government contracts is a booklet that you can obtain from the Government called "Armed Services Procurement Regulation Manual for Contract Pricing." This is published by the Department of Defense and is available for purchase from the Superintendent of Documents, U.S. Government Printing Office, Washington, D.C. 20402. You should also refer to Chapter 12 of this book since the type of Government contract will impact on your pricing strategy.

Chapter 11

HOW THE GOVERNMENT EVALUATES YOUR PROPOSAL

While price will always be important to some degree in determining the winner of a Government proposal, research and development and other proposals have many other factors that are of importance and are evaluated in judging the winner. Typically, the RFP or the RFQ will have a special section that contains technical evaluation criteria and award factors that the Government feels are important in the selection of a contractor to perform whatever services are sought. For example, Figure 43 shows the criteria contained in a recent Air Force RFP.

R&D proposals are generally evaluated on the basis of some common items that are contained in the evaluation factor section. These factors are technical approach, organization personnel and facilities of the bidder, and general quality and responsiveness of the proposal. However, these factors are not judged directly but through the scoring of subfactors, and the subfactors are weighted depending upon what the Government feels is important in the particular proposal under consideration.

In the evaluation factors example shown above, the Air Force indicated that relative order of importance for their proposal was first, technical merit/competence, then management capabilities, then cost/price, then past performance in adhering to contract requirements, and finally, other pertinent factors. Let us look now at only the technical merit/competence factors and see how a weighting in judging this proposal might be set up by the Government. Look at Figures 44a and b. For every major factor listed, there are subfactors. For example, under the factor Soundness of Approach, there are four subfactors, a through d. They are: adequacy of the plan, review and assess data; adequacy of analytical techniques; plan to upgrade, verify, and demonstrate the compouter code; and approach to assess potential problems. Referring back to what was written in the RFP, we see that under D4, the soundness of approach factor has a relative importance of 1. In Figure 44 the four subfactors a through d of Soundness of Approach are given the weights 5, 10, 3, and 3, respectively, giving a total weight of 21. In the same figure, the Understanding of the Problem factor has subfactors a through e, which are given weights of 5, 3, 3, 2, and 2, respectively, totaling 15. This matches the relative importance of 2 given to this factor in the RFP.

Now let's see how these weighting factors might be used to determine an overall winner. In Figure 43, note that four proposals have been submitted. Proposal A

SECTION D - <u>EVALUATION FACTORS FOR AWARD</u>

D-1. <u>EVALUATION AND AWARD FACTORS IN RELATIVE ORDER OF</u>
<u>IMPORTANCE</u>.

     The Government will select the best overall offer,
based on the following which are cited in their relative
order of importance: (1) Technical merit/competence in
accordance with Paragraph D-4 below; (2) Management capabilities including D-4(a) and D-3 below as appropriate; (3)
Cost/price; (4) Past performance in adhering to contract
requirements; (5) Other pertinent factors. Paramount consideration will be given to technical merit/competence.

D-2. <u>INFORMATION REQUIRED FOR EVALUATION</u>.

     (a) Statements of Information are required to be ade-
quate to enable Government evaluation of your organization's
technical and financial capabilities. Pertinent scientific
and technical information will be included in the technical
proposal as required by Section C. Cost and price information will be submitted with supporting documents, as required
in Section C.

     (b) The entire offer, both technical and financial,
should be as brief as practicable. The utilization of filler
pages and unnecessary attachments therefore is not to be
encouraged.

Figure 43. Section D/Evaluation factors for award.

D-4. SPECIAL EVALUATION FACTORS

Relative Importance   Factor

1   Soundness of Approach

a. Adequacy of plan to identify,
    review, and assess ground tests
    and spacecraft flight data.

b. Adequacy of analytical tech-
    niques to be employed for con-
    ducting sensitivity studies and
    in assessing chamber/flight data,
    testing capabilities and impact
    on spacecraft mission effective-
    ness.

c. Well planned, logical, systema-
    tic and comprehensive plan to
    upgrade, verify, and demonstrate
    the computer code.

d. Well planned, logical, and sys-
    tematic approach to assess
    potential problems for specific
    spacecraft systems and to perform
    sensitivity studies.

2   Understanding of the Problem

a. Understanding of the overall and
    detailed objectives of the pro-
    gram.

Figure 43 (*Continued*)

b. Understanding of liquid, solid and electric propulsion processes and known or potential contamination sources.

c. Understanding of contamination mechanisms and their effect on spacecraft materials, components and mission effectiveness.

d. Understanding of the problems and limitations of modelling the production, transport and surface-interaction effects of contaminants from liquid, solid, and electric propulsion systems.

e. Understanding of vacuum-chamber testing techniques, diagnostic instrumentation and spacecraft performance-monitoring devices

3   Compliance with Requirements
Adequate response to statement of work. Clarity of program plan. Substantiation of exceptions to work statement and how they will enhance program success.

4   Special Technical Factors
Unique concepts or new ideas which enhance the program success.

Figure 43 (*Continued*)

EVALUATION FACTORS

Technical Merit/Competence

Factor	Weight
1. Soundness of Approach	
a. Adequacy of plan to identify, review and assess data	5
b. Adequacy of analytical techniques	10
c. Plan to upgrade, verify and demonstrate the computer code	3
d. Approach to assess potential problems	3
2. Understanding of the Problem	
a. Understanding of objectives of the program	5
b. Understanding of propulsion processes and contamination sources	3
c. Understanding of contamination mechanisms and their effect	3
d. Understanding of problems and limitations of modeling	2
e. Understanding testing techniques	2
3. Compliance with Requirements	10
4. Special Technical Factors	8

Figure 44a. Evaluation factors.

Evaluation Factors	Weight	Proposal A	Proposal B	Proposal C	Proposal D
Part I Technical Merit/Competence					
1. Soundness of approach					
a. Adequacy of plan	5	70	90	90	80
b. Adequacy of analytical techniques	10	85	75	80	70
c. Plan to upgrade, verify, and demonstrate	3	80	80	70	80
d. approach to assess potential problems	3	NO DATA	50	70	80
Weighted total					
Weighted average					
a. Objectives of the program	5	100	90	90	100
b. Propulsion process and contamination sources	3	90	100	90	80
c. Contamination mechanisms	3	60	65	60	60
d. Problems and limitations	2	80	80	70	70
e. Testing techniques	2	50	50	60	50
Weighted total					

Figure 44b. Typical evaluation work sheet rating of subfactors.

314

received a score of 70 for adequacy of plan; 85 for adequacy of analytical techniques; and 80 for the plan to upgrade, verify, and demonstrate. Note that, according to the evaluator, no data could be located for Proposal A's approach to assess potential problems and no data was written in on the evaluation work sheet shown in the figure. Proposal B received 90 for adequacy of plan; 75 for adequacy of analytical techniques; 80 for plan to upgrade, verify, and demonstrate; and 50 for approach to assess potential problems; and so on. Each proposal received different scores for each subfactor listed under Soundness of Approach. The next factor was Understanding of the Problem with its five subfactors, *a* through *e*. They also received ratings from the evaluator beginning with Proposal A, with objectives of the program scoring 100, and so on.

Now turn to Figure 45. This figure shows a typical evaluation work sheet used for computations of the ratings of subfactors already accomplished. Let's look at Proposal A. Proposal A received a rating of 70 for adequacy of plan, 70 X a weight of 5 = 350 points. Proposal B received a rating for 90 for adequacy of plan, so again we multiply 90 X 5, giving Proposal B 450 points for this subfactor, and so on. For every subfactor, we compute the rating and multiply it by the previously established weight. Note that Proposal A had no data under subfactor *d*, approach to assess potential problems; that is, no data could be located. Thus under this particular subfactor no points were awarded for Proposal A. You can see that even if a few points had been given here it would have made a significant difference in the final score.

To score a proposal we add up the number of points. For example, Proposal A has 1440 points. Proposal B has 1590 points. Proposal C has 1670 points, and Proposal D has 1580. We also add up the weightings, which for Proposal A came to a total of 21. In the next line we divide the total number of points by the weighted total. So for Proposal A we would divide 1440 by 21. This gives us a weighted average of 68.7. In a similar fashion we compute the weighted average for Proposal B at 75.7, Proposal C at 79.5, and Proposal D at 75.2. The evaluator does the same thing, going through major factors and the major parts of the proposal until a weighted average for the entire evaluation is completed for each proposal. If the weighted average for Part 1 alone represented the entire proposal, then Proposal C would win with a weighted average of 79.5.

While this method is not used for every proposal evaluated by the Government, similar methods are used. For example, instructions for preparation of one of the Air Force's evaluation forms contains the following descriptive terms for each rating given. "Unsatisfactory" means that the rating is unsatisfactory and may by itself render a bid unacceptable for procurement. "Poor" is better than unsatisfactory, but clearly not average. This rating is given for mediocre responses that reflect little insight and imagination and inspire little confidence or respect. This response on a factor under consideration would be deemed inappropriate or inadequate and represent a minimal contribution. "Average" means a really good rating, when considering an industry as a whole. It is given whenever a proposal

Evaluation Factors	Weight	Proposal A	Proposal B	Proposal C	Proposal D
Part I Technical Merit/Competence					
1. Soundness of approach					
a. Adequacy of plan	5	$70 \times 5 = 350$	$90 \times 5 = 450$	$90 \times 5 = 450$	$80 \times 5 = 400$
b. Adequacy of analytical techniques	10	$85 \times 10 = 850$	$75 \times 10 = 750$	$80 \times 10 = 800$	$70 \times 10 = 700$
c. Plan to upgrade, verify, and demonstrate	3	$80 \times 3 = 240$	$80 \times 3 = 240$	$70 \times 3 = 210$	$80 \times 3 = 240$
d. Approach to assess potential problems	3	NO DATA	$50 \times 3 = 150$	$70 \times 3 = 210$	$80 \times 3 = 240$
Weighted total	21	1440	1590	1670	1580
Weighted average		$\frac{1440}{21} = 68.6$	$\frac{1590}{21} = 75.7$	$\frac{1670}{21} = 79.5$	$\frac{1580}{21} = 75.2$
2. Understanding the problem					
a. Objectives of the program	5	$100 \times 5 = 500$	$90 \times 5 = 450$	$90 \times 5 = 450$	$100 \times 5 = 500$
b. Propulsion process and contamination sources	3	$90 \times 3 = 270$	$100 \times 3 = 300$	$90 \times 3 = 270$	$90 \times 3 = 270$
c. Contamination mechanisms	3	$60 \times 3 = 180$	$65 \times 3 = 195$	$60 \times 3 = 180$	$60 \times 3 = 180$
d. Problems and limitations	2	$80 \times 2 = 160$	$80 \times 2 = 160$	$70 \times 2 = 140$	$70 \times 2 = 140$
e. Testing techniques	2	$50 \times 2 = 100$	$50 \times 2 = 100$	$60 \times 2 = 120$	$50 \times 2 = 100$
Weighted total	15	1210	1205	1160	1190

Figure 45. Typical evaluation work sheet computations.

reflects a good commanding position on that selection factor. "Very good" implies a response that is exceptional in its major aspects and that at least on that factor would represent the quality expected of an undisputed leader in this field, a clearly superior contribution. "Excellent" implies a response that is outstanding in its major aspects and that at least on that factor would represent a quality well beyond any that could normally be expected—a clearly outstanding contribution. "No data" means that certain relatively minor data were omitted and carries an O rating. This is used when data is missing that is required to complete the evaluation of the bidder and unsuccessful efforts have been made by the procuring organization to get it.

This description of an Air Force method of evaluation and describing factors goes on to give additional information. For example, a "poor" rating is not assessed solely on the basis that the idea or concept presented is considered to be incomplete. If it can be understood, it is evaluated on its merits. When appropriate, factors may be rated as "no data" or "unsatisfactory." However, if factors are to be scored, no points are assigned to these categories. "Average" and similar ratings apply to the quality of the proposal, not to the amount of information available. When a lack of sufficient data prevents the evaluator from rating a factor, the "no data" column is checked and that data required to permit completion of the assessment is identified in the evaluator's narrative.

The above information should tell you four things:

- The Government evaluates proposals against specific criteria and specific weightings established prior to the meeting of the Source Selection Board.
- These criteria differ from proposal to proposal.
- The information contained in the proposal regarding the relative importance of various factors and subfactors, while important, does not tell the whole story until you know exactly how the subfactors are rated.
- Obtaining the evaluation criteria to be used in evaluating your proposal is well worth your while.

There are other points of some importance regarding how the Government evaluates your proposal and how you might maximize your chances of winning. If you can do it, it is useful to learn the makeup of the Government evaluation team. Who is on this team will vary greatly. Why is it important to know? During the preproposal marketing phase you want to make certain you allocate the proper amount of time and marketing resources to those individuals who will actually be evaluating your proposal. Marketing to the wrong individuals is a waste of your resources, and if you fail to market to certain individuals it could cause you to lose the contract.

Different services in Government agencies have different rules regarding makeup of proposal and source selection teams. For example, NASA in its source evaluation board manual says this about the composition of source evaluation boards:

Source evaluation board shall be comprised of an appropriate mix of qualified management, technical, scientific, contracting, and business experts. Each board shall have a legal adviser. While in general the chairman and board and committee members are drawn from the installation having cognizance of the procurement, personnel from other NASA installations or other Government agencies are to be used when their services are required and available. It is desirable that voting members of the board include people who will have key assignments on the project to which the procurement is directed. Source Evaluation Board membership normally need not exceed seven voting members, including the chairman. If additional support is needed, the use of committees, panels, or other subgroupings is authorized. The number of each supporting personnel shall be kept as small as the nature of the subject matter to be covered permits. Whenever feasible, assignments to Source Evaluation Board membership shall be on a full-time basis. Where this is not feasible Source Evaluation Board membership and duties are to take precedence over other regular duties.

The Department of Energy Source Evaluation Board handbook states the following about board membership:

In keeping with the importance of source evaluation and selection process, Source Evaluation Boards shall be composed of highly qualified technical and business personnel. When appropriate, personnel from other Government agencies may serve as board members. The board chairman and secretary normally will be from the program organization having cognizance of the procurement. The secretary will not have a vote. One member of the board will be from the procurement organization to provide continuity in negotiation of the resulting contract; the procurement member shall be that individual who will negotiate the contract wherever practicable. It is desirable that at least one person who will be given a key technical assignment on the project to which the procurement is directed be designated a board member. The Assistant General Counsel for Procurement will designate a legal nonvoting member as a representative of the Office of General Counsel for each Source Evaluation Board. Since the legal member does not have a vote, his presence will not be required at all meetings of the board. However, he will be available on an as-needed basis and his advice will be sought in all important and potentially controversial actions of the board. The board should be small in size, normally not exceeding five voting members. Each voting member will have one vote.

The Air Force Systems Command says the following:

The technical evaluation teams consist of at least three technical personnel with specific knowledge of the technology being procured and of the required capabilities of the offerers. One evaluator will be designated the team chief and when it is determined that the evaluation of specific parts of the technical proposal is desirable as opposed to an overall evaluation, a separate technical evaluation team will evaluate each part. Fewer than three evaluators may be used in exceptional instances where additional qualified evaluators are not available for procurements under $100,000. At least two evaluators must always be used. These occurrences will be documented by appropriate explanation and justification must be approved by the technical approving authority. Nongovernment personnel will not be used as evaluators, but may be used on an advisory consultant basis, if they are acting in an official capacity or under contract for that purpose.

Note that the composition of the evaluation teams and source selection boards are somewhat different for different agencies. In order to find out the rules, you should ask a contracting officer of the Government agency with which you are dealing under which specific regulation the procurement evaluation will be made. Find out which official handbook will be used to assist the evaluator and request a copy of it. Do this as early as possible during the preproposal marketing activity phase of the project.

Proposals may be rated "unacceptable" regardless of the final composite rating when the technical proposal is determined to be nonresponsive or when any one evaluation subfactor that is thought to be significant by the Government has a particularly low numerical score.

If the proposal is otherwise acceptable and the Government feels that acceptance of the proposal may be in its best interest, it may attempt to negotiate a specific inadequacy rating with the potential contractor. But this rule can also be used to eliminate undesirable contractors. That is, if you propose to do more than is required, you could be eliminated as being nonresponsive, as pointed out earlier.

Generally, cost data is not furnished to the evaluation team at the same time that it does its technical evaluation. The reason for this is to avoid contaminating the technical evaluation with what the Government feels are nontechnical factors. However, there is no official requirement to withhold the information and there is no question that cost does impact upon whether you as a prospective contractor really understand the scope of the problem. Along these lines you should recognize that you can be eliminated for what the Government feels is an excessively low cost proposal because this might mean that your figures are not realistic. And conversely, you could lose because a competitor submits a much lower cost proposal. This is one of the reasons that it is so important to do preproposal marketing activities adequately. You must be able to bid a proposal at a price that is precisely within the scope of the contract and scaled at a price the Government anticipates.

When the technical evaluation is completed by the technical source selection board, this panel advises the contracting officer as to which proposal is most advantageous to the Government from a technical viewpoint. Several different conflicting regulations may apply at this time, and even here the contracting officer is left some room for judgment by the technical board. For example, take the Defense Acquisition Regulations. One regulation states that it is a policy of the Department of Defense to buy at prices calculated to result in the lowest ultimate overall cost to the Government. However, another regulation states that the primary consideration in determining the award is which contractor can perform the contract in the manner most advantageous to the Government.

Obviously, the evaluation procedures described allow considerable judgment as to which contractor is selected, even though quantitative numbers are assigned to the various subfactors and, as indicated, you can lose if you bid too low, too high, or even if you promise to do too much in your technical proposal.

However, it would be a mistake to think that awards can be "bought" or made entirely on the basis of personal influence with the Government. First, civil service regulations give protection to the individual Government employee. A Government official at a higher level making an arbitrary decision for one contractor may very well find himself in difficulties with his Inspector General. This is one reason that even though lower-level Government people may be fired or passed over for promotion because they "blew the whistle" on a rare higher-level arbitrary contract award, they're usually reinstated with full back pay when the full legal procedure of the civil service has run its course. The second reason that it is a mistake to think that you can "buy" or use personal influence to win a contract is that the regulations permit any unsuccessful bidder to protest an award. The ability to protest also tends to keep everyone honest. These two factors act as a check against abuses that may be inherent in allowing so much judgment in the selection of contractors.

If you know the rules of the game as spelled out in the regulations of the Government agency that you are dealing with and in the RFPs or RFQs, you can play the game to win by developing a unique proposal strategy. For example, for a large research and development procurement in which price was given great importance, one firm won the contract by bidding low and trying for minimal acceptability in all technical aspects. Amazingly, this contract was won with minimum pre-proposal marketing activities. However, they did everything else right, recognized their weaknesses, realized what criteria would be used in judging the proposal, and determined that the only successful way to win was to avoid being judged nonresponsive and to submit a very low but credible proposal. This was done by submitting a proposal that was low in cost and totally responsive, but not technically innovative. But a completely opposite strategy might also have been effective. That is, the firm might have bid high but with a very, very strong technical proposal. This might have worked if the technical aspect was a major evaluation criteria. I have often seen this strategy work. One company won against five other companies with the highest bid because their technical solution was so strong in all of its aspects.

Following the techniques and rules contained in this chapter and knowing how the Government is going to evaluate your proposal is the frosting on the cake. If you have done everything else right, knowing exactly how the Government is going to judge you will allow you to put your resources where they count and will make for high scores and a very high win rate.

Chapter **12**

THE TYPES OF GOVERNMENT CONTRACTS AND WHEN EACH IS BEST FOR YOU

HOW IMPORTANT IS THE TYPE OF CONTRACT?

A Government contract is simply an agreement between you as the seller of goods or services and the Government as the buyer. Like any other contract, it specifies what each side will do in the transaction. Now that you have written and submitted and all but won the contract, you may consider that the contract itself is of somewhat less importance. However, in entering into the contract, both you and the Government are defining your legal rights and limitations. This means that what kind of contract you enter into is of considerable importance to you. It is no exaggeration to say that the type of contract in itself can determine whether your project will be profitable or not, how the Government sees your performance, and whether or not you will be able to obtain future Government business.

The type of contract that you should make with the Government depends on the circumstances at the time of the agreement. Under certain conditions, one type of contract may work to your advantage; under different circumstances the same contract may work against you. Under a third set of circumstances this same contract may work against both your interest and the Government's. You should never accept a contract that works against your overall interests, and you should probably not accept one that works against the Government's—certainly not unless you have made your opinions known to the Government.

If you want to know how easy it is for a company to get into trouble, consider this example. In the early 1970s, the Air Force had a severe problem with bird strikes in the cockpit area of F-111 fighter-attack aircraft. With the aircraft flying at low levels and high speeds, birds would crash right through the plan's canopy, creating a considerable hazard to the pilots. As a partial solution to the problem, the Air Force decided to develop a helmet that completely protected the pilot's face through the use of a clear high-impact plastic material that had been developed by General Electric. This tough material would protect the pilot's face while allowing him to see and retain control of the aircraft even after a severe impact by a bird.

The responsible Air Force agency drew up complete specifications based on the optical characteristics inherent in the short protective visor that was then in use and covered only the pilot's eyes. Because the Air Force felt it knew exactly what was wanted, and because it developed complete paper specifications of the bird-strike helmet and visual/optical requirements of the protective visor, a firm fixed-price contract was anticipated.

A competitive RFP was released to industry, and one of the leading helmet-development companies in the country won the contract. The company bid the contract at a price that they felt would be necessary to win, cover all costs, and show a very slight profit. Meeting the visual/optical requirements of the contract's specifications in the complex shape required by full-face coverage, however, had never been done before. The helmet-development company's strategy for handling this problem was to include a pad of funds under the cost, and to request more time for delivery of prototypes than provided for in the RFP. The Government granted this. However, the company took no exception to the type of contract anticipated by the Government, and in fact a firm fixed-price contract was signed.

Problems started shortly after construction of tooling for making the face protector. No matter what procedure or formulation was tried, meeting the visual/optical requirements for this very complex shape could not be accomplished. The pad of funds that the contractor had included for developmental costs was soon gone, and the company was spending its own money. The schedule slipped repeatedly, and delivery of the prototype was late. And did not prove successful. In the end the company renegotiated the contract with the Air Force and a solution without meeting the exact visual/optical requirements was found. Instead of being profitable, this contract cost the company money; instead of being a new product for the company to sell, the helmet never went into production; instead of impressing the customer with the company's ability to meet the technical requirements and deliver the item on time, this contract had the opposite effect. Yet the very same events could have taken place under a different type of contract and:

- The contract would have been profitable for the company.
- The company would have completed all terms of the contract satisfactorily.
- The company's reputation would have remained intact, or even been enhanced.

Clearly the type of contract is of no small importance.

WHAT KIND OF CONTRACTS ARE AVAILABLE?

There are tow basic categories of Government contracts pertaining to method of payment and a number of contracts that can be categorized by the method by which the Government incurs the contractual obligation. Let's look at the two basic categories pertaining to method of payment first. These are: fixed price contracts and cost reimbursement contracts.

The Four Different Types of Fixed Price Contracts

If you've done some Government contracting before, you might have thought that there was only one kind of fixed price Government contract, because there is one that the Government uses more than any other, the firm fixed-price contract. But Government regulations actually provide for the use of four basic types of fixed price contracts. These are:

1. Firm fixed price.
2. Fixed price with economic price adjustment.
3. Fixed price incentive.
4. Fixed price redeterminable.

All of these contracts limit the price for a completed job, but each makes a different allocation of the risks involved in fulfilling the terms of the contract. You can see how the risk to you as the contractor varies conceptually in Figure 46. In the firm fixed-price contract, you bear all the risk of both cost and performance. But as you move to the right in the figure, you begin to share the risk with the Government and your cost risk is reduced. In the fixed price with economic price adjustment contract, you still bear the risk for cost except for that part of the cost covered by an economic price adjustment cost. Further to the right, with the fixed price-incentive contract, your cost risk is reduced to costs above an established cost ceiling. At a point still further to the right in fixed price

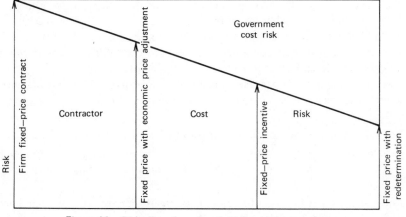

Figure 46. Risk allocation of costs in fixed price contracts.

redeterminable contracting, determining cost is done in one of two ways. It may be done on a prospective basis, but is broken down into price periods. Thus your risk is reduced, because after every price period you have a better idea of the cost for the next price period. Or it may be done retroactively, in which case you share all of the cost risk with the Government all the way up to the ceiling price. Above the ceiling price, of course, the risk is all yours. Now let's look at each type of fixed price contract a little more closely.

The Firm Fixed-Price Contract

Basically, in the firm fixed-price contract, the Government agrees to pay a specified price when the items called for by the contract have been delivered and accepted With few exceptions, no price adjustment is made for the original work after the award of the contract, regardless of your actual cost in performing the contract.

What are the exceptions? (These exceptions can cause the price to be reduced as well as increased.) They include inaccurate pricing data (someone made a verifiable mistake), the application of liquidated damages provisions, adjustment for defective workmanship and material, latent defects, contract modifications, and variations in quantity produced.

The Government requires that two conditions exist before using this type of contract:

- Reasonably well-defined specifications must be available.
- What the Government considers to be a fair and reasonable price for the procurement must be established.

If the Government uses an IFB, both of these conditions are considered to be present since established specifications are needed for anyone to bid, and adequate competition bidding on the IFB means that a fair and reasonable price, as defined by the Government, will be arrived at. This means that a contract resulting from an IFB will almost invariably be a firm fixed-price contract. But what if the contract is a negotiated procurement, that is, one resulting from an RFP or an RFQ? Here matters are less clear cut, since one or more conditions that permitted the Government to advertise (that is, release an IFB) are not available.

However, it may still be possible to negotiate a firm fixed-price type of contract with the Government under the following conditions:

- You can make historical price comparisons with similar or identical items.
- Certain cost or pricing data is available, which will permit you to develop realistic cost estimates in which the Government has a high degree of confidence.
- Any performance uncertainties can be so clearly identified that their impact upon the price can be evaluated to the Government's satisfaction.

Under the firm fixed-price contract, you as the contractor assume all the cost risk. However, if you can reduce the costs from those estimated at the time of contract award, you have the potential of making a considerable profit with this kind of contract. Therefore the more certain you are of your costs, and your potential for reducing them, the more willing you should be to take a firm fixed-price contract.

Assume you go on contract to supply 1000 widgets by a certain date and you have determined costs by producing the widgets in the same way that they have been made for the last fifty years—but you think you may know a cheaper way of production. Once on contract, sure enough you find a new production method that cuts production costs by 50%. As long as you meet all the terms and specifications of the contract, the increased profits resulting from the dramatically decreased costs are all yours. On the other hand, of course, if your cost estimates are lower than the actual cost, your profit is going to be reduced.

The Fixed Price with Economic Price Adjustment Contract

This type of contract is a good one if you can get it, but the Government doesn't like to use it because of the difficulties in administering it. However, if unfavorable economic conditions continue we are likely to see more of this type of contract, and have more success in persuading Government customers that this type of contract is often necessary.

A fixed price contract with economic price adjustment is used when a high degree of economic uncertainty exists during the period of contract performance. In other words, prices for labor and/or materials are liable to go way up, go way down, or fluctuate wildly or uncertainly. Exactly how contractual price is to be adjusted depends upon the contingencies provided for in the contract. Generally, the contingencies provided for include three types of adjustments:

1. Adjustments based on established prices. The contract price is adjusted based on an increase (or a decrease) from an agreed-upon level in established prices of either component parts or the end-items themselves.
2. Adjustments based on actual labor or material costs experienced. If actual labor or material costs go up or down, the contract price does the same thing.
3. Adjustments based on an index of labor or material costs. Which indices are applicable are specified in the contract. It could be the Bureau of Labor Statistics Wholesale Price Index. If this index went up or down, the contract price would do the same.

The Fixed Price Incentive Contract

The Government thought up this type of contract to try to harness the profit motive in the business world by providing an incentive for the contractor to improve his performance in cost, quality, or delivery. The most common form of incentive contract is cost alone, but other aspects of the contract may also be linked. This usually occurs in large developmental contracts.

Basically, the fixed price incentive contract provides for the adjustment of profit through the establishment of the final contract price up to a negotiated price ceiling after the performance of the contract.

There are two main types of fixed price incentive contracts:

- The firm target contract known as FPIF (Fixed Price Incentive Firm).
- The successive targets contract known as FPIS (Fixed Price with Successive Targets).

The Fixed Price Incentive Firm (FPIF) Contract

The FPIF contract has the following elements: a target cost, a target profit, a target price, a price ceiling, and a sharing formula. Generally, the target cost is arrived at by negotiation so that in the opinion of the Government, you have about a 50% chance of making the target cost. Once you have completed the contract, you submit a statement of costs incurred, which the Government audits to confirm their allowability. Your statement and the auditor's advisory report are the starting points for an analysis of your performance on contract and a negotiation that results in the established cost of the contract. After the final cost figure is established, profit is determined by the previously agreed to cost-sharing formula.

Let's take a look at how this would work. In Figure 47, the target cost has been established at $100,000, target profit at $15,000, target price at $115,000, a price ceiling at $130,000, and a sharing formula of 50/50.

Now if you end up with $100,000 (that is, right on target) you are at point A in the figure. Your profit will be $15,000, and the total price of the contract to the Government will be $100,000 plus $15,000, or $115,000. Let's say, however, that you really did a magnificent job in controlling costs, found a cheaper way of doing it, bought materials at less cost than anticipated, and so on, and came up with a final cost of $80,000. Now you are at point B. Your profit would be increased to $25,000. This is because your costs were $20,000 below target costs. One half, $10,000, goes to Uncle Sam, and $10,000 goes to you. That $10,000 plus your original target profit of $15,000 equals $25,000. What would the total price of the contract to the Government be? It would be $80,000 plus $25,000, or $105,000. There is another way at arriving at this figure. The target price was $115,000 and you've split the cost saving of $20,000 50-50 with the Government. Therefore the new price is $115,000 minus $10,000, or $105,000.

Now what happens if you overrun the cost? Let's say your actual cost was $120,000, or point C. Now your profit is down to $5,000 and the price of the contract is $125,000.

You can continue on down the 50/50 cost-share line until you reach the price

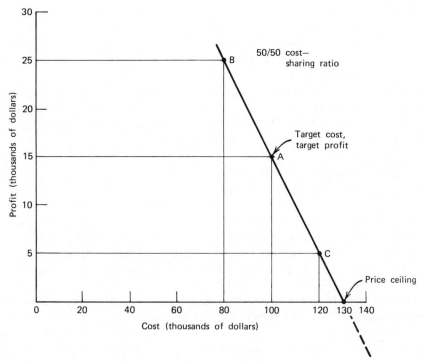

Figure 47. Cost sharing on an FPIF contract.

ceiling of $130,000. At that point your profit is zero, and from then on you are essentially in a firm fixed-price situation in which all you can do is lose. Every penny of cost comes out of your pocket.

The Fixed Price with Successive Targets (FPIS) Contract

This type of fixed price incentive contract isn't used as frequently as the FPIF contract because it is designed for use in a specific situation involving the procurement of the first or second production quantity of a newly developed item. In this situation, long lead times for production may make it desirable to contract for follow-on quantities of a new item before design or even production parameters are fixed. The cost and pricing data is not sufficiently accurate so that a FPIF contract may be negotiated. However, the required data is expected to be available at some relatively early point in the follow-on contract. Under these circumstances, the Government frequently feels that it is in its best interest to negotiate a FPIS contract rather than a cost-plus incentive fee contract or some other alternative.

Under the FPIS concept, you are given an overall ceiling price and some degree of cost responsibility and profit incentive prior to the time that sufficiently acurate cost and pricing data becomes available. At the outset, you and the Government negotiate an initial target cost, an initial target profit, a price ceiling, a formula for fixing the firm target profit, and a production point in units when you will start applying the formula. The formula also provides for a ceiling and floor on the firm target profit.

When the production point for applying the formula is reached, you negotiate the firm target cost (remember, up until then all you have is an initial target cost). The firm target profit is then determined automatically by using the formula.

At this point, you can go one of two different routes.

1.   You can negotiate a firm fixed-price contract.
2.   You can negotiate a FPIF contract.

Which type of contract you should prefer depends on your situation at the time. If the risk of a cost overrun is small, and you see where costs might be easily reduced, a firm fixed-price contract is preferable. If controlling the costs are a bit riskier, you'll want to share some of this risk with the Government. This means an FPIF contract.

You will note that both types of fixed price incentive contracts require considerable negotiation with representatives of the Government. To succeed in this you must be up in your negotiating skills, and it is also to your advantage to be negotiating with friends. Put another way, if your relations with this particular Government agency is at all in doubt, a firm fixed-price contract or one modified for economic fluctuations may be a better way to go.

The fact of negotiations after contract award also introduces us to the concept of post-award marketing. This means that the marketing job is not complete just because the contract has been awarded. Not only must you continue to work for customer satisfaction in a technical sense, but you must make certain that he knows what you are doing regarding costs, and you should start working well ahead of time to get his agreement and commitment to these actions. By this I mean, for example, that if an item is borderline as to whether or not it will be an allowable cost on a contract, you should start your informal negotiations on this item with your customer as soon as the cost in incurred, not months later during formal allowable-cost negotiations.

The Fixed Price Redeterminable Contract

As I said earlier, there are really two types of fixed price redeterminable contracts, prospective and retroactive. The prospective type is actually two or more firm fixed-price contracts that are negotiated at fixed times during the performance of the contract. Each successive contract is negotiated as more experience is gained as a result of prior contract performance. How does this work in practice? There is an initial price negotiation prior to going on contract. During this negotiation you and the Government:

- Establish the total estimated cost of the job.
- Establish a firm price for the initial period of performance.
- Establish intervals at which the price will be prospectively determined.
- Decide whether a price ceiling will be used, and if it is, the dollar amount of the ceiling.
- Decide whether the prospective price redetermination can be downward, upward, or in either direction.

The retroactive type of fixed price redeterminable contract involves adjusting the contract price after the work has been done. It is similar to the fixed price incentive contract in that a ceiling price is agreed upon prior to contract award, and actual costs, which are audited, serve as the starting point for negotiations to determine the final contract price. There is, however, a major difference between the tyo types of contracts. You will recall that with the fixed price incentive contract there is a precontract award cost responsibility share formula. No such animal exists with the fixed price redeterminable retroactive type contract. You and the Government determine cost responsibility at the final negotiation of price. In other words, price is dependent upon a subjective determination of how you perform, specifically known costs, and a subjective evaluation of profit.

You may consider this high-risk business, but it is less risky than you may think so long as you can document your costs. The Government considers this type of contract very risky for its interests since you do not have a direct monetary incentive to control costs.

Both types of fixed price redeterminable contracts are limited by Government regulation to short-term contracts for research and development priced at no more than $100,000.

You should keep several things in mind if you anticipate this type of fixed price contract. First, like other more sophisticated Government contracts, it's going to require additional negotiation. If you're going to go this route, you must be a good negotiator and you should do everything possible to ensure that the Government agency you are dealing with is friendly to your interests. Next, you must document your costs and be certain that the costs you anticipate will be allowable under Government regulations. Therefore be certain to ask which Government regulations will govern cost allowability. Finally, you must have some written assurance from the Government that price redetermination will take place as soon as possible after the work is completed. You want to get paid, and you certainly don't want money tied up over a long period of time while waiting for negotiations to take place.

Cost Reimbursement Contracts

You should only accept a fixed price contract when uncertainties are few and you have a reasonably good idea of all the job factors, both cost and technical, and are confident that you can do what you contract to do. But depending on your business, there will come a time when this is not the case. The magnitude of the uncertainties will be such that the risk is just too great. You would have to be something less than a good businessman to accept a fixed price arrangement of any type under these conditions.

Fortunately, there is a solution, provided that the Government is either already convinced or you can convince its representatives about the uncertainties involved. This is the cost reimbursement category of contracts. Its principal characteristic is the method of payment: you get reimbursed for your costs. Depending upon the terms of the contract, this may be done at the completion of the contract. However, reimbursement for costs is normally accomplished during contract performance by invoicing the Government for payment. The vouchers are, of course, audited for reasonableness and allowability under Government regulations. But assuming costs are both reasonable and allowable, the contracting officer orders payment and you get paid for costs prior to contract completion on an as-you-go basis. A cost type of contract could have saved the helmet contract discussed earlier.

Usually, there is a cost limitation clause in the contract, so the cost remimbursement contract does not give you authority to run completely wild. However, if you need more money to continue the work, and a cost limitation clause cuts off your cost reimbursement, you can stop work until additional funds are provided.

This points out a major difference between fixed price and cost reimbursement contracts. Under fixed price contracts, you must do what you said you would do and deliver when you said you will or you will be subject to contract default action by the Government. Not so under the cost reimbursement contract. Usually you are only required to promise your best efforts. The Government takes almost all the risk.

Now with all these attractions, why wouldn't you always want to take a cost reimbursement contract over a fixed price type? Well, for one thing, you can't make more profit on the first by thinking up a remarkable way to cut your costs. The Government pays your costs, and only your costs, whether you dream up a way of cutting them by 50% or not. Secondly, because the Government assumes most of the risk, your profit is limited by both law and regulation. What you make above cost, the Government terms your "fee." By law (10 U.S.C. 2306(a)) your fee on a cost reimbursement contract is limited to 10% of target costs for supply or service contracts and 15% of target costs for experimental, research, development, and test (RDT and E) contracts. Regulation (such as Defense Acquisition Regulations [DAR] 3–405.4(c)) extends these fee limits to cost plus incentives fee contracts. Moreover, although it may appear that "best effort" lets you off the hook for performance, since what is and is not "best effort" is open to question, this is not totally true. As a Government contractor you are encouraged to make your efforts truly your best by the carrot of potential future Government contracts and the stick of being cut off from future Government business.

Further, since cost reimbursement contracts are most frequently applied to research and development (in which the contractor may be seeking to make his real money not on the R&D contract, but on the follow-on production contract), there is considerable incentive to perform above and beyond the fee, which in theory is the main contractor motivator. Also, you must have, or establish, an accounting system that is acceptable to the Government, and costs will be autdited periodically and before final payment. In fact, the General Accounting Office may even take exception to those costs that have already been approved and paid for during one of the periodic voucher payments. Finally, there is a considerable administrative burden on you since property, including raw materials, work-in-progress, and so on, purchased by you and for which you will be reimbursed, passes from you to the Government. That means that you will have to establish extensive records and controls for property accountability.

However, if you are willing and able to live with the disadvantages you can try to get a cost reimbursement contract with the Government if one or more of the following situations exists:

- Research and development work is involved.
- The scope of the required work cannot be accurately described.
- The cost of the required work cannot be accurately estimated.
- There is some doubt that the work can be successfully completed.
- The product specifications are insufficient or not complete.

There are five basic types of cost reimbursement contracts:

1. Cost Plus Fixed Fee (CPFF).
2. Cost Plus Incentive Fee (CPIF).
3. Cost Plus Award Fee (CPAF).
4. Cost Contracts.
5. Cost Sharing Contracts.

The Cost Plus Fixed Fee (CPFF) Contract

At one time, especially during World War II, this was an extremely popular form of contract because the terms of cost, being undefined, allowed for a good deal of flexibility in procuring a wide variety of armaments. However, in 1962 Robert McNamara of the Department of Defense took a good look at CPFF and decided it was too advantageous a deal for contractors and did not motivate them to control costs. In fact, according to one school of thought a CPFF contract would actually motivate the contractor to increase direct costs. First, since overhead expenses are paid in proportion to direct costs, by increasing these costs he could move toward greater overhead absorption. Second, high costs could help justify high estimates on future contracts, especially if the contractor was a sole source supplier and there were no competitive pressures to keep contract prices down.

As a result, today CPFF contracts are generally confined to research studies and other limited contractual situations in which it is either difficult or impossible to define the objectives of the program accurately. In fact, it usually is not possible for you to get a CPFF if preliminary exploration studies have shown a high probability that the development, whatever it may be, is completely feasible, or if the Government has fully developed its performance objectives and desired completion schedule. However, if you decide that this type of contract is in your best interests, it's worth asking for it and supplying enough information to allow the Government agency you are dealing with to justify it to higher authority.

There are two basic forms of CPFF contracts. The first describes the scope of work as a clearly defined task or job, complete with a goal and a delivery schedule for an end-item. The other form, known as "level of effort," describes the scope of work in very general terms and obligates you only to devote a specified level of effort over a certain time period.

The Cost Plus Incentive Fee (CPIF) Contract

When use of the CPFF contract was discouraged for the reasons noted above, the cost plus incentive fee contract was put forth as a more appropriate alternative. It retains the flexibility of the CPFF and still alows you to avoid cost risk. However, this type of contract is designed to offer you an incentive for your best efforts at cost performance.

Recalling that incentives are part of FPIF and FPIS contracts, we might start by asking, "What's the difference?" There are three main differences:

1. There is no ceiling price in the CPIF contract.
2. Costs are reimbursed according to the regulations and the terms of the contract, not negotiated as they are in fixed price incentive contracts. Finally, remember that both law and regulation limit the fee that you can receive in any type of cost reimbursement contract.
3. Under the CPIF contract, both the maximum fee and minimum fee that you can earn are negotiated, along with a target fee, target cost, and cost average. The fact that a maximum and minimum fee is established based on a target cost means that at certain cost points, both low and high, fee becomes fixed. At either of these points, sharing stops and you are, in effect, in a CPFF situation.

To figure out the share formula on the CPIF contract, all you need to know is the difference between the maximum and minimum fee and the cost range. For example, if the maximum fee is $1500, the minimum fee is $500, and the cost range $6700, then your share is *maximum fee – minimum fee = cost range.*

$$\frac{\$1000}{\$6700} = 0.15$$

Now, if the target cost was $10,000, target fee $800, and your actual final cost was $9000, your profit would be $800 + (0.15) (10,000 – 9000) = $950.

In practice several sharing formulas may be used in a single contract to provide incentives for you as a contractor to take certain actions. For example, you could get a progressively greater share below target cost as you minimize cost and approach the maximum fee points, but must lose an even greater share as costs increase and you approach the minimum fee. The Government might desire such a plan in a CPIF contract when it feels that the probability of a substantial overrun is greater than the probability of a substantial underrun. This pattern of sharing gives you as contractor an economic incentive to control costs and minimize the overrun. Of course, whether it is in your interests to accept such a CPIF contract or not depends on what probability you assign to the possibility of a substantial overrun. If you feel that the actual probability of a cost overrun is low, then you might want to accept a greater share of responsibility for the risk and accept the chance of losing a greater percentage of cost above target cost from your target fee in exchange for a greater percentage of cost below target cost, added to your fee for a cost underrun.

The Cost Plus Award Fee (CPAF) Contract

The cost plus award fee contract also is designed to give you an incentive to do something while on contract that the Government wants you to do. It provides a means of applying incentives in contracts when finite measurement of performance necessary for a cost-plus incentive fee type of contract are not possible. Such a situation might occur with maintenance, operation, and service contracts as well as with research and development activities.

The fee paid to you in a CPAF contract consists of two parts. The first part is a fixed fee that you will be paid regardless of how well or how poorly you perform. The second part is the award amount, in theory sufficient to motivate you toward excellence in contract performance.

What criteria are used to evaluate you depends on what the Government wants to emphasize in the contract. Therefore the evaluation criteria will vary widely from contract to contract. For example, if technical performance is of primary importance to the Government, evaluation criteria might include ingenuity, quality, technical management, engineering competence, and thoroughness. If time of delivery is the Government's main concern, adherence to schedule, action on anticipated delays, and operational planning might be used.

Obviously, objective analysis of performance by the Government is not always possible because well-defined parameters that are both physically and mathematically measurable may not exist. In such cases, subjective evaluation methods are used that rely on the evaluators' impressions about the quality level of your performance. This is very difficult to do, and you and your evaluators may not agree at all about how well you performed a task. The key to making this system work for you is to define the criteria fully in the contract so that the meaning and intent of the criteria is thoroughly understood by both you and the Government. Also, you should ensure that the criteria used contains as many specifics as possible, such as milestones, targets, goals, and objectives that will be considered during the Government's evaluation. Finally, as each task is accomplished by you, you should inform the Government evaluators, give them your evaluation of the task, and supporting evidence. The idea is to be certain that you both see the performance in the same way, and that Uncle Sam knows what your own evaluation of the work is, and why, *before* he makes his evaluation.

You are furnished evaluation reports made on you by the Government in order to give you an opportunity to comment on the evaluators' findings. However, the amount of award fee that you will receive is a unilateral determination made by the Government and is not subject to the disputes clause of the contract.

Usually the contract provides for evaluations at stated intervals during the contract, so you will be able to keep pretty good tabs on what the Government really thinks about your work. Periodic evaluation is more important than it may seem, because some Government representatives whom you will work with won't express negative feelings in person—only on paper, when it is too late for you to correct. Also, partial payment of fees will generally correspond to evaluation periods. Therefore it's up to you to make certain that evaluation is slated for intervals during performance of the contract, and that this is specified in the contract.

The elements of a cost-plus award fee contract include:

- An estimated cost.
- A fixed base fee commensurate with minimum acceptable performance.
- A variable add-on to the fixed base fee.
- A minimum total fee.
- Criteria against which your performance or contract will be measured.

Government regulations limit the maximum amount of the fixed base fee to not more than 3% of the estimated cost of the contract, excluding the fee. The maximum amount of the total fee (the fixed base fee plus the variable add-on fee) is limited by law to 10% of cost for supply or service contracts and 15% for experimental, research, development, and test (RDT and E) costs.

Typical fee arrangements for CPAF contracts are shown in Figure 48. In arrangement A, the contractor receives 2% fixed base award fee regardless of performance. Below 61 performance points, that's all he receives. At 71 performance points, he receives 50% of the available variable award fee in addition to the fixed base award fee for a total award fee of 6% of cost. The percentage of available variable award fee and total award fee paid increases directly with performance points

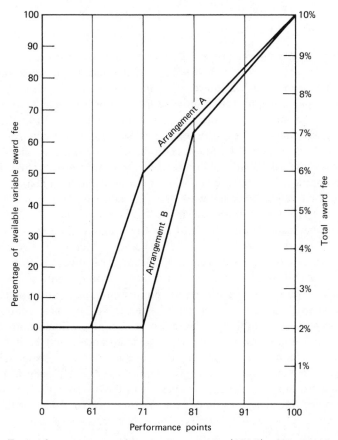

Figure 48. Typical fee arrangements for cost-plus award fee (CPAF) supply or service contracts.

until 100 performance points and the 10% of cost for total award fee limit are reached. The fee for arrangement B is calculated in a similar fashion.

Cost Contracts

The final type of cost reimbursement contracts are cost contracts in which the Government agrees to reimburse you for all allocatable and allowable costs incurred in the performance of the contract, but you don't get any fee at all.

Why would anyone want to go on a cost contract with the Government and agree to zero profit? Uncle Sam recognizes two reasons for contractors agreeing to a cost contract:

- Research contracts with educational institutions and not-for-profit organizations.

- Contracts providing facilities such as industrial property, buildings, plant equipment, and so on, to contractors.

The nature of the subject matter of some research contracts is such that it is intrinsically attractive to certain members of the faculty of some educational nonprofit institutions, such as universities. In such cases, Uncle Sam is perfectly willing *not* to pay a fee, his rationale being that if a project is in an area of study that interests the scientists of such an institution, reimbursement of the research cost may be acceptable to the institution and considered compensation enough.

Regarding the provision of facilities to contractors, Government policy is for contractors to furnish all facilities that are needed in order to successfully fulfill the terms of a contract. However, some facilities not available from non-governmental organizations are required for the work on some contracts. Also, it may be cheaper for the Government to furnish certain facilities than to pay the contractor to provide for the facilities himself. Thus the Government has a reason to furnish facilities under certain conditions—but why should the contractor agree to no fee in return for the usage of Government facilities? The answer is that it may be worthwhile to you as a contractor when you have other contracts that require such facilities. You make no profit on one contract, but more profit on the others.

In addition to these reasons, you might agree to go on a cost contract if you might benefit in some other way besides profit, or if profit were in some way deferred to the future. An example of the first instance might be if the results of the work performed under Government contract had some commercial appreciation, such as a new production process that could save money in producing your commercial line of products. An example of the deferred profit motive might be that in doing research you would learn something about producing the product that your competitors wouldn't know. Thus your costs on production contracts in the future might be lower than your competitors.

Cost Sharing Contracts

Under a cost sharing contract, you not only get no fee but you are reimbursed only for a certain percentage of your allowable costs, this percentage depending upon the regulations in force at the time and the contract. Like the cost contract, the cost sharing contract recognizes that you may benefit substantially from a Government contract without making an immediate profit. All the reasons that it might be in your interest to negotiate a cost contract are true with a cost sharing contract—but this type of contract makes the endeavor even more of a joint enterprise with the Government.

No-cost Contracts, Time and Material Contracts, Labor-hour Contracts, and Indefinite Delivery Contracts

These contracts don't fit either of the two main categories. A no-cost contract with the Government is one in which you foot the entire bill. Your reason for doing this is that you may want the Government to test a certain item for adoption, and charging nothing is a convenient way of getting the items for testing inspection, or whatever into Government hands. I am against no-cost items on principle. I believe it leads to a lack of respect for the product you are furnishing for testing. (After all it's "free"—right?) I believe it's better to charge something, or to furnish the product on a loan basis. However, if you do decide to use no-cost contracts as one of your marketing tools, I would recommend that you limit them to small dollar values. As one company that furnished a large number of prototype items valued at several hundred thousand dollars found out, it is possible to exert great effort on behalf of the Government without ever getting a production contract.

Time and materials and labor-hour contracts have some features of fixed price contracts and other features of cost contracts. With the time and materials type, you are paid for direct labor-hours at specified fixed hourly rates that are derived from direct and indirect labor, overhead, and profit, but you are reimbursed for materials at cost plus a materials handling charge. To give the Government some control, a price ceiling is established as a part of the contract.

This type of contract is generally used only in situations where it is not possible to estimate the extent of the work, how long the work will last, or exactly how much it will cost. Typical examples of its use are in emergency maintenance and repair, engineering design, and overhaul work.

The big advantage of this contract to you is also the Government's disadvantage, and for this reason this contract is rarely used. The major advantage to you is that since you are getting paid a fixed price per hour, the more hours you work the more profit.

Labor-hour contracts are identical except that you aren't required to furnish any materials.

Indefinite delivery contracts are used when the Government wants something on a recurring basis, but doesn't know exactly when or exactly how many will be wanted. The contract establishes all the known terms, but orders are not placed until the need arises. The advantage to the Government of this type of contract is that it permits Uncle Sam to maintain minimum level stocks in storage depots and direct shipment by the contractor to a number of different Government users.

Performance Incentive Contracts

The performance incentive contract incorporates features of both the fixed price incentive fee and cost-plus incentive fee types of contracts, but the big difference is that it is designed to reward you by increased fees or profit for surpassing specified performance goals. "Performance" by Government definition covers a lot of ground including performance of the product, timeliness of delivery, product capability and serviceability, economy of product maintence, or anything else that the Government feels is important in the acquisition covered by the contract. The minimum performance that the Government will accept is specified and required by the contract, and that part of the contract you must accomplish within a basic and agreed-upon price limitation. This means that you get paid one price for accomplishing the basic performance requirements of the contract and the incentive feature is applied to what the Government considers to be desirable goals. For filling these desirable goals you are given what might be considered a bonus.

Usually this type of contract is applied to complex weapons systems where performance potential is of major interest and importance to the Government.

Value Engineering Incentive Contracts

Value engineering is a branch of engineering that seeks to reduce costs by a critical appraisal of all elements of the design, manufacture or construction, inspection, installation, and maintenance of an item and its components. Most Government contracts have a clause that is in effect a value engineering incentive contract to encourage you to recommend changes that will reduce a product's cost without reducing its preformance effectiveness. For example, let's say that you are under contract to supply the Government with 1 million plastic hinges. The specification for the plastic formulation requires a chemical additive that has become very expensive. You know of a different chemical additive that can be substituted that costs half the price and yet will not degrade the properties of the hinges in any way. You can propose substitution of the new additive and a change of the specification in a value engineering change. If the change that you recommend is accepted, a change order is issued under the changes clause of the contract. The contract price is reduced in accordance with the cost reduction worked out between you and the Government. Depending on the contract, you will share in the amount of the cost saving by increased profit on the contract. Further, if this is a basic change in which the Government will save money on all future procurements of the same item, in many cases you will be paid for this savings for a certain number of future procurements even though someone else wins the contract. Therefore it's always a good idea to have some sort of value engineering clause written into your contract and to keep your eyes open for changes to the contract that will lower cost without reducing performance.

GOVERNMENT METHODS OF INCURRING
CONTRACTUAL OBLIGATION

The Government may use various methods of contracting with you for your goods and services. These may include:

- Definite contracts.
- Letter contracts.

- Basic agreements.
- Basic order agreements.
- Purchase orders.

Definitive Contracts

Definitive contracts are what we've been talking about up to now. All the terms and obligations including performance, price, and delivery are spelled out to the maximum extent possible.

Letter Contracts

Letter contracts are used to authorize you to begin work when negotiation of a definitive contract would take too long to meet the urgent need of the customer. A letter contract gets you started at once; then, as soon as it is practical to do so, a regular definite contract is negotiated.

Basic Agreements

Basic agreements are not contracts, but they do establish general ground rules that will be incorporated into definitive contracts for supplies or services in the future. They have two main uses:

1. As a timesaver, if the Government plans on entering into a number of separate contracts with you in the future.
2. If the Government has had a number of recurring negotiating problems with you.

The important thing to remember about basic agreements is that they cannot be modified or superseded by individual contracts or purchase orders subject to the basic agreement without modifying the basic agreement itself.

Basic Ordering Agreements

The basic ordering agreement is similar to the basic agreement, except that it goes further. It includes a description of the supplies or services to be furnished, the method for determining the price, and those Government activities that will do the ordering.

Basic ordering agreements are frequently used to order spare parts or where specific items, quantities, and prices are not known but past experience indicates that substantial future requirements will result in future procurements during a specified period. The advantage of this agreement to the Government is that the administrative time required for placing the procured article in a production status will be significantly shortened. This in turn decreases the amount of support inventory required and the possibility that parts purchased by the Government will become obsolete as a result of design changes between the purchase of the parts and their use.

Purchase Orders

The purchase order can be used for purchases up to $10,000—and it is a very simple procedure that doesn't take as long as a more formal written contract. You get an official form describing what is wanted in simple terms. The purchase order is primarily intended for small, everyday, inconsequential buys, but it is occasionally used by the Government to speed things up when it wants to do business with someone and time is pressing. A series of several purchase orders, each for less than $10,000, has also been used to circumvent the $10,000 legal limit for services rendered. If time is pressing and your customer really wants the work done, it is a potential way for you to get on contract fast.

HOW TO DECIDE ON WHICH TYPE OF CONTRACT

The major consideration in deciding on the type of contract you as the contractor prefer is whether or not the item can be made or the services can be performed, and how easy it will be to do so.

  If you know that you can do the job and can secure a price that will adequately cover the contingencies and risks in the job, in addition to your costs and profit, then a firm fixed-price contract is best. As various uncertainties arise that add risk to your ability to perform the contract within a specific cost estimate, a cost contract in which you share the risk with the Government becomes more attractive.

  But you should also see selection of the contract type through the Government's eyes. Here are the key factors that the Government considers when deciding on the type of contract it prefers in any situation:

- Motivating you to keep costs down. The Government is interested in ensuring that you are motivated toward being cost-conscious in contract performance. Thus in the interest of keeping costs down, the Government will try to select a type of contract in which your ultimate profit is in reverse relationship to the cost of performance.

- Performance and cost uncertainty. For many reasons, the Government, even in its own self-interest, does not want you to lose money on a contract, or fail, or even to come away resolved never to do business with the Government again. Therefore the Government will be interested in selecting a type of contract in which uncertainties of cost and performance are not more of a risk than it feels you should be taking.

- The environment in which the contract is being awarded. Uncle Sam is going to consider such factors as the size of your company. But this could work to your advantage. For example, the Government knows that a small contract will probably get more attention from a small company than from a multibillion dollar giant. If you are the only company that can do a certain job, you're going to get a better deal than if there are ten other companies ready, willing, and able to do the same thing. Similarly, if the Government thinks you can afford to break even or lose money now because you're going to get it all back with interest later, be ready for some tough negotiating.

- Your accounting system. The Government considers this a limiting factor. If you don't have an accounting system suitable to a certain type of contract, or can't or won't get one, the Government is going to steer you away from that type of contract.

- The negotiation process. The Government recognizes that there must be mutual agreement about which type of contract will be most appropriate for the contract under consideration. Since price is totally dependent on what is to be priced, and what is to be priced implies risk and uncertainty, there is considerable room for give and take during the negotiation process. One Government manual says this about the contract: "It must represent the best judgment of both contracting parties concerning the contractual arrangement most likely to result in maximum effective performance at minimum cost or price to the Government."

HOW TO USE THE INFORMATION ON CONTRACT TYPES
FOR MAXIMUM EFFECTIVENESS

I've discussed a wide range of contract types in this chapter. Here's how to use this information for maximum effectiveness. First, decide what type of contract is in your best interests before you start negotiating. Do this even if you have bid against another type of contract required by the RFP or RFQ. Even though frequently the type of contract is not negotiable, you never know until you ask. Also characteristics of the contract including fee, ceiling, floor, etc. are negotiable. You may be able to get what you want anyway under a slightly different type of contract. Pick several fall-back positions in case your first choice is unacceptable. Knowing the Government criteria requirements for each type and its motivation for selecting any single type, get all your facts and figures together to support your case. When you enter negotiations, present your preference along with your justification. You will find that spending a little time in selecting and negotiating for the type of contract you prefer rather than trying to do what may not even be possible under a type of contract anticipated by the Government will be more than worth your while in dollars, time, your company's reputation, and your own ulcers.

Chapter 13

WHAT CONTRACTORS DO WRONG AND HOW TO DO IT RIGHT BY UNCLE SAM (THE SMALL BUSINESS ADMINISTRATION)

Your Uncle Sam realizes that he can save a lot of money if he can reduce your costs of marketing and doing business with him. In order to help improve your performance and avoid many of the problems in Government contracting, the Small Business Administration prepared a brochure entitled "Contractor Paths to Grief with Some Solutions."

This brochure analyzes the actual experiences of bidders who have suffered losses or defaults while performing Government contracts, as well as suggestions and guidelines designed to both avoid these problems and provide remedies when problems occurred. No mass of lofty theory, "Contractor Paths to Grief" was developed under the direction of the Industrial Support Services Division of the Office of Procurement and Technical Assistance by the ten Assistant Regional Directors for Procurement Assistance and their staffs.

Here are the problems, problem-avoiding procedures, and remedies exactly as provided by these highly qualified authors:

1. FAILURE TO READ WITH METICULOUS CARE THE SOLICITATION, ITS ATTACHMENTS, AND SPECIFICATIONS

Government contracts are well-known for detail and numerous specifications that require careful analysis. Requests for Proposal (RFP's) and Invitations for Bid (IFB's) include standard forms and special provisions, with many contract clauses incorporated by reference. Inexperienced contractors are often unaware of the importance of the clauses, and failure to understand often leads to grief. As soon as the contract is awarded, changes in the requirements can begin to take place and may continue for the life of the contract.

Below are some cases wherein failure to read the soliciation attachments and specifications with care has resulted in contractors' losses.

A small manufacturer in California was awarded a $25,000 contract to manufacture Aircraft Drag Chutes. After a sizable number of the items had been completed and submitted to the Government for inspection, it was found that the specified nylon thread had not been used in the manufacturing process due to failure by the contractor to read and follow specifications. The items were subsequently rejected. The contractor requested a waiver of the sewing requirements; however, the waiver was not granted on the basis that the size thread used would not withstand the stress occurring in slowing the aircraft. Repair procedures were also considered inadequate and unacceptable by the using activity, as the repairs would weaken the already defective areas. After three years of effort, a default termination, which resulted in losses in time, material, and legal fees, was issued.

A small firm, located in Central Texas, was awarded a contract to overhaul over 100 line items. There were various reels on the contract, mostly inertia reels.

There was one line item on the contract, however, called an In-Flight Refueling Reel. The contractor bid approximately $20 per reel to overhaul all reels. When the in-flight refueling reels began to arrive, the handling and uncrating costs alone exceeded $20 per reel. The contractor attempted to overhaul all reels. The result was bankruptcy.

A small manufacturer bid on aerospace hardware which included a metal fabricated cylinder with a door. The door was to be sealed with a gasket and bolted. The surface where the cylinder interfaced with the door called for a surface which was almost a mirror finish. This was far in excess of standard industrial practice. The manufacturer could not meet the specifications and had assumed that what the Government required was a commercial cylinder with a leak-proof door, which he knew he could make. The Government wanted something more than was within the manufacturer's capabilities. The contract was terminated for default.

Remember, the Government's way of doing business comes with the contract. This way may be different from commercial practice. The newcomer should determine all that is expected before bidding. Resources for contract administration and for handling extensive documentation are needed for many prime contracts.

Information on Government buying methods; specfications, materials allocation, delivery and supplier problems; counsel on bidder's rights and obligations, appeal procedures, termination and default actions; help on contractual, financial and contract administration advice and advice on size criteria is provided without cost through SBA's offices.

2. EXCESSIVE OPTIMISM IN ASSESSING THE TASK THE RISK, AND IN-HOUSE CAPABILITIES

Small business, in its endavor to increase sales volume and anticipated profit may at times be overly optimistic in assessing the task, the risk and in-house capabilities when bidding on a Government contract, either as a prime or subcontractor. In assessing the risk, the bidder must take a realistic approach in determining whether it has the overall capability, both technical and financial, to perform on a selected procurement.

Delay in receipt of goods and supplies from vendors or subcontractors could cause the contract to be in delinquent status, which in turn could be cause for termination of the contract. These factors must be taken into consideration if a small business entrepreneur is to succeed in establishing a profitable business entity.

There must be sufficient cash available either on hand or through granting of credit by suppliers and/or financial institutions.

Given sufficient capital, a small business can always expand its in-house capabilities; however, management must decide whether increased staff, and the additional equipment and space can be used productively beyond the completion of the immediate contract. A solicitation may be a one-time procurement.

Overall, small business, involving itself in Government procurement, must approach each solicitation critically and assess the following:

1. Are your people competent and are they available for this job?
2. Are your facilities adequate, and are they available?
3. What has been your experience on similar jobs?
4. Are the Government drawings complete?
5. Are your people familiar with the quality control standards and procedures?
6. Can you meet the delivery schedule?
7. Can you handle the job financially?

3. BIDDING ON UNRELIABLE DRAWINGS, PURCHASE DESCRIPTIONS, AND SPECIFICATIONS

A major problem encountered by small business firms is requests to submit a fixed price bid on solicitations which may contain unreliable drawings, purchase descriptions and specifications. The normal period provided to prepare a bid on a Government contract is 30 days. During that time, it is difficult to perform a complete drawing review and identify problems associated with incomplete drawings, purchase description and or specification. The following is provided to make you aware of some clues which may indicate that there are problems in the documents supplied with the solicitation:

A. Drawings

The date listed on a drawing will provide some insight into an unreliable drawing. If a drawing is 20 years old and the last revision is dated 12 years ago, it can be assumed that the required design has many changes not shown. Contact the technical personnel and ask questions.

If the drawing reflects numerous specification references, notes related to other documents or other drawings, it can be assumed that the item depicted on the drawing is unusual and not an item to which commercial practice applies. The specifications listed on the drawings for materials are critical, since the material and finish of metal parts will affect tooling machine time, manufacturing process, and cost to produce.

Experienced producers can identify unreliable drawings. However, a newcomer should obtain as much technical advice and production experience as possible before bidding solely on the basis of a set of drawings. Reliance on drawings alone to estimate costs may lead to a loss contract.

Any problems which are identified by proposed vendors or subcontractors should be resolved with the technical staff prior to submission on your bid. The information compiled prior to award will eliminate the difficulties which may be encountered after award. With all the facts, you may decide not to bid.

B. Purchase Description

A purchase description is the heart of the solicitation and identifies the item to be purchased and may or may not relate to drawings or specifications which provide characteristics of the item to be purchased.

If the purchase description states that the unit must be equal to a commercial unit identified by a manufacturer model number, the unit supplied must meet the specifications of the commercial unit.

In form, the purchase description may resemble a specification with the following contents:

SCOPE OF WORK—Provides a description of the equipment or service that will lead to achievement of the objectives.

APPLICABLE DOCUMENTS—Specifications such as MIL-E-16400, and standards such as MIL-STD-243.

REQUIREMENTS—This is a detailed listing of factors covering performance, electrical and mechanical design, reliability and maintainability, and human factors engineering.

QUALITY ASSURANCE PROVISIONS—These may be based on MIL-Q-9858A, for example.

PREPARATION FOR DELIVERY—Describes packaging, packing and delivery requirements.

C. Specifications and Standards

Specifications seek a level of quality. They are clear and accurate descriptions of the technical requirements for materials, products, or services. They specify the minimum requirements for quality and construction of material and equipment necessary for an acceptable product. Generally, specifications are in the form of written descriptions, drawings, prints, commercial designations, industry standards, and other descriptive references. They are an integral part of the purchase contract.

Standards are descriptive criteria to assure material uniformity and interchangeability of parts and may be used in specifications, invitation for bids, proposals, and contracts.

A basic problem with specs and standards is the proliferation and the different numbering systems. However, they may be divided into four rather distinct groups.

1. Military
2. Federal
3. Governmental
4. Other than Government sources: industry, standards, associations, professional, societies

All of them may appear in procurement documents.

Be sure that your bid is based on the latest revision to the specification. Many small business firms have built units to the basic version of the specification and assumed that no revisions were made to the equipment, only to have the product rejected. An actual example of this problem is a situation in which a firm submitted a bid price on a procurement on an item which it was currently producing. After the date on which the firm received the original award, a revision was appended to the specification, changing the output electrical power level from 1 Watt to 10 Watts. The change did not affect the units being produced on the original contract but did change the new units being purchased. The firm submitted its bid based on the specification cited in its original contract, but was required to supply a unit which cost twice as much to produce.

It is wise not to assume the requirements; obtain all of the documents referenced in the solicitation and utilize these documents to compile your bid. Many specifications may be obtained from the Naval Publications and Printing Service Office, 700 Robbins Avenue, Philadelphia, Pennsylvania 19111. Obtain vendor and subcontractor quotations on all items to the specifications. A recent case clearly illustrates this point. A solicitation cited a packaging requirement which was unfamiliar to the bidder. It asked a local packaging firm to bid the requirement without citing the specification listed in the IFB. After the award the firm provided the packaging firm with the specification and was advised by the packaging firm that it did not have the equipment capability to meet the IFB requirement. The firm suffered a major loss on the contract because it did not obtain quotions to the specification cited in the solicitation.

4. BIDDING BASED ON GUESS ESTIMATING, INSTEAD OF COST ESTIMATING BASED ON FACTUAL DATA

Experience has shown that some small business concerns prepare a cost estimate based on previous award prices. The presumption is that prior contractors had profitable contracts. The concern that underbids the last award price by a small percentage is risking a loss contract.

Sometimes the bid price is arrived at by historical prices on comparable items, and the market is not checked for current costs for materials and components.

There are instances in which a small business concern will bid low to obtain a contract in the hope of follow-on business; the procurement agency will offer a production solicitation for an item on which a large firm produced the prototype. This may have included much R&D work. The solicitation will include an item description and performance requirement and contain a "technical data package" (prepared by the original contractor). The new bidder, wanting to get in on the ground floor of a new item with anticipated large future requirements, may bid low with the hope that he can break even on the first contract, but will be in a position, due to a head start on competition, to make money on future reprocurements. The tragedy is that there are instances where the data package is less complete than the bidder realizes, and failure to perform results in termination for default, sometimes with the eventual bankruptcy of the firm.

Skill in estimating costs realistically is perhaps the most important capability of the Government contractor, because it is his price that gets him the contract when competing with others equally qualified. Some typical cost estimating factors are:

- Subcontractor and vendor costs
- Overhead and overhead trend
- Learning curves for labor and salaried personnel
- Estimate of man-hours
- Availability of Government Furnished Material and Equipment (GFM and GFE)
- Material cost trend
- Labor and salary rates and predictable changes
- Judgment based on experience with similar jobs
- Profit

The "pig in a poke" approach to bidding often results in lamentation when the contract is granted. The solution is obvious: bid carefully.

5. BIDDING UNDER TOO MUCH PRESSURE OF TIME

When a contractor bids under the pressure of time, the results can be disastrous. The contractor finds himself committed to contractual requirements that cannot be met profitably or in a timely manner. Preparing a profitable, responsive bid requires close and careful study of the bid set which includes all specs and standards. Invitations have deadlines however, and there seems to be no time to get needed specs, obtain supply quotations, and resolve conflicts. In brief, the quotation is made with little or no visibility. The solution lies in setting up a system for a quick bid/no bid decision, and if the word is "bid", a rapid system for retrieving specs. Referenced specs should be read carefully. Suggested reading for bidders is Standard Form 32 which contains the general provisions for fixed-price supply contracts.

In one actual case, a contractor bid on an Air Force contract for aircraft access ladders. Although the time allowed to bid was sufficient, there was not enough time to gather all the various specifications. After award of the contract, a review of the specifications indicated that the welding required had to be done by certified welders. The firm was unable to qualify. It then became necessary to subcontract the welding portion of the contract at an increased cost of almost 30%.

Waiting until the preparation of a bid is a poor time to start assembling vendor support. For example, one small construction contractor was afforded the opportunity to offer on a 1.8 million dollar contract. Because of the short lead time in procurement, the contractor was unable to avail himself of a competitive bidding procedure with his subcontractors and in several cases, he was locked into a single subcontractor. In subsequent negotiations, without the opportunity to reassess alternate subcontractors, the procurement was lost to another bidder.

In another case, the small businessman had not taken the time to assemble cost accounting records so that production costs in terms of time and material were readily available. When the short lead time solicitation arrived, the firm resorted to a hasty estimate based on a best guess rather than factual performance records. A loss resulted.

A relatively insignificant error in addition can be multipled into the difference between profit and loss when extended by production quantities. In two actual cases, the cumulative total of the man-hours displayed in the required manning schedules did not correctly correspond to the price bid. Under the pressure of time, the bidders did not feel compelled to double check their addition and were required to perform the man-hours bid at the low bid price.

The contractor should realize that no matter how attractive the solicitation appears on the surface, it should not be bid unless time permits the bidder to adequately study all of the task specifications and evaluate completely all costs essential to the production of the bid item or service.

6. PERFORMING ON A PREVIOUS "ESTABLISHED SOURCE" CONTRACT

The apparently lucrative Government contract performed by an established and experienced producer can lead to disaster for a new contractor unfamiliar with the technical requirements.

For the purpose of illustration, consider the following case: For several years, a large firm had been under contract with the U.S. Air Force to furnish a quantity of electronic devices. This source had developed a successful relationship with its material and component suppliers and with the Government technical, purchasing and inspection personnel. The concern had completed a "first article" which passed all requirements of the test specification and received approval to commence production. Its learning curve had reached a high degree of efficiency, and costs had been reduced to a point where maximum profit was realized. Clarification by all concerned of drawings and specifications had been achieved, which all but eliminated rejections and assured a minimum of expensive rework of defective units.

On the next procurement for this device, a small firm was successful in winning the Air Force contract. For the small firm, this meant starting all over again. Although it was considered technically capable, it had not made this item before.

During negotiations, the small contractor obtained approval of the contracting officer to use a critical component manufactured by a company located outside the United States. After several months delay and great expense to the contractor, the foreign company was unable to furnish an acceptable component sufficient to meet the rigid test parameters required for the first article. The small firm was now delinquent and facing possible termination for default. In order to remove the delinquent status of the contract and avoid termination, the contractor was required to pay a substantial monetary consideration to the Air Force. This is a normal procedure in Government contracting under these circumstances. This was done with the understanding and agreement that the new delivery schedule for completion of the first article must be met or termination of the contract would be necessary.

In desperation the contractor decided to purchase the component from another supplier, and approval of the contracting officer was obtained. In a last ditch effort to avoid further loss of time and expense, special arrangements were made to provide financial and engineering support to the new component supplier.

After a number of tests, specification waivers, and a great deal of added expense to the contractor, the first article performance test requirements still could not be achieved and termination for default of the contract resulted.

To satisfy the Government's needs for the equipment, the contracting officer reprocured the electronic device from the former established source at a much greater price. The defaulted small contractor not only suffered tremendous financial losses while unsuccessfully attempting to perform the contract, but was also responsible under the terms and conditions of the "default clause" for the reprocurement costs incurred by the Government.

When competing for federal contracts which have been performed by firms considered "established sources," extreme caution should be exercised. Particular attention should be given to a possible short delivery schedule and a thorough research of the technical requirements, availability of acceptable components and the general/special terms and conditions of the contract.

7. ACCEPTING AN IMPOSSIBLE TIME FRAME

If you can't do it—don't bid. Because of eagerness to receive a contract award, contractors may inadvertently or intentionally accept an impossible time frame or delivery schedule for contract performance. The net result is frequently serious financial losses or even bankruptcy.

Prior to the acceptance of a contract you must ascertain that you can make delivery of the supplies or perform the services within the time specified in the contract, and also be assured that continued progress can be made so that performance will not be endangered.

All fixed price supply contracts contain a default clause which, in part, provides the Government with the right to terminate all or any part of the contract for default if the contractor (1) fails to make delivery of the supplies or perform the services within the time specified in the contract, and, (2) fails to make progress so as to endanger performance of the contract.

In the event the Government terminates the contract in whole or in part, the Government may procure the supplies or services similar to those so terminated, and the contractor is liable to the Government for any excess costs for such similar supplies or services.

The following is an example of a case in which a contractor failed to make progress so as to endanger the performance of the contract. This resulted in the Government terminating the contract for default, and holding the contractor liable for excess costs:

Contractor A entered into a contract on March 1 for the delivery of four aluminum castings. The delivery schedule set forth in the invitation to bid and in the resultant contract specified delivery of the first casting on April 15, with the balance to be delivered at 30-day intervals, with the completion date of the contract on or before July 15. The unit price set forth in the contract was $3,500.00, with a total contract amount of $14,000.00. At the time the bid was prepared a shortage of skilled labor existed in the area. Foundry workers and pattern makers were scarce. Knowledge of these shortages were the responsibility of the contractor, and consideration should hve been given to these factors prior to accepting the short delivery schedule. Subsequent to entering into the contract, the contractor found that due to labor shortages, his subcontractor for the casting pattern would not be able to complete the pattern until May 1, which would result in a delay of six weeks in the delivery of the first casting.

Due to the urgent need of the castings by the Government, the Government, in accordance with the default provisions of the contract, terminated the contract for default and repurchased the castings from the next low bidder at a unit price of $4,300.00 each. Contractor A was held liable by the Government for the additional $800.00 per unit, or a total of $3,200.00.

8. ACCEPTING TASKS BEYOND THE STATE OF THE ART

Creative and exploratory procurements are negotiated with performance specifications. Proposals are required and the end products are study and feasibility reports, breadboards, prototypes or test and evaluation models. The Government buys technical competency.

The procurement process takes place in three distinct steps:

1. *The presolicitation phase,* which begins with procurement planning and culminates in the procurement package. This package consists of the bid set and its source material.
2. *The solicitation-award phase,* in which prospective bidders are selected and given a bid set. The bidders respond with quotations/proposals

and an award is made to the one most responsive to the needs of the Government.

3. *The post-award contract administration phase* during which the contract, as administered by the Government, controls the performance of the contractor.

The activity of procurement is divisible into two basic functions: technical and administrative. These functions areaccomplished in the Government by the Government Engineer and the Contracting Officer, respectively. Both have the prime responsibility of meeting the technical objectives of the procurement, and each has his counterpart in industry.

Needless to say, *The Government Engineer is the ultimate customer, the one that must be satisfied at all stages of the procurement cycle.* His counterpart in industry is the scientist or engineer who manages the technical program for his firm.

After award of the contract, it is imperative that the contractor maintain close contact with the Government Engineer through the Contracting Office. This close relationship is important in order to avoid costly contractor errors and misconceptions about the project. Tasks beyond the state of the art do not have drawings and specifications detailing what is required; technical communication is extremely important. It would serve no purpose if an end item is delivered that is not what the procuring activity intended, be the requirement a report, a breadboard model or hardware.

The following is an example of what can happen. This project required the contractor to design a series of statistically valid experiments necessary to empirically relate passenger ratings of ride quality with measures of the motions of vehicles. The development of the experimental designs required a thorough understanding in the areas of statistical design, vehicle dynamics, and physical factors contributing to ride quality. Although some work had been accomplished in this area, the particular tasks outlined above had never been accomplished before. A cost plus fixed fee contract for approximately $60,000 was awarded to Contractor A. Monthly reports and a final report in 12 months were required.

The initial monthly reports showed satisfactory progress as did the first interim report. When the monthly reports for the 6th and 7th months were not received, inquiry by the procuring activity revealed that the engineer who wrote the proposal and was most capable was not assigned to the program. Instead of communicating actual progress with the procuring activity, the contractor withheld information that little progress was being made. As a result, instead of submitting a final report containing innovative thinking, the report merely reiterated past accomplishments. The option to extend the contract for an additional 12-month period was not exercised.

The important second phase of the program was then advertised as a small business set-aside, and award was made to another contractor.

Free communication between the contractor and the project engineer could have resulted in an additional 12 months work for Contractor A rather than award to a competitor.

9. BUYING PRODUCTION QUANTITIES OF COMPONENTS BEFORE THE DESIGN HAS BEEN TESTED AND ACCEPTED

Many contracts, particularly those that require a first article submission, place the risk of success or failure upon the contractor, even though the design may not have been tested prior to release for procurement. The first article testing is evidence to the procuring agency that the contractor has the know-how to produce what the Government needs.

Armed Services Procurement Regulation 1-1902(c) states, in essence, the following: Pending approval of the first article, acquisition of materials and/or components or commencement of production is normally at the sole risk of the contractor. Only the Contracting Officer may authorize prior material acquisition or early production. Failure of the contractor to produce an acceptable first article can have disastrous effects upon a small business concern's financial condition.

The following example is cited: The M503 fuze was originally designed and manufactured by an Army loading plant. In handling, the fuzes became prematurely armed prior to actual use. A revised design was made and a large business was the first contractor. The first lot of 100 were fired and rejections exceeded 10%. Further engineering was done, and in 1970, it was felt that data was sufficiently complete to warrant competitive bidding, and a small business concern was awarded the contract.

Obviously, the design was faulty for immediately thereafter numerous change orders were issued and not one of the units was usable. In spite of this, a second award was made to this same small business in 1971. There were several engineering change orders, and three stopwork orders were issued after considerable materials had been purchased by the contractor. Only 35,000 of the 200,000 fuzes delivered were usable.

Again in the face of the above problems, the company accepted another contract for 612,000 assemblies. Considerable material was again purchased. This contract was terminated for convenience after 127,000 were delivered.

At the present time, there are numerous claims against the Government which will require years to settle before the contractor can recover the losses.

The above example is typical of the problems that can have serious adverse effects upon a small business concern when involved with a production contract for an item that has not been fully tested. Contractors should approach their projects with caution and be sure that they understand all provisions of the procurement regulations to minimize expenditure of company resources.

10. REMEDIAL ACTION

The determination as to whether a contractor is in just a little trouble, or in deep trouble, is the Administrative Contracting Officer's (ACO's). He recommends and applies remedial action; he cannot, however, take a really drastic step, such as termination, without approval from higher up. No such measures are taken without careful (and well documented) consideration.

If the contractor does not agree with the rulings of the ACO, he may appeal within 30 days, under the disputes clause of his contract. His appeal ends up with the Board of Contract Appeals, which consists of a group of attorneys specializing in contract law. The environment in which they hear cases is an informal one: the contractor can plead his own case, or be represented by an attorney. The case is heard under adversary proceedings, and a decision is rendered by the Board. The Board is the final authority for the agency, but if the contractor wishes to carry the matter further, his case will be heard by the U.S. District Court, or the U.S. Court of Claims.

The sums involved in disputes have ranged from less than $1,000 to millions of dollars.

Some typical problems and adjustments contracting officers are authorized to make are listed below:

PROBLEMS WITH REMEDIES

Contractor Missed Delivery: "In Default"

1. Revise schedule, with consideration.
2. Permit continued performance by a third party.
3. Terminate contract.
   a. No cost settlement.
   b. Reprocurement against contractor's account.
   c. Collect liquidated damages.

Items Delivered Do Not Conform to Requirements

1. Relax requirements.
2. Enforce conformance.
3. Get consideration.

Contractor Cannot Get Needed Materials

Expedite by:

   a. Government assistance of subcontractors
   b. Locating other sources of supply
   c. Establishing priorities
   d. Supplying from government stock
   e. Allowing substitutes

Late Delivery of GFE/GFM or Facilities

Make an equitable adjustment of contract.

Chapter 14

HOW TO NEGOTIATE WITH UNCLE SAM

Doing business with Uncle Sam can be profitable or costly to your firm. It all depends on the contract that you negotiate with the Government. For example, the type of contract itself can be critical, as I discussed in detail in Chapter 12. As you recall, you may have a fixed price contract or a cost contract and it may be redeterminable or not. If you are negotiating a fixed price contract, it provides for a firm, fixed price. It can't be adjusted because of the cost problems that you have during the performing of the contract. It places maximum risk on you. You are responsible for all costs over and above the firm, fixed price. Whether you gain or lose on the contract is entirely in your hands.

Of course there are variations to the firm fixed contract, which we discussed earlier. If you have a redeterminable contract, it sets the target at a ceiling price and provides that under certain circumstances that the price can be redetermined and that the redetermination may result in a lower or a higher price, although it may not exceed the ceiling. Or you may have a cost contract, which provides for payment of allowable costs that you will incur during performance of the contract. Each different type of contract calls for different negotiation of goals so that at the end of the contract you will be profitable and not suffer a loss.

Contract negotiation also depends upon specifications for the product or service that you are going to furnish to the Government. Your liability as a contractor will vary depending on the type of specifications in the contract as well as the type of contract you sign. Government specifications fall into three basic categories: (1) design specifications, (2) performance specifications, and (3) purchase descriptions.

Sometimes best effort or design goal clauses are put into a contract so that specifications can be modified. In any case, you must evaluate the facts and circumstances in a particular procurement to determine whether such clauses are appropriate for the contract that you are negotiating or perhaps should be requested for the contract.

Let's talk about each of these types of specifications for a moment since they are important both as to the type of contract that you negotiate and to the contract's ultimate profitability.

DESIGN SPECIFICATIONS

Design specifications are basically "how to" specs. They tell you exactly how the Government wants you to make the product in very precise terms. For example, they will state exact measurements, tolerances, the materials you will use, in-process tests that may be accomplished, product finish tests that may be accomplished, quality control and inspection requirements, and so on. Usually the Government will accept responsibility for the correctness of the design specifications. In other words, if you follow the specifications that the Government gives you to the letter and the product does not end up exactly as the Government desires, the Government will accept responsibility for this fact.

PERFORMANCE SPECIFICATIONS

Performance specifications state the performance characteristics that will be required of the item that the Government is buying. For example, armor must stop a certain amount of projectiles. Electronic transmitting equipment must be able to transmit for a certain distance. A battery must have a certain shelf life. These are performance specifications. If a contract has the performance specifications it usually does not state design, measurements, and tolerances. When the contract has such performance specifications, you as a supplier must accept responsibility for design, engineering, and achievement of all stated performance requirements. In other words, the Government doesn't care how you meet these performance specifications as long as they meet the long-range requirements that are stated in the contract. However, sometimes both performance and design specifications are required. Then your problem is more difficult because you must meet both kinds.

PURCHASE DESCRIPTIONS

Purchase descriptions are used only when it is impractical or uneconomical to prepare a full specification. Remember that since these specifications are reasonably detailed, it takes some time and work for the Government to do this. Usually purchase descriptions tell the contractor to use a stated name brand, model, or part number or its equivalent in putting together the end item. As long as you follow these instructions and use a desired item as specified in the contract by the Government, the responsibility for the performance of the end item is that of the Government. However, if for any reason you substitute another brand or model, then you must bear responsibility for this substitution in meeting the requirements of the contract.

Profit Limitations

There are certain limitations to profit when dealing with the Government. You should know what they are before you begin to negotiate. Profit is limited by law on certain types of contracts:

- On cost-plus fixed fee research and development contracts, profit is limited to 15% of the total estimated cost.
- On cost-plus fixed fee supply contracts, profit is limited to 10% of the total estimated cost.
- On agricultural/engineering services contracts, profit is limited to 6% of the total estimated cost.

There are no statutory profit limits on negotiated fixed price contracts. However, by custom and sometimes by policy, negotiated profit rates normally range from 8 to 15% of the total negotiated cost and no more.

Who You Must Negotiate With

Although negotiation of any government contract is to a certain extent a negotiation with the end-item user, you must deal with the technical personnel who put the data package together and evaluate your proposal as well as the contracting office. In a legal sense, the contracting officer is the only Government employee who is authorized to obligate the Government for a particular contract. In addition, the contracting officer administers and authorizes changes in the contract if and when he agrees or finds them to be necessary.

Again, relating to something that I stated at the outset, you should keep in mind that a contracting officer cannot bind the Government if he operates beyond his authority. The extent to which he can act for the Government is spelled out in his certificate of employment. If and when you are ever doubtful about the scope of his authority you can always ask to see this certificate.

However, this is something that you should do only if you have extreme doubt. Usually an individual who is, in fact, a contracting officer will have the authority to do what he says he can do and he knows what this authority is in very precise terms.

However, you must be extremely careful not only during negotiations but throughout the performance of the contract to recognize that the contracting officer is the only person who is authorized to commit the Government financially. Therefore you should be very careful when other Government personnel such as engineers, inspectors, quality control people, and others give you instructions or directions. This will happen frequently, not only during negotiations when the contracting officer is present, but also during performance of contract when he is not present. Any instructions that you are given during the course of your contract may not actually commit the Government to pay for changes, modifications, or additions. Therefore your action on receipt of such directions should normally be a friendly but nice note to the contracting officer indicating who has instructed you to do what and what it will cost, and asking written confirmation that the Government wants this done. Even if the change that is requested is small and you do not intend to charge the Government for it, you should document this change in this fashion so that the Government takes responsibility for this change.

I once had a Government engineer insist on a change in which the holes in a protective mask would be moved a quarter of an inch. My own engineer told me that this change, while it would cost very little at this stage, would cost a great deal if the holes had to be moved back later. Further, my engineer was confident that the holes were in the correct place in their original location. Therefore I sent a letter to the contracting officer confirming that we would make this change at no charge, but that if they proved to be incorrect and the holes had to be re-located the Government would have to accept financial responsibility for the later relocation. As it turned out, it was fortunate that I did this because the holes were indeed incorrectly placed and we did have to relocate them to their original location. This ultimately cost the Government approximately $20,000, which, had we not documented the change in a letter, would have been our own responsibility and our own loss.

THE FORMS OF NEGOTIATIONS

Negotiations may take one of two basic forms, written or oral discussions. Further, the oral discussions may be broken down into face-to-face discussions or discussions over the telephone.

You should know that contracting officers are required to conduct written or oral discussions with all responsible offerers who submit proposals within a certain competitive range. There are exceptions to this basic requirement. For example, one of the exceptions is that the requirement for written or oral discussions need not be applied to procurements in which it can be clearly demonstrated from the existence of adequate competition or accurate prior cost experience with a product or service that acceptance of the most favorable initial proposal would result in a fair and reasonable price. We talked about this a little earilier in the chapter on pricing. However, in order for the contracting officer to use this exception, the RFP must have notified you as well as your competitors of the possibility that an award might be made without discussion and, if an award is made on this basis, then it must be made without any written or oral discussion with *any* offerer.

The important thing about the contracting officer's requirement to conduct discussions with all responsible offerers with proposals within a competitive range is that it lets you know you are within that range. The difficult part to ascertain is what that range is. We have no way of judging that since it is up to the contracting officer himself. But you should know that it is the contracting officer who is responsible for determining which proposals are within the competitive range, and that the determination of the competitive range is based on his judgment, on price or cost, on technical and other important factors, and must include all proposals that have a reasonable chance of being selected for the award. One Government manual discussing proposals and competitive range says, "A proposal must be regarded as being within the competitive range unless it is so deficient or out of line in price or technical merit as to preclude further meaningful negotiations."

Another factor in these negotiations is that you will usually be advised of the deficiencies in your proposal and will have the opportunity to correct or resolve them. The Government defines a deficiency as that part of an offerer's proposal that would not satisfy the Government's requirements. Advising you of a deficiency does not imply that the Government will also advise you as to how to correct it. The decision about what you must do in the light of this advice is strictly up to you. The Government also recognizes that correction or resolution of a deficiency may require you to submit revised price or cost information.

Officially the Government discourages auction techniques; that is, indicating a price that must be met to obtain further consideration or informing you that your price is not low in relation to a competitor or repeatedly calling for "best and final" offers is not encouraged by the Government. However, you will find very frequently that the Government will do this. You must make the decision then as to whether the Government is bluffing or whether your price is really out of line with the competition. You must make this decision based on your total experience with that contracting officer, on what you learned about your product or service during the months of preproposal marketing, and on what your feelings of strength are versus your competitors and in the eyes of the Government.

When the Government concludes discussions with all competitors that are determined to be within the competitive range, usually a final cut-off date is established that all competitors must meet for a written "best and final" offer. All remaining competitors are notified of this cut-off date. There is a distinction here between what you put in your "best and final" offer and the discussions prior to this with the contracting officer. Generally, written or oral discussions may well be used by the Government for evaluation or selective purposes. However, the final contract negotiations translate and restate this information in a contractually binding form.

The Government defines six steps in the process of reaching final contract negotiations after the receipt of your proposal. These are:

1. Evaluation and ranking of offers in the light of evaluation criteria specified in the RFP.
2. Identification of those offerers whose proposals are determined to be within a competitive range.

3. Identification and elimination of unacceptable proposals; that is, those proposals containing such deficiencies in price and/or technical merit as to preclude further meaningful negotiations.
4. Conducting written or oral discusstions with the competitors identified in step 2 and, if necessary, permitting revision of individual proposals in order to correct isolated deficiencies.
5. Notifications of each offerer with whom discussions have been conducted on the final common cut-off date for submissions of a written "best and final" offer.
6. Selection of the source or sources for award or for final negotiations if appropriate.

The Government's Objectives in Negotiation

Before you negotiate with someone, it is important to understand his objectives, motivations, and goals. In understanding this I would like to quote from the *Armed Services Procurement Regulation Manual for Contract Pricing.* This is what Uncle Sam himself says to his contracting officers who must negotiate with you, the potential contractor.

> "There are two parties to a negotiation. You represent the Government and it is in your interest to make a contract that promises to pay the contractor a fair and reasonable price if he delivers the needed equipment or services on time. You are trying to create a contractural climate that will encourage this and will also encourage the contractor to control and then reduce the costs of contract performance. You equate price with quality and try to get the required quality at the most reasonable price. This may mean the lowest price or as low as possible under the circumstances."

Now I must tell you that as a Government contractor who has bid on countless contracts and has negotiated contracts for industry and participated in contract negotiations as a member of Government negotiating teams, that I have never in all my years of experience seen the Government negotiate a higher price. The Government—as can be expected in a party with which you are negotiating—will invariably seek a lower price, and this will be its definition of "fair and reasonable." I am certain, having just said this, that those of you who may be in the Government will state that this is just not true and will point out instances in which the Government has apparently sought a higher price for the benefit of the contractor. I must state in all fairness that I do not think that this is totally accurate, that where a higher price has been negotiated, the Government has obtained something on the other end that it desired. Thus any price increase was not done for the contractor's benefit but because the Government representative felt that something good (or better) would accrue to the Government.

Another Government objective along these lines has to do with intellectual property such as your ideas, inventions, or whatever. The Government wants to avoid getting itself into a sole source position, that is, having to deal with only you and no other contractor. As a consequence, a basic Government objective is to negotiate for the rights to any type of proprietary property. Of course, it is in your interest to retain control over such property. In general, you can retain control if you can show that the property in question is already proprietary to your commercial product line. In general, you cannot retain control of such property (such as an invention or a manufacturing process) if it was or is to be developed at Government expense. In any case, you should be careful of this and should consult an attorney familiar with these aspects of Government contracting before beginning negotiations.

The key in all negotiation is preparation. On the Government's side the Government contracting officer is going to assemble all his data. He is going to get the pricing data from you or the cost data if he needs it. He is going to do his homework, check his facts, prepare his case, have a certain objective, and anticipate arguments from you and develop responses to these arguments. You, as the contracting negotiator, must do the same. You must also gather any pricing and cost and competitive data that you have available, and other data from the industry. And you must do your homework, check your facts, prepare your case, have a distinct negotiation objective, anticipate arguments that the Government will come up with, and develop responses to these arguments. You must develop a strategy for the impending negotiation conference and it should be based on a thorough understanding of the characteristics of the Government's goals, what the Government wants and why, the situation that exists at the time, and all the data that you obtained during your preproposal marketing phase of getting the contract.

Now how can you do this at the same time that you are preparing your proposal? The answer is that you cannot do it during this period. Usually proposal preparation time is 30 days or less, and as I pointed out in the chapters on proposal preparation, you will be fully engaged during this period in not only putting your proposal together but in ensuring that the proposal is produced in sufficient time to arrive at the Government's facilities by the required date. But as soon as this material is mailed to the Government, you should begin to gather together all the additional facts that you lacked during your proposal preparation and organize and prepare for negotiation.

As pointed out earlier, the Government may negotiate by telephone. I was amazed when I first got into the contracting business on the Government end as a program manager to note that my contracting office once negotiated a half-million dollar contract on the phone in about 15 minutes. He succeeded in getting the price reduced by 10 to 15% merely by asking the words, "Can you do any better?" My advice to you is not to negotiate based on an initial phone call unless the contract is really simple and you really have the facts well in hand. If the

Government contracting officer calls and wishes to begin negotiations, why not tell him that you do not have the facts immediately at your fingertips and ask him if you can call him back at some later fixed time when you can assemble this information? Or if it is better for him to call and he offers to do so, set aside a certain time span during which you will be available for his telephone call and have the required information. You should also utilize this time to ensure that your own people are available during this telephone call in case they are needed for an opinion or to supply facts.

The Negotiation Plan

For any negotiations you should develop a plan of attack in order to obtain the contract at the price you desire. The negotiation plan includes an overall objective and a target price. You should know your bottom-line price, below which you can afford to go without losing money. You should then work out a strategy to reach your planned objective. For example, your strategy in reaching the planned price objective may start with a presentation of similar costs for other programs in order to build credibility for the price that you are offering. From these initial prices, which you can show are reasonable and have been paid in the past, you may lead into your company's experience with this product and build your credibility for how much you know about manufacturing or producing it. Finally, your strategy may be to represent the price that was already offered in your proposal. Or you may go in with an entirely different strategy. You may let the contracting officer ask for a reduced price, or listen to what he is saying and come back in response with a new offer.

Once having developed the strategy, you then work out the tactics in order to accomplish each individual part of your strategy. If you are negotiating by yourself, you should work through the problem on your presentation and also think about what the other side may do to counter your strategy or tactics. You should also attempt to present your strategy to another member of your company who can probe and ask questions so that you can anticipate questions that might arise from the Government. If you are taking a team with you to negotiate face to face, then you should decide how you are going to work together as a team so that each member understands exactly what his job is and what he is to do in accomplishing the tactics in support of the overall strategy. Everyone on the team must know what is possible and who will make the final decision and how this decision will be made during the negotiation process. You should also plan where you can give in on a negotiating position and where you definitely will not give in, but will hold fast. And while you are doing this always keep in mind that the Government is going through the same process of preparation, that they will prepare in the same fashion that you are preparing for this contest, so that you will finally come up with a "fair and reasonable price"; not only what the Government feels is fair and reasonable, but what you feel is fair and reasonable as well.

Gamesmanship in Negotiation

There is no question that even with the best interests of both parties at heart that there will be gamesmanship in negotiation, and the games that you play and the importance of winning them will largely decide whether you are profitable, how profitable you will be, or whether you will lose money on a Government contract. Therefore please read this section very closely and consider gamesmanship ploys that you may choose to use and how you will handle these ploys when the Government uses them.

Making the Other Party Appear Unreasonable

This is a basic ploy and it is one that the Government will frequently use at the very beginning of negotiations. For example, during one negotiation that I participated in, the Government representative opened by stating that while I, as a member of industry, was concerned only with my company, that the contracting officer, on the other hand, represented the entire Government of the United States, and was by regulation required to negotiate a fair and reasonable cost for both of us. Thus while I was working for my company, he was really working for both sides. This was one way of making me appear unreasonable, while he appeared to be fair and aboveboard. In response to the contracting officer's opening statement I stated that I applauded his stance inasmuch as I had been instructed by my Board of Directors that since this was a Government contract and therefore in the public interest, I was to consider my own company's *and* the Government's interest—and to make sure that the contract that resulted was fair and reasonable to both sides. My statement, of course, brought laughter to everyone in attendance, but it relieved me from the burden of appearing unreasonable.

Placing the Other Party on the Defensive

There are many ways in which you can place the other party on the defensive. Usually this is done by asking a question that will force an answer that the respondent is unprepared for. For example, one tactic that I have seen a Government customer sometimes try is to place you on the defensive when his authority is limited for certain contracts to less than $100,000 unless he goes higher. He might tacitly get an agreement from you sometime during the negotiation process that the contract will not exceed $100,000. Then, at the very end when you have the contractual price negotiated at almost $100,000, the contracting officer might make a statement such as this: "You are not going to embarrass me by making this price so close to $100,000 that my superiors will suspect what we are doing?" And you, being on the defensive, may answer no and agree to shave off several hundred or several thousand dollars. I just want to remind you that this is several hundred or several thousand dollars of your profit and that the proper answer to such a question is, "I'm sorry. I've negotiated in good faith and that is the price."

Blaming a Third Party

Using this technique, either you or the Government can say, "I agree with what you are saying, but I can't get this contract through," and usually the speaker will blame some higher authority who is not at the negotiation and therefore cannot be consulted. For example, you could say to the Government, "I agree that we should be able to do this for $10,000 and not $11,000 as my boss insists, but my boss told me that if I come back and we don't have this contract for at least $11,000, I don't have a job." Or the Government can do the same thing. The negotiator will agree that it can be done for $11,000, but his boss does not agree to a figure over $10,000, and his job will be in jeopardy if he goes for the higher figure.

The Good Guy-Bad Guy Syndrome

This is a device that I think began with interrogation of prisoners of war or suspected criminals. First, one interrogator would be the "bad guy," act extremely bad tempered, perhaps kick the prisoner around a little, scream, yell, and then stalk from the room. Then the "good guy" would enter. The good guy would offer the prisoner a cigarette, commiserate with him on what a monster the other interrogator was, and suggest that perhaps the prisoner could give some bit of information or make some small confession just to appease the other interrogator.

The same technique is used during negotiation. Some negotiating teams will consist of a good guy and a bad guy. The bad guy will continue to put pressure on you, will press you at every point, will scream that you are lying, and do anything else that he can think of to irritate and really make life difficult for you. He may or may not leave, but he is always counterbalanced by a good guy on the same team. This good guy will say, "Gee, I think it is terrible the way he is treating you. It is awful. However, if we can just give him a little bit, perhaps we can get him to agree on the big issues. Can you give in on this? Then we can stop him going for these other things." Remember that the good guy is also an adversary. Frequently the good guy and the bad guy will switch roles at the very next negotiation, so don't fall for this one.

Straw Issues

Straw issues are issues that really don't amount to a hill of beans, but they are introduced by one side or the other as the final position. These straw issues may be totally unreasonable. The reason for introducing them is that when the real position of your negotiating opponent is introduced, it will seem so much better that you will agree to it much more readily. The Russians are known to frequently negotiate this way. Sometimes the treaties that have resulted from our negotiations with them have been quite favorable. Yet when we ask our negotiators how they could have possibly agreed to such terms, their response is something like "But you should have seen what the Russians' first position was." The first position may very well have been a straw issue, one that the other side did not expect us to accept, but which they backed with such force that when another position was introduced that still was to their advantage, we accepted gratefully, thinking that we had negotiated our adversaries into a better position for ourselves.

The Walk Out

The walk out is a tactic that is not used frequently because it may be very difficult to get the negotiations going again if it fails. Again, this is a tactic that both you and the Government can use. The Government can say that there is nothing more to be said, we can't go any higher, and get up and leave. Or you can do the same thing. This tactic should not be used impulsively because it may be difficult to get back together again. But must you keep walking once you start? Of course not. You can always turn around, if you don't hear that call of surrender and say, "Wait a minute, maybe there is another way of approaching this thing." That's one way of getting back into negotiations without losing too much face. The difficult thing about the walk out is that to make it strong, strong enough to be credible and then turn around and come back, you may as a consequence lose your credibility for the rest of the negotiations.

The Recess

The recess is always a good tactic because it does not break off negotiations and it does not necessarily mean anything. I have used the tactic in negotiations. Sometimes at a difficult point I called for a recess and we did nothing but smoke cigarettes, drink coffee, and talk about matters that had absolutely nothing to do with the negotiations. But a recess may give the other side a chance to worry a little about what you are deciding during the break. I have seen the simple act of calling a recess in negotiation win both the point and the day.

The Time Squeeze

So here it is Friday afternoon and you've got to catch a plane. This tactic is used often by the Government and Government contractors as well. It is one that you should be aware of and if you are visiting or being visited by the Government, be ready for it and do not be deceived by it. The time squeeze is used when you are in a hurry to make a contract. At the very last minute when a critical point comes up, the Government will announce, "We can't continue negotiations past 4:30, all our staff must go home." Or the contractor may say, "We must fly back to our plant. We don't have reservations for tomorrow." This puts pressure on the other side to come to a decision at almost any cost. As a contractor you should be aware of this and you should plan on staying additional days beyond the time you think may be required for the negotiations. Your answer if someone tries the time squeeze on you is, "Let's make sure we can get it right. If we can't finish today, let's extend until tomorrow, or if you must leave, then let's get together next week or the week after that. We want to do the right kind of job for you, and I don't think we can really do that if we are negotiating against the clock."

I have detailed these specific gimmicks and ploys because they are facts. In fact, they are discussed thoroughly in *The Armed Services Procurement Regulation Manual for Contract Pricing.* So you can bet that the Government is going to be familiar with these bargaining process strategems and may use them in negotiations with you.

This same Government manual advises Government contracting officers who are conducting negotiations with potential contractors to do or not to do certain things. Let's look at this advise that the Government manual gives to negotiators.

1. Don't dictate, but negotiate. You represent the Government; be a reasonable person.

2. Don't expose anyone to ridicule or insult.

3. Don't try to make anyone look bad.

4. Don't be predictable in your approach.

5. Do be discriminating, accept good offers. Don't feel you always have to knock something off the price.

6. Do fight hard on important points. Win the war, not the battles. Don't start fights you have no chance of winning or which even if you do win, would not be worth the fight.

7. Do remember you usually are in at least as good a negotiating position as a company's representatives. The resources of the Government are extensive and diversified. Experience that you gain doing business with many companies can give you what you may lack in depth of knowledge of a single company's situation. The company usually needs your business at least as much as you need his product or service.

8. Do be courteous and considerate. Do what you say you will. Have integrity.

9. Do know when to talk and when to listen. Do stop talking when you have made your point, won your case, reached agreement.

10. Do remember that negotiation is a two-way street and that prenegotiation preparation is the most important attribute of successful buying.

I would like to say that I think these ten points are excellent ones for you and me as ongoing and potential Government contractors to follow in our negotiation with the Government.

Dr. Chester L. Karrass is the director for the Center for Effective Negotiating in West Los Angeles, California. He has conducted hundreds of negotiating seminars for thousands of business executives both here and abroad, and is the author of two books on negotiation that I will mention at the end of this chapter. Here are ten points that Karrass says you should follow if you want to be a successful negotiator:

1. Negotiation is not a contest. With a little effort a better deal can be found for both parties at the same time.

2. Don't start a negotiation with a chip on your shoulder or a discourteous note. President John F. Kennedy once said, "Civility is not a sign of weakness; there is no point to abusing an opponent. An attack on a man's ego serves only to heighten resistance; he will harness his energies to protect not only his assets, rights and privileges, buthis self-importance." A negotiator jeopardizes his objectives by attacking an opponent's dignity or invalidating his self-worth. If you are angry, write the opponent a long letter, then tear it up. The longer the letter, the better you feel.

3. Never let an issue be discussed unless you are prepared for it. The temptation to play by ear must be resisted. Nobody is smart enough to know what to do unless he thinks about it first.

4. Never fear to negotiate no matter how great the differences are. It is impossible for both parties to recognize where and how a deal can be made. The final outcome may become apparent only after extended discussions. President Kennedy said, "Let us never negotiate out of fear, but let us never fear to negotiate." An agreement is possible even when its structure is not the least bit apparent.

5. Don't negotiate with the second rate team. Too much is at stake to use mediocre assistance. A team leader must select people whom he respects. It is more important to have tough-minded experts at your side than nice guys.

6. As a manager, don't let complaints about your negotiators cause you to overreact. Complaints by the opponent are probably a sign that all is going well for your side.

7. Never go into an important negotiation without inoculating your team. No plan is complete without considering how you will defend yourself against arguments. Inoculation may be achieved in a variety of ways, one of which is the devil's advocate approach. Despite the importance of running through the opponent's arguments beforehand, I have seen it done only rarely. Discipline yourself to do it; you will be glad you did.

8. Don't concentrate on cost analysis exclusively. Worth analysis is even more important. The more you demand from your people in terms of quality, analysis, and preparation, the more they will deliver.

9. Don't assume that the opponent knows what he is gaining from a settlement. Take the time to spell out each of his short- and long-term benefits as clearly as possible and you may be making it easier for him to sell the deal to his own people.

10. Don't talk, listen.

I would recommend reading the following books if you do a lot of serious negotiation with Uncle Sam. The first two are by Dr. Chester L. Karrass, *The Negotiat-*

ing Game and *Give and Take,* published by Thomas Y. Crowell Co. of New York. *Fundamentals of Negotiating* is by Gerald I. Nierenberg and is published by Hawthorn Books, Inc. of New York. The last is called *Negotiation of Contracts* by Paul R. McDonald. This book can only be obtained by writing to the publisher, Procurement Associates, Inc., 733 No. Dodsworth Avenue, Covina, CA 91724.

Chapter 15

HOW TO PREPARE FOR A PRE-AWARD SURVEY

A pre-award survey is an evaluation of your capability to perform under the terms of a proposed contract. By regulation, the mere fact that you are being surveyed by the Government does not necessarily mean that it will result in a contract award. In fact, the Government can and does sometimes survey more than one company while under negotiation for a single contract. However, a pre-award survey obviously is not a bad sign. If you are being given such a survey you have not been eliminated from competition.

The purpose of this survey is to determine whether you are capable of producing or delivering the item for which the contract calls. The contracting officer may ask for a pre-award survey because he wants to be certain that your company can fulfill the contract before he signs a contract with you. According to Defense Acquisition Regulation 1-904.1, "No purchase shall be made from and no contract shall be awarded to any person or firm unless the contracting officer makes an affirmative determination that a prospective contractor is responsible."

We talked about the Government's definition of a responsible contractor earlier in this book. You will recall that basically it is that you have adequate financial resources or the ability to obtain these resources during contract performance, that you are able to comply with the proposed delivery schedule (taking into consideration all your other business commitments), that you have a satisfactory record of prior contract performance, that you have a satisfactory record of integrity, and that you are otherwise qualified to receive an award under the applicable laws and regulations.

In brief, the contracting officer wants to be certain that although he awards the contract at the lowest price, that he is not going to get into any trouble because of default, late delivery, or some other unsatisfactory performance on your part later on. In other words, the contracting officer wants to be sure that you as a contractor will deliver exactly what the Government intends to buy and that other contractual obligations are met in the process. Having said all this, I must also add that on some proposed contracts pre-award surveys are routinely accomplished regardless of the contracting officer's certainty of your ability to perform the contract.

Accordingly, for one reason or another, the contracting officer requests that a pre-award survey be made of your company. This survey is made by a team of production, technical, and financial specialists who will review your capabilities in each area and prepare reports on the survey of these aspects of your business.

You will of course be notified before the team's arrival and will have some time to prepare for a visit; however, typically the time for preparation is not overlong since the Government wants to get on with the contract as soon as possible and will do so as soon as it can evaluate and confirm your company's ability to perform.

You may wonder who is going to conduct the survey. The survey is generally conducted by the Defense Contract Administration Services (DCAS), which in most cases will be charged with administering the contract after the award, if it is a defense contract. When nondefense contracts are involved, surveys are usually made by GSA personnel or by a specialist from that branch of the Government or agency with which you are dealing. But DCAS sometimes will do the pre-award survey for other Government agencies, if requested.

There are 14 major factors that may be investigated during a survey. These are listed in Figure 49, DD Form 1524, "Pre-award Survey of a Prospective Contractor General." These 14 factors are: technical capability, production capability, plant facilities and equipment, financial capability, purchasing and subcontracting, accounting system, quality assurance capability, transportation, plant safety, security clearance, labor resource, performance record, ability to meet required schedule, and other. "Other" is a catchall for any additional items that the Government wishes to check. The Figures 49 through 54, DD Form 1524-1 through 1524-5, give the complete details of each of the factors that are surveyed. However, as noted earlier, in most cases you will not be surveyed on all of the factors, only on certain ones.

The basic concept from your standpoint as a potential contractor is that the pre-award survey should be seen as another opportunity to sell. In other words it may be viewed as pre-contract, post-proposal marketing activities with the Government. Even if you are the only contractor, you must successfully pass this survey if you are going to get the contract. However, if there are still several contractors negotiating with the Government, this is a chance for you to get in one last lick at helping the contracting officer decide that you are the best choice to do the program for the Government.

You can expect the survey team to discuss everything in detail with you regarding work flow, production estimates, purchasing, labor, packaging, shipping, storage space, receiving docks, suppliers, methods, safety, subcontractors, quality assurance, your financial situation, and even background of your key personnel. You can also anticipate that the survey team will attempt to verify all the information that you give them that may affect performance of the contract. How deeply this verification will go depends upon the dollar value of the contract, how important the contracting officer feels about the various aspects of the survey, and the attention to detail of the survey team itself.

PRE-AWARD SURVEY OF PROSPECTIVE CONTRACTOR
GENERAL

| 1. SERIAL NO. (For CAO use only) | Form Approved
Budget Bureau No. 22-R253 |

SECTION I - REQUEST (By Purchasing Office)

| 2. NAME AND ADDRESS OF SURVEYING ACTIVITY | 3a. IFB, RFP, OR NIP REQ | 3b. TOTAL BID OR PROPOSED PRICE |
| | 3c. TYPE OF CONTRACT | |

4. NAME AND HOME ADDRESS OF FIRM PROPOSED AS CONTRACTOR

(Bidder represents that he ☐ is ☐ is not a small business concern.)

| 5. PLANT AND LOCATION (If different from Item 4) | 6. NAME, TITLE, PHONE NO. AND AREA CODE OF FIRM'S CONTACT FOR SURVEY |

| 7. CONTRACTOR EMPLOYER'S IDENTIFICATION NO. | 8. PARENT FIRM EMPLOYER'S IDENTIFICATION NO. | 9. REQUESTING ACTIVITY, BUYER'S NAME AND PHONE NUMBER |

| 10. DATE OF REQUEST | 11. DATE REPORT TO BE RETURNED | 12. SURVEY SHALL BE ☐ COMPLETE ☐ PARTIAL (As checked in Sec III, Column a) |

SECTION II - DATA (By Purchasing Office)

ITEM NO.	FEDERAL STOCK NO. AND NOMENCLATURE		TOTAL QUANTITY	UNIT PRICE	PHASED TOTAL REQUIREMENTS				
a	b		c	d	e	f	g	h	i
		IFB/RFP							
		BID/PROP							
		IFB/RFP							
		BID/PROP							
		IFB/RFP							
		BID/PROP							

SECTION III - FACTORS TO BE INVESTIGATED AND INVESTIGATION RESULTS
(Column a for purchasing office use, columns b and c for contract administration use)

FACTORS	CHK a	SAT b	UNSAT c	FACTORS	CHK a	SAT b	UNSAT c
1. TECHNICAL CAPABILITY				8. TRANSPORTATION			
2. PRODUCTION CAPABILITY				9. PLANT SAFETY			
3. PLANT FACILITIES AND EQUIPMENT				10. SECURITY CLEARANCE			
4. FINANCIAL CAPABILITY				11. LABOR RESOURCE			
5. PURCHASING AND SUBCONTRACTING				12. PERFORMANCE RECORD			
6. ACCOUNTING SYSTEM				13. ABILITY TO MEET REQUIRED SCHEDULE			
7. QUALITY ASSURANCE CAPABILITY				14. OTHER (Explain in Remarks)			

REMARKS

THE PROPOSED CONTRACTOR ☐ HAS ☐ HAS NOT REQUESTED FINANCIAL ASSISTANCE FROM THE GOVERNMENT.

SECTION IV - CONTRACT ADMINISTRATION OFFICE RECOMMENDATION

1. RECOMMENDATION

☐ COMPLETE AWARD ☐ PARTIAL AWARD (Quantity _____) ☐ NO AWARD

Cite on reverse side those Sections of the report which substantiate entries in Section III, Columns b and c above, and/or recommendation for a partial award or for no award.

2. APPROVAL	DATE
	PHONE NO.
(Chairman, Pre-Award Survey Board)	

Figure 49. Form DD 1524/Pre-Award Survey of a Prospective Contractor General.

<table>
<tr><td colspan="2">PRE-AWARD SURVEY OF PROSPECTIVE CONTRACTOR
PART I - PRODUCTION</td><td>PROPOSED CONTRACTOR</td><td>SERIAL NUMBER</td><td>Form approved
Budget Bureau No. 22-R253</td></tr>
</table>

PART I - PRODUCTION | *(If more space is required, continue on reverse and identify items)*

SECTION I - COMPANY ORGANIZATIONAL DATA

1. TYPE OF COMPANY	2. YEAR ESTABLISHED	3. FACILITY SECURITY CLEARANCE
☐ CORPORATION ☐ PARTNERSHIP ☐ OTHER		

SECTION II - MANAGEMENT

1. KEY PERSONNEL *(Attach available organization charts showing relationship between management, production and inspection.)*

NAMES (Place (*) after persons furnishing information) a	TITLE AND LOCATION b	NO. OF YEARS WITH FIRM c

2. FIRM HAS AND/OR UNDERSTANDS THE ITEMS BELOW *(Explain "No" on the reverse)*	YES	NO		YES	NO	3. CLASSIFICATION OF SUPPLIER *(Check appropriate box)*
a. SPECIFICATIONS			f. PACKAGING REQUIREMENTS			☐ MANUFACTURER ☐ DISTRIBUTOR
b. EXHIBITS			g. FIRST DELIVERY REQUIRE-MENTS			☐ ASSEMBLER ☐ REGULAR DEALER
c. DRAWINGS						☐ FABRICATOR ☐ MANUFACTURER'S AGENT
d. QUALITY CONTROL REQUIRE-MENTS			h. SHIPPING REQUIREMENTS			☐ JOB SHOP ☐ JOBBER
e. TECHNICAL DATA REQUIREMENTS						CORPORATE AFFILIATIONS *(List and explain on reverse)* ☐ YES ☐ NO

SECTION III - PERSONNEL

1. TYPES OF EMPLOYEES	ON BOARD TOTAL	ON BOARD FOR PROPOSED CONTRACT	ADDITIONAL REQUIRED	AVAILABLE YES	AVAILABLE NO	SOURCE
a. SKILLED PRODUCTION EMPLOYEES						
b. UNSKILLED PRODUCTION EMPLOYEES						
c. ENGINEERING EMPLOYEES						
d. ADMINISTRATIVE EMPLOYEES						
TOTALS						

2. SHIFTS ON WHICH WORK IS TO BE PERFORMED: ☐ FIRST ☐ SECOND ☐ THIRD

3. UNION AFFILIATION AND EXPIRATION DATE OF AGREEMENT	4. RELATIONSHIP WITH LABOR INDICATES PROBLEMS AFFECTING TIMELY PERFORMANCE OF PROPOSED CONTRACT *(If "Yes", explain on reverse)* ☐ YES ☐ NO

SECTION IV - PLANT FACILITIES

1. SIZE OF TRACT	2. SQUARE FEET UNDER ROOF	3. NUMBER OF BUILDINGS

4. DESCRIPTION AND TYPE OF BUILDING *(Include expiration date(s) of any leased facilities - Continue on reverse)*

5. SPACE	SQUARE FEET	ADEQUATE	INADEQUATE
a. TOTAL FOR MANUFACTURING			
b. MANUFACTURING SPACE AVAILABLE FOR BID ITEM			
c. TOTAL FOR STORAGE			
d. STORAGE FOR INSPECTION LOTS			
e. STORAGE FOR GFP			
f. STORAGE FOR SHIPPING QUANTITIES			
g. TOTAL STORAGE SPACE AVAILABLE FOR BID ITEM			
h. STORAGE THAT CAN BE CONVERTED TO MANUFACTURING *(If required)*			

6. MISCELLANEOUS PLANT OBSERVATIONS *(Explain "No" on reverse)*	YES	NO
a. BUILDING(S) ARE FIRE RESISTANT		
b. BUILDING(S) UNDER MUNICIPAL FIRE PROTECTION		
c. PREMISES APPROVED BY MUNICIPAL FIRE DEPARTMENT		
d. SECURITY MEASURES EXIST *(Burglar alarm, safes, watchman services, etc. adequate for G.F.P. and classified document(s))*		
e. GOOD HOUSEKEEPING MAINTAINED		
f. POWER AND FUEL SUPPLY ADEQUATE TO MEET PRODUCTION REQUIREMENTS		
g. TRANSPORTATION FACILITIES AVAILABLE FOR SHIPMENT OF PRODUCT		
h. SAFETY MEASURES ADEQUATE FOR PERFORMANCE OF PROPOSED AWARD		
i. ADEQUATE MATERIELS HANDLING EQUIPMENT AVAILABLE		

Figure 50a, b, c. Form DD 1524-1/Pre-Award Survey of Prospective Contractor Part I-Production.

PRE-AWARD SURVEY OF PROSPECTIVE CONTRACTOR PART I - PRODUCTION	PROPOSED CONTRACTOR			SERIAL NUMBER
	(If more space is required, continue on reverse and identify items)			

SECTION V - PRODUCTION EQUIPMENT

1. MAJOR TYPES OF MANUFACTURING EQUIP REQUIRED FOR BID ITEM (Include GFP) *a*	QTY ON HAND *b*	CONDI-TION (G,F,P) *c*	SOURCE IF NOT ON HAND *d*	VERIFIED DELIVERY DATE TO MEET PRODUCTION *e*
2. SPECIAL TOOLING (Include GFP)				

SECTION VI - MATERIALS AND PURCHASED PARTS

1. PARTS/MATERIALS WITH LONGEST LEAD TIME *a*	SOURCE *b*	VERIFIED DELIVERY DATE TO MEET PRODUCTION *c*

2. AN ESTABLISHED MATERIAL CONTROL SYSTEM IS IN OPERATION (If "No", explain how material is controlled)

☐ YES   ☐ NO

3. GOVERNMENT PROPERTY, IF FURNISHED, CAN BE ADEQUATELY CONTROLLED AND RECORDED

☐ YES   ☐ NO

SECTION VII - SUBCONTRACTING

ITEM DESCRIPTION *a*	SOURCE *b*	VERIFIED DELIVERY DATE TO MEET PRODUCTION *c*

Figure 50 (*Continued*)

PRE-AWARD SURVEY OF PROSPECTIVE CONTRACTOR PART I - PRODUCTION	PRODUCTION CONTRACTOR	SERIAL NUMBER

SECTION VIII - PRODUCTION CONTROL

AN ESTABLISHED PRODUCTION CONTROL SYSTEM IS IN OPERATION (If "No", explain how production is controlled)

☐ YES   ☐ NO

SECTION IX - RELATED PREVIOUS PRODUCTION (Government)

PAST YEAR PRODUCTION		GOVERNMENT CONTRACT NUMBER 1/	GOVERNMENT AGENCY	QUANTITY OR VALUE
ITEM NOMENCLATURE a	FSN b	c	d	e

1/ Place asterisk (*) after government contract number(s) having unsatisfactory performance.

SECTION X - CURRENT PRODUCTION

GOVERNMENT AND CIVILIAN CONCURRENT PRODUCTION SCHEDULE USING SAME EQUIPMENT AND/OR PERSONNEL AS BID ITEM

1. ITEM(S) BEING PRODUCED (Include Government Contract Number if applicable)	MONTHLY SCHEDULE OF CONCURRENT DELIVERIES (Quantity)										
	1ST	2ND	3RD	4TH	5TH	6TH	7TH	8TH	9TH	10TH	BAL
2. ITEM(S) PENDING AWARD											

SECTION XI - RECOMMENDATION

1. RECOMMENDATION REGARDING PRODUCTION ASPECTS

☐ COMPLETE AWARD   ☐ PARTIAL AWARD (Quantity _____)   ☐ NO AWARD

2. IF PARTIAL, OR NO AWARD IS RECOMMENDED, CITE THOSE SECTIONS OF REPORT WHICH SUBSTANTIATE THE RECOMMENDATION AND LIST ANY OTHER BACKUP INFORMATION IN THIS SPACE, ON REVERSE SIDE, OR ON ATTACHED SHEET IF REQUIRED.

SURVEY MADE BY (Signature and office)	PHONE AREA CODE & NO.	DATE

Figure 50 (Continued)

PRE-AWARD SURVEY OF PROSPECTIVE CONTRACTOR	PROPOSED CONTRACTOR		SERIAL NUMBER	Form approved Budget Bureau No. 22-R253
PART II - QUALITY ASSURANCE	*(If more space is required, continue on reverse and identify items)*			

SECTION I - GENERAL

1. NAME OF FACILITY	2. LOCATION

SECTION II - COMPANY DATA

1. QUALITY ASSURANCE CAPABILITY AND ORGANIZATION *(Describe briefly)*

2. QUALITY ASSURANCE OFFICIALS CONTACTED *(Names and titles)*

3. IDENTICAL OR SIMILAR ITEM HAS BEEN PRODUCED OR SERVICED BY THIS CONTRACTOR
☐ YES ☐ NO

SECTION III - EVALUATION STATEMENTS *(Explain negative entries in Section IV)*

1. CONTRACTOR UNDERSTANDS THE FOLLOWING AS THEY PERTAIN TO THE PROPOSED PROCUREMENT

	YES	NO		YES	NO
a. EXHIBITS			*e.* SPECIFICATIONS		
b. TECHNICAL DATA REQUIREMENTS			*f.* PACKAGING REQUIREMENTS		
c. DRAWING			*g.* OTHER *(Identify)*		
d. APPROVAL REQUIREMENTS					

2. THE FOLLOWING QUALITY ASSURANCE SPECIFICATIONS WILL APPLY TO PROPOSED PROCUREMENT

3.	YES	NO
a. CONTRACTOR HAS CONSIDERED INSPECTION AND TEST PERSONNEL THAT MAY BE REQUIRED.		
b. CONTRACTOR HAS ARRIVED AT AN ESTIMATE OF ADDITIONAL INSPECTION AND TEST PERSONNEL THAT MAY BE REQUIRED.		
c. CONTRACTOR HAS THE NUCLEUS OF TRAINED INSPECTION AND TEST PERSONNEL NECESSARY.		
d. QUALITY CONTROL, INSPECTION, AND TEST PERSONNEL ARE FURNISHED ADEQUATE INSTRUCTIONS COVERING INSPECTION, TEST AND CONTROL OF PRODUCT QUALITY.		
e. CONTRACTOR HAS NECESSARY INSPECTION AND TEST EQUIPMENT.		
f. CONTRACTOR HAS CONSIDERED INSPECTION AND TEST EQUIPMENT THAT MAY BE REQUIRED.		
g. CONTRACTOR HAS ARRIVED AT AN ESTIMATE OF ADDITIONAL INSPECTION AND TEST EQUIPMENT THAT MAY BE REQUIRED.		
h. SUITABLE GAGES AND OTHER INSPECTION, MEASURING AND TESTING DEVICES ARE PROVIDED AND MAINTAINED IN PROPER CONDITION.		
4. QUALITY CONTROL OR INSPECTION FUNCTION HAS BEEN EFFECTIVELY PLANNED IN CONJUNCTION WITH OTHER PLANNING AND CONTROL FUNCTIONS.		
5. SYSTEM IN EFFECT DOES PROVIDE FOR EFFECTIVE RELEASE OF TECHNICAL REQUIREMENTS, REVISIONS, AND CHANGES THERETO REQUIRED FOR PRODUCTION, INSPECTION AND TEST PERSONNEL.		

Figure 51a, b. Form DD 1524-2/Pre-Award Survey of Prospective Contractor Part II-Quality Assurance.

PRE-AWARD SURVEY OF PROSPECTIVE CONTRACTOR PART II - QUALITY ASSURANCE	PROPOSED CONTRACTOR	SERIAL NUMBER		
			YES	NO
6. AN EFFECTIVE SYSTEM IS ESTABLISHED FOR ANALYSIS OF PRODUCT CHARACTERISTICS IN DETERMINING AND PLANNING FOR INSPECTION AND TESTS REQUIRED.				
7. EFFECTIVE IN-PROCESS CONTROLS ARE ESTABLISHED FOR MINIMIZING PRODUCTION OF DEFECTIVE MATERIAL.				
8. ADEQUATE MEASURES ARE PROVIDED FOR SEGREGATING DEFECTIVE MATERIAL AND TAKING CORRECTIVE ACTION TO PREVENT REPEATED MANUFACTURE OF DISCREPANT MATERIAL.				
9. EFFECTIVE CONTROL IS ESTABLISHED FOR SELECTING QUALIFIED SUPPLIERS AND IN ASSURING RECEIPT OF QUALITY MATERIAL.				
10. ADEQUATE MEASURES ARE PROVIDED FOR PRESERVATION, PACKAGING AND SHIPMENT OF MATERIAL.				
11. ADEQUATE QUALITY CONTROL AND INSPECTION RECORDS ARE MAINTAINED SHOWING INSPECTIONS AND TESTS PERFORMED AND RESULTS THEREOF.				
12. RECORDS AVAILABLE INDICATE THAT CONTRACTOR HAS A SATISFACTORY QUALITY PERFORMANCE RECORD FOR THE PAST SIX MONTHS ON GOVERNMENT AND WHERE RELEVANT, COMMERCIAL PRODUCTION.				
13. USED OR RECONDITIONED MATERIAL AND FORMER GOVERNMENT SURPLUS MATERIAL WILL BE FURNISHED BY CONTRACTOR. (If yes, explain on reverse.)				
14. CONTRACTOR WILL REQUIRE UNUSUAL ASSISTANCE FROM THE GOVERNMENT. (If yes, explain on reverse.)				

SECTION IV - QUALITY ASSURANCE RECOMMENDATION

RECOMMENDATION REGARDING QUALITY CONTROL ASPECTS   ☐ AWARD   ☐ NO AWARD

SURVEY MADE BY (Signature and office)	PHONE AREA CODE & NO.	DATE

Figure 51 (*Continued*)

PRE-AWARD SURVEY OF PROSPECTIVE CONTRACTOR PART III - FINANCIAL CAPABILITY	PROPOSED CONTRACTOR		SERIAL NUMBER	Form Approved Budget Bureau No. 22-R253
	LOCATION			

1. LATEST BALANCE SHEET		2. LATEST PROFIT AND LOSS STATEMENT

a. DATE	b. FILED WITH	a. CURRENT PERIOD (From - To)

FINANCIAL POSITION		b. STATEMENT FILED WITH

c. CASH	$	NET SALES	
d. CURRENT ASSETS			
e. CURRENT LIABILITIES		c. CURRENT PERIOD	$
f. WORKING CAPITAL		d. FIRST PRIOR FISCAL YEAR	
g. NET WORTH		e. SECOND PRIOR FISCAL YEAR	
h. TOTAL LIABILITIES		NET PROFITS BEFORE TAXES	
i. CURRENT RATIO (Current assets to current liabilities)		f. CURRENT PERIOD	$
j. ACID TEST RATIO (Cash, temporary investments held in lieu of cash, and current receivables to current liabilities)		g. FIRST PRIOR FISCAL YEAR	
		h. SECOND PRIOR FISCAL YEAR	
k. TOTAL LIABILITIES TO NET WORTH		i. OTHER PERTINENT INFORMATION	

3. DATE FISCAL YEAR ENDS	4. BALANCE SHEETS AND PROFIT AND LOSS STATEMENTS HAVE BEEN CERTIFIED:	
	a. THROUGH (Date)	b. BY

5. CONTRACTOR'S FINANCIAL ARRANGEMENTS			
(Check appropriate box)	YES	NO	d. DOES INDEPENDENT ANALYSIS OF CONTRACTOR'S FINANCIAL POSITION SUPPORT THE CONTRACTOR'S STATEMENTS IN ITEM a, b, AND/OR c ? (If "No", explain Continue on reverse, if necessary.) ☐ YES ☐ NO
a. USE OF CONTRACTOR'S OWN RESOURCES			
b. USE OF BANK CREDIT			
c. OTHER (Specify)			

6. FINANCIAL AID TO BE REQUESTED FROM GOVERNMENT IN CONNECTION WITH PERFORMANCE OF THIS CONTRACT			
(Check appropriate box)	YES	NO	d. (Explain affirmative answers to items a, b, and c.)
a. PROGRESS PAYMENT			
b. GUARANTEED LOAN			
c. ADVANCE PAYMENTS			

7. FINANCIAL AID CURRENTLY OBTAINED FROM GOVERNMENT		
(Check appropriate box)	YES	NO
a. IS CONTRACTOR RECEIVING GOVERNMENT FINANCING AT PRESENT?		
b. IF ANSWER TO ITEM a ABOVE IS "YES" IS LIQUIDATION CURRENT?		

8. AMOUNT OF UNLIQUIDATED PROGRESS PAYMENTS OUTSTANDING	9. AMOUNT OF GOVERNMENT GUARANTEED LOANS WITH DOLLAR AMOUNT BEING USED AT PRESENT	a. AUTHORIZED	b. IN USE
$		$	$
$	10. AMOUNT OF GOVERNMENT ADVANCE PAYMENTS WITH DOLLAR AMOUNT BEING USED AT PRESENT	$	$

11. GOVERNMENT AGENCIES INVOLVED	12. APPLICABLE CONTRACT NUMBERS

Figure 52a, b, c. Form DD 1524-3/Pre-Award Survey of Prospective Contractor Part III-Financial Capability.

PRE-AWARD SURVEY OF PROSPECTIVE CONTRACTOR PART III - FINANCIAL CAPABILITY	PROPOSED CONTRACTOR	SERIAL NUMBER
	(If more space is required, continue on reverse and identify items)	

13. COMMENTS OF BANK OF PROSPECTIVE CONTRACTOR

14. COMMENTS OF TRADE CREDITORS

15. COMMENTS AND REPORTS OF COMMERCIAL FINANCIAL SERVICES AND CREDIT ORGANIZATIONS, SUCH AS DUN & BRADSTREET, STANDARD & POOR, ETC.

16. MOST RECENT CREDIT RATING

a. DATE

b. BY

17. OTHER SOURCES *(Business and financial reputation, and integrity of the prospective contractor, or if not established, of the principal executives, as determined by other sources.)*

Figure 52 *(Continued)*

PRE-AWARD SURVEY OF PROSPECTIVE CONTRACTOR PART III - FINANCIAL CAPABILITY	PROPOSED CONTRACTOR	SERIAL NUMBER

18. DOES PRICE APPEAR UNREALISTICALLY LOW?

☐ YES   ☐ NO

19. OUTSTANDING LIENS OR JUDGMENTS

20.   SALES

CATEGORY	CURRENT DOLLAR BACKLOG OF SALES *a*	ANTICIPATED ADDITIONAL DOLLAR SALES FORECAST FOR NEXT 18 MONTHS *b*
a. GOVERNMENT *(Prime and Subcontractor)*		
b. COMMERCIAL		
TOTALS		

21. RECOMMENDATION REGARDING FINANCIAL ASPECTS

☐ COMPLETE AWARD   ☐ PARTIAL AWARD *(Quantity* _____ *)*   ☐ NO AWARD

(If partial or no award is recommended, cite those sections of report which substantiate the recommendation and list any other backup information in this space.) (If more space is required, continue on reverse or on separate sheet.)

SURVEY MADE BY *(Signature and office)*	PHONE AREA CODE AND NO.	DATE

Figure 52   *(Continued)*

378

PRE-AWARD SURVEY OF PROSPECTIVE CONTRACTOR PART IV - ACCOUNTING SYSTEM	PROPOSED CONTRACTOR	SERIAL NUMBER	Form Approved Budget Bureau No. 22-R253		
(Check appropriate box)			YES	NO	NOT APPLICABLE
1. EXCEPT AS STATED BELOW, IS THE CONTRACTOR'S ACCOUNTING SYSTEM IN ACCORD WITH GENERALLY ACCEPTED ACCOUNTING PRINCIPLES APPLICABLE IN THE CIRCUMSTANCES?					
2. DOES THE CONTRACTOR'S ACCOUNTING SYSTEM PROVIDE FOR:	a. PROPER SEGREGATION OF COSTS APPLICABLE TO THIS CONTRACT AND TO OTHER WORK OF THE CONTRACTOR				
	b. DETERMINATION OF COSTS AT INTERIM POINTS TO PROVIDE DATA REQUIRED FOR CONTRACT REPRICING PURPOSES OR FOR NEGOTIAT- ING REVISED TARGETS				
	c. EXCLUSION FROM COSTS CHARGED TO THIS CONTRACT OF AMOUNTS WHICH ARE NOT ALLOWABLE UNDER THE TERMS OF ASPR XV OR OTHER CONTRACT PROVISION				
	d. IDENTIFICATION OF COSTS BY CONTRACT LINE ITEM AND BY UNITS IF REQUIRED BY THE CONTRACT				
	e. SEGREGATION OF PREPRODUCTION COSTS FROM PRODUCTION COSTS				
3. DOES THE CONTRACTOR'S ACCOUNTING SYSTEM PROVIDE FINANCIAL INFORMATION	a. REQUIRED BY CONTRACT CLAUSES CONCERNING "LIMITATION OF COST" (ASPR 7-203.4 / 7-402.3) OR "LIMITATION ON PAYMENTS" (ASPR 7-108.1 (t), etc.)				
	b. REQUIRED TO SUPPORT REQUESTS FOR PROGRESS PAYMENTS				
4. IS THE ACCOUNTING SYSTEM DESIGNED, AND ARE THE RECORDS MAINTAINED IN SUCH A MANNER THAT ADEQUATE, RELIABLE DATA ARE DEVELOPED FOR USE IN PRICING FOLLOW-ON PROCURE- MENTS?					

5. REMARKS (Clarification of above, additional deficiencies, and other pertinent comments. If more space is required, continue on reverse or on blank sheets.)

SURVEY MADE BY (Signature and office)	PHONE AREA CODE AND NO.	DATE

Figure 53. Form DD 1524-4/Pre-Award Survey of Prospective Contractor Part IV-Accounting System

PRE-AWARD SURVEY OF PROSPECTIVE CONTRACTOR PART V - MONITOR REPORT	PROPOSED CONTRACTOR		SERIAL NUMBER	Form Approved Budget Bureau No. 22-R253

1. IS PROSPECTIVE CONTRACTOR INCLUDED ON THE CONSOLIDATED LIST OF DEBARRED, INELIGIBLE, AND SUSPENDED CONTRACTORS, OR ANY OTHER CURRENT CONTROL LIST? *(If "Yes", identify list and state reason for inclusion thereon.)*

☐ YES   ☐ NO

2. INDICATE THOSE PROCEDURES OF THE PROSPECTIVE CONTRACTOR WHICH HAVE PREVIOUSLY BEEN REVIEWED BY GOVERNMENT PERSONNEL

(Check appropriate boxes)	REVIEWED		ACCEPT-ABLE		(Check appropriate boxes)	REVIEWED		ACCEPT-ABLE	
	YES	NO	YES	NO		YES	NO	YES	NO
a. PURCHASING SYSTEM					e. QUALITY PROGRAM				
b. ESTIMATING SYSTEM					f. INSPECTION SYSTEM				
c. ACCOUNTING SYSTEM					g. OTHER (Specify)				
d. CONTROL OF GOVT. PROPERTY									

3. BASED ON ALL INFORMATION RECEIVED, RECOMMEND ☐ COMPLETE AWARD, ☐ PARTIAL AWARD, ☐ NO AWARD
(Where partial, or no award is recommended, state justification. Use reverse if more space is required.)

MONITOR (Signature and office)	PHONE AREA CODE AND NO.	DATE

Figure 54.   Form DD 1524-5/Pre-Award Survey of Prospective Contractor Part V-Monitor Report

If at all possible, you should attempt to meet the pre-award survey team personally when it arrives at your company. If you are unable to, your chief assistant should do so. Prepare a briefing covering the major areas that the survey team will check on and be ready to answer questions in all areas. Naturally you should get the appropriate background information together and have it readily available. For example, the survey team may check into your organization. You should have an organization chart handy and be prepared to tell the team about the background of all the key personnel who are filling blocks on the organization chart.

You can expect questions about production personnel if your contract concerns production. The team will want to know about the personnel involved in production, whether you have specification exhibits, drawings, quality control requirements, packaging requirements, and first delivery requirements, and whether you understand what you will be required to do. They will want to know the numbers and types of personnel that you have on board for production such as skilled and unskilled production workers, and engineering and administrative employees. They will want to know about and will examine more closely actual or potential labor relations problems that may affect the program. They will look into your plant facilities for production including the space for manufacturing; space available for the bid item; the space available for storage for inspection lots, storage for Government-furnished property, storage for shipping quantities, and storage that can be converted to manufacturing.

The survey team will ask questions regarding your buildings and whether they are fire resistant, whether they are under municipal fire protection, and whether the premises are approved by the municipal fire department. They will ask about security measures such as burglary alarms, safes, watchman services, and so on. They will check whether you are maintaining good housekeeping, whether power and fuel supply is adequate to meet production requirements, whether transportation facilities are available for shipment of the product. They will ask about safety measures and if adequate materials handling equipment is available.

The type of equipment you intend to use and its efficiency will also be reviewed in detail. You should prepare a list of this equipment before the team arrives and be prepared to show or even demonstrate it, if requested.

The pre-award survey team will also ask about materials and purchase parts, what the longest lead time is, what your sources are, whether you have verified the delivery date to meet production needs, and whether you have verified your costs and have these documented in writing from the supplier. The same goes for special tooling and subcontracting activities. You can also expect that methods of manufacturing will be discussed and the Government specifications will be compared to the way that you intend to produce the item. If there are ambiguities in the specifications, then you will have an opportunity to discuss it with the Government at this time.

If you have had previous contracts with the Government, the survey team will review your past performance. They will want to know what you produced, what the federal stock number was, the Government contract number, which agency it was for, and also the quantity or value. If you have never done Government work before, the survey team may evaluate how you have served your nongovernment customers. You should expect this, and have a record available that you can show, including names and telephone numbers, so that the individuals can be contacted by members of the survey team if they so desire.

The survey team will also review your current production activities, when various items are due, and even other potential Government contracts where the award is still pending.

You can expect the survey team to give you a quality assurance inspection. During the inspection the team will review your inspection system and look at your test equipment, the training of your inspectors, the availability of a quality control manual, a control system for marketing defective material, and how inspectors are supervised. You will be questioned to determine whether you understand aspects of quality control that are contained in the proposed contract such as technical data requirements, drawings, approval requirements, specifications, packaging requirements, and so forth. You will be questioned to determine whether you have considered inspection and test personnel that may be required for the contract. If you have arrived at an estimate of additional inspection test personnel that may be necessary, the Government will want to know if you have the nucleus of trained inspection test personnel necessary. The same consideration will be expected regarding test inspection equipment on hand and additional inspection equipment that may be required. The condition of gauges and other inspection, measuring, and testing devices that you have will also be checked to be certain that they are maintained in the proper condition. Finally, you will be checked to see that your quality control system provides for effective release of technical requirements, revisions, and changes required for production, inspection, and test personnel. You can also expect that your past records will be checked to indicate that you have a satisfactory quality performance record of the past six months on Government, and where relevant, commercial production contracts. All of these items should be prepared prior to the arrival of the pre-award survey team.

Anticipate that your financial capability will be looked into very closely. This inspection will include a credit report from, say, Dun and Bradstreet. You will also be required to file a financial statement within a few days of the request. The Government considers that financial stability is one of the most important determinations that the contracting officer can make. Basically, the Government wants to ensure your ability to pay for the materials and labor needed to produce the end-item or services under the contract. Prepare for this by having your accountant prepare a balance sheet ahead of time showing assests and liabilities, or have a very recent one available. Provide documentation from your bank to confirm any statements that you make on your financial condition. All aspects including cash flow, working capital, and credit rating are important factors that will be reviewed by the survey team. You may also expect that trade creditors such as your bank, commercial financial services, and credit organizations may be contacted. If your bid was very low, you will be particularly scrutinized. Be prepared to back up a very low bid with hard documented figures. This can make the difference between a satisfactory and unsatisfactory pre-award survey.

In addition to your financial system, the survey team will look at your accounting system. They will check to ensure that your accounting system is in accord with generally accepted accounting principles including the following:

- Whether your accounting system provides for proper segregation for costs applicable to the proposed contract and to other work that you are doing.
- Whether the determination of cost is provided at interim points to supply data required for contract repricing purposes or for negotiated revised targets.
- Whether your system provides for the exclusion of costs charged to this contract that are not allowable under the terms of Government regulations or other contract provisions.
- Whether your system provides for indentification of cost by contract line item and by units, if required by the contract.
- Whether it provides for segregation of reproduction costs from production costs.
- Whether your accounting system is designed and the records maintained in such a manner that adequate reliable data are developed for use in pricing follow-on procurements.

When the pre-award survey team completes their review of your company, they will prepare reports. These reports and recommendations, when coordinated by their supervisors, are combined into a formal pre-award survey report that is submitted to the contracting officer. This report includes all of the details that we have discussed previously and that the team has reviewed during its visit to your company. Based on this formal pre-award survey report, the contracting officer decides whether you can be a responsible producer for the Government in this particular situation. If he decides that you can and you win the contract, he will notify you formally that you have a contract and you can then proceed according to the term of the contract. The contracting officer will also notify you if the results are negative.

Will the pre-award survey team discuss their findings with you prior to submitting their report to the contracting officer? Government regulations only permit discussion with a prospective contractor of questionable areas that in the opinion of the survey team require clarification during the survey. However, this is up to the survey team, so they may or may not discuss findings with you at this time. Some survey teams prefer not to discuss any findings with you, saying that such discussion is strictly the business of the contracting officer.

If your bid is low and is rejected as a result of a pre-award survey team's visit to your company, you do have recourse. According to Government regulations, the contracting officer must refer you to the Small Business Adminstration if you are a rejected bidder and a small business. As pointed out earlier, the SBA will then review your case and will act, if required, to issue a certificate of competency that certifies that you can fulfill the contract. See Chapter 3.

David Hoffman, who was assistant chief of procurement and management assistance in the Philadelphia regional office of the Small Business Administration, offers the following reminder list as items that you should use as a checklist to be readily available for a pre-award survey team when one visits you. Here are the items:

1. Manpower. Include the availability of technical and supervisory personnel, special skills, and know-how.
2. Facilities and equipment. List your equipment and include the commitments that you have made for additional facilities and equipment.
3. Quality assurance. This should show the systems used and whether they have been approved by any Government agencies.
4. Production scheduling. Show by PERT, Gantt, or similar charts how you plan to meet the schedule.
5. Schedule of total workload. Include anticipated and repeat work, and dollar value of remaining backlog.
6. Bill of materials. Include on the list components to be made in your plant and a list of those you need to buy from suppliers.
7. Inventory. Check existing inventory for usability on the proposed contract.
8. Material suppliers and subcontractors. Include written or telegraphic confirmations on delivery dates of major and critical items.
9. Cost breakdown and analysis. Cost should be described in enough detail to allow evaluation of cash flow sheets.
10. Cash flow sheets. These should be included from the proposed contract for the plant's total workload and they should be reconciled with the production schedule, the plant's commitments for materials, and other financial commitments.
11. Financial statements. Include your most recent profit-and-loss statement and balance sheet.

If the preparation for the pre-award survey is done correctly, you will have no problem with the survey itself. Keep uppermost in your mind that the pre-award survey should not be considered by you as a chance that the Government has to unveil your weaknesses, but rather as another opportunity for you to demonstrate just how good you really are.

Summary

YOU CAN MAKE
MILLIONS OF DOLLARS

In the previous chapters of this book, I have covered every aspect of doing business with the Government that will help you to make millions of dollars while serving the needs of your country at the same time. But the instructions, techniques, and secrets I have given you are just that unless you put them to use. Only you can do this. Unless you take action, the contents of this book are just so many words on paper. If you do take action and follow the directions I have given you, I am confident that you can and will make millions.

COMMON ACRONYMS
AND ABBREVIATIONS

AAC	Alaskan Air Command
ADC	Aerospace Defense Command
ADP	Automatic Data Processing
AEC	Atomic Energy Commission
AFCS	Air Force Communications Service
AFLC	Air Force Logistics Command
AFOSR	Air Force Office of Scientific Research
AFSC	Air Force Systems Command
AGE	Aerospace Ground Equipment
AMA	Air Materiel Area
ARRADCOM	Army Armament Research Development Command
ARRCOM	Army Armament Materiel Readiness Command
ARS	Advanced Records System
ASL	Atmospheric Sciences Laboratory
ASPR	Armed Services Procurement Regulation (replaced by DAR, see below)
ATC	Air Training Command
AVRADCOM	Army Aviation Research and Development Command
BMEWS	Ballistic Missile Early Warning System
CAS	Cost Accounting Standards
CBD	Commerce Business Daily
CERCOM	Army Communications and Electronics Materiel Readiness Command
CNO	Chief of Naval Operations
CO	Contracting Officer
COC	Certificate of Competence
CONAD	Continental Air Defense Command
CORANDCOM	Army Communications Research and Development Command
CP	Cost Plus Contract
CPAF	Cost Plus Award Fee
CPFF	Cost Plus Fixed Fee

CPIF	Cost Plus Incentive Fee
CSTAL	Combat Surveillance and Target Acquisition Laboratory
DAR	Defense Acquisition Regulation (replaced ASPR)
DARS	Defense Acquisition Regulation System
DCAA	Defense Contract Audit Agency
DCASMA	Defense Contract Administration Services Management Area
DCASR	Defense Contract Administration Services Region
DIDS	Defense Integrated Data System
DLA (CAS) HQ	Defense Contract Administration Services
DLA	Defense Logistics Agency
DOD	Department of Defense
DOE	Department of Energy
DOL	Department of Labor
DOT	Department of Transportation
EAM	Electric Accounting Machine
ECM	Electronic Countermeasures
ERADCOM	Army Electronic Research and Development Command
ETDL	Electronic Technology and Devices Laboratory
EWL	Electronic Warfare Laboratory
FAA	Federal Aviation Administration
FAR	Federal Acquisition Regulation (replaced FPR below)
FBM	Fleet Ballistic Missile
FDA	Food and Drug Administration
FEA	Federal Energy Administration
FP	Fixed Price Contract
FPAF	Fixed Price Award Fee
FPIF	Fixed Price Incentive Fee
FPR	Federal Procurement Regulation (replaced by FAR above)
FRA	Federal Railroad Administration
FSC	Federal Supply Classification
FSS	Federal Supply Schedule
GAO	General Accounting Office
GFE	Government Furnished Equipment
GSA	General Services Administration
HDL	Harry Diamond Laboratories
HEW	Department of Health, Education, and Welfare
HSA	Health Services Administration
HUD	Department of Housing and Urban Development
IFB	Invitation for Bid
IR and D	Independent Research and Development
LEAA	Law Enforcement Assistance Administration
MAC	Military Airlift Command

MAP	Military Assistance Program
MERANDCOM	Army Mobility Equipment Research and Development Command
MIRADCOM	Army Missile Research and Development Command
MIRCOM	Army Missile Materiel Readiness Command
MOL	Maximum Order Limitation
MSC	Military Sealift Command
NADC	Naval Air Development Center
NARADCOM	Army Natick Research and Development Command
NASA	National Aeronautics and Space Administration
NAVAIR	Naval Air Systems Command
NAVELEX	Naval Electronics Systems Command
NAVFAC	Naval Facilities Engineering Command
NAVSEA	Naval Sea Systems Command
NAVSUP	Naval Supply Systems Command
NHTSA	National Highway Traffic Safety Administration
NICP	National Inventory Control Point
NIDA	National Institute for Drug Abuse
NIH	National Institute of Health
NIMH	National Institute of Mental Health
NLM	National Library of Medicine
NMP	National Maintenance Point
NOL	Naval Ordnance Laboratory
NRL	Naval Research Laboratory
NUSC	Naval Underwater Systems Center
NVEOL	Night Vision and Electro-Optics Laboratories
OCE	Office Chief of Engineers
OE	Office of Education
O and M	Operations and Maintenance
OMB	Office of Management and Budget
ONR	Office of Naval Research
OSD	Office of Secretary of Defense
OSHA	Occupational Safety and Health Administration
PHS	Public Health Service
QPL	Qualified Products List
RDTE	Research, Development, Test, and Evaluation
RFI	Request for Information
RFP	Request for Proposal
RFQ	Request for Quotation
SAC	Strategic Air Command
SBA	Small Business Administration
SOW	Statement of Work
SWL	Signals Warfare Laboratory

TAC	Tactical Air Command
TARADCOM	Army Tank-Automotive Research and Development Command
TARCOM	Army Tank-Automotive Materiel Readiness Command
TECOM	Army Test and Evaluation Command
T and M	Time and Material
TSARCOM	Army Troop Support and Aviation Materiel Readiness Command
USA	United States Army
USAF	United States Air Force
USCG	United States Coast Guard
USDA	United States Department of Agriculture
USN	United States Navy
USPS	United States Postal Service

Appendix

EXTRACTS FROM THE U.S. GOVERNMENT PURCHASING AND SALES DIRECTORY

MILITARY DEPARTMENTS WITH MAJOR RESEARCH AND DEVELOPMENT ACTIVITIES

Department of the Army

U.S. Army Safeguard System Command

The U.S. Army SAFEGUARD System Command (SAFSCOM) is a Class II Activity under the supervision and command of the SAFEGUARD System Manager (SAFSM). The Commanding General, SAFSCOM, with headquarters in Huntsville, Alabama, is responsible for accomplishing the development, acquisition and installation of the approved SAFEGUARD Ballistic Missile Defense (BMD) System, and to accomplish necessary effort in carrying out a prototype demonstration program for Site Defense of MINUTEMAN (SDM), within the guidance and direction of the SAFSM who is headquartered in Arlington, Virginia. The CG, SAFSCOM also commands and operates the Kwajalein Missile Range (KMR), a Department of Defense National Range located in the Marshall Islands in the Pacific, under the guidance and direction of the Chief of Research and Development, Department of the Army.

Principal Interests: Research, development, test and evaluation of the SAFEGUARD BMD System; continuous system analysis and feasibility studies to insure development of optimum protection against the current and future postulated threat; generation, collection, and analysis of technical, strategic and economic data for defining the "threat" on which effectiveness of the SAFEGUARD BMD System is determined; analysis of the threat against which the effectiveness of Site Defense of MINUTEMAN is evaluated; analysis and feasibility studies to insure that the components developed for the prototype demonstration of SDM will provide optimum protection against

current and future threats; development, establishment, maintenance and operation of range facilities and equipment to meet the requirements of approved range users.

Address:

Commanding General
U.S. Army SAFEGUARD System Command
P.O. Box 1500
Huntsville, Ala. 35807

U.S. Army Materiel Development and Readiness Command

The U.S. Army Materiel Development and Readiness Command (DARCOM) is responsible for the complete life cycle of U.S. Army hardware including research, development, procurement, production, supply, and maintenance. Headquarters DARCOM, Alexandria, VA, provides supervisory, planning, and budgetary direction to the several major subordinate commands and other installations and activities independent of the commands where contracts are executed and administered. Those elements of DARCOM in which research and development programs are carried out are summarized below:

U.S. Army Aviation Research and Development Command

Principal Interests: Basic and applied research concerning assigned materiel development to include end item aircraft, airframe structural components, ground support equipment, wheel and brake systems, etc., gas turbine, jet engines, internal combustion radial and horizontally opposed aircraft engines, and aircraft hydraulic pumps, starters, etc.

Address:

Commander
U.S. Army Aviation Research and Development Command
St. Louis, MO 63166

1. Headquarters, U.S. Army Air Mobility Research and Development Laboratories

Principal Interests: Accomplishes basic, applied, exploratory and advanced development research in the field of subsonic aerodynamics applicable to aircraft, missile and other aerodynamic devices.

Adresses:

Commander
Headquarters, U.S. Army Air Mobility Research and Development Laboratories
Moffett Field, Calif. 94035

Director
Ames Directorate
U.S. Army Air Mobility Research and Development Laboratories
Ames Research Center
Moffett Field, Calif. 94035

Director
Eustis Directorate
U.S. Army Air Mobility Research and Development Laboratories
Fort Eustis, Va. 23604

Director
Langley Directorate
U.S. Army Air Mobility Research and Development Laboratories
Langley Research Center
Hampton, Va. 23365

Director
Lewis Directorate
U.S. Army Air Mobility Research and Development Laboratories
Lewis Research Center
Cleveland, Ohio 44135

U.S. Army Electronics Command

Principal Interests: Responsible for the research, development of communication and elec-tronic equipment and systems. Principal interests are communications, communications security, electronic warfare, aviation electronics (avionics), night vision, combat surveillance, target acquisition, electronic intelligence, photographic and mircrofilming, air-defense electronics, identification-friend or foe (radar) systems, automatic data processing, radar, meteorological and electronic radiological detection material (except fire control, radar, computers, and closed-circuit computer system integral to a weapon system), electric power generation equipment, and related assigned special-purpose and multi-system test equipment, component parts and materials. Conducts continuing research in the fields of missile electronics warfare, missile vulnerability, and missile surveillance. Coordinates the missile electronics counter-measures efforts of the U.S. Army.

Address:

Commander
U.S. Army Electronics Command
Fort Monmouth, N.J. 07703

U.S. Army Missile Research and Development Command

Principal Interests: Conducts a basic and applied research program with respect to assigned material and such other research projects as may be assigned. Assigned material includes free rockets, guided missiles, ballistic missiles, target missiles, air-defense missile-fire coordination equipment, special-purpose and multisystem test equipment, missile-launching and ground-support equipment, and missile-fire control equipment.

Address:

Commander
U.S. Army Missile Research and Development Command
Redstone Arsenal, Ala. 35809

U.S. Army Armament Research and Development Command

Principal Interest: Basic and applied research concerning weapons, including aircraft weapon systems, artillery weapons, infantry weapons, and crew-served weapons (including those weapons mounted on any type of vehicle, tank-like weapons systems), self propelled artillery and conducts or manages research, design and development of artillery, artillery mounts, recoil mechanisms, carriages, leaders, handcarts, arms racks, certain target material, common tools, tool sets, shop equipment, design and development of individual weapons, machine guns, grenades, munitions, conventional, nuclear and chemical/biological.

Address:

Commander
U.S. Army Armament Research and Development Command
Dover, N.J. 07801

U.S. Army Tank-Automotive Research and Development Command

Principal Interests: Conducts applied research development and engineering of tank-automotive vehicles and components for the Army and other Department of Defense activities. Typical R&D programs include power train components, suspension systems, trucks, trailers, tires, new concepts for mobility, armor concepts, weapons systems for tanks and combat vehicles, and all types of vehicle engines and accessories.

Address:

Commander
U.S. Army Tank-Automotive Research and Development Command
Warren, MI 48090

U.S. Army Mobility Equipment Research and Development Command

Principal Interests: Accomplishes basic and applied research and development with respect to assigned items of equipment, e.g., rails, marine and amphibious equipment, construction, electric power generation, bridging and assault stream crossing, fire fighting, prefabricated buildings, waste disposal, heating and air conditioning, night vision, camouflage and concealment, mine warfare, barrier and intrusion detection, demolitions, water purification, petroleum products including storage and distribution, industrial engines, and land navigation.

Address:

Commander
U.S. Army Mobility Equipment Research and Development Command
Fort Belvoir, Va. 22060

U.S. Army Natick Research and Development Command

Principal Interests: Accomplish research and development in special aspects of the physical engineering, environmental, and life sciences, to meet military requirements for soldiers' equipment in the commodity categories of clothing, foot wear, and body armor; organic materials, textiles, tentage and equipage; subsistence and food services equipment; containers and materials handling equipment; POL handling and dispensing equipment; field support equipment including printing and composing equipment, equipment and techniques for air drop of Army personnel, supplies and equipment. As assigned, support other components of DA and the DLA, with respect to applications engineering and standardization programs, for designated commodity areas.

Address:

Commander
U.S. Army Natick Research and Development Command
Natick, Mass. 07160

U.S. Army Harry Diamond Laboratories

Principal Interests: Performs basic and applied research in, (but not restricted to), the fields of radiating or influence fuzing, time fuzing (electrical, electronic, decay or fluid) and selected command fuzing; for target detection and signature analysis; and for the target-intercept phase of terminal guidance. Performs weapon systems synthesis and analysis to determine characteristics that will effect fuze design to achieve maximum immunity to adverse influences, including counter-counter measures, nuclear environment, battlefield conditions and high-altitude and space environments. Performs basic and applied research, in support of assigned missions, on instrumentation, measurement and simulation; on materials, components and subsystems, including electronic timers for weapons; and on selected advanced energy transformation and control systems. Conducts basic research in the physical sciences. Performs basic and applied research on fluid devices and systems.

Address:

Commander
U.S. Army Harry Diamond Laboratories
2800 Powder Mill Road
Adelphi, Md. 20783

U.S. Army Materials and Mechanics Research Center

Principal Interests: Manages and directs that portion of the DARCOM materials research program conducted within its own laboratories, including basic scientific research, and research in metals, ceramics and other materials. Coordinates the total materials research program of DARCOM. Coordinates and manages a program of testing techniques, in conjunction with the quality-assurance program, and executes assigned portions of standardization programs.

Address:

Commander
U.S. Army Materials and Mechanics Research Center
Watertown, Mass. 02172

Ballistic Research Laboratories

Principal Interests: Conduct basic and applied research in interior and intermediate ballistics, kinematic analyses of automatic weapons mechanism, exterior and terminal ballistics. Determines the vulnerability of all types of military targets, both materiel and personnel, to various lethal mechanisms. Prepares firing tables for all Army weapons except designated guided missiles.

Address:

Commander
Ballistic Research Laboratories
Aberdeen Proving Ground, Md. 21005

Army Materiel Systems Analysis Agency

Principal Interests: Conducts systems analysis studies in order to develop measures of small arms system effectivenesses; evaluates concepts and proposals in accordance with these measures, and develops techniques and methodology associated with the systems analysis function. Participates in the design and analysis of experiments to define performance as a function of system parameters. Establishes the requirement for data banks on subjects basic to systems analysis activities and provides systems analysis input data, such as hit probabilities, probabilities of incapacitation, etc., for larger systems studies performed by other agencies or services.

Address:

Commander
Army Material System Analysis Agency
Aberdeen Proving Ground, Md. 21002

Human Engineering Laboratories

Principal Interests: Performs research in life sciences regarding human factors in quantifying the capabilities and limitations of human performance in tasks associated with small arms. Conducts experiments and analysis to obtain data which define such performance as a function of weapon design parameters. Conducts simulation of the environmental hazards, such as noise, blast, etc., to which a firer is subjected during use of the weapons in order to assess their effort on human performance. Assists design agencies in the application of human factors engineering principles to design and development of end items.

Address:

Commander
Human Engineering Laboratories
Aberdeen Proving Ground, Md. 21005

U.S. Army Test and Evaluation Command

The Commanding General, U.S. Army Test and Evaluation Command is responsible for planning and conducting engineering and service tests of Army materiel for DARCOM.

1. Aberdeen Proving Ground

Principal Interests: Conduct of research and development, production and post production testing of components and complete items of weapons, systems, ammunition, and combat and support vehicles. Also tests numerous items of individual equipment in use Army wide.

Address:

Commanding Officer
Aberdeen Proving Ground
Maryland 21005

3. Jefferson Proving Ground

Principal Interests: Processing, assembling and acceptance testing of ammunition and ammunition components. Receives, stores, maintains and issues assigned industrial stocks, including calibrated components.

Address:

Commanding Officer
Jefferson Proving Ground
Madison, Ind. 47250

4. White Sands Missile Range

Principal Interests: Conducts testing and evaluation of Army missiles and rockets. Operates the United States' only land based National Range to support missile and other testing for the Army, Air Force, Navy and National Aeronautics and Space Administration.

Address:

Commanding General
White Sands Missile Range
New Mexico 88002

5. Yuma Proving Ground

Principal Interests: Conduct of research and development, production and post production testing of components and complete items of weapons, systems, ammunition, and combat and support vehicles. Desert environmental tests of some items, air drop and air delivery tests and participation in engineering and expanded service testing of combat and support items.

Address:

Commanding Officer
Yuma Proving Ground
Arizona 85364

Office of the Chief of Engineers

The Chief of Engineers, Department of the Army, is responsible for basic and applied research and development for construction and related activities. The Office of the Chief of Engineers provides supervisory, planning, and budgetary direction to the subordinate activities where the programs are executed and administered.

1. U.S. Army Engineer, Waterways Experiment Station

Principal Interests: Conducts engineering research, development and investigations in the fields of hydraulics, flexible pavements, soils and concrete.

Address:

Director
P.O. Box 631
Vicksburg, Miss. 39180.

2. U.S. Army Cold Regions Research and Engineering Laboratory

Principal Interests: Conducts basic and applied research for construction in snow, ice, and frozen ground.

Address:

Commander/Director
Hanover, N. H. 03755

3. U.S. Army Construction Engineering Research Laboratory

Principal Interests: Conducts research and engineering studies in materials, utilities, foundations, and structural requirements for construction of buildings.

Address:

Director
P.O. Box 4005
Champaign, Ill. 61820

4. U.S. Army Engineer Topographic Laboratories

Principal Interests: Conducts research and development in the field of topography.

Address:

Commander
Fort Belvoir, Va. 22060

5. U.S. Army Coastal Engineering Research Center

Principal Interests: Conducts research and development in all fields of coastal engineering.

Address:

5201 Little Falls Road, NW.
Washington, D.C. 20016

Office of the Surgeon General

The Surgeon General, Department of the Army, is responsible for research and development in areas of basic and applied medical and scientific research applicable to medical sciences, supplies and equipment. Contracts are executed and administered by one command.

1. U.S. Army Medical Research and Development Command

Principal Interests: Basic and applied research and development relating to medical sciences, supplies and equipment.

Address:

Commanding General
U.S. Army Medical Research and Development Command
Office of the Surgeon General
Washington, D.C. 20315

Department of the Navy

The Navy's research and development programs are accomplished primarily through the Naval Material Command which includes the Naval Air Systems Command, Naval Electronic Systems Command, Naval Engineering Facilities Command, Naval Sea Systems Command, and the Naval Supply Systems Command; the Bureau of Navy Personnel; the Naval Medical Research and Development Command; and the Office of Naval Research.

These activities support research and development programs within their specific fields of interest. This is accomplished through the use of government installations as well as through work performed under contract by business concerns and educational and nonprofit institutions.

Office of Naval Research

This office is concerned with the support of research and technology which is potentially relevant to the missions of the Navy and Marine Corps. Contract awards usually result from unsolicited proposals submitted by scientific organizations. The interests of the office are covered under two major headings:

1. Naval Research

Principal Interests: Physics, electronic and solid state sciences, logistics, mathematical sciences, operations research, statistics and probability, information and computer sciences, fluid dynamics, physiology and biomedicine, medical and dental sciences, organizational effectiveness, engineering psychology, personnel and training research,

Arctic research, geography, earth physics, atmospheric sciences, metallurgy, chemistry, energy research, structural mechanics and oceanography.

2. Naval Technology

Principal Interests: Research and exploratory developments on new technology, concepts and systems for flight, surface and undersea vehicles and their various subsystems, including sensors. Aerodynamics, controls, advanced flight and underwater weapon design, mines and mine warfare, countermeasures, displays, acoustics, signal processing, and advanced power or propulsion concepts are areas of interest. Work is also supported in operational analysis to solve operational forces problems and to provide guidance and new alternatives in Navy planning.

Address:

Chief of Naval Research
Department of the Navy
800 North Quincy St.
Arlington, Va. 22217

Bureau of Naval Personnel

Principal Interests: Applied research in personnel administration and related behavioral sciences contributing to improved management and utilization of manpower.

Address:

Chief of Naval Personnel
Department of the Navy
Washington, D.C. 20370
Tel: 202/694–1053

Naval Medical Research and Development Command

Principal Interests: Aviation medicine, trauma care, fleet occupational health care, human performance, dental research, submarine and diving medical research, and infectious disease.

Address:

Commanding Officer
Naval Medical Research and Development Command
Department of the Navy
National Naval Medical Center
Bethesda, Maryland 20014
Tel: 301/295–1053

Naval Air Systems Command

Principal Interests: Design, development, testing and evaluation of naval airframes, aircraft engines, components, and fuels and lubricants therefor; airborne versions of electronic equipment, pyrotechnics, and minesweeping equipment; air launched weapon systems and underwater sound systems; aircraft drone and target systems; catapults, arresting gear, visual landing aids, photographic equipment, meteorological equipment, ground handling equipment for aircraft, parachutes, flight clothing, and survival equipment.

Address:

Commander
Naval Air Systems Command
Department of the Navy
Washington, D.C. 20361
Tel: 202/692–3064

Naval Electronic Systems Command

Principal Interests: Research, development, test and evaluation for command, control and communications; underseas and space surveillance; electronic warfare; navigational aids; electronic test equipment; electronic materials, components and devices.

Address:

Commander
Naval Electronic Systems Command
Department of the Navy
Washington, D.C. 20360
Tel: 202/692–6413

Naval Facilities Engineering Command

Principal Interests: Research and development program is directed toward items of new or improved materials, equipment, or engineering techniques which will significantly improve solutions to specific engineering problems pertaining to the technical planning, design, construction, operation, and maintenance of the shore facilities and related material and equipment.

Address:

Commander
Naval Facilities Engineering Command
Department of the Navy
200 Stovall Street
Alexandria, Virginia 22332
Tel: 202/325–8537

Naval Sea Systems Command

Principal Interests: Research, development, testing, and evaluation in the fields of ship structures, hydromechanics, ship machinery, nuclear propulsion, shipboard surveillance, navigation, communications, mine and torpedo countermeasures, noise, vibration, shock, materials, fuels and lubricants, oceanography, and data processing techniques and equipment. Research, design, development, test and evaluation in the fields of surface and air launched undersea weapons systems, complete shipboard weapons systems, submarine weapons loading, handling and launching systems; components including guns, ammunition, mines, torpedoes, associated radar fire control systems, weapons direction equipment and launchers. Research, exploratory development and advanced development (non system oriented) for explosives, propellants, acoustics, and actuating technology therefor, electromagnetics, explosive ordnance demolition and special equipment for explosive ordnance disposal.

Address:

Commander, Naval Sea Systems Command
Department of the Navy
Washington, D.C. 20362
Tel: 202/692–1157

Naval Supply Systems Command

Principal Interests: Research and development in supply systems management techniques, including mathematical and statistical analyses, materials handling, clothing and textiles, transportation, and logistics data processing systems.

Address:

Commander
Naval Supply Systems Command
Department of the Navy
Washington, D.C. 20376
Tel: 202/697-4561

Naval Research Laboratory

Principal Interests: Conducts scientific research and development in materials, equipment, techniques, and systems for the Navy; major fields of interest are electronics, materials and general sciences, space science technology, and oceanology.

Address:

Director
Naval Research Laboratory
4555 Overlook Avenue SW.
Washington, D.C. 20375
Tel: 202/767-3698

Civil Engineering Laboratory

Principal Interests: Principal Navy research, development, test and evaluation center for shore and seafloor facilities and the support of Navy and Marine Corps construction forces.

Address:

Commanding Officer
Naval Civil Engineering Laboratory
Naval Construction Battalion Center
Port Hueneme, Calif. 93043
Tel: 805/982-4696

Naval Underwater Systems Center, New London Laboratory

Principal Interests: Principal research, development, test, and evaluation center for underwater combat systems.

Address:

Commanding Officer
Naval Underwater Systems Center,
New London Laboratory
New London, Conn. 06320
Tel: 203/442-0771, Ext. 2202

Naval Coastal Systems Laboratory

Principal Interests: Research, development, test, and evaluation for the application of science and technology associated with military operations carried out primarily in the coastal regions, and to perform investigations in related fields of science and technology.

Address:

Commanding Officer
Naval Coastal Systems Laboratory
Panama City, Fla. 32401
Tel: 904/234-4392

Naval Surface Weapons Center, White Oak Laboratory

Principal Interests: Basic and applied research in physics, chemistry, aeroballistics, and mathematics in areas that relate to weapons; development and evaluation of both conventional and nuclear weapons.

Address:

Commander
Naval Surface Weapons Center,
White Oak Laboratory
Silver Spring, Md. 20910
Tel: 202/394-1865

Naval Underwater Systems Center, Newport Laboratory

Principal Interests: Plan and conduct programs of warfare and systems analyses, research, development, test evaluation and fleet support in underseas surveillance systems, navigation and related science and technology.

Address:

Commanding Officer
Naval Underwater Systems Center
Newport Laboratory
Newport, Rhode Island 02840

Naval Ship Engineering Center

Principal Interests: Research and development programs in advanced and engineering development for materials ship production, safety and damage control, new ship systems design, hull structures and fluid dynamics, electrical and mechanical and auxiliary systems and ship propulsion and control and electronic command surveillance systems. Responsibility limited to non-nuclear propulsion.

Address:

Commander
Naval Ship Engineering Center
Department of Navy
Washington, D.C. 20362

Naval Air Test Center

Principal Interests: Conducts test and evaluation of aircraft weapons systems and their components.

Address:

Commanding Officer
Naval Air Test Center
Patuxent River, Md. 20670
Tel: 301/863-4207

Naval Air Propulsion Test Center

Principal Interests: Test and evaluate air breathing gas turbine propulsion systems and components and accessories and fuels and lubricants; and perform applied research and development leading to new propulsion systems and the correction of design deficiencies and service problems.

Address:

Commanding Officer
Naval Air Propulsion Test Center
Trenton, N.J. 08628
Tel: 609/882-1414, Ext. 373

Naval Air Development Center

Principal Interests: Visual, fixed-base, and dynamic simulation systems for: terrain avoidance; carrier landing of aircraft; personnel search, detection, and rescue; and reconnaissance. Aircrew personal safety; protective and survival equipment; flotation and anti-exposure systems; emer-gency escape, restraining, and oxygen breathing systems. Aircraft structures; missile weapons systems; instrumentation; and test equipment. Missile propulsion; aerial targets; towed bodies; weapons suspension and landing equipment; flight and engine instruments; inertial platforms; photo reconnaissance and detection systems. Aircraft hydraulic systems and fluids; compressed and liquified gases; elastomers; sealants; adhesives; plastics; laminating resins; sandwich constructions; textiles; fibers; polymer synthesis; lubricants; bonded films; bearings; fluid systems; structural alloys; high temperature materials; inorganic matrix composites; corrosion protective coatings. Magnetics; electro-optics; electronic navigation; fire-control; missile guidance; electronic warfare; radar; radomes; antennas; data processing; underwater acoustics; sonobuoys; microelectronic circuitry; data transmission; digital logic communication; electric accessories. Air-to-air, strike, and support warfare analyses; antisubmarine warfare systems; analog and digital computers.

Address:

Commander
Naval Air Development Center
Warminster, Pa. 18974
Tel: 215/672-9000

Naval Air Engineering Center

Principal Interests: Research, engineering, development, development test, evaluation, systems integration, limited production, and fleet engineering support in launching, recovery, and landing aids for aircraft and in ground support equipment for aircraft and airborne weapons systems; and support of Department of Defense standardization and specifications programs.

Address:

Commanding Officer
Naval Air Engineering Center
Lakehurst, New Jersey 08735
Tel: 201/323-2744 or 657-4912

Naval Surface Weapons Center, Dahlgren Laboratory

Principal Interests: Research, development, test and evaluation in the field of exterior, interior and terminal ballistics, ordnance systems, and ordnance materials.

Address:

Commander
Naval Surface Weapons Center,
Dahlgren Laboratory
Dahlgren, Va. 22448
Tel: 703/663-7584

Naval Weapons Center

Principal Interests: Research, development, test, and evaluation relating to air warfare and missile systems including technology-base effort in missile propulsion, warheads, fuzes, avionics and fire control, missile guidance; and participation as lead laboratory or DPM on various total-weapons system developments.

Address:

Commander
Naval Weapons Center
China Lake, Calif. 93555
Tel: 714/939-3555

Naval Missile Center

Principal Interests: To perform test, evaluation, development support and exercise engineering cognizance over certain naval weapons, weapon systems, and related components.

Address:

Commanding Officer
Naval Missile Center
Point Mugu, Calif. 93042
Tel: 805/982-8914

Naval Ocean Systems Center

Principal Interests: Research, development, test and evaluation for command control, communications, ocean surveillance, surface and air-launched undersea weapons systems and supporting terminologies.

Address:

Commander
Naval Ocean Systems Center
San Diego, Calif. 92152

Naval Training Equipment Center

Principal Interests: Responsible for the procurement of training aids and equipment for the Army, Navy, Marine Corps, Air Force and other Government activities, including the following: (i) research investigations and exploratory development in simulation technology and techniques, (ii) investigations and studies in the fields of training psychology, human factors and human engineering, (iii) design and engineering development of training equipment, weapons system trainers and simulators, and (iv) technical data and related ancillary support materials and services.

Address:

Commanding Officer
Naval Training Equipment Center
Orlando, Fla. 32813
Tel: 305/646-5464

Naval Ship Research and Development Center

Principal Interests: Research, development, test, and evaluation of naval vehicles, including system development and analyses, fleet support and investigations into related field of science and technology, including hydromechanics, aeromechanics, structures, computer technology, machinery and materials.

Address:

Commander
Naval Ship Research and Development Center
Bethesda, Maryland 20084
Tel: 202/227-1417

Naval Weapons Support Center

Principal Interests: Research development, design, engineering, and in-service engineering pertaining to pyrotechnics, chemical and demolition devices, and other designated ordnance items. Specialized studies in operations research and manufacturing technology. Additional endeavors in the applied sciences field.

Address:

Commanding Officer
Naval Weapons Support Center (Code 50)
Crane, Ind. 47522

Naval Avionics Facility

Principal Interests: Research, development, pilot and limited manufacturing and depot maintenance on avionics and related equipment.

Address:

Commanding Officer
Naval Avionics Facility
6000 E. 21st Street
Indianapolis, Ind. 46218
Tel: 317/353–3011

Naval Explosive Ordnance Disposal Facility

Principal Interests: Conducts exploratory development studies and programs to provide technology base to support the consolidated Department of Defense explosive ordnance disposal (EOD) mission. Defines tool and technology requirements in terms of technical development parameters to guide tool development program. Conducts advance development projects resulting in the development of EOD tools and equipment for all Armed Services. Conducts and/or monitors technical evaluation (functional, environmental, and limited operational evaluation) of prototype tools and equipment. Provides technical capability to deal with Armed Services field problems.

Address:

Commanding Officer
Naval Explosive Ordnance Disposal Facility
Indian Head, Md. 20640
Tel: 301/743–4530

Naval Ordnance Missile Test Facility

Principal Interests: Supports research, development, test, and evaluation programs in the flight testing of guided missiles and to support endo and exo-atmospheric research in the launching of rockets.

Address:

Commanding Officer
Naval Ordnance Missile Test Facility
White Sands Missile Range, N. Mex. 88002
Tel: 915/678–3531

Naval Ship Missile Systems Engineering Station

Principal Interests: Research, development, test, and evaluation of programs for ships guided weapons systems.

Address:

Commanding Officer
Naval Ship Missile Systems Engineering Station
Port Hueneme, Calif. 93043
Tel: 805/982–5801

Naval Ordnance Station

Principal Interests: Research, development, test, and evaluation of ammunition, pyrotechnics and solid propellants used in missiles, rockets, and guns.

Address:

Commanding Officer
Naval Ordnance Station
Indian Head, Md. 20640
Tel: 301/743–4650

Naval Weapons Station

Principal Interests: Explosive loading development.

Address:

Commanding Officer
Naval Weapons Station
Yorktown, Va. 23691
Tel: 703/887–4767

Naval Oceanographic Office

Principal Interests: Research and development in area of oceanographic, hydrographic, and geodetic equipment, techniques and systems.

Address:

Commander
Naval Oceanographic Office, NSTL Branch (Code 4130)
Bay St. Louis, Miss. 39522
Tel: 601/688–4162

Department of the Air Force

Management of Air Force research and development is under the direction of the Air Force Systems Command. The major portion of Air Force research and development is procured through Air Force Systems Command divisions and its centers.

Space and Missile Systems Organization

Principal Interests: Plans, programs, and manages the development and acquisition of missile and space systems and related equipment.

Address:

Commander (BC)
Space and Missile Systems Organization
Los Angeles Air Force Station
P.O. Box 92960, Worldway Postal Center
Los Angeles, Calif. 90009

Space and Missile Test Center

Principal Interests: Test Range instrumentation procurement within this broad field may require research, development and product engineering, or any combination of these tasks in radar, telemetry, electro-optics, range instrumentation, ships, aircraft, impact location, data handling, data reduction, communication, range and mission control, range safety, weather timing and firing, and frequency control and analysis.

Address:

Commander (BC)
Space and Missile Test Center
Vandenberg Air Force Base
Lompoc, Calif. 93437

Aerospace Medical Division

Principal Interests: Procurement of research, development and testing in the following areas: Life sciences, human factors, aerospace medicine, biosciences, biomedicine, behavioral sciences, space medicine, biotechnology, human engineering, human resources, aviation medicine, space biology and medical equipment.

For Procurement Information Contact:

Directorate of R&D Procurement (BC)
Aeronautical Systems Division
Wright-Patterson Air Force Base, Ohio 45433

Electronics Systems Division

Principal Interests: Procurement of research and development relating to command and control systems, and related equipment, systems for data collection, transmission and display, development work necessary to permit exercise of weapon, command, executive control associated with Air Force aerospace operations.

Address:

Commander (BC)
Air Force Electronic Systems Division
Hanscom Air Force Base
Bedford, Mass. 01731

Aeronautical Systems Division

Principal Interests: Development and acquisition of aeronautical systems, sub-systems, their components, and related government-furnished aerospace equipment (GFAE) including, but not limited to, aircraft engines, aircraft wheels and brakes, airborne communication systems, aircraft bombing and navigation systems, aircraft instruments; aeronautical reconnaissance systems, sub-systems, special reconnaissance projects, and mobile land based tactical information processing and interpretation facilities.

Address:

Commander (BC)
Air Force Aeronautical Systems Division
Wright-Patterson Air Force Base, Ohio 45433

Directorate of Research and Development Procurement (an Organization Element of Aeronautical Systems Division)

Principal Interests: Procurement of exploratory and advanced research and development in the areas of air breathing, electric and advanced propulsion, fuels and lubricants, power generation. Transmission and reception (above 15 GC) molecular electronics, bionics, lasers, vehicle environment, photo materials and optronics, position and motion sensing devices, navigation, guidance, reconnaissance and avionics, communications. Flight dynamics, structures, aerodynamics, aerothermodynamics, control displays and crew sta-

402

tion, aerodynamic accelerators and escape, alighting and orbital attachment, airframe and equipment bearing, flight testing techniques. Material sciences metals and ceramics, nonmetallic materials, manufacturing technology. Subareas of life support, aerospace medicine and human performance, environmental effects, techniques and equipment for well being, protection and performance enhancement in subareas of biodynamic forces and energies, altitude thermal, toxic hazards, bionics, human engineering and training. Basic research in selected areas of applied mathematics, organic, inorganic radiation and molecular chemistry, plasma, atomic, theoretical, nuclear and solid state physics, metallurgy and ceramics, heat transfer, energy conversion and fluid dynamics.

Address:

Directorate of R&D Procurement (BC)
(An organizational element of Aeronautical Systems Division)
Wright-Patterson Air Force Base, Ohio 45433

Air Force Flight Test Center

Principal Interests: Supports advanced development programs in four principal areas:

(1) Flight testing and evaluation of all new aircraft planned for inventory production and aerospace research vehicles, including fixed wing, VTOL, STOL, lifting body, and other experimental manned flight vehicles.

(2) Training experimental and aerospace research pilots.

(3) Development testing and evaluation of new parachutes (Personnel and Cargo), deceleration and retardation devices, and aerial delivery and recovery systems.

(4) Development, testing, and evaluation of rocket propulsion systems, including static test of complete engines, and investigation and synthesis of new propellant formulations—liquid, solid; and hybrid. The principal technical organizations and their subsidiary elements conducting R & D activities at the AFFTC are: (1) Technical Support Office (TS)—Technical Support Development Division (TSE) (2) USAF Aerospace Research Pilot School (AV)—R&D Division (AVR) (3) 6511th Test Group (Parachute) (TG), located at El Centro, California—Engineering Division (TGTE) (4) Air Force Rocket Propulsion Laboratory (AFRPL)—Liquid Rocket Division

(RPL/LK), Solid Rocket Division (RPL/MK), Test and Support Division (RPL/TS), Technology Division (RPL/RT).

Address:

Commander (BC)
Air Force Flight Test Center
Edwards Air Force Base, Calif. 93523

Air Force Contract Management Division Kirtland Procurement Center

Principal Interests: Test and engineering pertaining to Nuclear Weapon Systems equipment. Specific engineering interests include: Nuclear effects simulation, analysis of nuclear effects and the reaction of equipment to these effects, telemetry, instrumentation weapons/aircraft flight characteristics, high speed camera techniques. The Center is concerned with test and evaluation on systems, subsystems, and support equipment for nuclear safety, reliability, compatibility, survivability and vulnerability. The Center provides Air Force resources to support AEC/DOD nuclear test operations or training exercises both in the United States and overseas. This support includes providing the staff nucleus for exercises and developing operational concepts and plans.

Address:

Commander (BC–39)
Kirtland Procurement Center
Air Force Contract Management Division
Kirtland Air Force Base, N. Mex. 87115

Air Force Weapons Laboratory

Principal Interests: Research in the areas of weapons effects, kill mechanisms, radiation hazards, and delivery techniques. Delevopment and evaluation programs for advanced non-conventional weapon and nuclear power systems integration, nuclear weapon components, training devices, suspension and release systems, ground handling equipment, nuclear safety studies and civil engineering research. The design and development of weapons effects simulation devices and techniques.

Address:

Commander (BC–39)
Kirtland Procurement Center
Air Force Contract Management Division
Kirtland Air Force Base, N. Mex. 87115

Air Force Eastern Test Range

Principal Interests: The Air Force Eastern Test Range Research & Development central procurement program is confined primarily to range test instrumentation. Principal interests are: Test range instrumentation involving radar, trajectory computers and recorders, tracking and target analysis, wire communications, radio communications, programming timing and firing systems, telemetry receiving, data storage, data separation and presentation, optics and telemetry data reduction; develops, maintains and operates the Test Range and provides support for the Department of Defense missile and space programs.

Address:

Commander (BC)
Air Force Eastern Test Range
Patrick Air Force Base, Fla. 32925

Rome Air Development Center

Principal Interests: Surveillance, electronic intelligence, communications, computer and data processing techniques, textual data processing, intelligence extraction from aerial reconnaissance, data presentation, high power electromagnetic generators, receivers, transmission line components, microelectronics applications, reliability and maintainability, survivability, propagation, vulnerability reduction, electronic countermeasures, and electromagnetic weapons.

Address:

Commander (BC)
Rome Air Development Center
Griffis Air Force Base
New York, N.Y. 13441

Armament Development and Test Center

Principal Interests: Procurement of research, development and test related to the evaluation of guns and other aircraft weapons, new explosives, non-nuclear munitions, bomb warheads, chemical-biological weapons, dispensers, target, and scorers, equipment and the application of equipment or new techniques for counter-insurgency operations, testing of Air Force tactics and techniques, test ranges for aircraft and missile systems testing and an electro-magnetic test environment for ECM and ECCM.

Address:

Commander (BC)
Armament Test and Development Center
Eglin Air Force Base, Fla. 32542

Arnold Engineering Development

Principal Interests: Arnold Center is an Air Force Systems Command center with test laboratories in which atmospheric conditions, orbital, space flight, and ballistic conditions can be simulated. The Center functions as a service to the aerospace industry, to educational institutions, and to military and civilian agencies of the Federal Government which are concerned in aerospace research and development. Tests conducted at the Center aid in the development of aircraft, missile, satellite and space programs. Five major laboratories have a total of thirty-six testing units, including wind tunnels, high altitude propulsion test cells, space simulation chambers, impact ballistic ranges and research units. Conditions of flight can be simulated ranging from sea level conditions to those encountered in an orbital altitude of approximately three hundred miles, and velocities from the subsonic to well above Mach 20. Equipment or vehicles tested can range in size from a small-scale model to a full-scale vehicle with its propulsion system installed and operating. Research associated with high temperatures and unique mechanical, electrical, and thermodynamic investigations relating to high-altitudes propulsion test cells, wind tunnels and space simulation chambers is frequently carried out by contracts with industry or educational institutions. Examples of research carried out by contract are: Development of a magnetohydrodynamic generator burner system; a study to develop a hypervelocity impact data recorder; a study of MHD channel flows; a study to develop preliminary design criteria for a space guidance environmental facility; study and develop diagnostic techniques; study of surface catalysis in non-equilibrium flows; a study of a hypervelocity light gas gun augmentation technique; feasibility study of high density shock tunnel augmented by a magnetohydrodynamic accelerator; a study to develop criteria for the design of an arc heater mixing chamber; study of leak detection in a large aerospace systems environmental chamber.

Research Opportunities

Industrial concerns and non-profit organizations having research capabilities in major scientific fields, and whose personnel include competent scientific investigators may submit basic research proposals to the below office.

The Air Force Office of Scientific Research encourages and supports fundamental research designed to increase understanding of the natural sciences and to stimulate the recognition of new scientific concepts. The primary concern of the AFOSR is with the ability of the investigators and their research preferences. Particularly desired is the original and unique scientific approach likely to clarify or extend understanding of the sciences which are of interest to the principal technical Directorates of AFOSR.

The principal Directorates and major Divisions of AFOSR are: Directorate of Aeromechanics and Energetics (NA)—Aeromechanics Division (NAM)—Energetics Division (NAE). The Directorate of Electronic and Solid State Sciences (NE). The Directorate of Life Sciences (NL). The Directorate of Mathematical and Information Sciences (NM). The Directorate of Physics (NP)—General Physics Division (NPP)—Geophysics Division (NPG).

The AFOSR accepts unsolicited proposals for basis research grants or contracts. Any scientific investigator may make a preliminary inquiry to obtain advice on the degree of interest in his area of research, or may submit a specific research proposal. A proposal should indicate the field of investigation and the objectives sought, describing previous work and related grants or contracts held, if any; in addition, it should outline the approach planned for the research and should include estimates of the time and cost requirements. The principal investigator should be named and an outline of his professional background included.

Each proposal will be evaluated by the appropriate Directorate from the standpoint of its probable value to the Air Force basic research program, of the current availability of funds, and of other relevant factors. In some cases it may be necessary for the Directorate to request additional details prior to rendering a decision as to sponsorship.

Address:

Directorate of Procurement (BC)
Air Force Office of Scientific Research
Bolling Air Force Base
Washington, D.C. 20322

STANDARD FORM 129
JANUARY 1966 EDITION
FPR (41 CFR) 1-16.802

BIDDER'S MAILING LIST APPLICATION

INITIAL APPLICATION
REVISION

Fill in all spaces. Insert "NA" in blocks not applicable. Type or print all entries. See reverse for instructions.

TO (Enter name and address of Federal agency to which form is submitted. Include ZIP code)	DATE

1. APPLICANT'S NAME AND ADDRESS (Include county and ZIP code)	2. ADDRESS (Include county and ZIP code) TO WHICH SOLICITATIONS ARE TO BE MAILED (If different from item 1)

3. TYPE OF ORGANIZATION (Check one)

INDIVIDUAL	PARTNERSHIP	NON-PROFIT ORGANIZATION	4. HOW LONG IN PRESENT BUSINESS
CORPORATION, INCORPORATED UNDER THE LAWS OF THE STATE OF			

5. NAMES OF OFFICERS, OWNERS, OR PARTNERS

PRESIDENT	VICE PRESIDENT	SECRETARY
TREASURER	OWNERS OR PARTNERS	

6. AFFILIATES OF APPLICANT (Names, locations, and nature of affiliation. See definition on reverse)

7. PERSONS AUTHORIZED TO SIGN BIDS, OFFERS, AND CONTRACTS IN YOUR NAME (Indicate if agent)

NAME	OFFICIAL CAPACITY	TEL. NO. (Incl. area code)

8. IDENTIFY EQUIPMENT, SUPPLIES, MATERIALS, AND/OR SERVICES ON WHICH YOU DESIRE TO BID (See attached Federal agency's supplemental listing and instructions, if any)

9. TYPE OF BUSINESS (See definitions on reverse)

MANUFACTURER OR PRODUCER	REGULAR DEALER (Type 1)	REGULAR DEALER (Type 2)
SERVICE ESTABLISHMENT	CONSTRUCTION CONCERN	RESEARCH AND DEVELOPMENT FIRM

☐ SURPLUS DEALER (Check this box if you are also a dealer in surplus goods)

10. SIZE OF BUSINESS (See definitions on reverse)

SMALL BUSINESS CONCERN *	OTHER THAN SMALL BUSINESS CONCERN	
* If you are a small business concern, fill in (a) and (b):	(a) AVERAGE NUMBER OF EMPLOYEES (Including affiliates) FOR FOUR PRECEDING CALENDAR QUARTERS	(b) AVERAGE ANNUAL SALES OR RECEIPTS FOR PRECEDING THREE FISCAL YEARS

11. FLOOR SPACE (Square feet)		12. NET WORTH	
MANUFACTURING	WAREHOUSE	DATE	AMOUNT

13. SECURITY CLEARANCE (If applicable, check highest clearance authorized)

FOR	TOP SECRET	SECRET	CONFIDENTIAL	NAMES OF AGENCIES WHICH GRANTED SECURITY CLEARANCES (Include dates)
KEY PERSONNEL				
PLANT ONLY				

THIS SPACE FOR USE BY THE GOVERNMENT	CERTIFICATION
	I CERTIFY THAT INFORMATION SUPPLIED HEREIN (Including all pages attached) IS CORRECT AND THAT NEITHER THE APPLICANT NOR ANY PERSON (Or concern) IN ANY CONNECTION WITH THE APPLICANT AS A PRINCIPAL OR OFFICER, SO FAR AS IS KNOWN, IS NOW DEBARRED OR OTHERWISE DECLARED INELIGIBLE BY ANY AGENCY OF THE FEDERAL GOVERNMENT FROM BIDDING FOR FURNISHING MATERIALS, SUPPLIES, OR SERVICES TO THE GOVERNMENT OR ANY AGENCY THEREOF. SIGNATURE
	NAME AND TITLE OF PERSON AUTHORIZED TO SIGN (Type or print)

406

INFORMATION AND INSTRUCTIONS

Persons or concerns wishing to be added to a particular agency's bidder's mailing list for supplies or services shall file this properly completed and certified Bidder's Mailing List Application, together with such other lists as may be attached to the application form, with each procurement office of the Federal agency with which they desire to do business. If a Federal agency has attached a supplemental Commodity List with instructions, complete the application as instructed. Otherwise, identify in Item 8 the equipment, supplies, and/or services on which you desire to bid. *The application shall be submitted and signed by the principal as distinguished from an agent, however constituted.*

After placement on the bidder's mailing list of an agency, a supplier's failure to respond *(submission of bid, or notice in writing, that you are unable to bid on that particular transaction but wish to remain on the active bidder's mailing list for that particular item)* to Invitations for Bids will be understood by the agency to indicate lack of interest and concurrence in the removal of the supplier's name from the purchasing activity's bidder's mailing list for the items concerned.

TYPE OF BUSINESS DEFINITIONS
(See Item No. 9)

A. MANUFACTURER OR PRODUCER means a person (or concern) owning, operating, or maintaining a factory or establishment that produces, on the premises, the materials, supplies, articles, or equipment of the general character of those listed in Item No. 8, or in the Federal Agency's supplemental Commodity List, if attached.

B. REGULAR DEALER (Type 1) means a person (or concern) who owns, operates, or maintains a store, warehouse, or other establishment in which the materials, supplies, articles, or equipment of the general character listed in Item No. 8 or in the Federal Agency's supplemental Commodity List, if attached, are bought, kept in stock, and sold to the public in the usual course of business.

C. REGULAR DEALER (Type 2) in the case of supplies of particular kinds *(at present, petroleum, lumber and timber products, machine tools, raw cotton, green coffee, hay, grain, feed, or straw, agricultural liming materials, tea, raw or unmanufactured cotton linters).* "REGULAR DEALER" means a person (or concern) satisfying the requirements of the regulations (Code of Federal Regulations, Title 41, 50–201.101(b)) as amended from time to time, prescribed by the Secretary of Labor under the Walsh-Healey Public Contracts Act (Title 41 U.S. Code 35–45). For coal dealers, see Code of Federal Regulations, Title 41, 50–201.604(a).

D. SERVICE ESTABLISHMENT means a concern (or person) which owns, operates, or maintains any type of business which is principally engaged in the furnishing of nonpersonal services, such as *(but not limited to)* repairing, cleaning, redecorating, or rental of personal property, including the furnishing of necessary repair parts or other supplies as part of the services performed.

E. CONSTRUCTION CONCERN means a concern (or person) engaged in construction, alteration or repair (including dredging, excavating, and painting) of buildings, structures or other real property.

DEFINITIONS RELATING TO SIZE OF BUSINESS

A. SMALL BUSINESS CONCERN. A small business concern for the purpose of Government procurement is a concern, including its affiliates, which is independently owned and operated, is not dominant in the field of operation in which it is bidding on Government contracts and can further qualify under the criteria concerning number of employees, average annual receipts, or other criteria, as prescribed by the Small Business Administration. (See Code of Federal Regulations, Title 13, Part 121, as amended, which contains detailed industry definitions and related procedures.)

B. AFFILIATES. Business concerns are affiliates of each other when either directly or indirectly (i) one concern controls or has the power to control the other, or (ii) a third party controls or has the power to control both. In determining whether concerns are independently owned and operated and whether or not affiliation exists, consideration is given to all appropriate factors including common ownership, common management, and contractual relationship. (See Items Nos. 6 and 10.)

C. NUMBER OF EMPLOYEES. In connection with the determination of small business status, "number of employees" means the average employment of any concern, including the employees of its domestic and foreign affiliates, based on the number of persons employed on a full-time, part-time, temporary, or any other basis during the pay period ending nearest the last day of the third month in each calendar quarter for the preceding four quarters. If a concern has not been in existence for four full calendar quarters, "number of employees" means the average employment of such concern and its affiliates during the period such concern has been in existence based on the number of persons employed during the pay period ending nearest the last day of each month. (See Item No. 10.)

COMMERCE BUSINESS DAILY

The Commerce Business Daily, published by the Department of Commerce, contains information concerning proposed procurements, sales, and contract awards. For further information concerning this publication, contact your local Commerce Field Office.

<table>
<tr>
<td colspan="2">U. S. POSTAL SERVICE

BIDDER'S MAILING LIST APPLICATION</td>
<td colspan="2">NOTE: See Instructions on reverse before completion. Type or print all entries. Insert "NA" in items not applicable.</td>
</tr>
<tr>
<td>TO:</td>
<td colspan="3">Western Area Supply Center, Data Automation Division, Attn: Bidder's Mailing List
P.O. Box 19065, Topeka, Kansas 66624</td>
</tr>
</table>

1.	A. PARENT COMPANY *(Name Only)*		EMPLOYER IDENTIFICATION NO.
	B. DIVISION *(Name Only)*		EMPLOYER IDENTIFICATION NO.
NAME AND ADDRESS	ADDRESS TO WHICH SOLICITATIONS ARE TO BE MAILED		
	C. ATTENTION		
	D. STREET OR BOX NUMBER		
	E. CITY, STATE AND ZIP CODE		

2. APPLICANT'S ADDRESS IF DIFFERENT FROM ITEM 1

3.	TYPE OF ORGANIZATION *(Check One)*	4. HOW LONG IN PRESENT BUSINESS
☐ A. INDIVIDUAL ☐ B. PARTNERSHIP ☐ C. NON-PROFIT ORGANIZATION ☐ D. CORPORATION: INCORPORATED UNDER THE LAWS OF THE STATE OF		

5.	NAMES OF OFFICERS, OWNERS, OR PARTNERS *(Type or Print)*	
PRESIDENT	VICE PRESIDENT	SECRETARY
TREASURER	OWNERS OR PARTNERS	

6. AFFILIATES OF APPLICANT *(Names, locations, and nature of affiliation)*

7.	PERSONS AUTHORIZED TO SIGN BIDS, PROPOSALS, AND CONTRACTS IN YOUR NAME *(Indicate if agent)*	
NAME	OFFICIAL CAPACITY	TEL. NO. *(Include Area Code)*

8. IDENTIFY ITEMS ON WHICH YOU DESIRE TO BID BY MARKING THE CORRECT ITEM CODES AS SHOWN ON THE ATTACHED PS FORM 7429A. PS FORM 7429A MUST BE RETURNED WITH APPLICATION FOR APPLICANT TO BE PLACED ON BIDDER'S LIST.

9. TYPE OF BUSINESS *(See definitions on reverse)*	A. MANUFACTURER OR PRODUCER	B. REGULAR DEALER *(Type 1)*	C. REGULAR DEALER *(Type 2)*
	D. SERVICE ESTABLISHMENT	E. CONSTRUCTION CONCERN	F. RESEARCH AND DEVELOPMENT FIRM
	G. SURPLUS DEALER *(Check this block if you are also a dealer in surplus goods)*		

10.	SMALL BUSINESS/MINORITY ENTERPRISE IDENTIFICATION CODE *(Check One)*	
☐ A – SMALL BUSINESS CONCERN *(But not a minority enterprise)*	☐ B – MINORITY ENTERPRISE *(Whether or not a small business concern)*	☐ D – A BUSINESS CONCERN WHICH DOES NOT QUALIFY AS EITHER A SMALL BUSINESS OR MINORITY ENTERPRISE

CERTIFICATION

I CERTIFY THAT INFORMATION SUPPLIED HEREIN *(including all pages attached)* IS CORRECT AND THAT NEITHER THE APPLICANT NOR ANY PERSON *(or concern)* IN ANY CONNECTION WITH THE APPLICANT AS A PRINCIPAL OR OFFICER, SO FAR AS IS KNOWN, IS NOW DEBARRED OR OTHERWISE DECLARED INELIGIBLE BY ANY AGENCY OF THE FEDERAL GOVERNMENT FROM BIDDING FOR FURNISHING MATERIALS, SUPPLIES, OR SERVICES TO THE POSTAL SERVICE OR ANY AGENCY OF THE FEDERAL GOVERNMENT.

NAME AND TITLE OF PERSON AUTHORIZED TO SIGN *(Type or print)*	SIGNATURE	DATE

408

BIDDER'S MAILING LIST APPLICATION

COMMODITY AND GEOGRAPHIC LOCATION

CHECK-OFF

1.   An "X" preceding any geographic location listed
in Section 1 will limit the applicant to receipt of
solicitations for bids, proposals, or quotations issued
by those postal facilities located within the geographic
locations so designated. The absence of any "X" mark in
Section 1 will result in an applicant being given Postal
Service-wide solicitation consideration.

2.   An "X" preceding any commodity or service item code
listed in Section 2 will place the applicant on the U. S.
Postal Service Bidder's List for the items so designated.
Failure to mark any item code in Section 2 with an "X" voids
this application.

N O T I C E

This form must always accompany PS Form 7429, March 1975
or later revision.

SECTION 1

BIDDER'S GEOGRAPHIC MARKETING LIMITATIONS
(Leave blank if marketing area is national
in scope.)

___ 0X   New England and New Jersey
___ 00   Puerto Rico and the Virgin Islands
___ 01   Western Massachusetts
___ 02   Eastern Massachusetts and Rhode Island
___ 03   New Hampshire
___ 04   Maine
___ 05   Vermont
___ 06   Connecticut
___ 07   Northern New Jersey
___ 08   Southern New Jersey

___ 1X   New York, Pennsylvania, and Delaware
___ 10   Manhattan, Bronx, Staten Island
___ 11   Brooklyn, Queens, Long Island
___ 12   Eastern New York State
___ 13   North Central New York State
___ 14   Western New York State
___ 15   Southwestern Pennsylvania + DuBois
___ 16   Northwestern Pennsylvania + State College
___ 17   Central Pennsylvania
___ 18   Northeastern Pennsylvania
___ 19   Southeastern Pennsylvania and Delaware

___ 2X   Maryland, Virginia, West Virginia, North
          Carolina, South Carolina, and the District
          of Columbia
___ 20   Washington, D. C., and Suburbs
___ 21   Maryland
___ 22   Northern Virginia
___ 23   Southeastern Virginia
___ 24   Southwestern Virginia
___ 25   Southern West Virginia + Martinsburg
___ 26   Northern West Virginia
___ 27   Northern North Carolina
___ 28   South Carolina
___ 29   South Carolina

__	3X	Tennessee, Mississippi, Alabama, Georgia, and Florida
__	30	Northern and Northeastern Georgia
__	31	Central and Southern Georgia
__	32	Northern Florida + Melbourne
__	33	Southern Florida
__	34	Unassigned
__	35	Northern Alabama
__	36	Southern Alabama + Anniston
__	37	Eastern Tennessee + Nashville
__	38	Western Tennessee + Cookeville and Northern Mississippi
__	39	Southern Mississippi
__	4X	Michigan, Indiana, Ohio, and Kentucky
__	40	North Central to Southeastern Kentucky
__	41	Northern and Eastern Kentucky
__	42	Southern and Western Kentucky
__	43	Northwestern through East Central Ohio
__	44	Northeastern Ohio
__	45	Southern and Western Ohio
__	46	Northern and Central Indiana
__	47	Eastern, Western, and Southern Indiana
__	48	Eastern and East Central Michigan
__	49	Northern, Western, and Southern Michigan
__	5X	Montana, North and South Dakota, Minnesota, Wisconsin, and Iowa
__	50	Central and Southern Iowa
__	51	Western Iowa
__	52	Eastern Iowa
__	53	Southern and South Central Wisconsin
__	54	Northern Wisconsin
__	55	South Central and Eastern Minnesota
__	56	Southwestern and Western Minnesota
__	57	South Dakota
__	58	North Dakota
__	59	Montana
__	6X	Illinois, Missouri, Kansas, and Nebraska
__	60	Northeastern Illinois + Chicago
__	61	Northwestern through East Central Illinois
__	62	Western, Central, and Southern Illinois
__	63	Eastern Missouri
__	64	Western Missouri
__	65	Central through South Central Missouri
__	66	Eastern Kansas
__	67	Western Kansas
__	68	Eastern Nebraska
__	69	Western Nebraska

__	7X	Arkansas, Louisiana, Oklahoma, and Texas
__	70	Southern Louisiana
__	71	Northern Louisiana and Southern Arkansas
__	72	Northern Arkansas
__	73	Western Oklahoma
__	74	Eastern Oklahoma
__	75	Northeastern Texas
__	76	North Central Texas
__	77	Southeastern Texas
__	78	South Central Texas
__	79	Western Texas
__	8X	Colorado, Utah, Arizona, New Mexico, Nevada, Wyoming, and Idaho
__	80	Eastern Colorado
__	81	Western Colorado
__	82	Wyoming
__	83	Idaho
__	84	Utah
__	85	Southern Arizona
__	86	Northern Arizona
__	87	North Central and Western New Mexico
__	88	Eastern and Southern New Mexico
__	89	Nevada
__	9X	Washington, Oregon, California, Alaska, Hawaii and Pacific Islands
__	90	Los Angeles
__	91	Van Nuys-Burbank-Pasadena-Alhambra
__	92	Southern California
__	93	South Central California
__	94	San Francisco Bay Area
__	95	Northern California
__	96	Hawaii, and Pacific Islands
__	97	Oregon
__	98	Washington
__	99	Alaska

S E C T I O N 2

COMMODITY AND SERVICE LISTING

Mail Processing Equipment - List A

Non-fixed mechanization support equipment

___ AAAA   .culling and facing conveyors
___ AAAB   .culling machines
___ AAAC   .facing and canceling machines
___ AAAD   .flat sorters
___ AAAE   .letter sorting systems
___ AAAF   .multi-slide sorters (parcel or sack)
___ AAAG   .edger/stacker feeder systems
___ AAAH   .distribution rings (parcel)

Mail handling support equipment

___ ABAA   .canceling machines (class A, B, C)
___ ABAB   .Model 89 portable conveyors
___ ABAC   .Model H & L portable conveyors
___ ABAD   .roller gravity portable conveyors
___ ABAZ   .other portable conveyors
___ ABAE   .sack and pouch label machines
___ ABAF   .long and short stackers
___ ABAG   .tying machines
___ ABAH   .extendable conveyors, telescoping, fixed base

Material transport equipment
(also see Expendable Equipment - List P)

___ ACAA   .industrial batteries, battery chargers, and motors
___ ACAB   .hamper dumpers
___ ACAC   .industrial and baggage type trailers
___ ACAD   .intercommunications equipment
___ ACAE   .platform and yard equipment
___ ACAF   .scooters (electric)
___ ACAG   .skids
___ ACAH   .tractors, lifts, and fork lifts (electric)
___ ACAJ   .tray carts
___ ACAK   .carts (other than utility)
___ ACAL   .containers, Bulk Mail
___ ACAM   .pallets

Workroom furniture and equipment
(also see Expendable Equipment - List P)

__ ADAA   .parcel post rewrap equipment
__ ADAB   .work tables, desks, and similar equipment

City delivery service equipment
(also see Expendable Equipment - List P)

__ AEAA   .city delivery carts
__ AEAB   .containers for parcel post shuttle
__ AEAC   .co-op racks
__ AEAD   .customer boxes, delivery (neighborhood)
__ AEAE   .apartment house mail boxes

Motor Vehicles - List B

__ BAAA   Carrier mechanization vehicles

__ BBAA   Bulk transfer vehicles

__ BCAA   Law enforcement vehicles

__ BDZZ   Other vehicles

Vehicle auxilliary equipment

__ BEAA   .snow plows for vehicles
__ BEAB   .power tailgates
__ BEAC   .trailer couplers
__ BEAD   .service trailers

Customer Service Equipment - List C

Lobby equipment
(also see Expendable Equipment - List P)

__ CAAA   .bulletin boards
__ CAAB   .lobby desks

Window service equipment

__ CBAA   .automatic cashiers
__ CBAB   .cabinets (stamp, form, etc.)
__ CBAC   .money order machines and related equipment
__ CBAD   .postage meters
__ CBAE   .scales, all sizes (except SSPU)

414

Self-service equipment (SSPU)
(also see Expendable Equipment - List P)

___	CCAA	.coin counting and sorting machines
___	CCAB	.core units
___	CCAC	.currency - coin change machines
___	CCAD	.parcel depositories
___	CCAE	.scales, parcel post
___	CCAF	.vending machines - 3 postage value
___	CCAG	.vending machines - 5 postage value
___	CCAH	.vending machines - multi-commodity

Postal Support Equipment - List D

Office machines and equipment

___	DAAA	.accounting machines including adding machines and calculators
___	DAAB	.duplicating equipment including addressograph and photocopying-photostatic machines
___	DAAC	.dictating equipment
___	DAAD	.time recorders, electric
___	DAAE	.typewriters (other than data processing)

Office furnishings

___	DBAA	.office furniture including desks, tables, chairs, couches, davenports, bookcases, wardrobes, and lamps
___	DBAB	.floor covering including tile, carpeting, and padding

Audio/visual type equipment

___	DCAA	.CCTV cameras and monitors
___	DCAB	.cabinets, carts, film storage
___	DCAC	.cameras, copy, movie, still
___	DCAD	.communications system, address, lecture
___	DCAE	.photo processing - darkroom equipment
___	DCAF	.projectors, movie, slide, opaque, etc.
___	DCAG	.recorders, tape, TV, etc.
___	DCAH	.simulator models

Protective equipment
(also see Expendable Equipment - List P)

___	DDAA	.firearms
___	DDAB	.safes

Protective equipment (cont'd)
(also see Expendable Equipment - List P)

___ DDAC   .vault entrances
___ DDAD   .financial enclosure and overhead wire
___ DDAE   .security force dogs
___ DDAF   .security test equipment

Personnel equipment

___ DFAA   .lockers
___ DFAB   .civil defense equipment
___ DFAC   .employee cafeteria equipment
___ DFAD   .first-aid cabinets
___ DFAE   .medical unit equipment
___ DFAF   .photo identification equipment

Custodial equipment

___ DGAA   .custodial supply carts
___ DGAB   .floor polishers (large electric)
___ DGAC   .mopping equipment (tank type)
___ DGAD   .snow plows and blowers, gasoline powered
___ DGAE   .sweepers, powered
___ DGAF   .vacuum cleaners (heavy duty)
___ DGAG   .lawn mowers, powered

Maintenance shop equipment

___ DHAA   .electronic and other test equipment
___ DHAB   .metal and woodworking machines
___ DHAC   .power tools

Building equipment

___ DJAA   .air-conditioning units
___ DJAB   .air compressors
___ DJAC   .emergency lighting and power
___ DJAD   .lift platforms
___ DJAE   .fans
___ DJAF   .lighting, localized/general

Vehicle maintenance equipment

___ DKAA   .body repair units
___ DKAB   .engine analysis equipment
___ DKAC   .engine repair equipment

Vehicle maintenance equipment (cont'd)

___	DKAD	.jacks and lifts
___	DKAE	.overhead lubrication reels
___	PXAA	.steam cleaners (See Expendable Equipment)
___	DKAG	.tire changers and operators
___	DKAH	.truck washing equipment
___	DKAJ	.wheel alignment equipment

Automatic data processing (purchase or lease)

___	DLAA	.ADP systems design
___	DLAB	.ADP hardware
___	DLAC	.ADP software
___	DLAD	.ADP training
___	DLAE	.ADP programming
___	DLAF	.ADP time sharing
___	DLAG	.ADP keypunching
___	DLAH	.ADP performance monitors
___	DLAJ	.ADP typewriter systems
___	DLAK	.ADP terminal devices
___	DLAL	.ADP optical scanners
___	DLAM	.micro-film readers and printers

Rental of Equipment - List E

___	EAAA	.AP and UPI ticker service
___	EBAA	.photocopy equipment rental
___	ECAA	.duplicating equipment rental
___	EDAA	.vehicle hire, rental, or lease

Services - List F

___	FAAA	.cleaning supply rental
___	FBAA	.computer maintenance
___	FCAA	.expert consultant
___	FDAA	.elevator maintenance
___	FEAA	.electric motor rebuild
___	FFAA	.electronic equipment repair
___	FGAA	.electric power installation and repair
___	FHAA	.employee recruitment
___	FJAA	.employee training
___	FKAA	.employee uniform quality control
___	FLAA	.engineering and technical studies
___	FMAA	.engineering and technical services (except A & E)
___	FNAA	.exhibit and display design
___	FPAA	.food service

Services (Cont'd)

___	FRAA	.HVAC service
___	FSAA	.insurance placement
___	FTAA	.job cleaning service
___	FWAA	.landscaping
___	FXAA	.laundry service
___	FAAB	.machine shop service
___	FAAC	.moving and storage
___	FAAD	.painting
___	FAAE	.plumbing services
___	FAAF	.professional studies and surveys (non-technical)
___	FAAG	.quality control testing
___	FAAH	.research and development - hardware
___	FAAJ	.research and development - feasibility
___	FAAK	.secretarial services
___	FAAL	.safety program services
___	FAAM	.sales promotion and advertising
___	FAAN	.security and fire equipment installation and service
___	FAAP	.trash and snow removal
___	FAAR	.test and examination services - personnel
___	FAAS	.training film and instructional material
___	FAAT	.vehicle maintenance service
___	FAAW	.vehicle shop equipment repair
___	FAAX	.vehicle parts rebuild and overhaul
___	FBAB	.vehicle painting
___	FBAC	.vehicle storage
___	FBAD	.vehicle towing
___	FBAE	.vehicle tire recapping
___	FBAF	.vehicle washing
___	FBAG	.waste oil removal
___	FBAH	.window washing
___	FBAJ	.medical services
___	FBAK	.auctioneering
___	FBAM	.asphalt surfacing
___	FBAN	.carpentry and flooring
___	FBAP	.concrete surfacing
___	FBAR	.fencing
___	FBAS	.masonry
___	FBAT	.roofing and siding

Building Supplies - List G

Cleaning supplies

___	GAAA	.brooms
___	GAAB	.brushes
___	GAAC	.dust pans
___	GAAD	.cloths, scrub and wiping
___	GAAE	.mops and mopping units
___	GAAF	.cloths, sweeping, treated, non-woven

418

Cleaning supplies (cont'd)

___ GAAG   .chamois skins, natural and imitation
___ GAAH   .sponges
___ GAAJ   .receptacles, all types
___ GAAK   .feather dusters, all types
___ GAAL   .pads, floor machines (steel wool, etc.)
___ GAAM   .garden hose
___ GAAN   .polish
___ GAAP   .renovator, floor
___ GAAR   .floor finish, resin
___ GAAS   .detergents
___ GAAT   .buckets
___ GAAW   .trash bags

Washroom supplies

___ GBAA   .disinfectants and deodorants
___ GBAB   .toilet tissue
___ GBAC   .towels and towel cabinets
___ GBAD   .hand soap
___ GBAE   .soap dispensers

Postal Supplies - List H

Maintenance parts and supplies

___ HAAA   .air and hydraulic systems and components
___ HAAB   .bearings - ball and roller
___ HAAC   .bearings - pillow block
___ HAAD   .capacitors and resistors
___ HAAE   .compressed gases (except heating, for which see Fuel and Utility Services - page 14 of 16)
___ HAAF   .computer electronic repair parts
___ HAAG   .conveyor belting
___ HAAH   .conveyor belt fasteners
___ HAAJ   .diodes and transistors
___ HAAK   .electric wire and cable
___ HAAL   .electronic sensors
___ HAAM   .electron tubes
___ HAAN   .electrical conduit and fittings
___ HAAP   .fasteners (bolts, nuts, screws, washers)
___ HAAR   .forging and castings
___ HAAS   .gauges - pressure, temperature
___ HAAT   .gaskets
___ HAAW   .gear drives and reducers
___ HAAX   .gears and sprockets
___ HABA   .HVAC controls
___ HABB   .integrated circuits
___ HABC   .lubricants - industrial
___ HABD   .lumber
___ HABE   .lamps - fluorescent and incandescent

Maintenance parts and supplies (cont'd)

___ HABF	.lighting fixtures
___ HABG	.motors
___ HABH	.plate and window glass
___ HABJ	.pipe, tubing and fittings
___ HABK	.paint, lacquer and thinner
___ HABL	.packings and seals
___ HABM	.printed circuit boards
___ HABN	.power drive chain links
___ HABP	.rollers
___ HABR	.switches and relays
___ HABS	.steel wire, rope, and cable
___ HABT	.structural steel shapes and plates
___ HABW	.sheet and coil steel
___ HABX	.sheet and coil aluminum
___ HACA	.sheet and coil brass and copper
___ HACB	.springs
___ HACC	.solvents - industrial
___ HACD	.v-belts
___ HACE	.valves - fluid
___ FACF	.valves - gas
___ HACG	.volt and ohm meters
___ HACH	.miscellaneous carpentry supplies
___ HACJ	.miscellaneous electronic components
___ HACK	.miscellaneous industrial electrical supplies
___ HACL	.miscellaneous industrial HVAC supplies
___ HACM	.miscellaneous industrial plumbing supplies
___ HACN	.miscellaneous masonry supplies
___ HACP	.miscellaneous painting supplies
___ HACR	.miscellaneous telecommunications equipment parts
___ HACS	.casters

Vehicle parts and supplies (new and rebuilt)
(except when installed or provided to a specific
vehicle by a service station or garage, for which
see Services - List F)

___ HBAA	.alternators, regulators, generators, and starters
___ HBAB	.anti-freeze (bulk and in containers)
___ HBAC	.brake lining and shoes
___ HBAD	.brake system components
___ HBAE	.brake drums
___ HBAF	.brake fluid
___ HBAG	.batteries and battery acid
___ HBAH	.bearings
___ HBAJ	.body and frame components
___ HBAK	.clamps, hose
___ HBAL	.connectors, fuel and hydraulic

420

Vehicle parts and supplies (new and rebuilt) (cont'd)
(except when installed or provided to a specific
vehicle by a service station or garage, for which
see Services - List F

__	HBAM	.distributors
__	HBAN	.drive shafts
__	HBAP	.differentials, axles, and components
__	HBAR	.electrical switches
__	HBAS	.electrical wiring
__	HBAT	.exhaust system components
__	HBAW	.engines and components
__	HBAX	.filters - oil, air, fuel
__	HBBA	.fan belts and hoses
__	HBBB	.fuses
__	HBBC	.fuel pumps, carburetors, and fuel system components
__	HBBD	.fuel tanks
__	HBBE	.gasoline and diesel fuel in bulk
__	HBBF	.gaskets - cork and composition
__	HBBG	.grease fittings
__	HBBH	.gauges and sending units
__	HBBJ	.heaters and components
__	HBBK	.ignition system electrical components
__	HBBL	.hardware and fasteners
__	HBBM	.lamps, lamp housings, bulbs, reflectors
__	HBBN	.lubricants, automotive
__	HBBP	.motor oil and transmission fluid
__	HBBR	.mirrors and brackets
__	HBBS	.radiators
__	HBBT	.spark plugs
__	HBBW	.seals
__	HBBX	.shock absorbers and components
__	HBCA	.springs and components
__	HBCB	.steering - power and mechanical with components
__	HBCC	.steering linkage and components
__	HBCD	.tires and tubes
__	HBCE	.tire repair material
__	HBCF	.tubing - flexible metal
__	HBCG	.transmissions, components and linkage
__	HBCH	.thermostats
__	HBCJ	.universal joints
__	HBCK	.upholstery, seats, and seat covers
__	HBCL	.wheels and rims
__	HBCM	.wiper motors
__	HBCN	.wiper blades and arms
__	HBCP	.water pumps
__	HBCR	.windshield and window glass
__	HBCS	.warning devices - flares and reflectors

General postal supplies

___ HCAA   .ammunition
___ HCAB   .belts and holsters
___ HCAC   .briefcases - plastic and leather
___ HCAD   .cash boxes
___ HCAE   .canvas baskets
___ HCAF   .cash and stamp drawers
___ HCAG   .computer magnetic tape
___ HCAH   .computer paper punch tape
___ HCAJ   .computer punch cards
___ HCAK   .computer printout paper
___ HCAL   .computer self-adhesive print labels
___ HCAM   .computer disk packs
___ HCAN   .computer printer inked ribbons
___ HCAP   .collection box inserts
___ HCAR   .canvas mail pouches
___ HCAS   .corrugated paper containers
___ HCAT   .envelopes
___ HCAW   .flags
___ HCAX   .medical supplies
___ HCBA   .office supplies
___ HCBB   .packing materials
___ HCBC   .paper stock
___ HCBD   .printing inks
___ HCBE   .protective clothing
___ HCBF   .rubber bands
___ HCBG   .rubber stamps and stamping devices
___ HCBH   .satchels and straps
___ HCBJ   .seals and signs
___ HCBK   .trays- plastic
___ HCBL   .trays - fiberboard
___ HCBM   .trays - cardboard
___ HCBN   .twine and rope
___ HCBP   .typewriter ribbons
___ HCBR   .wire and band tying and bailing material
___ HCBS   .dog repellant
___ HCBT   .thread
___ HCBW   .ID badges

Fuel and Utility Services - List J
(for automotive fuel see Vehicle Parts and
Supplies - List H)

___ JAAA   .coal
___ JBAA   .electricity
___ JCAA   .fuel - oil and kerosene
___ JDAA   .gas - city (natural or manufactured)
___ JEAA   .propane (includes butane or LP)
___ JFAA   .water and sewer (city)

Communication Services - List K

__ KAAA .federal telecommunications systems
__ KBAA .telephone service (other than FTS)
__ KCAA .telegraph and teletype service

Printing - List M

__ MAAA .publications
__ MBAA .miscrofilming
__ MCAA .blue-line & black-line whiteprints, sepia,
         intermediates, etc.
__ MDAA .postal forms
__ MRAA .posters and placards
__ MTAA .postal maps
__ MAAC .letterhead stationery
__ MAAF .tags
__ MAAG .labels
__ MZZZ .miscellaneous printing and duplicating

Facility Acquisition, Construction, Architect-Engineer Services - List N

__ NAAA .architect and engineer services
__ NBAA .construction - fire protection systems
__ NBAB .construction - mechanization
__ NBAC .construction - new postal facility
__ NBAD .construction - alterations and additions
__ NBAE .construction - "WCIP"

U.S. DEPARTMENT OF COMMERCE DISTRICT OFFICE DIRECTORY

OFFICE OF FIELD OPERATIONS
February 1977

ALABAMA

Birmingham—Gayle C. Shelton, Jr., Director, Suite 200–201, 908 South 20th Street, 35205, Area Code 205 Tel 254–1331, FTS 229–1331

ALASKA

••Anchorage—Sara L. Haslett, Director, 412 Hill Building, 632 Sixth Avenue 99501, Area Code 907 Tel 265–5307

ARIZONA

••Phoenix—Donald W. Fry, Director, Suite 2950 Valley Center Bank Bldg., 201 North Central Avenue 85004, Area Code 602 Tel 261–3285, FTS 261–3285

ARKANSAS

•Little Rock (Dallas, Texas District) —1100 North University, Suite 109 72207, Area Code 501 Tel 378–5157, FTS 740–5157

CALIFORNIA

Los Angeles—Eric C. Silberstein, Director, Room 800, 11777 San Vicente Boulevard 90049, Area Code 213 Tel 824–7591, FTS 799–7591
  •San Diego—233 A Street, Suite 310 92101, Area Code 714 Tel 293–5395, FTS 895–5395
San Francisco—Philip M. Creighton, Director, Federal Building Box 36013, 450 Golden Gate Avenue 94102, Area Code 415 Tel 556–5860, FTS 556–5868

COLORADO

Denver—Norman Lawson, Director, Room 165, New Customhouse, 19th & Stout Street 80202, Area Code 303 Tel 837–3246, FTS 327–3246

CONNECTICUT

Hartford—Richard C. Kilbourn, Director, Room 610–B, Federal Office Building, 450 Main Street 06103, Area Code 203 Tel 244–3530, FTS 244–3530

FLORIDA

Miami—Roger J. LaRoche, Director, Room 821, City National Bank Building, 25 West Flagler Street 33130, Area Code 305 Tel 350–5267, FTS 350–5267
  •Clearwater—128 North Osceola Avenue 33515, Area Code 813 Tel 446–4081
  •Jacksonville—604 North Hogan Street 32202, Area Code 904 Tel 791–2796, FTS 946–2796
  •Tallahassee—Collins Bldg., Rm. G–20 32304, Area Code 904 Tel 488–6469, FTS 946–4320

GEORGIA

Atlanta—David S. Williamson, Director, Suite 600, 1365 Peachtree Street, N.E. 30309, Area Code 404 Tel 881–7000, FTS 257–7000
••Savannah—James W. McIntire, Director, 235 U.S. Courthouse & P.O. Building, 125–29 Bull Street 31402, Area Code 912 Tel 232–4321, Ext. 204, FTS 248–4204

HAWAII

Honolulu—John S. Davies, Director, 286 Alexander Young Building, 1015 Bishop Street 96813, Area Code 808 Tel 546–8694

IDAHO

•Boise (Portland, Oregon District)— P.O. Box 9366, 83707, Area Code 208 Tel 384–1326, FTS 554–1326

ILLINOIS

Chicago—Gerald M. Marks, Director, 1406 Mid Continental Plaza Building, 55 East Monroe Street 60603, Area Code 312 Tel 353–4450, FTS 353–4450

INDIANA

Indianapolis—Mel R. Sherar, Director, 357 U.S. Courthouse & Federal Office Building, 46 East Ohio Street 46204, Area Code 317 Tel 269–6214, FTS 331–6214

IOWA

Des Moines—Jesse N. Durden, Director, 609 Federal Building, 210 Walnut Street 50309, Area Code 515 Tel 284–4222, FTS 862–4222

KANSAS

•Wichita (St. Louis, Missouri District)—Wichita State University, Clinton Hall, Room 341, 67208, Area Code 316 Tel 267–6160, FTS 752–6160

KENTUCKY

•Frankfort (Memphis, Tennessee District)—Capitol Plaza Office Tower, Room 2332, 40601, Area Code 502 Tel 875–4421

LOUISIANA

New Orleans—Edwin A. Leland, Jr., Director, 432 International Trade Mart, No. 2 Canal Street 70130, Area Code 504 Tel 589–6546, FTS 682–6546

MAINE

•Portland (Boston, Massachusetts District)—Maine State Pier, 40 Commercial Street 04111, Area Code 207 Tel 775–3131, FTS 833–3236

MARYLAND

Baltimore—Carroll F. Hopkins, Director, 415 U.S. Customhouse, Gay and Lombard Streets 21202, Area Code 301 Tel 962–3560, FTS 922–3560

MASSACHUSETTS

Boston—Richard F. Treadway, Director, 10th Floor, 441 Stuart Street 02116, Area Code 617 Tel 223–2312, FTS 223–2312

MICHIGAN

Detroit—William L. Welch, Director, 445 Federal Building, 231 West Lafayette 48226, Area Code 313 Tel 226–3650, FTS 226–3650
  •Ann Arbor—Graduate School of Business Administration, University of Michigan Room 288, 48105, Area Code 313 Tel 944–3297, FTS 374–5638
  •Grand Rapids—17 Fountain Street N.W. 49503, Area Code 616 Tel 456–2411/33 FTS 372–2411

MINNESOTA

Minneapolis—Glenn A. Matson, Director, 218 Federal Building, 110 South Fourth Street 55401, Area Code 612 Tel 725–2133, FTS 725–2133

MISSISSIPPI

•Jackson (Birmingham, Alabama District)—P.O. Box 849, 2003 Walter Sillers Building 39205, Area Code 601 Tel 969–4388, FTS 490–4388

MISSOURI

St. Louis—Donald R. Loso, Director, 120 South Central Avenue 63105, Area Code 314 Tel 425–3302–4, FTS 279–3302
  •Kansas City—Room 1840, 601 East 12th Street 64106, Area Code 816 Tel 374–3142, FTS 758–3142

MONTANA

•Butte (Cheyenne, Wyoming District)—210 Miners Bank Building, Park Street 59701, Area Code 406 Tel 723–6561, Ext. 2317, FTS 585–2317

•DENOTES SATELLITE OFFICE.
••DENOTES CHANGE.

NEBRASKA

Omaha—George H. Payne, Director, Capitol Plaza, Suite 703A, 1815 Capitol Avenue 68102, Area Code 402 Tel 221–3665, FTS 864–3665

NEVADA

Reno—Joseph J. Jeremy, Director, 2028 Federal Building, 300 Booth Street 89509 Area Code 702 Tel 784–5203, FTS 470–5203

NEW JERSEY

Newark—Clifford R. Lincoln, Director, 4th Floor, Gateway Building, Market Street & Penn Plaza 07102, Area Code 201 Tel 645–6214, FTS 341–6214

NEW MEXICO

Albuquerque—William E. Dwyer, Director, 505 Marquette Ave., NW, Suite 1015, 87102, Area Code 505 Tel 766–2386, FTS 474–2386

NEW YORK

Buffalo—Robert F. Magee, Director, 1312 Federal Building, 111 West Huron Street 14202, Area Code 716 Tel 842–3208, FTS 432–3208

New York—Arthur C. Rutzen, Director, 37th Floor, Federal Office Building, 26 Federal Plaza, Foley Square 10007, Area Code 212 Tel 264–0634, FTS 264–0600

NORTH CAROLINA

Greensboro—Joel B. New, Director, 203 Federal Building, West Market Street, P.O. Box 1950 27402, Area Code 919 Tel 378–5345, FTS 699–5345

  •**Asheville**—151 Haywood Street 28802, Area Code 704 Tel 254–1981, FTS 672–0342

OHIO

Cincinnati—Gordon B. Thomas, Director, 10504 Federal Office Building, 550 Main Street 45202, Area Code 513 Tel 684–2944, FTS 684–2944

Cleveland—Charles B. Stebbins, Director, Room 600, 666 Euclid Avenue 44114, Area Code 216 Tel 522–4750, FTS 293–4750

OKLAHOMA

•**Oklahoma City (Dallas, Texas District)**—4020 Lincoln Boulevard 73105, Area Code 405 Tel 231–5302, FTS 736–5302

OREGON

Portland—Lloyd R. Porter, Director, Room 618, 1220 S.W. 3rd Avenue 97204, Area Code 503 Tel 221–3001, FTS 423–3001

PENNSYLVANIA

Philadelphia—Patrick P. McCabe, Director, 9448 Federal Building, 600 Arch Street 19106, Area Code 215 Tel 597–2850, FTS 597–2866

Pittsburgh—Newton Heston, Jr., Director, 2002 Federal Building, 1000 Liberty Avenue 15222, Area Code 412 Tel 644–2850, FTS 722–2850

PUERTO RICO

San Juan (Hato Rey)—Enrique Vilella, Director, Room 659-Federal Building 00918, Area Code 809 Tel 763–6363 ext. 555, FTS 759–7040/45

RHODE ISLAND

•**Providence (Boston, Massachusetts District)**—1 Weybossett Hill 02903, Area Code 401 Tel 277–2605, ext. 22, FTS 838–4482

SOUTH CAROLINA

Columbia—Philip A. Ouzis, Director, 2611 Forest Drive, Forest Center 29204, Area Code 803 Tel 765–5345, FTS 677–5345

  •**Charleston**—Suite 631, Federal Building, 334 Meeting Place 29403, Area Code 803 Tel 577–4361, FTS 677–4361

TENNESSEE

Memphis—Bradford H. Rice, Director, Room 710, 147 Jefferson Avenue 38103, Area Code 901 Tel 521–3213, FTS 222–3213

  •**Nashville**—Room 1004, Andrew Jackson Office Building 37219, Area Code 615 Tel 749–5161, FTS 852–5161

TEXAS

Dallas—C. Carmon Stiles, Director, Room 7A5, 1100 Commerce Street 75242, Area Code 214 Tel 749–1515, FTS 749–1513

Houston—Felicito C. Guerrero, Director, 2625 Federal Bldg., Courthouse, 515 Rusk Street 77002, Area Code 713 Tel 226–4231, FTS 527–4231

  •**San Antonio**—University of Texas at San Antonio, Div. of Continuing Education 78285, Area Code 512 Tel 229–5875, FTS 229–5875

UTAH

Salt Lake City—George M. Blessing, Jr., Director, 1203 Federal Building, 125 South State Street 84138, Area Code 801 Tel 524–5116, FTS 588–5116

VIRGINIA

Richmond—Weldon W. Tuck, Director, 8010 Federal Building, 400 North 8th Street 23240, Area Code 804 Tel 782–2246, FTS 925–2246

  •**Fairfax**—8550 Arlington Blvd., 22030, Area Code 703 560–4000

WASHINGTON

Seattle—Judson S. Wonderly, Director, Room 706, Lake Union Building, 1700 Westlake Avenue North 98109, Area Code 206 Tel 442–5615, FTS 399–5615

WEST VIRGINIA

Charleston—J. Raymond DePaulo, Director, 3000 New Federal Office Building, 500 Quarrier Street 25301, Area Code 304 Tel 343–6181, ext. 375, FTS 924–1375

WISCONSIN

Milwaukee—Russell H. Leitch, Director, Federal Bldg/U.S. Courthouse, 517 East Wisconsin Avenue 53202, Area Code 414 Tel. 224–3473, FTS 362–3473

WYOMING

Cheyenne—Lowell O. Burns, Director, 6022 O'Mahoney Federal Center, 2120 Capitol Avenue 82001, Area Code 307 Tel 778–2220, ext. 2151, FTS 328–2151

SBA FIELD OFFICES

ADDRESSES AND TELEPHONE NUMBERS

REGION		CITY	STATE	ZIP CODE	ADDRESS	(TELEPHONE NUMBERS FOR PUBLIC USE ONLY)
	RO	Boston	Mass.	02114	150 Causeway St., 10th Floor	(617) 223-3224
	DO	Boston	Mass.	02114	150 Causeway St., 10th Floor	(617) 223-3224
	POD	Holyoke	Mass.	01040	302 High Street - 4th Floor	(413) 536-8770
I	DO	Augusta	Maine	04330	Federal Building, 40 Western Ave., Room 512	(207) 622-6171
	DO	Concord	N.H.	03301	55 Pleasant St., Room 213	(603) 224-4041
	DO	Hartford	Conn.	06103	One Financial Plaza	(203) 244-3600
	DO	Montpelier	Vt.	05602	Federal Building, 87 State St., Room 210	(802) 223-7472
	DO	Providence	R.I.	02903	57 Eddy St., Room 7th Fl	(401) 528-1000
	RO	New York	N.Y.	10007	26 Federal Plaza, Room 3214	(212) 264-1468
	DO	New York	N.Y.	10007	26 Federal Plaza, Room 3100	(212) 264-4355
	POD	Melville	N.Y.	11746	425 Broad Hollow Rd. Rm. 205	(516) 752-1626
	DO	Hato Rey	Puerto Rico	00919	Chardon and Bolivia Streets, PO Box 1915	(809) 753-6363
	POD	St. Thomas	Virgin Island	00801	U.S. Fed. Ofc. Bldg., Veterans Dr., Rm. 283	(809) 774-8530
II	DO	Newark	N.J.	07102	970 Broad St., Room 1635	(201) 645-2434
	POD	Camden	N.J.	08104	1800 East Davis Street	(609) 757-5183
	DO	Syracuse	N.Y.	13202	Federal Building-Room 1073-100 South Clinton Street	(315) 423-5370
	BO	Buffalo	N.Y.	14202	111 West Huron St., Room 1311, Federal Building	(716) 842-3240
	BO	Elmira	N.Y.	14901	180 State Street - Rm. 412	(607) 733-4686
	POD	Albany	N.Y.	12210	99 Washington Ave., Twin Towers Bldg., Room 921	(518) 472-6300
	POD	Rochester	N.Y.	14614	Federal Building, 100 State Street	(716) 263-6700
	RO	Philadelphia	Bala Cynwyd, Pa.	19004	231 St. Asaphs Rd., 1 Bala Cynwyd Plaza, Suite 646 West Lobby	(215) 597-5888
	DO	Philadelphia	Bala Cynwyd, Pa.	19004	231 St. Asaphs Rd., 1 Bala Cynwyd Plaza, Suite 400 East Lobby	(215) 597-5888
	BO	Harrisburg	Pa.	17102	1500 North 2nd Street	(717) 782-3840
	BO	Wilkes-Barre	Pa.	18702	Penn Place, 20 N. Pennsylvania Ave.	(717) 826-6497
	BO	Wilmington	Del.	19801	844 King Street, Federal Building, Rm. 5207	(302) 571-6294
III	DO	Baltimore	Towson Md.	21204	Oxford Bldg., 8600 LaSalle Road, Rm. 630	(301) 962-4392
	DO	Clarksburg	W. Va.	26301	109 North 3rd St., Room 301, Lowndes Building	(304) 623-5631
	BO	Charleston	W. Va.	25301	Charleston National Plaza, Suite 628	(304) 343-6181
	DO	Pittsburgh	Pa.	15222	Federal Building, 1000 Liberty Ave., Room 1401	(412) 644-2780
	DO	Richmond	Va.	23240	Federal Building, 400 North 8th St., Room 3015	(804) 782-2617
	DO	Washington	D.C.	20417	1030 15th St. N.W. Suite 250	(202) 655-4000
	RO	Atlanta	Ga.	30309	1375 Peachtree St., N.E.	(404) 881-4943
	DO	Atlanta	Ga.	30309	1720 Peachtree Street, N.W., 6th Floor	(404) 881-4325
	DO	Birmingham	Ala.	35205	908 South 20th St., Room 202	(205) 254-1344
	DO	Charlotte	N.C.	28202	230 S. Tryon Street	(704) 372-0711
	POD	Greenville	N.C.	27834	215 South Evans Street Rm. 206	(919) 752-3798
	DO	Columbia	S.C.	29201	1801 Assembly St., Room 131	(803) 765-5376
IV	DO	Jackson	Miss.	39201	Providence Capitol Bldg., Suite 690, 200 E. Pascagoula St.	(601) 969-4371
	DO	Biloxi	Miss.	39530	111 Fred Haise Blvd., Gulf Nat. Life Insurance Bldg. 2nd Floor	(601) 435-3676
	DO	Jacksonville	Fla.	32202	Federal Building, 400 West Bay St., Room 261, PO Box 35067	(904) 791-3782
	DO	Louisville	Ky.	40202	Federal Building, 600 Federal Pl., Room 188	(502) 582-5971
	DO	Miami	Coral Gables Fla.	33134	2222 Ponce De Leon Blvd., 5th Floor	(305) 350-5521
	POD	Tampa	Fla.	33602	1802 N. Trask Street, Suite 203	(813) 228-2594
	DO	Nashville	Tenn.	37219	404 James Robertson Parkway, Suite 1012	(615) 251-5881
	BO	Knoxville	Tenn.	37902	502 South Gay St., Room 307, Fidelity Bankers Building	(615) 637-9300
	POD	Memphis	Tenn.	38103	Federal Building, 167 North Main St., Room 211	(901) 521-3588
	POD	West Palm Beach	Fla.	33402	Federal Building, 701 Clematis St., Room 229	(305) 659-7533
	RO	Chicago	Ill.	60604	Federal Building, 219 South Dearborn St., Room 838	(312) 353-0355
	DO	Chicago	Ill.	60604	Federal Building, 219 South Dearborn St., Room 437	(312) 353-4528
	BO	Springfield	Ill.	62701	One North, Old State Capital Plaza	(217) 525-4416
	DO	Cleveland	Ohio	44199	1240 East 9th St., Room 317	(216) 522-4180
	DO	Columbus	Ohio	43215	34 North High Street, Tonti Bldg.	(614) 469-6860
V	BO	Cincinnati	Ohio	45202	Federal Building, 550 Main St.	(513) 684-2814
	DO	Detroit	Mich.	48226	477 Michigan Ave., McNamara Building	(313) 226-6075
	BO	Marquette	Mich.	49855	540 W. Kaye Ave., Don H. Bottum University Center	(906) 225-1108
	DO	Indianapolis	Ind.	46204	575 North Pennsylvania St., Rm. 552 New Fed. Bldg.	(317) 269-7272
	DO	Madison	Wis.	53703	122 West Washington Ave., Room 713	(608) 252-5261
	BO	Milwaukee	Wis.	53233	735 West Wisconsin Ave., Room 690, Continental Bank Bldg.	(414) 224-3941
	POD	Eau Claire	Wis.	54701	500 South Barstow St., Room 89AA, Fed. Off. Bldg. & U.S. Courthouse	(715) 834-9012
	DO	Minneapolis	Minn.	55402	12 South 6th St., Plymouth Building	(612) 725-2362

REGION		CITY	STATE	ZIP CODE	ADDRESS	(TELEPHONE NUMBERS FOR PUBLIC USE ONLY)
	RO	Dallas	Tex.	75242	1720 Regal Row, Regal Park Office Bldg., Rm. 3C36	(214) 749-2531
	DO	Dallas	Tex.	75670	1100 Commerce St., Room 300	(214) 749-3961
	POD	Marshall	Tex.	75670	100 South Washington Street, Federal Building G-12	(214) 935-5257
	DO	Albuquerque	N. Mex.	87110	5000 Marble Ave., N.E., Patio Plaza Bldg.	(505) 766-3430
	DO	Houston	Tex.	77002	One Allen Ctr., 500 Dallas Street	(713) 226-4341
	DO	Little Rock	Ark.	72201	611 Gaines St., Suite 900	(501) 378-5871
VI	DO	Lubbock,	Tex.	79401	1205 Texas Ave., 712 Federal Office Bldg. & U.S. Courthouse	(806) 762-7011
	BO	El Paso	Tex.	79901	4100 Rio Bravo, Suite 300	(915) 543-7200
	DO	Lower Rio Grande Valley	Harlingen, Tex.	78550	222 East Van Buren Street	(512) 423-3011
	BO	Corpus Christi	Tex.	78408	3105 Leopard St.	(512) 888-3011
	DO	New Orleans	La.	70113	1001 Howard Ave., Plaza Tower, 17th Floor	(504) 589-2611
	POD	Shreveport	La.	71101	Fannin Street, U.S. Post Office & Courthouse Building	(318) 226-5196
	DO	Oklahoma City	Okla.	73102	Fed. Bldg., 200 N.W. 5th St., Suite 670	(405) 231-4301
	DO	San Antonio	Tex.	78206	727 E. Durango, Rm A-513	(512) 229-6250
	RO	Kansas City	Mo.	64106	911 Walnut St., 23rd Floor	(816) 374-3318
	DO	Kansas City	Mo.	64106	1150 Grande Ave. - 5th Floor	(816) 374-5557
VII	DO	Des Moines	Iowa	50309	New Federal Building, 210 Walnut St., Room 749	(515) 284-4422
	DO	Omaha	Neb.	68102	Nineteenth and Farnum Streets, Empire State Building	(402) 221-4691
	DO	St. Louis	Mo.	63101	Suite 2500, Mercantile Tower, One Mercantile Center	(314) 425-4191
	DO	Wichita	Kan.	67202	110 East Waterman Street, Main Place Building	(316) 267-6311
	RO	Denver	Colo.	80202	Executive Tower Bldg, 1405 Curtis Street, 22nd Floor	(303) 837-0111
	DO	Denver	Colo.	80202	721 19th St., Room 426A	(303) 837-0111
	DO	Casper	Wyo.	82601	Federal Building, Room 4001, 100 East B St.	(307) 265-5550
VIII	DO	Fargo	N. Dak.	58102	Federal Building, 653 2nd Ave., North, Room 218	(701) 237-5131
	DO	Helena	Mont.	59601	618 Helena Avenue	(406) 449-5381
	DO	Salt Lake City	Utah	84138	Federal Building, 125 South State St., Room 2237	(801) 524-5800
	DO	Sioux Falls	S. Dak.	57102	National Bank Building, 8th & Main Ave., Room 402	(605) 336-2980
	BO	Rapid City	S. Dak.	57701	515 9th St., Federal Bldg. (Room) 246	(605) 343-5074
	RO	San Francisco	Calif.	94102	450 Golden Gate Ave., Box 36044	(415) 556-7487
	DO	San Francisco	Calif.	94105	211 Main Street	(415) 556-7490
	BO	Fresno	Calif.	93721	Federal Building, 1130 O. St., Room 4015	(209) 487-5000
	POD	Sacramento	Calif.	95825	2800 Cottage Way	(916) 484-4726
	DO	Las Vegas	Nev.	89101	301 E. Stewart	(702) 385-6011
IX	POD	Reno	Nev.	89505	50 South Virginia St., Rm. 308	(702) 784-5234
	DO	Honolulu	Hawaii	96813	1149 Bethel St., Room 402	(808) 546-8950
	BO	Agana	Guam	96910	Ada Plaza Center Building	**(-) 777-8420
	DO	Los Angeles	Calif.	90071	350 S. Figueroa St., 6th Floor	(213) 688-2956
	DO	Phoenix	Ariz.	85004	112 North Central Ave.	(602) 261-3611
	DO	San Diego	Calif.	92188	880 Front Street, Federal U.S. Building, Room 4-S-33	(714) 293-5444
	RO	Seattle	Wash.	98104	710 2nd Ave., 5th Floor, Dexter Horton Building	(206) 442-1455
	DO	Seattle	Wash.	98174	915 Second Ave., Federal Building - Room 1744	(206) 442-5534
	DO	Anchorage	Alaska	99501	1016 West 6th Ave., Suite 200, Anchorage Legal Center	**(907) 272-5561
X	BO	Fairbanks	Alaska	99701	501½ Second Avenue	**(907) 452-1951
	DO	Boise	Idaho	83702	216 North 8th St., Room 408	(208) 384-1096
	DO	Portland	Oreg.	97204	1220 S.W. Third Avenue, Federal Building	(503) 221-2682
	DO	Spokane	Wash.	99210	Court House Building, Room 651	(509) 456-3777

**Dial Operator for Assistance

10 Regional Offices (RO)   18 Branch Offices (BO)
63 District Offices (DO)   15 Post-of-duty (POD)

INDEX